Foundations of Computer-Aided Design

Foundations of Computer-Aided Design

Chinyere Onwubiko
OREGON STATE UNIVERSITY

WEST PUBLISHING COMPANY
St. Paul · New York · Los Angeles · San Francisco

Copyediting: Linda Thompson
Text and cover design: Wendy Calmenson
Cover image: © Dan McCoy/Rainbow
Art and composition: Rolin Graphics
Indexing: Virginia Hobbs

COPYRIGHT ©1989 By WEST PUBLISHING COMPANY
50 W. Kellogg Boulevard
P.O. Box 64526
St. Paul, MN 55164-1003

96 95 94 93 92 91 90 89   8 7 6 5 4 3 2 1 0

Library of Congress Cataloging-in-Publication Data

Onwubiko, Chinyere Okechi.
    Foundations of computer-aided design / Chinyere Onwubiko.
        p.   cm.
    ISBN 0-314-48134-6
    1. Computer-aided design.   Title.
TA174.058 1989
620'.00425'0285—dc 19

88-28646
CIP

To Mr. Charles Holder of Bay Springs, Mississippi
an eternal friend, whose love for our Lord
Jesus Christ motivated him to provide me
(a total stranger by every human standard)
both material and immaterial support to acquire
the foundation necessary to write this book.

C O N T E N T S

CHAPTER 3   PRINCIPLES OF SOFTWARE DESIGN   **39**

In July of 1977, an international conference was held in Middlesbrough, England, in which the major theme was computer-aided design (CAD) education. Many models were proposed for CAD education in universities and colleges. Most of the suggested models failed to make a careful distinction between training and education. Webster's dictionary helps to differentiate between the two concepts. "Training stresses instruction and drilling with a specific end in view," whereas "education applies to the manner of imparting information or skill so that others may learn." Therefore, it follows that CAD educational objectives should differ from those of the CAD practitioner in the process of training an individual to use computer-aided design in a particular industry.

Before drawing up a syllabus, the objectives of CAD education should be determined. There are at least two primary goals: (1) To provide information to the "would-be designers of CAD systems," and (2) to provide information to "would-be users of CAD systems." In my opinion, it is more difficult to accomplish the second goal satisfactorily because of the diversities in, or lack of standardization of, hardware and software packages used in CAD and because of the rapidly changing CAD hardware technology. The first goal, which is more easily accomplished, is the purpose of this book.

A typical syllabus aimed at providing instruction to the would-be designers of CAD systems should be drawn after defining the function of designers of CAD systems. Their functions include evaluation and selection of hardware and software packages of a CAD system. They should also be capable of writing their own application software packages when none are available. Therefore, the syllabus should contain at least:

- A discussion of available CAD tools
- An introduction to design optimization
- An introduction to the principles of shape description

This book is written as a first step to fulfilling these minimum requirements. It is written for the senior-level engineering course in computer-aided design and assumes the students have a good background in computer programming and have, or are in the process of completing, the ABET-required design sequence of their curriculum. Although this book is written primarily for senior-level students in mechanical engineering, it is generic enough in the coverage of the topics presented to be used by most engineering disciplines. Many people consider computer-aided design purely computer graphics or automated drafting. But this book takes the view CAD involves the entire design process rather than a phase in the design process.

The book treats subjects ranging from the definition of computer-aided design to its applications in industry. In Chapter 1, computer-aided design is defined and the concept of design is reviewed. Chapter 2 covers the tools necessary for computer-aided design. Chapter 3 introduces the principles of software design. Chapter 4 is a treatment of the solution of nonlinear algebraic equations. Chapter 5 gives a brief introduction to computer graphics. Chapter 6 is an introduction to computational geometry, with emphasis on curve designs, including many references to computational geometry. Chapters 7 through 9 deal with optimization. Chapter 10 is an introduction to finite element analysis, explaining the need and purpose of finite element. Chapter 11 provides an introduction to solid geometric modeling and gives, in detail, a typical application of computer-aided design. Exercises are also included at the end of Chapters 3 through 10.

An important feature of this book is that it contains detailed flowcharts for easy programming. Sample programs are also included. The book is designed to be completed in one semester.

ACKNOWLEDGMENTS

I am grateful to Dr. Decatur Rogers, my former department chairman, who encouraged me to write this book. He actually put me on the spot when he announced to the entire faculty that I would be writing a book in the area of computer-aided design. From then on I had no choice but to start the painful exercise of writing a textbook.

I am indebted to many of my reviewers for their critical suggestions especially Professors L. Levine of UCLA, Rollin Dix of Illinois Institute of Technology, Ali Manesh of University of Arkansas, and Thomas Cook of Oklahoma State University (whose specific suggestion on design philosophy helped in the modification of Chapter 1). Special thanks go to Professor Ray Johnson who helped me to understand his method of optimization presented in Chapter 9. I appreciate Dr. Barr's permission to use his concept of Superquadrics.

I am grateful to my acquiring editor Mr. T. M. Slaughter for his confidence and support throughout the process of writing this book. Special thanks also go to the production team of West Publishing Company, especially Jean Cook, and to Pat Lewis. The role played by Mrs. Gloria Crowther in editing the manuscript in its early stages is highly appreciated.

Many more persons in my famly deserve credit than I have acknowledged. To Ngozi: Your understanding throughout the process of writing this book is highly appreciated especially when you had to drive 85 miles to take care of my temporary place of residence just to be sure I ate properly and had the opportunity to spend those long hours on the computer.

Finally, I salute my former mechanical engineering students at Oregon State University and Praire A & M University for their input during the process of writing this book.

C.O.O.

Foundations of Computer-Aided Design

Introduction

1.1 DEFINITION OF COMPUTER-AIDED DESIGN

The advent of the computer has simplified many design processes. While computer-aided design (CAD) and computer-aided manufacturing (CAM) are usually treated as one subject, this book treats CAD as a distinctly different subject from CAM. CAM is viewed as automation of the manufacturing process; CAD is also an automation process, but one having different components.

The term computer-aided design means many things to many people. Some define CAD as computer-aided drafting. Others prefer to use the term computer-aided design and drafting (CADD). Though there is no agreement as to terminology, **computer-aided design** can be defined as follows: an automation process in which computer systems are used to aid in the design process from conception and synthesis, through analysis, optimization and drafting, to building and testing of prototypes.

1.2 THE DESIGN PROCESS

To understand computer-aided design properly, one must comprehend the process of design itself. In simplest terms, design is a method of providing a solution to an identified need. The design process can be considered a sequence of dilemmas ranging from confusion to despair to discovery. The process of designing anything is a very tedious and iterative procedure. There are various ways of presenting the design process; Deutschman et al. [1], for example, gave nine steps (see Figure 1.1). These nine steps are, in effect, incorporated in the six steps given by Shigley [2], which are:

1. Recognition of a need
2. Definition of the problem
3. Synthesis
4. Analysis and optimization
5. Evaluation
6. Presentation

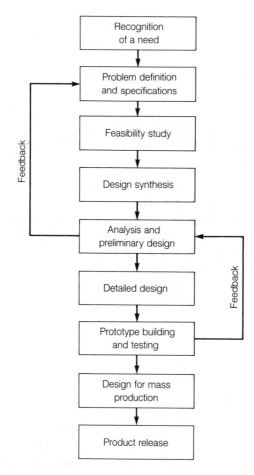

FIGURE 1.1

Design sequence.

Recognition of a need, which is the first step in the design process, originates from many sources. Perhaps the greatest sources of needs are government agencies, such as the Defense Department, which desire up-to-date military equipment. Needs can be as simple as a self-propelled wheel chair and as complex as a defense system against a missile. Addressing an established need requires some specifications. Specifications may include physical and functional requirements and economic constraints. Since no design process can begin without establishing the problem, it is important that the problem be properly defined.

Synthesis is closely tied to creativity, since creativity is the synthesis of old and/or new ideas and concepts in such a way as to produce a desired effect. Synthesis is a selection and compromise process. It may involve choosing one among several options without any modification or modifying options before selection. Synthesis requires a sound technical background, since it normally involves input from several applied sciences. Some of the required information may come from a scientific background, whereas the rest of the information comes from the creativity and experience of the designer. Of course, no synthesis can take place without analysis and optimization.

Analysis and optimization require the use of mathematical models. Analysis involves calculations to determine sizes or parameters, along with materials needed to satisfy the defined need. Analysis may involve highly iterative processes that require good mathematical techniques. These mathematical processes are presented in Chapter 4. Optimization, which involves selection of the best possible solution, is discussed in Chapters 7, 8, and 9.

The evaluation phase deals with measuring the completed design against the specifications given in the problem statement. It usually involves prototype building and testing to ascertain operating performance or factors such as reliability. The result of the evaluation phase may yield a satisfactory design, or it may lead to further modification in the design. Any changes and/or modifications are incorporated into the prototype assembly for continued testing and evaluation. This process of continuous revisions and improvements to the design is repeated until satisfactory performance has been achieved.

The final stage in the design process is the presentation of the design, which involves communicating it through such means as graphics. Depending on the product and the design environment, some "selling" of the design may be required. The design is really not complete if one cannot sell it; therefore, a great deal of effort should be applied in the presentation of a design.

The design process thus far described has been the traditional approach. However, the proliferation of computer systems and analysis software has given rise to new philosophies and models for the design process. For example, an account of the simplified version of the steps in design as recommended by the German Society of Engineers has been given by Rankers [4]. In the light of the models for the design process, a more general approach to design, specifically mechanical system design, may be represented as shown in Figure 1.2. Discussion of some of these steps is given in the next section. However, we can immediately note that Figure 1.2 reveals clearly the iterative nature of this design process, which makes it well suited for a CAD environment.

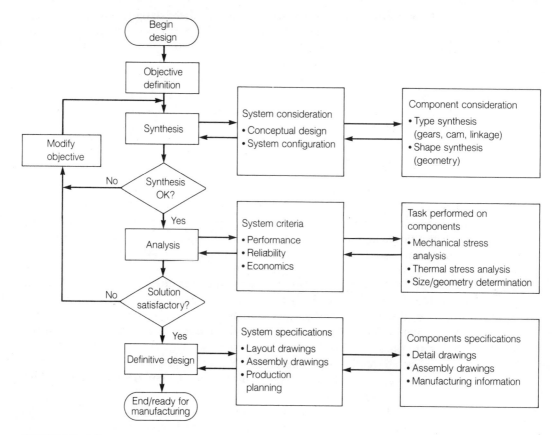

FIGURE 1.2

Mechanical system design in CAD environment.

1.3   ELEMENTS OF COMPUTER-AIDED DESIGN

Computer-aided design involves two main factors, the system factor and the human factor. The CAD system consists mainly of hardware and software.

Hardware, which consists of the physical components of the computer system, includes:

- The host computers
- Display devices
- Interactive devices
- Output devices

A detailed description of the hardware components of the CAD system is given in Chapter 2.

Software is a set of written instructions, procedures, and rules that directs the operation of the computer. Emphasis is laid on the development of software throughout the subsequent chapters of this book.

The human factor concerns the training of the designer or the engineer, without whom the CAD system becomes a useless tool. The designer behind the system is involved with three components of computer-aided design:

- Computer-aided analysis
- Computer-aided visualization
- Computer-aided synthesis

The elements of computer-aided design are shown in Figure 1.3.

COMPUTER-AIDED ANALYSIS

Computer-aided analysis is the use of specialized and/or general-purpose software programs to perform the normal calculations in a design process. Problems that would be difficult to solve manually, either because of their complexity

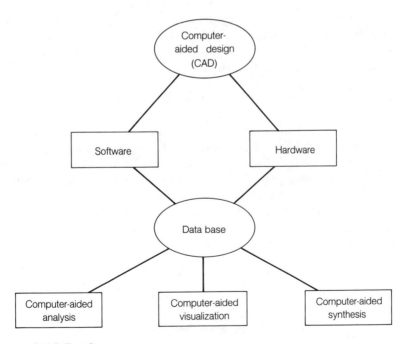

FIGURE 1.3

Elements of computer-aided design.

or their magnitude, are easily solved using the computer as a tool. Consider the difficulty involved in trying to invert a 100×100 matrix. If one undertakes this task manually, the time required to accomplish the inversion may be more than a month, and at its completion, the solution may not be accurate. From this illustration, it is obvious that by using the computer to perform such tedious and time-consuming work, the designer is free to give more attention to the results. As a result of relief from routine calculations, there may well be an increase in the designer's efficiency and the creativity.

COMPUTER-AIDED VISUALIZATION

There are various ways of treating computer-aided visualization, but the simplest, which is given by Mistree [3], is summarized here. Computer-aided visualization includes the use of a computer as:

- An automated drafting tool and in computer graphics;
- An aid in other graphical communications, such as preparation of bar charts and plots;
- A means of making real-time observations of the response of a model to prescribed inputs.

Automated drafting is simply using the computer to do what is normally done with conventional drafting tools such as a T-square and set square. Automated drafting allows the designer quickly to create the drawing of the elements or parts that are being designed. The term *computer graphics* is often used to mean automated drafting; however, this is not quite correct. Computer graphics means the use of the the computer to define, store, manipulate, interrogate, and present pictorial output. Automated drafting (which may be better called interactive computer graphics) allows the user also to interact with the picture in real time.

Graphical communication and real-time observation are essential in a design process. Both aid the designer in synthesis as well as in analysis. Real-time observation is especially crucial if there is any form of simulation in the design phase. For example, John Deere Company uses the effect of real-time observation in simulating the dynamic impact on various parts of a tractor as it travels over rough terrain. Parts that are prone to failure are detected and are redesigned. This procedure saves money and avoids waste of materials. In fact, the heart of computer-aided design is computer-aided visualization. Computer-aided visualization makes design very interesting, allowing the designer to measure completely the effect of such things as tolerances in the overall design of a product. Changes in parts can be made easily while still in the design phase.

COMPUTER-AIDED SYNTHESIS

The primary purpose of synthesis in the design process is to provide information needed to improve the system design. Many times the synthesis process yields several alternative solutions; the one considered most profitable must then be selected. This selection process requires considerable insight into the nature and performance of the system being designed as well. The effect of variation of the design parameters on the entire system may be evaluated by simulation. It may even be necessary to vary the structure and/or the configuration of the system. The interpretation of the simulation results would normally lead to making some judgments concerning the design. Certainly this is not an easy task; often the insight required to make such judgments comes from many years of design experience.

Computer-aided synthesis requires the use of the computer to support human judgment. In the future the greatest impact on computer-aided synthesis may come from the use of *artificial intelligence*, the so-called expert systems. These are programs that can solve problems by utilizing the same domain knowledge and heuristics used by experts [5,6]. Expert systems can perform the tasks of experts because they simulate expert judgement. An expert system consists of three main parts: (1) A knowledge base, the source of facts and heuristics associated with a given problem; (2) a context, a global data base with histories of what actions have been taken in the past for a particular problem; and (3) an inference mechanism, a process (or algorithm) for reaching decisions based on the information of the knowledge base.

Expert systems would no doubt revolutionize the process of synthesis during the design phase. Good decisions require as much information as possible. It is unlikely that any one designer could possess all the necessary information for a particular situation, yet it could be possible for much of it to be resident in the data base of a computer system. If well constructed, such a system could allow reliable decisions in synthesis to be made in a relatively short time, even for difficult problems. Yet before getting very excited about this prospect, one must remember that expert systems are still in the developmental stage. In the meantime, good synthesis and analysis software exists. For example, in kinematics, there are presently well-developed and commercially available synthesis design packages that can be used until expert systems are fully operational. (A good example of such a package is LINKAGES, developed at the University of Minnesota.)

1.4 ADEQUATE AND OPTIMUM DESIGN

When the engineer follows the steps outlined in Section 1.2, he or she should arrive at a solution. There are two questions that need to be posed before the design can be considered complete. The first question is related to the adequacy of the design, and the other concerns the possibility of improving the design.

Is the design an adequate one? **Adequate design** can be defined as the selection of sizes and/or material needed to satisfy the functional requirements while keeping costs and undesirable effects within tolerable limits. Adequate design is usually based on engineering information available from equations, graphs (in handbooks), and the experience of the designer. Often an adequate size may be discarded in favor of a standard size because of economic considerations. In some instances this approach may be satisfactory, but it is unsatisfactory under certain conditions. For example, in the design of a machine element such as a shaft, the size specified may really be the best solution, given the functional constraints imposed on the original design. In other cases, regardless of how efficient the design may be, it becomes necessary to modify the design in order to achieve a more desirable objective.

The idea of modification is aimed at answering the question of whether the adequate design is the best possible design, given all the constraints imposed on the design. To answer this question requires an understanding of the concept of **optimum design.** By definition, optimum design is the selection of sizes and/or materials in order to minimize an undesirable effect or to maximize a functional requirement. Optimum design requires clear definition of the objective or goal. In most optimum designs, the governing factor is to minimize the cost of production while maintaining satisfactory system performance. In mechanical systems for flight, the objective could be to make the total system as light as possible without sacrificing strength requirements. The objective may be to transmit as much power as possible while keeping the power transmission components, such as the gear set, as compact as possible. Optimum design usually involves complex calculations that require the use of high-speed computers and the skills to use them.

1.5   BENEFITS OF COMPUTER-AIDED DESIGN

Computer-aided design in the automobile and aircraft industries has revolutionized the design process. Of the many benefits of computer-aided design, some are easy to quantify, and others are not. Here is a partial list.

INCREASE OF DESIGN EFFICIENCY AND EFFECTIVENESS

The benefit of computer-aided design is most noticeable in the efficiency and effectiveness of the designers. Although these two terms are similar, there is a functional difference best given by Mistree [3]: **Efficiency** is a measure of the ability of the designer to apply the design methods as well as possible in relation to a predetermined performance criteria (for example, time or cost). **Effectiveness** has been defined as a measure of the designer's ability to partition a design problem into parts that optimize the use of the designer's judgment, the mathematical tools and the computer-human interaction.

Efficiency and effectiveness are increased with computer-aided design because those chores that are tedious and time-consuming can easily be handled through the use of the computer. Because of the use of the computer in the design, the designer is not discouraged from applying any techniques that may involve complex calculations, such as finite element analysis. In addition, various methods of optimization may be applied in an attempt to produce an optimal design.

SIMPLIFICATION OF THE DESIGN PROCESS

Many design projects require the interaction of the various designers—for example, the engineer with the drafter. This interaction may require that design concepts be developed first in one division and then transmitted to another, a process that can be inefficient and frustrating. However, with the use of computer-aided design, all data are stored in the data base of the system and can be called up by any of the designers to examine the status of the design. In addition, computer-aided visualization is a tremendous aid in kinematics designs because machine motions can be easily visualized.

ECONOMY OF MATERIAL AND LABOR

Traditionally, the last stage in the design of a product may be the building and the testing of prototypes. Building of prototypes helps to spot faulty designs and often may lead to modifications. Of course, if the prototype does not function properly, materials have been wasted, so this practice can be very expensive. The use of computer-aided design helps to minimize the cost associated with product development. More importantly, computer-aided design makes it possible to simulate some aspects of the performance of a proposed product early in the design phase. Several alternatives, in fact, can be evaluated without building any of them.

BETTER DOCUMENTATION

It is considered a good engineering practice to document every design step properly. This documentation makes it possible to make modifications and to spot any errors or mistakes. It is also important that working drawings be properly labeled and dimensioned as well as readable and clear. The use of computer-aided design makes it possible both to produce good working drawings and to preserve clearly the results of some of the computations involved in the design process. Also, it is easier to edit drawings and correct mistakes on the computer than it would be to do so manually. In addition, computer-aided design assists in communications between groups because it forces them to use the same language in describing phenomena of design and results.

REFERENCES

1. Deutschman, A. D., W. J. Michels, and C. Wilson. *Machine Design*. New York: Macmillan Publishing Company, 1975.

2. Shigley, J. E., and L. D. Mitchell. *Mechanical Engineering*. New York: McGraw-Hill Book Company, 1983.

3. Mistree, F. "Computer-Based Design Synthesis," ASEE Annual Conference Proceedings, 1982.

4. Haugh, E. J., editor. *Computer Aided Analysis and Optimization of Mechanical System Dynamics*. New York: Springer-Verlag, 1984, 421–425.

5. Nau, D. S. "Expert Computer Systems." *Computer* (February 1983): 63–85.

6. Van Horn, Mike. *Understanding Expert Systems*. New York: The Waite Group Inc., 1986.

Tools for Computer-Aided Design

2.1 HISTORICAL BACKGROUND

During the 1960s, the automotive and aerospace industries introduced the computer into the design phase of automobiles and airplanes. The use of the computer in drafting and design underwent a radical change with the development of the Sketchpad system by Dr. Ivan Sutherland. This system involves a data structure, cathode ray tube (CRT) plotting, and human interaction with the machine.

In 1970, the Applicon Corporation made available the first complete CAD system; then other companies followed, such as ComputerVision and Calma. However, the cost of these systems limited their use to large companies. With recent rapid advances in the development of the microprocessor and minicomputers, the cost of these systems has been reduced. Because of this, many educational institutions are now acquiring these tools.

The mathematical background needed for computer-aided design is not new; the only thing that can be considered new is the system itself, which is composed of both hardware and software. Nevertheless, the CAD system is a tool, and will always remain a tool, for the engineer/designer.

2.2 COMPUTER AND GRAPHICS IMAGES

Before discussing the various hardware components of a CAD system, we need to understand interactive computer graphics. Besides picture production, interactive computer graphics includes the designer using pictures to communicate with the computer. There are two major ways of producing a picture: vector representation and raster (pixel) representation.

A vector is a directed line segment. In vector representation each picture/image is defined in terms of lines that make up the picture, each line being defined by the coordinates of its endpoints. In such representation, curves or circles are represented by a series of short, straight line segments or by polynomial approximations, so a circle is drawn as an n-sided polygon. The number n determines how smooth the circle appears to the observer.

The term **raster** means grid, or net. To represent a picture in a raster form, the entire picture is decomposed into small homogenous cells on a grid. Each of these cells contains one of a range of colors and shades, popularly known as picture elements (PELs), or **pixels.** The quality of a raster picture depends on the resolution (the number of pixels per unit area) and the shades and range of colors allowable in each picture element. If the pixels are small and have a great variety of colors and shades, the picture is more pleasing than if the pixels are large with few shades and colors.

Each of these methods presents some desirable features. The storage requirement for vector graphics is considerably smaller than that of raster graphics, since only the coordinates of the endpoints of a line need be stored. Also, because pictures are represented as a series of straight lines, the vector graphics method is a faster and more precise image-processing approach and lends itself to the more natural process of geometric entity creation. On the other hand, the raster (pixel) representation, though requiring more memory, is better suited for fine picture detailing such as color shading.

Understanding these two ways of developing a picture/graphics image is helpful in selecting some of the hardware components of a CAD system suitable for a particular application. For example, a vector input device is more suitable for communicating picture information to the computer if the object can be considered linear or can be approximated by a series of straight lines, as in the cases of circles or polygons.

2.3   HARDWARE COMPONENTS*

In this chapter only the hardware components are discussed. These consist of:

1.   Host computer
2.   Input devices
3.   Output devices

*Some of these materials are taken from *Introduction to Computer Graphics* by Tektronix, Inc., and are used with permission.

A complete CAD workstation consists of these three components. A schematic representation of a typical CAD workstation is shown in Figure 2.1 (see also Figure 2.2).

There are several books that treat the subject of the host computer; therefore, we discuss only the input and output devices. In some cases the input and the output devices can be combined into a single unit called a **terminal**. This is very similar to a combination of a TV set and a typewriter keyboard (see Figure 2.3). Terminals may be viewed from two aspects: operation mode and display technology.

The term **operation mode** refers to whether the terminal is dumb or intelligent. Dumb terminals provide input and display; their use is decreasing. Intelligent terminals contain their own microprocessors, which enables them to perform many tasks, such as graphics computations, that would otherwise be done by the host computer. Some important features of intelligent terminals that determine their usefulness include (1) screen resolution, (2) color range, (3) speed of the microprocessor, and (4) communication capabilities for connection to a computer. Both the accuracy of performance and the speed of the computer are affected by the word size and memory size.

Most commercially available terminals are based on the cathode ray tube (CRT) technology. There are, however, other display technologies available, such as plasma display. We briefly discuss plasma display technology after treating CRT technology. For more studies in other display technologies, the reader should consult the suggested reading references.

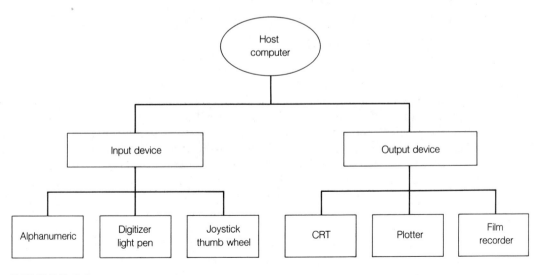

FIGURE 2.1

Schematic of CAD workstation.

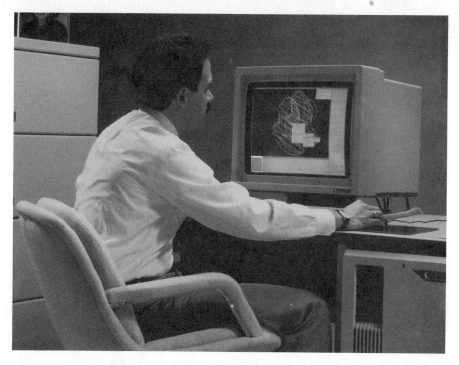

FIGURE 2.2

A CAD workstation. (Courtesy of Computervision Corp.)

CATHODE RAY TUBE

It appears that for many years to come the CRT will continue to be the dominant display device for many CAD systems. The ubiquity of the CRT is due to several factors. Among these are its speed of response, high-quality resolution, adaptability to several scanning techniques (stroke, random, or raster), reliability, visibility in high ambient light, and longevity. Despite these advantages, the CRT has some drawbacks: It cannot store information and maintain a high brightness level for a prolonged period of time, and its display is not digital, and it wears out. These qualities may be desirable in certain applications.

A simplified representation of one type of widely used CRT is shown in Figure 2.4. In essence, the CRT consists of four parts: an electron gun, a focusing device, a deflection system, and a phosphor-coated viewing screen. The operation of the CRT can be explained in simple terms: An electron beam emitted from heated cathode strikes the phospor, causing it to glow. The data to be displayed are applied in the form of a video signal to the electron beam current-controlling electrode of the electron gun, in synchronization with the deflection signals. In this way, the screen provides a visual display that corresponds to the electrical signal contained in the electron beam.

FIGURE 2.3

A CAD terminal. (Courtesy of Computervision Corp.)

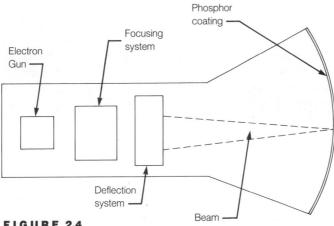

FIGURE 2.4

A schematic of a CRT.

The electron gun is the source of the high-density electron beam, the current of which can be modulated. The electron beam is actually produced by the application of an electric field to the surface of the cathode. The electron gun may be of two forms, crossover or laminar flow. The **crossover** gun is designed in such a way as to provide an intense electron beam that abruptly converges to the phosphor screen, whereas the **laminar flow** gun, specifically the direct-replacement flow gun, provides a more uniform, intense source of electron emission.

The focusing device may consist of either magnetic coils or an electrostatic lens, depending on the method used in focusing the electron beam. If magnetic coils are used, then focusing is achieved by forces created in the magnetic field as the divergent electron beam enters the magnetic field. If, however, the focusing is electrostatical, then by application of appropriate voltage, the lens causes the divergent electron beam to focus on the screen.

The deflection system, like the focusing system, consists of either magnetic coils or metal plates, depending on the means of deflection. If the deflection is by means of the magnetic fields, then two pairs of coils, mounted in such a way as to provide both vertical and horizontal deflection, are used. Deflection of the electron beam to a desired point on the screen is achieved by adjusting the current in the magnetic coils. If, however, deflection is achieved by electrostatic means, then two sets of metal plates mounted at right angles to each other are used to produce horizontal and vertical deflection. CRTs for computer graphics applications use a combination of an electrostatic focusing system and a magnetic deflection system because this combination has been found to have good resolution characteristics.

The viewing screen is comprised of a thin layer coated with phosphor particles and a thin film of aluminum deposited over the phosphor. The purpose of the aluminum is to establish electrical potential at the screen. The type of phosphor used depends on the desired application. For example, if animation is of particular interest, the CRT may be constructed from a phosphor with low persistence (time it takes an emitted light to decay to 10% of its original intensity).

COLOR CRTs

Earlier display devices based on CRT technology were monochrome. Soon it was realized that for more aesthetically pleasing displays (compare the viewing pleasure of black-and-white TV with that of color TV) and because of more complex information generated by the computer, full-color capabilities must be incorporated into the display devices. There are many methods in use for incorporating color into the CRT. We will discuss only the two most widely used: mask and beam penetration.

MASK METHODS

The **mask** method makes use of three electron guns for three different colors, red, blue, and green; a mask; and a faceplate coated with phosphors. The method of arranging the electron guns and the type of perforation of the mask distinguish the three types of mask systems in use. If the three electron guns are arranged in a triangular, or delta, configuration and the mask has round holes, it is the **delta gun** system (see Figure 2.5). In the delta system, the faceplate consists of round phosphor dots arranged in sets of red, blue, and green colors. By either a selective turning on and turning off of the three electron guns or adjustment of the intensities of the beams, different colors are obtained.

The mask system in which the electron guns are located in a line, with vertical slots on the mask, and the faceplate consists of vertical strips of phosphor is the **in-line gun trinitron** (see Figure 2.6). The advantage of the trinitron over the delta gun is that it has an improved vertical resolution because of the absence of horizontal structural obstructions. The convergence of the beams is much simpler than in the delta gun.

Another configuration of the mask method is the **precision-in-line system.** This is similar to the trinitron (see Figure 2.7). However, its mask uses slits with horizontal supports. These supports make the mask very rigid, allowing it to be curved spherically. This system offers a simpler solution to the problem of convergence of the three beams over the entire faceplate (screen) than the delta gun. This simplification is the result of a special design feature, a deflection yoke, which—in addition to deflecting the three beams—helps them to converge.

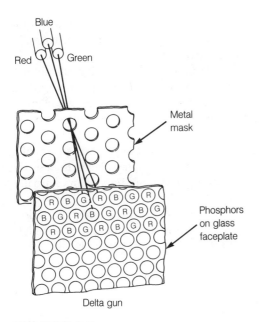

FIGURE 2.5

Delta gun system.

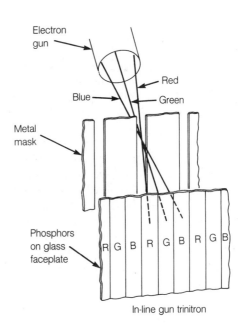

FIGURE 2.6

The in-line gun trinitron system.

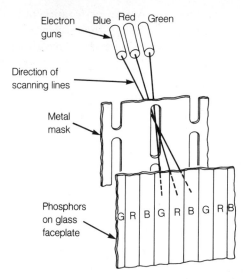

Electron guns — Blue Red Green

Direction of scanning lines

Metal mask

Phosphors on glass faceplate

G R B G R B G R B

FIGURE 2.7

The precision in-line system.

BEAM PENETRATION METHOD

In the **beam penetration** system, two layers of phosphor, separated by a barrier, are placed between an aluminum film and a glass faceplate. The aluminum is the innermost layer, closest to the electron gun. Color generation is controlled by the beam energy coming from a single electron gun.

The entire system normally is equipped with two primary-colors phosphors, which operate best at different voltages or beam energies. For example, at low voltage, the color red usually dominates, and at high voltage the color green does. Other hues are formed at intermediate voltages by the combination of the two dominant primary colors. Because of the fact that the stroke-written lines in the penetration color CRTs are smooth and continuous and do not suffer color infringement, they are useful in raster scan graphics displays. Nevertheless, the penetration color CRTs have other limitations. The more notable ones are inability to display blue and the low brightness of red.

By way of comparison, the two types of color CRTs, mask and penetration, have high resolution. The penetration color CRTs are better suited for high-quality color stroke-written displays. On the other hand, the mask color CRTs are used for full-color raster displays.

STORAGE TUBE TERMINALS

Storage tube terminals are equipped with a direct-view storage tube manufactured by Tektronix, Inc. The direct-view storage tube is also called a **bistable** storage tube display, probably because of the method of manufacturing the tube.

During the manufacturing process, a grid electrode is deposited as an integral part of the phosphor layer on the screen, resulting in a bistable phosphor. A storage tube is noted for retaining an image for a considerable period of time without being refreshed. An image is **refreshed** if it is rewritten many times so that it appears to the observer to be steady on the screen. The storage tube has some advantages that make it attractive, including low cost, ability to display a large amount of data without flickering, and good (high) resolution (number of points per inch that the computer plots). The storage tube's refresh capability takes a considerable load off the unit responsible for supplying a continual picture on the screen. Hence, these units can be simpler—particularly in their memory elements. In addition, a low-cost hard copy of the picture can easily be obtained. Nevertheless, the storage tube has some disadvantages, such as low brightness and contrast, lack of multicolor capability, and unsuitability for light-pen applications. Perhaps the greatest disadvantage is the fact that editing and interacting with pictures on the CRT is very difficult, which is primarily due to the fact that the screen cannot be selectively erased. To make a change in a picture requires that the entire picture be erased and repainted, which takes some time. Recent models, in addition to the storage mode, now include a nonstore or write-through mode to help alleviate some of these difficulties.

RASTER (GRAPHICS) TERMINALS

The operation of the raster graphics terminal is similar to that of a television set. An electron beam from an electron gun bombards the inner surface of the CRT, causing the phosphor coating on the CRT to glow. The creation of the picture element on the raster terminal depends on whether the terminal is monochrome raster or color raster. The mode of operation for the monochrome raster terminal and the color raster terminal are somewhat different.

In the monochrome raster, an electron beam from a single electron gun sweeps the face of the CRT by moving through a series of parallel horizontal lines (raster lines). As the beam sweeps each raster line, it is turned on and off very precisely to create the portion of the picture that falls on that raster line (see Figure 2.8). In the case of the color raster, three electron beams (from three electron guns), which cause three separate phosphors to glow red, green, and blue, sweep the face of the CRT simultaneously. A special convergence circuitry is used to maintain the proper timing, direction, and focus for each beam, in order to produce a crisp, clear picture. Colors other than red, blue, and green are produced by causing the red, green, and blue phosphors to glow in appropriate intensities and combinations.

Whether it is monochrome or color, the glow of the phosphor is short-lived (a fraction of a second). To keep the phosphor glowing, the terminal continually refreshes the display by repeating the electron beam bombardment several times per second. If the refresh rate is too low, the phosphor begins to fade before the refresh cycle, causing the display to flicker. Some terminals have refresh rates as low as 30 hertz; some, like the Tektronix 4100 series, have refresh rates of 60

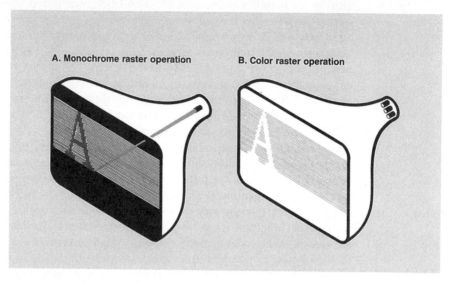

A. Monochrome raster operation   B. Color raster operation

FIGURE 2.8

Basic raster operation. (Courtesy of Tektronix, Inc.)

hertz, which ensures a bright, stable, flicker-free display. Flicker is an undesirable feature because it is very tiring to the eyes. Monochromatic flicker is worse than color flicker.

The display characteristics of the raster terminal are digitally controlled, since the terminal itself is driven by digital circuitry. Each of the electron beams is turned on and off very rapidly and precisely to create a pattern of dots (pixels) on the screen. The color, the intensity, and the on/off operation of a pixel are controlled by graphics commands. If a group of closely spaced pixels are illuminated, it appears to the human eye as a single image. The number of pixels that the terminal can display along each of its axes determines the display resolution. A low-resolution terminal can display 200 pixels along the horizontal axis and 200 pixels along the vertical axis, for a total of 40,000 pixels per screen (this resolution is popularly designated as 200 $\times$ 200 pixels). A medium-resolution terminal may be 640 $\times$ 480 pixels (i.e., 640 pixels along the horizontal axis and 480 along the vertical axis). Higher-resolution terminals are capable of displaying 1,000 pixels along each axis. Generally, sharper, crisper displays are obtained from terminals with higher pixel resolutions.

PICTURE DISPLAY ON RASTER TERMINAL

As we have previously noted, any picture displayed on a raster consists of a collection of lighted pixels. Picture display then requires that the terminal have information as to which pixel to turn on, in which color, and of what intensity.

This operation seems complicated, and it is, but the user does not have to specify one by one which pixels to turn on. These computations are generally done by the host computer or by the intelligent graphics terminals through the **firmware** (programs stored in read-only memory [ROM] chips) instruction sets in the terminal ROM chip. Their main function is to interpret graphics commands so that the terminal knows what graphics action to take. Once the terminal analyzes the command, checking for error, it checks whether the parameter values are within range; then it translates the command into internal picture data, which the terminal's display circuitry can understand; next, the picture data is stored in the display memory. To display the picture, the display circuitry scans the display memory and translates the data into signal timing and intensities for each electron gun. A picture is obtained when the terminal's circuitry then displays this data as a collection of illuminated pixels on the screen.

From our discussion so far, it would seem that the raster terminal displays only graphics information; this is not so. For example, the Tektronix 4100 series terminals contain, among other memory requirements, a graphics area and a dialog area. The graphics area displays information from the graphics memory, whereas the dialog area displays textual information such as error or warning messages. Since the dialog area fills quickly, it is designed so that when it is full, the original text "scrolls up" out of sight, making way for a new text. This text is not lost; rather, it is stored in the dialog memory. The dialog area can be made visible or invisible by the use of a dialog key. This ability makes it possible to make the dialog area transparent, with the result that any graphics information behind it is still visible.

RASTER TERMINAL AND GRAPHICS PRIMITIVES

We have noted that the creation of pictures requires that individual pixels be turned on and off. The implication is that to draw even a straight line, for example, we must decide ahead of time which pixels on the terminal must be turned on. With this approach, interactive computer graphics would be very difficult. Fortunately, the raster terminals are equipped so that the calculations for generation of **graphics primitives** (fundamental units of graphics displays, such as line segments, arcs, circles, and markers) are predefined in the terminals.

Each graphics primitive is then generated by a command. A straight line between the two points (200, 300 and 1000, 2000) in terminal coordinates can be drawn by such a command as

```
MOVE 200,300
DRAW 1000,2000
LINE (300,500) - (600,900)
```

In drawing the straight line, we have defined a vector. The raster terminal is equipped with the vector primitive graphics that make it easy not just to draw a line but also to specify its style (such as dotted or dashed) and color.

In a similar fashion, an arc or a circle may be drawn. However, it is important to realize that a curve or a circle is drawn by the use of a series of straight lines, which means that smoothness of a circle (or a curve) obtained depends on the pixel resolution of the screen and the number of straight line segments used.

THE RASTER SCAN TERMINAL

The raster scan terminal uses a standard television monitor method for display. The graphic image is created by a series of pixels. These dots are traced out in a series of parallel horizontal lines until the display surface is covered. This line-by-line sweep across the entire display surface is the scanning raster. If the horizontal line is written from the top to the bottom of the display surface, it is called **sequential scanning.** Sequential scanning may produce flicker if the refresh rate is such that it does not match the persistence of the phosphor. The raster scan terminal has a scan converter, the function of which is to convert the line and character information to a form compatible with the raster presentation.

The advantages of the raster scan are its low cost and its ability to display a large amount of information without flicker. It allows for the representation of both static and dynamic objects in the same display surface. This is possible because during each refresh cycle each individual pixel is addressed. The disadvantages of the raster scan can be traced to this feature of pixel-by-pixel addressing. For example, raster scan requires a lot of storage and calculation for each pixel, especially if an object is to be displayed in colors. Its circuitry design is very tasking, since large amounts of data must be transferred from the display memory to the screen (monitor).

THE REFRESH TERMINALS

The refresh terminal is very suitable in engineering designs requiring the simulation of dynamic motion. Its display of the graphics image is different from that of a TV in that the beam traces a set of variously placed lines anywhere on the screen.

The images on a refresh terminal are repainted (refreshed) many times per second in order to maintain bright, crisp, and sharp images. If the refresh rate is less than 30 times per second, a phenomenon called flicker results. An excessive number of vectors (a very dense data base) could cause the refresh rate to slow.

In addition to the CRT, the refresh terminal has two other essential elements: a picture memory and a display generator. The function of the first is to hold the data necessary to draw the picture. The display generator draws the picture on the CRT. The images have short duration, which makes the refresh CRT very suitable for simulation of dynamic motion.

The primary advantage of the refresh terminal is that it allows interaction with the image in real time. Editing is very simple, and selective erasure can easily be implemented. In addition, the refresh terminal can be used with all kinds of input devices, especially the light pen. As previously mentioned, the primary disadvantage is that it is not flicker-free, and it is also very expensive at present.

PLASMA DISPLAY

The plasma display device, often called the gas-discharge display, is another technology that may impact CAD systems. In its simplest form, the configuration of a plasma display consists of a gas cavity and two substrates. Each substrate consists of parallel conductors on which is overlayed a transparent dielectric. The conductors are arranged in such a way that the conductor in one substrate is perpendicular to that on the other substrate. The gas cavity usually contains a gas mixture, which is predominantly neon-argon. By proper application of voltage to the conductors, the gas in the cavity breaks down and produces a short burst of light or a glow. The voltage is then changed to sustain the glow.

The plasma display is generally of one of two kinds, AC or DC (see Figure 2.9); the most recent plasma displays come equipped with both. There are several characteristics that make the plasma display suitable for computer graphics applications. The display cells can operate in memory or refresh modes, making refreshing unnecessary, and they have increased brightness. In addition, there is less flicker and less small-scale image motion. The primary disadvantage seems to be high cost. Interested readers may consult the suggested readings for more details on plasma displays.

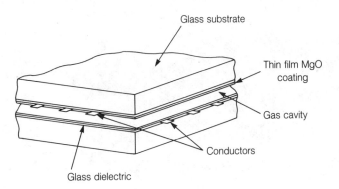

FIGURE 2.9

Typical AC plasma panel construction.

2.4   INPUT DEVICES

Input devices are the tools used to enter data into the main computer for the purpose of communication (interaction) between the user and the host computer. These devices make it possible to interrogate the data base, to modify existing designs, and/or to create new designs. The more commonly used input devices are the alphanumeric keyboard, the light pen, the joystick, the mouse, and the digitizing tablet.

ALPHANUMERIC KEYBOARD

The **alphanumeric keyboard** is similar to the keyboard of a typewriter but differs from it in the number of keys. Most regular typewriter keyboards contain no more than 60 keys. The CAD keyboard generally contains more than 75 keys (see Figure 2.10).

The keyboard is used to enter nongraphic information, such as numerical data. Its most useful function is issuing commands. Most keyboards have special function keys that are used to move a cursor (tracking marker) and to zoom in on displayed entities. An important point to remember about the CAD keyboard

FIGURE 2.10

Alphanumeric keyboard (with a mouse). (Courtesy of Tektronix, Inc.)

function keys is that the function identified with each key is computer controlled. This means that the function can be changed as desired by the user. This makes it possible to include the function keys along with a **menu** on a digitizer surface (described later).

The alphanumeric keyboard is an input device with the rate of interaction depending on the user. If the user is not a good typist, the level of interaction will be very low; however, the rate is higher for a good typist. Though the alphanumeric keyboard is a good interactive input device, it is no match for the light pen.

LIGHT PEN

The most widely used interactive input device is the **light pen.** This device usually has a shape similar to a fountain pen (see Figure 2.11), making it easy for the user to handle.

The light pen is used either for creating new drawings on the screen or for editing existing drawings. It contains a light-sensitive element, which is usually a photodiode or a photo transistor, that functions by detecting changing light that appears on the screen. When a light pen is placed on a line on the screen and activated, an interrupt is sent to the computer; then, the computer software decides what action to take. The interrupt is a highly time-dependent function. If a storage tube is used, this time reference will be lost; therefore, the light pen is limited to use with the refresh CRT. A more detailed description of the principle of operation of the light pen can be found in a book by Scott [1].

JOYSTICK

The **joystick,** along with thumbwheels, trackballs, mouse, and dials, belongs to a class of input devices that move a cursor about on the screen. These devices allow the user to "point" to lines or objects directly on the screen but cannot be used to locate a very precise point on the screen.

The joystick, a spindle usually less than 6 inches in height, is vertically mounted on a base (see Figure 2.12). Most have at least four degrees of freedom, allowing forward, backward, and sideways movement. There are generally three types of joysticks: the displacement, the force-operated, and the switch-activated, of which the most commonly used is the displacement type.

DIGITIZER

The most versatile and accurate input device is the **digitizer.** A digitizing unit consists of a flat surface, usually called a *tablet*, and a pencil-like stylus, which can be moved over the surface of the tablet (see Figures 2.13 and 2.14). The tablet is an electronic unit consisting of a rectangular grid of embedded wires. The tablet operates by means of electric impulses generated in the wires, making it possible to sense the location of the stylus. The position of the stylus relative to the

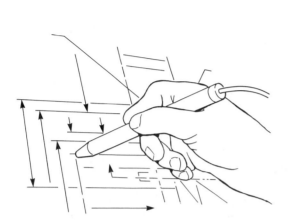

FIGURE 2.11

Light pen.

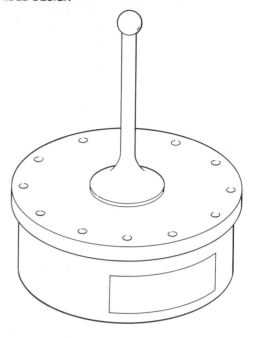

FIGURE 2.12

Joystick.

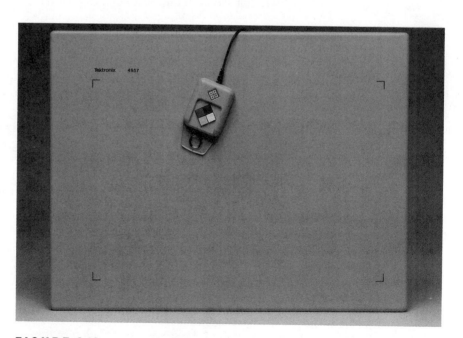

FIGURE 2.13

A graphics tablet with four-button cursor. (Courtesy of Tektronix, Inc.)

FIGURE 2.14

Pedestal graphics tablet for digitizing drawings. (Courtesy of Tektronix, Inc.)

tablet is, of course, determined by decoding the stylus signal. Usually, a small spot (cursor) appears on the screen to indicate the position of the stylus in relation to the tablet.

The digitizer, being an input device, is used to convert graphic data into digits or a binary form that is acceptable and processable by the computer. The digitizer can perform all the functions of a light pen or a joystick. It differs from the joystick in that it measures the absolute location of a point in relation to the permanent frame of reference provided by the tablet, whereas the joystick measures only changes in location of points. It is better than the light pen as a pointing device because with the digitizer the indication registers in the data base, whereas with the light pen the indication occurs in the display file. The digitizer is used mainly for tracing drawings or converting rough sketches into finished drawings. Conversion is made easier by overlaying a menu on a portion of or the entire table without disturbing the interaction between the stylus and the tablet. More details of the digitizer and its operation can be found in a book by Newman [2].

2.5   OUTPUT DEVICES

The output from a CAD system can be of two major types: temporary or permanent (hard copy). Temporary output is displayed only on the CRT, whereas permanent output is recorded by any of several devices, including plotters and graphic film recorders. The CRT display is used to make changes as desired before permanently recording the drawings or data. The accuracy and/or the resolution of a hard copy is generally better than that of the CRT.

In this book, discussion of hard copy is limited to plotters. Information concerning the graphic film recorder can be obtained from [1]. Plotters can be classified into two major categories: the **electromechanical** pen plotters and the **electrostatic** plotters.

ELECTROMECHANICAL PEN PLOTTER

Three types of pen plotters are currently in use: the drum, the flatbed, and the beltbed (see Figures 2.15 through 2.17). These all operate in an incremental mode, in which the plotting tool, not necessarily a pen, moves across the plotting surface (or paper) in a series of small steps of approximately 0.001 to 0.01 inch.

In the drum plotter, the paper is wrapped around the drum, which is rotated by a digital stepping motor. Two-dimensional motion is achieved as follows: Transverse motion is produced by the marking tool moving back and forth across the paper and longitudinal motion is obtained by rolling the paper back and forth with the marking tool making firm contact with the paper.

In the flatbed the paper placed on the flat surface is stationary, and the writing head moves simultaneously in two dimensions over the paper. In both the flatbed and the drum, the pen can usually also be moved at 45° relative to the paper. The beltbed plotter is a combination of both the drum plotter and the flatbed plotter.

There are attractive features available in pen plotters, including the capabilities of being equipped with multiple pen heads and of plotting various line widths and colors simultaneously. These features are useful not only to the engineer but also to the artist, whose primary concern is aesthetics. A disadvantage of electromechanical plotters is that they are very slow.

ELECTROSTATIC PLOTTER

The **electrostatic plotter** (see Figure 2.18) was introduced to overcome the slowness of the electromechanical plotter; however, it produces poorer quality drawings than the electromechanical plotter. Like the drum plotter, it produces drawing of unlimited length.

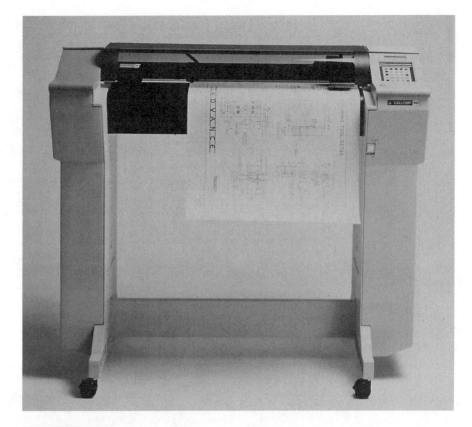

FIGURE 2.15

Drum plotter. (Courtesy of CalComp Group, California Computer Products, Inc.)

This type of plotter consists of a combination of wire nibs, or styli, at a density of up to 200 nibs per inch. The plotter operates as follows: A special type of paper is passed over the nibs, which deposit electrostatic charges on small areas of the paper. Because these charges are invisible, the paper is passed over dark liquid toner particles, which are attracted to the charged areas, producing visible marks. Any excess toner is removed and the paper is quickly dried.

The electrostatic plotter, in addition to having low resolution and accuracy, also requires considerably more computer storage to construct a picture than do the pen plotters. This is because it operates on raster technology, thereby presenting information one line at a time. It is also restricted to one color of ink and therefore is not used for color printing.

FIGURE 2.16

Flatbed plotter. (Courtesy of Xynetics, Inc.)

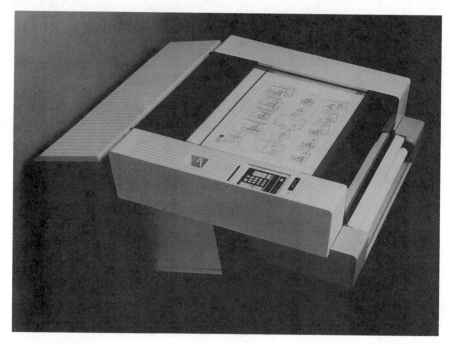

FIGURE 2.17

A beltbed plotter. (Courtesy of CalComp Group; Lockhead Company.)

(a)

(b)

FIGURE 2.18

(a) Electrostatic plotter. (Courtesy of Benson Inc.; A Schlumberger Co.)
(b) Electrostatic plotter. (Courtesy of Versatec; A Xerox Company.)

2.6 PERSONAL COMPUTER (PC) BASED CAD SYSTEMS

Most of the application programs for computer-aided design were originally written for mainframe and minicomputers. Because of this and because the hardware components described so far were initially very expensive, the use of CAD systems was once limited to large corporations and a few universities. This limitation has been removed by the introduction of both application programs based on the personal computer and less expensive input and output devices.

It is projected that in the future, 90% of CAD activities will be accomplished by the PC-CAD systems. Just as the area of computer-aided design is progressively changing, so also are the information and the software packages needed to execute computer-aided design. It is certain that hardware systems are useless without the appropriate application software packages. Therefore, any good software packages for computer-aided design on PCs must provide the functions of geometry creation, dimensioning, and labeling and geometry editing.

Geometry creation is the construction of shapes by making use of lines, arcs, and some primitive shapes such as circles. It may also include surface and curve designs. To be useful in curve design, the software packages must have splines and Bezier programs (the principles of splines and Bezier curves are discussed in Chapter 6).

Since most PC-CAD systems are mainly drafting tools, the feature of dimensioning and labeling is very essential. It is, therefore, desirable that the software package be capable of automatic dimensioning. If the system is to be used for detailing of complex parts such as injection molds, then ordinate dimensioning must be a feature of the software packages. Of course, these demands (automatic and ordinate dimensions) imply much sophistication and the use of expert systems programs that are capable of deciding the type of dimensional information needed for the particular design.

Design in general involves trial and error, requiring the ability to edit a drawing or to modify a design. Editing may require deleting and inserting parts, scaling or rotating the drawing for a view from a different perspective, and zooming in on an area for close examination. A good software package for PC-CAD systems must provide all these features. In addition, automatic cross-hatching is also a desirable feature.

The features just described are found in almost all CAD systems that are mainframe- or minicomputer-based. Other desirable features of a software package for PC-CAD systems include the ability to perform simple calculations (such as calculating areas, volumes, centroids, moments of inertia, and centers of mass) and finite element analysis. A software package for PC-CAD systems with all these features would be very expensive, which may exclude the majority of the users for which the packages are designed. One solution to this problem may be to develop a software package capable of linking up, through the use of a modem, with programs for mainframe-based CAD systems that have all these features.

There are many packages available for PC-CAD systems, and many more will be developed in the near future. Some of the more popular ones are AutoCad, VersaCad, SuperCad, Cadkey, and Anvil 1000 MD. We mention these packages not as an endorsement of them but because each possesses some of the features previously discussed, although none, at the time of writing this text, has all the features discussed. To select any of these software packages, an extensive evaluation must be done and many questions must be asked in light of the desired application of the package.

To set up a complete PC-CAD workstation, low-costing output devices should be considered. One such output device is the HP 7475A pen plotter. This is a multipen plotter that is very reliable and produces high-quality drawings (see Figure 2.19). Another output device that could be used is the **direct-screen color copier** (see Figure 2.20). Most of these copiers are based on ink-jet technology. Pictures are produced by placing colored dots onto specially prepared papers or transparency material. Because of this mode of producing pictures, these copiers are able to reproduce accurately both text and graphics created on the screen (see Figure 2.21).

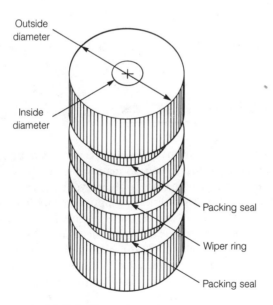

FIGURE 2.19

A sample output from HP 7475A pen plotter.

FIGURE 2.20

A direct screen color copier Tektronix 4695. (Courtesy of Tektronix, Inc.)

2.7   SELECTION OF CAD SYSTEMS

The market is flooded with various types of CAD systems, ranging from systems that are based on PCs to those based on mainframe computers. Every vendor claims to have the solution to the CAD problem, yet each system has only minor differences from all others. In addition, computer technology keeps changing, so that things considered impossible at the very early stages of computer-aided design are now simple matters. For example, the cost of CAD systems led many practitioners to believe that it was not for every industry, but the shift of CAD to PCs makes such an assumption invalid. Of course, the cost and the return on investment for CAD systems must always be considered in their selection. The aforementioned factors make it difficult to set up any set of criteria that can be considered as "the selection criteria." There are two main groups of CAD users, industrial and educational, each with different goals and, therefore, requiring different criteria.

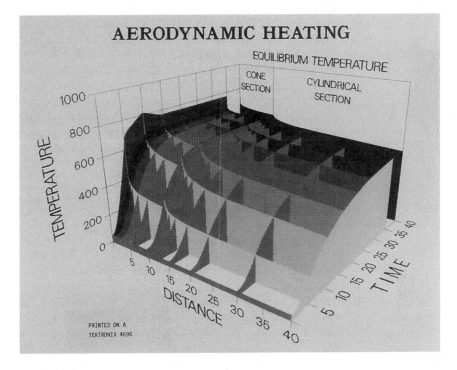

FIGURE 2.21

A sample output from a direct screen color copier. (Courtesy of Tektronix, Inc.)

The selection suggestions offered here are meant to be general. Although this book is written primarily for educational institutions, some of the criteria set forth here are geared toward the industrial practitioner. Detailed discussion on the selection process may be found in [3].

The first step in selecting a CAD system is to evaluate the goals and objectives of the user. Then one must decide which of the two approaches to use: The first is to build up the CAD system by assembling the different components and acquiring the software packages from various vendors; the second is to let one vendor deliver a complete package consisting of the various hardware components, software packages, and the installation of the complete system. It is said that all the buyer in the second approach has to do is to turn on the key; hence, this is called **turnkey.** The disadvantage of the first approach is that it is time-consuming, complex, and often frustrating, since some hardware components from one vendor may not easily interface with hardware and software from another. The primary disadvantage of the second approach is that it may be more expensive. In addition, the support services obtained from a turnkey system could be inadequate, depending on the particular vendor. Having evaluated one's needs and having decided which approach is more suitable, the next step is to evaluate the hardware and software components of various CAD systems, using certain guidelines given next.

1. **Hardware.** In evaluating the hardware components several issues must be addressed:

    *   The speed and cost of the computer on which the system is based.
    *   The expandability and growth capability of the system.
    *   The interactive capabilities.
    *   The ability to interface with other devices.
    *   The type of graphics terminals (dumb or intelligent).
    *   The response time and the resolution of some of the input and output devices.

2. **Software.** Special attention must be given to the language supported by the software package. Besides having all drafting features (such as scaling, windowing, rotating, translating, multiple views, and so on), the data base can be truly three-dimensional so that geometric modeling and finite element analysis can be performed. Of course, the buyer's application may not require these features. The software must be evaluated on whether or not it is user-friendly, amenable to expansion, and adaptable to user innovation. If one decides on the turnkey approach, then the service support of the vendor must be thoroughly investigated in terms of maintenance, training, and response to calls for assistance.

    For both hardware and software, one must also be aware that some vendors make false claims about the capabilities of their systems, and so asking many questions of users of the same or similar systems is recommended. Finally, before committing any resources to a system, one should have the vendor demonstrate its capabilities, using a typical problem in the operation for which the CAD system is to be utilized.

CONCLUDING REMARKS

The preceding chapters have examined the meaning of computer-aided design and the tools needed for it. Beginning in the next chapter, this book approaches computer-aided design from the educational, rather than the industrial, point of view. Computer-aided design has been very difficult to teach in the universities, not just because of the cost of CAD systems but because many of the universities are trying to match their courses with detailed requirements of specific industries. To the author, it seems that most educators are not properly differentiating between "education" and "training." For computer-aided design, the educational objectives should be to provide the fundamentals, so that the graduate will leave the academic environment with the ability to take the steps necessary to become a CAD practitioner in industry. Therefore, the remainder of the text addresses the theory behind some aspects of application software packages.

REVIEW QUESTIONS

1. What is the difference between vector and raster representation of images?

2. Define the following terms:
   a. Pixel
   b. Resolution

3. What is a good terminal?

4. Name two methods of incorporating color into the CRT.

5. Name three types of terminals. Give the advantages and disadvantages of each.

6. What feature makes plasma display technology attractive?

7. Compare and contrast electromechanical and electrostatic plotters.

8. Describe the process of selecting a CAD system. What criteria must be considered?

SUGGESTED FURTHER READINGS

1. *The CAD/CAM Handbook.* Bedford, Mass.: Computer Vision, 1980.

2. Demel, T., and M. J. Miller. *Introduction to Computer Graphics.* Pacific Grove, Calif.: Brooks/Cole Engineering Div., 1984.

3. Foley, J. D., and A. Van Dam. *Fundamentals of Interactive Computer Graphics.* Reading, Mass.: Addison-Wesley Publishing Company, 1984.

4. Hearn, D., and M. P. Baker. *Computer Graphics.* Englewood Cliffs, N.J.: Prentice Hall, 1986.

5. Refioglu, H. I. Ihan, editor. *Electronic Displays.* New York: Institute of Electrical and Electronics Engineers, Inc., 1983.

REFERENCES

1. Scott, J. E. *Introduction to Interactive Computer Graphics.* New York: John Wiley & Sons, Inc., 1982.

2. Newman, W. M., and R. Sproull. *Principles of Interactive Computer Graphics.* New York: McGraw-Hill Book Company, 1973.

3. Chasen, S. H., and J. W. Dow. *The Guide for the Evaluation and Implementation of CAD/CAM Systems.* Atlanta, Ga.: CAD/CAM Decision, 1979.

Principles of Software Design

3.1 INTRODUCTION

Some people believe that it is easier to make an engineer a good programmer than to teach engineering principles to a computer scientist. This being the case, it is important that someone capable of performing in a CAD environment possess a good working knowledge of software design. It is one thing to write a program, but it is a different thing to produce a quality program. The engineer should be able to write a program that will execute properly at first run. Many programs do not do so because of three types of errors: specification errors, programming errors, and processor discrepancies. If the engineer is not a good programmer, detection of the particular error becomes very frustrating. Therefore, the intention of this chapter is to introduce the reader to the basis of good software (program) design. This chapter may seem very elementary to the reader, who is expected to have had some computing experience, but doing the exercises at the end of the chapter will help the student to realize that writing a program for a given problem is quite different from producing a software for a CAD applications.

Software was defined in Chapter 1 as a set of written instructions, procedures, and rules that directs the operation of the computer. As such the terms *software* and *program* have become virtually interchangeable until recently, when read-only memory chips (ROM) were introduced. Programs that are stored in ROMs have been termed **firmware,** since these programs cannot be altered. Programs on other storage media, such as files, are called software. But because the programs the student is going to write are stored in files rather than in ROM chips, we will still use the word software and program interchangeably.

The primary purpose of any software used in computer aided design is to create a model of the design problem in the computer. Any computer model consists of data structure and algorithms. These two components, which are the essence of any software, are the subject of this chapter. This is in keeping with this book's objective, which is to equip the reader with principles (or tools) needed to function in a CAD environment. Most of the illustrations used are in FORTRAN language, but the principles given are applicable to any high-level language.

3.2 CHARACTERISTICS OF A GOOD SOFTWARE

It is important to understand what constitutes a good software in order both to develop and to select one of quality.

The following are characteristics of good software:

1. **Efficiency.** An efficient program is one that results in the effective use of the central processing unit (CPU) in terms of both time and storage. An efficient software may be costly to develop. In general, the efficiency of a software is related to the size, or complexity, of the program. A smaller program, if it is well designed, is likely to be more efficient than a large, complex program.

2. **Simplicity.** Well-designed software must be very easy to use, or user-friendly, so it is said that the user can "interface freely" with the software. The software should be written in a language that is suitable to the user or should be easy to learn. If software, especially a CAD package, cannot be easily learned, designers are likely to shy away from it, regardless of its capability.

3. **Flexibility.** Flexibility is a measure of the degree of difficulty involved in modifying a software to conform to a new specification. If software is properly designed, future modifications or changes become very easy. Hence the principle: Flexible software requires little maintenance.

4. **Readability.** Readability is a measure of how easily a user can comprehend the logic behind the software. To make a software readable requires proper documentation of the programming process within the program. Style and aesthetics become important in readability of the program; for instance, it is very helpful to leave as much space as possible between various parts of the program. The program must be free of ambiguities.

5. **Portability.** Portability has to do with the ease by which a program may be transferred from one system to another. This feature is highly desirable in the area of computer-aided design; unfortunately, most application programs in computer-aided design today are machine-dependent.

6. **Reliability.** Reliability is a measure of the functionality of the software with respect to a desired specification. Reliability is a very important aspect of

software design, especially because many processes/operations today that are software-dependent deal with human life. To avoid casualities, software must be reliable.

7. **Recoverability.** Well-designed software must not crash because of an error on the part of the user. When the user makes a mistake in the entry of data, the software must have a means of warning the user of the error and at the same time continue to function. This characteristic of a good software is known as recoverability.

These seven characteristics are given as guidelines and, therefore, are not exhaustive. Other features may be found in [1] through [3].

3.3 PRELIMINARIES

Any software consists of three parts: data, algorithm, and structure. The word data as used here represents a set whose members or elements are numerical values, names, symbols, and codes. Algorithm deals with how a set of data should be manipulated. Structure means organization. In effect, the three are related and provide the essential high quality of all good programs. Good software thus provides a good organization of data and algorithm. This relationship can be conceived as shown in Figure 3.1. If the data are properly structured, then less structuring of the algorithm is required and vice versa.

To structure data properly requires an understanding of data structures; therefore, more discussion is given in the next section.

3.4 DATA STRUCTURES

Data structure is the organization of data elements in such a way as to both maintain the logical association and relationship between them and provide access from one data element to another. Each data element may be one of three types:

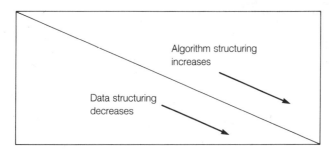

FIGURE 3.1

integer, real, or logical. Integer data elements have integer numeric values, and data elements of the real type consist of numeric values that contain decimal parts. Logical-type data elements have logical values of ".TRUE." and ".FALSE.".

Classification of data structure can be approached in different ways, depending on the application. For example, in computer graphics, related graphic and nongraphic data may be stored in the same data base. However, it may not be appropriate to use same data structure for both of these items. Recognizing that any complex data structure is constructed using simple ones, a simple classification is adopted here (for a more general approach to data structure classification, see [4]). The classification used here views data structure in two ways: fixed and variable. In fixed structures, the relationship between the data elements is invariant whereas in variable structures the relationship between data elements is subject to change.

FIXED DATA STRUCTURES

Discussion of fixed data structures is limited to vectors, arrays, strings, and records.

Vectors

A **vector** is a one-dimensional data structure with the same type of data elements. For example, the data elements are either all real numbers or all logical values. The size of a vector is determined by the number of elements it contains. These elements can be accessed through an index (usually a positive integer) associated with it (see Figure 3.2); e.g., the number 1000 can be accessed through the index number 3. If the programming language is FORTRAN, this number can easily be called or assigned to another entity, as shown in Figure 3.3.

Generally, but not always, the data elements of a vector are numbers. The number of data elements of a vector is fixed, which means that its component elements may be altered but no element can be deleted or added to the set.

Index	Elements
1	5
2	210
3	1000
4	347
5	428

F I G U R E 3.2

Identification of vector elements.

```
C   THE VARIABLE A REPRESENTS THE ELEMENTS OF FIGURE 3.2
C
      INTEGER A(20)
          .
          .
          .

C   X TAKES ON THE VALUE OF INDEX NUMBER 3
      X = A(3)
          .
          .
          .
```

FIGURE 3.3

Assignment of array element to another variable.

Array

An **array** is a set consisting of a fixed number of the same type of data elements. If an array is one-dimensional, then there is no difference between an array and a vector. An n-dimensional array can be thought of as a collection of vectors. The elements of an array are referenced by an ordered set of indexes. The index used depends on the dimension of the array: For example, a two-dimensional array requires a set of two-index values. The limit to the dimensions of an array is set by specifically the compiler of the computer system, some systems permitting arrays of more than three dimensions.

A two-dimensional array can be viewed as row and column vectors or as a table. For example, suppose that during the design of a shaft various materials are to be considered and you want the computer to output the diameter in a tabular form. Suppose that the final output appears as follows.

Design No.	Material			
	1	**2**	**3**	**4**
1	1.0250	1.0000	1.5000	1.3750
2	1.5600	1.2500	1.8750	1.7000
3	2.7500	1.6250	2.0000	1.9000
4	3.2500	2.5650	2.1750	2.1250

The portion of the computer program that will result in such an output may appear as follows:

```
* DESIGN OF SHAFTS USING VARIOUS MATERIALS
* DIA:= DIAMETER
```

```
      REAL DIA(4,4)
           .
           .
           .
      WRITE(6,20)

 20   FORMAT(40X, 'MATERIAL'/5X,'DESIGN #',10X,'1',30X,'2',
    . 10x,'3',10x,'4')
      DO 120 I = 1,4
      DO 120 J = 1,4
      WRITE(6,140)I,DIA(I,J)
120     CONTINUE
140     FORMAT(3x,I2,17X, (4(F10.4)))
           .
           .
```

The order in which the elements of an array with more than one dimension are stored in the computer memory must always be remembered during programming. The elements are stored with the first subscripts varied most rapidly and the last subscripts least rapidly. For example, in a two-dimensional array $P(2, 3)$, the storage of the elements is as follows:

$P(1, 1)$	$P(1, 2)$	$P(1, 3)$	$P(2, 1)$	$P(2, 2)$	$P(2, 3)$

It must be noted that, like the vector, the size of the array remains invariant, although each element may change. This feature can be very useful in storing data for computer graphics applications. For example, if one is dealing with rotation, all that is needed is to enter the rotation matrix in an array form and then change the angles when necessary. Rotation can be accomplished using the matrix given next:

$$[x'\ y'\ 1] = [x\ y\ 1] \begin{bmatrix} \cos\theta & \sin\theta & 0 \\ -\sin\theta & \cos\theta & 0 \\ 0 & 0 & 1 \end{bmatrix}$$

The rotation matrix is a three-dimensional array, and of all the nine elements, only four of them will actually change as the rotation is performed through various angles. This knowledge leads to the designing of a more efficient program.

Strings

A string is a sequence of characters (alphabetic or numeric) or symbols. In FORTRAN, a string is characterized by single quotes—e.g., 'CHEM' or 'A234'—but some FORTRAN compilers require the use of double quotation marks. In BASIC, any variable name followed by the dollar sign is a string, e.g., A$ or U$. The main use of strings is the processing of nonnumerical data. It is particularly .

useful in the development of interactive programs. For example, in BASIC, if you want a response in order to decide what course of action to take, a string such as the following may be used:

```
100 INPUT A$
   .
   .
   .
900 IF A$ = ''YES'' THEN 910 ELSE 2000
```

Record

We have noted that an array contains scalars of the same type, but there is always the need to organize a collection of arrays, and this is done by the use of a record. A record is an ordered set of different data elements. It allows data to be represented as a tree, such as

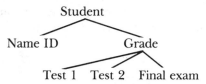

FORTRAN provides for the use of arrays but does not directly provide for the use of records. Therefore, the programmer must construct records from simple data array structures by defining the individual components of the record. For example, suppose that a record of students' grades is to be kept, using an identification number as shown:

ID No.	Grade (%)
1	83
2	60
.	.
.	.
.	.
N	79

A record data structure may be creased in FORTRAN using the program given next.

```
C A RECORD OF GRADES FOR STUDENTS IN A CLASS
C
C CLASS SIZE IS 35
      REAL GRADE (35)
      DO 2 I=1,35
      READ, GRADE(I)
  2   CONTINUE
```

VARIABLE STRUCTURES

Some of the data structures under this classification are list, stack, queue, and file.

List

A **list** is a one-dimensional data structure consisting of an assemblage of elements. A list can be one of two forms: linear or linked.

A **linear list** is made of elements whose adjacent members are contiguous (see Figure 3.4). It is quite similar to a vector, except that a linear list allows addition or deletion of elements, and it need not be homogeneous.

A **linked list** is a list in which each list element has a pointer to its successor. Usually a special pointer is used to mark the head of the list, and the end of the list is marked by a pointer whose value is a null (empty; see Figure 3.5). The link in a linked list may be useful in establishing any desired logical order for the data elements without changing the physical order of the elements (Figure 3.5). For example, suppose that we have an array A that contains some data; we do not want to print the contents sequentially, but we want to dictate the order in which

Cube	Cylinder	Sphere	Cone

FIGURE 3.4

A linear list of geometrical primitives.

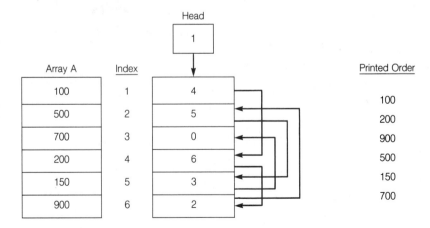

FIGURE 3.5

Use of a linked list.

the data should be printed out. A linked list structure for performing this task is shown in Figure 3.5, and a sample program for this is as follows:

```
* Portion of program illustrating the use of linked list
* Assuming that the array A and LINK exist.
          .
          .
          .
        ORDER = 1
30      CONTINUE
        IF (ORDER.NE.0) THEN
            WRITE(6,40)A(ORDER)
40              FORMAT(20X,I4)
                ORDER = LINK(ORDER)
                GO TO 30
        ELSE
                GO TO 100
        END IF
100     CONTINUE
          .
          .
          .
```

Stack

A **stack** is a linear list of elements that can be accessed at only one end, with all addition and deletion taking place at that one end. An alternate name for stack is LIFO (acronym for last-in first-out). For instance, in a warehouse where boards are placed in stacks, the first to be removed is the board that was last placed.

There are two main types of manipulations of stack: pushing and popping. Pushing is the process of adding an element to a stack, and popping is the process of deleting one.

Stack data structure is most useful for processes where there is an interruption of a main task for a subtask and consequent return to the main; this is called a subroutine. Stacks may also be used for arithmetic operations.

Queue

A queue is a linear list that can be accessed at two locations. Insertion can be performed only on one end (rear), while deletion is carried out on the other end (front); hence, another name for queue is FIFO (an acronym for first-in, first-out).

Since a queue is useful for operations where information is processed in the order in which it is received, it has many applications in operating systems where jobs are queued until an execution slot can be found for the queued individual jobs.

Files

A file is a list (or an array) of records. Since a record may involve hundreds or even thousands of storage units, it is easy to see that a file may require a large amount of storage space. For this reason it is quite inefficient to store files in a main memory; instead, they are stored in secondary (external) storage devices such as magnetic disks and tapes. When it becomes necessary to process the contents of a file, the file is brought into the main memory.

Because files are stored in external devices, a programmer must have the means of accessing these files, which means bringing them into the main memory of the computer. Two access methods are possible in FORTRAN: sequential and direct. The sequential access method permits only orderly retrievals of records in a given file. The direct access method allows random access of records in a file. This is because direct access files are stored in magnetic disks where the records in a file are arranged in a somewhat arbitrary order. Two FORTRAN statements used for transferring data from external memory to the main memory of the computer (or vice versa) are READ and WRITE.

Data structure has been briefly introduced here because of its role in designing software. However, the discussions are not exhaustive, and an interested reader may consult [4] and [5] for further studies of data structure.

3.5   THE DESIGN PROCESS

Before discussing the design process, it is important to remember what software is. Software is a set of written instructions that directs a computer to operate on a set of given data in order to achieve a desired result. Software design is a process of determining how best to instruct the computer to perform a given task. It encompasses every step taken before the actual writing of the necessary instruction in a given computer language.

The design of software can be approached in several steps. For our purpose, we have chosen to view the design process in four parts: analysis, algorithm design, coding, and testing. Each of these steps is examined in the subsequent sections.

ANALYSIS

Many people write programs that are unworkable and full of errors. One reason for this is the lack of analysis, which in this phase involves proper identification of the objective. The designer must take time to understand the task to be performed in order to have an unambiguous and complete statement of the problem.

In the analysis stage, the designer must clearly examine the specifications of the software, which deal mostly with the input and output of data. The selection of data structure or the structuring of the data may begin at this stage (which is why we examined data structure previously). Attention should be paid to the sources of data and the input devices, whether keyboard, tapes, or other peripherals (e.g., digitizer or mouse). The output devices, such as printer/plotter, screen (CRT), or microfilms, should also be considered. The input/output devices affect the manner of coding the program.

Analysis is therefore the key to well-designed software. It is the beginning stage for resolution of problems that may be encountered in the coding stage. A good analysis of the task minimizes coding difficulties. The overall plan for the design of the software should be properly documented.

In summary, the analysis should result in a layout of the design procedure. This procedure should define the purpose, data (input/output), test cases, and expected results of the test cases (see Figure 3.6).

ALGORITHM DESIGN

As we have previously mentioned, an algorithm deals with the manipulation of data. An algorithm is defined as an unambiguous set of instructions or executable actions or steps that must be taken in order to solve a particular problem.

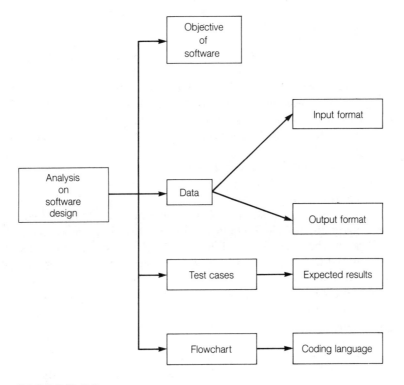

FIGURE 3.6

A typical result of the analysis stage in a software design process.

Therefore, algorithm design involves the development of these instructions in a logical manner, so that the execution of the given instructions results in the solution of the problem. The instructions may be written in English or in what is now called pseudolanguage, or model programming language. However, the best approach to algorithm design, especially for an unexperienced programmer, is the use of flowcharts. We therefore pause to give some attention to flowcharting.

FLOWCHART

The computer may be thought of as a "faithful dummy" that does exactly what it is told, following precisely and sequentially the instructions issued by the programmer. It has no way of telling if the steps of execution of the program are out of sequence. One way of producing an unambiguous sequence is through the use of flowcharts. A flowchart can be viewed as a diagramatic representation of the sequence of operations to be performed by the computer.

A flowchart is extremely useful when programming in an unstructured language such as BASIC. Even with structured languages, it may be useful, although one may have to convert the various constructs into appropriate flowcharts. A flowchart allows the programmer to detect any logical flaws in the program and, hence, enhances the logical thinking process during the design phase of a program. A good flowchart should allow a third party easily to understand the function of a given program.

A flowchart consists of symbols and lines called flow lines. The various symbols in use are shown in Figure 3.7. Certain characteristics of some of these symbols are worth noting. The input/output and process symbols normally have two flow lines—an entry and an exit. The terminal symbol has one flow line, either entering into it (if it is at the end of the flowchart) or leaving it (if it is at the start of the flowchart). The decision symbol has one entrance line and a maximum of three exit lines (two are more common). In the use of the decision symbol, it is imperative that no two branches (exit lines) should be equally valid choices, as this may create some confusion in the program or may even result in an erroneous solution.

Since a process symbol has only one entry line, it becomes necessary to merge the flow lines coming out of the decision symbol into a single line. The point where all the flow lines coming out of the decision box meet is called a **merge point.** There are two ways to represent the merging of the flow lines, shown in Figure 3.8. Under no circumstances should two flow lines enter an operation symbol. It is important to realize that once we have passed the merge point, we can no longer perform operations that will be applicable only to one of the flow paths. Besides, the merge point makes it easier to do a backward trace of the flowchart. It is obvious that once a merge point is located in a flowchart, the preceding operations must have been some form of logical operation.

The best way to construct a flowchart is first to view the computer program as consisting of three main phases, input, processing, and output. Then write short statements about each phase in relation to the problem definition. As an

The *terminal* symbol is used to represent the start or end of a program or a subroutine.

The *paper tape* symbol is used to represent punched paper tape input and/or output.

The *document* symbol is used to represent hard copy output in the form of a paper document or report.

The *generalized input/output* symbol is used to represent input or output in place of another, more specific symbol. It will be used for input designation in most of the samples in this text.

The *process* symbol is used to represent calculations, processing, input/output generalized functions, or any other function not specifically described by one of the symbols.

The *predefined* process is used to represent a subroutine or logical unit.

The *preparation* symbol indicates the initialization of a routine and the setting or modifying of an index.

The *decision* symbol is used to represent a comparison, question, or decision that determines an alternative path to be followed.

The *communication link* is used to represent a connection between two pieces of hardware via communication lines or wires.

The *flow* symbol is used to connect the other symbols. It indicates the sequence of operations.

The *connection* symbol is used to represent a temporary break in the flowchart. It is used to connect broken paths or different pages of the same flowchart.

The *punched card* symbol is used to represent punched card input and/or output.

F I G U R E 3.7

Standard flowchart symbols.

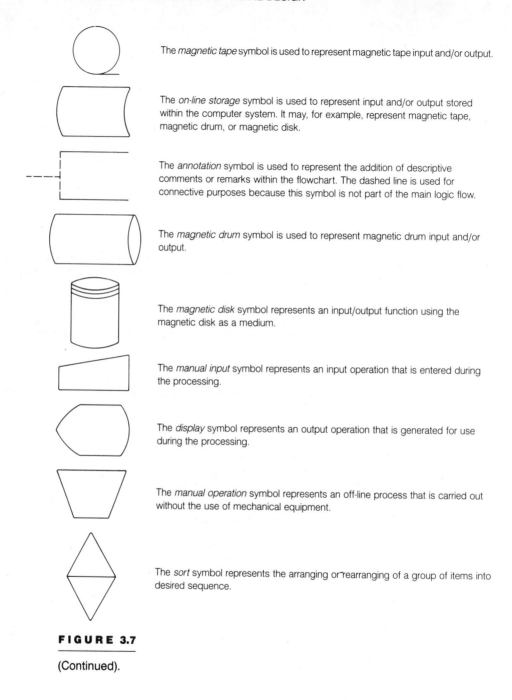

The *magnetic tape* symbol is used to represent magnetic tape input and/or output.

The *on-line storage* symbol is used to represent input and/or output stored within the computer system. It may, for example, represent magnetic tape, magnetic drum, or magnetic disk.

The *annotation* symbol is used to represent the addition of descriptive comments or remarks within the flowchart. The dashed line is used for connective purposes because this symbol is not part of the main logic flow.

The *magnetic drum* symbol is used to represent magnetic drum input and/or output.

The *magnetic disk* symbol represents an input/output function using the magnetic disk as a medium.

The *manual input* symbol represents an input operation that is entered during the processing.

The *display* symbol represents an output operation that is generated for use during the processing.

The *manual operation* symbol represents an off-line process that is carried out without the use of mechanical equipment.

The *sort* symbol represents the arranging or rearranging of a group of items into desired sequence.

FIGURE 3.7

(Continued).

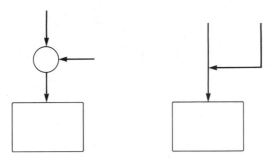

FIGURE 3.8

Representation of merging flow lines.

illustration, suppose we wish to construct a flowchart to solve a quadratic equation. We may proceed as follows:

1. Problem definition. Prepare flowchart to solve a quadratic equation.

2. Mathematical equation needed.

$$x = -b \pm \frac{(b^2 - 4ac)^{1/2}}{2a}$$

3. Input. a, b, and c.

4. Processing. We note that since we cannot take the square root of a negative quantity, we must make further decisions. Three cases arise:
    a. $b^2 = 4ac$
    b. $b^2 > 4ac$
    c. $b^2 < 4ac$
    We can combine cases (a) and (b), in which case the decision will result in either computing the root of the quadratic or not. We may anticipate that it is possible for some user of the program to enter $a = 0$ mistakenly. If this were to happen we would not want the program to crash, so we may put an error message that will say "This is not a quadratic equation."

5. Output. We can print either the solution of the equation or a statement showing that we have either an imaginary solution or the presence of error and then terminate the program. The flowchart for this simple problem is shown in Figure 3.9.

In summary, flowcharts should be used to indicate the flow of information and the logical relationships between various components of the software. Besides helping the designer to be sure that all aspects of the software specifications have been covered, flowcharts help reveal any inconsistencies in the programming logic.

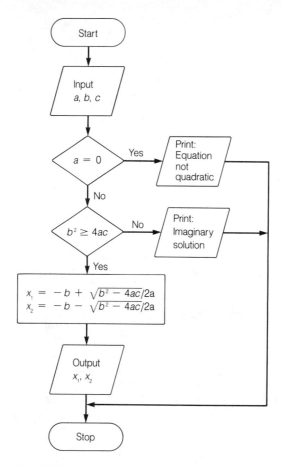

FIGURE 3.9

Flowchart for solving a quadratic equation.

CODING

Coding deals with the writing of the program itself. At this phase, the computer language to be used is selected based on the analysis of the problem. Regardless of the computer language selected, there are at least two things that are helpful: organization of the statements of the computer language selected (based on frequency of their use) and listing the restrictions of the compiler in relation to the program. For example, FORTRAN statements can be organized based on data, operations, constructs, and subprograms, but the FORTRAN compiler prefers the ordering shown in Figure 3.10. Note that in Figure 3.10, the position of the subprogram in relation to the main program is irrelevant, but for readability it makes sense to put all the subprograms after the main program.

Function statements
Data declarations
Data sharing
Data initialization
Main program — End
Subprogram — End

FIGURE 3.10

Typical ordering for FORTRAN compiler.

Since the coding phase is essential to obtaining a functional software, great care must be exercised in it. Perhaps one of the best approaches to producing an error-free program is to use **structured programming.**

Structured programming is an approach that concentrates on the organization (or structure) and logics involved in designing (or developing) a software. Detailed discussion of structured programming can be found elsewhere [6]; only a summary of this method is given here. The two main parts of structured programming are:

1. Top-down (modular programming)
2. Structural coding

TOP-DOWN DESIGN

In the development of large software packages, many persons are involved. Each person is assigned to develop a functional section of the entire software. Finally, the different sections are integrated. This approach would be very difficult were it not for the top-down design process, which is defined as the process of dividing a program into smaller subunits, called **modules,** which are organized in a hierarchial structure. Hierarchial structural organization means that the first-used module comes first and the last-used module comes last.

The process begins with the development of the main program (called the control program). During this, it is assumed that a subprogram for handling complex operations (calculations) exists. When the entire main program is developed, then attention is focused on each subprogram. The advantage of this approach is obvious: We do not get bogged down with details and lose our chain of thought while constructing the control program. It must be noted that even the subprograms may be subdivided into smaller units if the need exists. The use of the top-down design method helps us to develop error-free programs, following the old cliche "divide and conquer," because it is much easier to solve several simple problems than a complex one. The success of this method depends on the modularization, which can be termed **modular programming.**

MODULAR PROGRAMMING

From the previous discussion we note then that modular programming is a method of partitioning a program into small independent units called modules. A module is any collection of executable program statements that forms a closed subprogram capable of being called from any other part of the program or of being independently compiled. A module can also mean simply a set of statements which are operated on as an entity such as the IF THEN ELSE. A well-structured program depends on proper design of the constituent modules. There are several factors that must be considered in module design.

Module Size

The purpose of partitioning of a program is to create a series of manageable programs. Many experienced programmers advocate that the average size of a module should be about 60 lines of code; others contend that the appropriate size should be a page. Some other good rules of thumb, based on program size, are suggested in Table 3.1. On the high end, it is suggested that a module should not exceed 300 lines of code, because one with too many lines is difficult to comprehend.

Module Independence

It is desirable to make each module in the program be as independent as possible. This is useful particularly in eliminating what is called ripple effect, a change in one portion of a program causing a problem in other parts of the program.

Module Strength

Module strength deals with the relationships among the elements within a given module. If the relationship or interaction is very high, then there is a good chance for maintaining the independence of the module. There are several aspects of module strength, but perhaps the most important is functional strength. A functionally strong module is one that performs a specific function. Module strength will help reduce errors, and when errors do occur it will be easy to trace and correct them. For further study on design of modules, consult [8].

STRUCTURED CODING

The importance of coding in software design has already been noted. Any process that results in good coding should be properly examined. Structured coding

Program Size	Module Size
< 2000 lines	45 lines
< 10,000 lines	60 lines
> 10,000 lines	250 lines

TABLE 3.1

Suggested module size.

is one such process; it is a highly structured technique for writing programs. Good programmers do not write programs; rather, they structure programs.

Structured coding is based on the well-known structure theorem: Any proper program (a program with a single entry line and a single exit line) can be constructed using only three logic structures: sequence, IF THEN ELSE, and DO WHILE constructs. While it is true that, at least in theory, a proper program can be written using these three constructs, it is often more practical to include other constructs. Three major categories of constructs used in structured coding are discussed next.

Selection Constructs

Selection constructs are the constructs based on a choice of two courses of actions predicated on a certain condition. They are of three main types: IF THEN (Figure 3.11a), IF THEN ELSE (Figure 3.11b), and CASE (Figure 3.12).

The IF THEN construct is used in situations where we want to take an action or do nothing. As such the IF THEN constructs require the use of the logical IF.

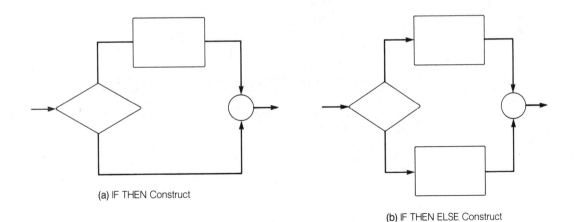

(a) IF THEN Construct

(b) IF THEN ELSE Construct

FIGURE 3.11

Selection construct.

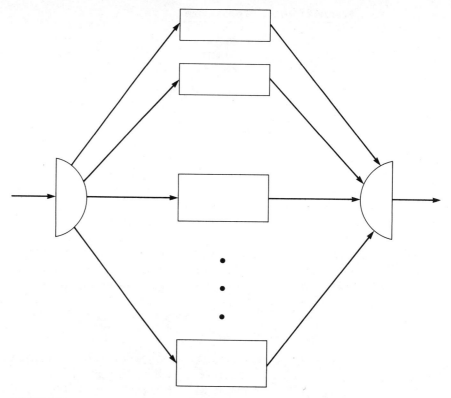

FIGURE 3.12

Case construct.

The complete form of an IF THEN construct is:

```
IF(logical statement) THEN
      Statements
         .
         .
END IF
```

If the logical statement is "true," then the statements contained between the IF THEN . . . END IF are executed. If, however, the logical statement is false, then no action is taken, and the next statement after the END IF is executed. Sometimes, when the IF THEN construct is used for an iterative process, GO TOs may be required. For example, suppose we want to solve for the root of a nonlinear equation (see Chapter 4) using the equation

$$x = x_o - \frac{f(x_o)}{f'(x_o)}$$

and a termination condition ε. We can use an IF THEN construct as shown:

```
* Program solve root of equation by Newton method
* Note only a portion of the program is given
            .
            .
            .
10    XNEW = XOLD - F(XOLD)/F'(XOLD)
      IF(F(XNEW).GT.E) THEN
            XOLD = XNEW
            GO TO 10
      END IF
            .
            .
            .
```

We have noted that the use of the IF THEN construct in FORTRAN requires the use of logical IF and GO TOs. A good program uses a minimum number of GO TO statements because of the difficulties of following the logic of a program with too many GO TOs. The use of GO TO is necessary in FORTRAN 77 because of the absence of the WHILE loop construct.

The IF THEN ELSE construct is an extension of the IF THEN construct, but unlike the IF THEN construct, a course of action is still taken, even if the logical statement is false. Its format is as follows:

```
IF(logical expression is true) THEN
            (statements)
                  .
                  .

ELSE
            (statements)
                  .
                  .

END IF
```

The IF THEN ELSE construct is also used with ELSE IF to execute several conditional statements. This format is of the form

```
IF(logical expression) THEN
      .
      .
```

```
            statements
                  .
                  .
                  .
     ELSE IF (logical expression) THEN
                  .
                  .
        statements
                  .
                  .
                  .
     ELSE IF(logical expression) THEN
                  .
                  .
        statements
                  .
                  .
                  .
     END IF
                  .
                  .
                  .
```

The CASE construct is used for multiple decisions— in effect, it is a series of logical IF statements. It can easily be implemented in such structured language as Pascal. FORTRAN does not directly provide for the use of the CASE construct. But this construct can be implemented by a combination of IF THEN ELSE and ELSE IF constructs (and GO TOs), as shown previously.

Repetition Constructs

The **repetition construct** is used when an iterative process is involved. There are two types: DO WHILE and DO. The DO WHILE construct requires a continual check of the termination condition. The process is repeated until the given condition is satisfied (true), at which point iteration stops. In FORTRAN, the DO WHILE involves the use of GO TO, logical IF, and a CONTINUATION statement. The DO construct is used when the exact number of iterations is known. It does not have to use a CONTINUE statement (i.e., for FORTRAN), though its use is encouraged. A sample of a portion of a program in FORTRAN for both DO WHILE and DO constructs is given in Figure 3.13, and the flowchart format is shown in Figure 3.14.

Subprograms

Subprograms (or procedures) are the essential features of structured programming. Any program of considerable length can be divided into a main program and many subprograms. The main program controls the order of execution of the rest of the subprograms. Each subprogram is in itself a complete program that can be compiled and tested differently; hence, each subprogram is a module.

```
C   SAMPLE PROGRAM STATEMENTS FOR REPETITION
C   CONSTRUCTS
            .
            .
            .
C    BEGIN DO WHILE
  20     CONTINUE
         IF(L.LE.30) THEN
         A = A + 1
            .
            .
            .
            .
         L = L + 1
         GO TO 20
         END IF
C    END DO WHILE
  80     CONTINUE
```

```
            .
            .
            .
         DO 40 I = 1,20
            .
            .
            .
         A(I) = A(I) + 1
  40     CONTINUE
```

(a) Example of DO WHILE
    construct

(b) Example of DO construct.

FIGURE 3.13

Repetition construct.

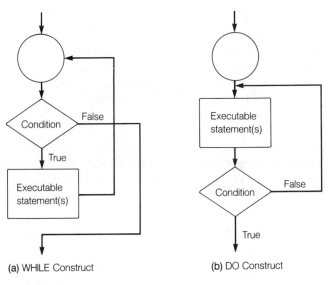

(a) WHILE Construct

(b) DO Construct

FIGURE 3.14

DO WHILE construct.

In FORTRAN, subprograms are of two kinds: subroutines and functions (note that Pascal uses procedures and functions). Although both of these are modules, there are differences between them. Functions are normally associated with a single value; subroutines are not. Furthermore, subroutines may be modularized but functions cannot (in the strictest sense of modules) be modularized. A subroutine is invoked by the main program through the use of a CALL statement, but a function is invoked by referencing its name. A function subprogram is usually preceded by a TYPE data statement (real or integer, logical, or character), but this is not the case with a subroutine, since it may be associated with different data types. We will examine the two subprograms shortly.

Because subprograms are the building blocks that should be used in modularizing programs, we need to understand some of their essential features. Regardless of the computer language in use, every subprogram has the following features:

1. **Boundaries.** The presence of boundaries makes it possible for a subprogram to physically separate statements. For example, FORTRAN (or Pascal) provides statements that mark the beginning and the end of a subprogram. The boundaries, once defined, remain fixed (in terms of defining the range of variables) during program execution.

2. **Interface points.** An interface point is the point where subprograms connect to the rest of the program. It is here that data exchange and flow of control take place.

3. **Locality of variables.** Variables in a subprogram are unique to the subprogram. The main program and other subprograms remain ignorant of the variables in a subprogram unless a COMMON (or equivalent) statement is used. Note that in BASIC the preceding feature does not apply.

4. **Transfer of control.** During the execution of a main program or subprogram, there may be an interruption of the main (or subprogram) to permit the execution of a particular subprogram; at this point a transfer of control is said to have taken place. When the particular subprogram has finished executing transfer of control back to the main program (or subprogram), the main program resumes from where it stopped (recall the application of stack). It is important to note that the rules for transfer of control are language-dependent; therefore, the programmer must be familiar with the rules governing control transfers in a chosen computer language.

We are now going to discuss briefly function subprogram and subroutines as applicable to FORTRAN. A FORTRAN function subprogram is of two forms: internal (or built-in functions) such as cosine (sine) or square root (SQRT), and external, which is user-defined. Our interest is primarily the user-defined function subprogram. The usual format of a function program is:

```
<Type> FUNCTION <Name> ([<Dummy argument list>])
               .
               .
               .
    END
```

The function is called by its name in the main program with the actual arguments supplied. In order to have a function subprogram perform properly, two rules must be observed. First, the function should not change the values of the actual arguments. Second, the dummy arguments should neither be assigned values nor used as actual arguments in the CALL statements. An example of a function subprogram for evaluating a given polynomial for different values of the independent variables is a follows:

```
*   Main Program calling the function subprogram.
*   Program evaluates a given Polynomial. The independent
*   variable ranges from 1.3 to 3.4 at increment of 0.1.
            .
            .
      Y = 1.3
10    CONTINUE
      IF(Y.LE. 3.4) THEN
      VALUE = EQUAT(Y)
      Y = Y + 0.1
      GO TO 10
      END IF
            .
            .

*   Function subprogram.
      REAL FUNCTION EQUAT(X)
      REAL X
      EQUAT = 3*X**3 - 2*X**2 + 1.5*X
      END
```

Subroutines in FORTRAN serve as the primary means of modularizing programs. They can themselves be modularized, which means that if the subroutine involves some other complex operations, the complex operations can also be carried out using another subroutine. Subroutines therefore can call other subroutines but may not call themselves. The general format of a subroutine is:

```
SUBROUTINE <Name> {([<Dummy argument list>])}
            .
            .
RETURN
END
```

Although a subroutine is a complete program, it cannot be executed without being invoked by another program (most frequently, the main program) through the use of a CALL statement in the form

```
CALL <Subroutine name> {([<actual argument list>])}
```

If a subroutine is modularized, the CALL format may be represented as

```
*   Calling program
```

```
            .
            .
            .
        CALL NAME1
            .
            .
            .
        END
*   Modularized subroutine Name1
        SUBROUTINE NAME1
            .
            .
            .
        CALL NAME2
        CALL NAME3
            .
            .
        CALL NAMEN
            .
            .
        RETURN
        END
```

Note that both the calling program and the subroutines are without arguments. This is permissible. The only catch is that since the main program must actually communicate actual parameters to the subroutines, a means must be provided to carry out the communication. Fortunately, this communication can easily be done by the use of the COMMON statement in both the calling program and the various subroutines. For more details on the use of COMMON, a fundamental book on FORTRAN programming should be consulted.

We have discussed structured programming as consisting of several parts, but it is the responsibility of the programmer to pull all these parts together in order to achieve good coding of the program. In structuring the program, it is advisable to structure the data and the selected algorithms in such a way as to permit easy access of information and data in the shortest possible time. For further studies of structured programming, see [2] and the other books and papers cited at the end of this chapter.

3.6 TESTING

The final step in producing workable software is testing of the program developed. Testing and debugging go hand in hand, but testing has the primary purpose of verifying that the program executes according to the design specifications. The program must provide correct solutions under all conditions. If a program is well designed and properly coded, this step can be relatively easy. In fact it is beneficial to do what is known as a "walk-through," which is having another experienced programmer go through your algorithm with some numerical values. This should be done before actual coding begins.

Testing helps to detect at least three classes of errors: logical, machine-dependent, and specification errors. Logical errors are due to incorrect algorithm design and may manifest themselves in such a way as infinite loops, incorrect jumps to an address, or incorrect initialization. Machine-dependent errors may be rounding errors (caused by the fact that real computers cannot always represent decimal values accurately) or sometimes, overflow (a condition resulting from assignment of more data to a location area than the area can accommodate). Some overflow errors may also be due to incorrect data or incorrect initialization. Specification errors are associated with functional and programming specification; they may be caused by improper or incomplete definitions. Improper definition could mean that integer data was entered for real data. Logical and specification errors may easily be avoided if an early testing method is applied.

There are various methods for testing a program, but our discussion is limited to two approaches: phased testing and incremental testing (see [9]). **Phased testing** tests a group of subprograms (or modules) together. Using this method involves coding and testing each module (subprogram) separately, compiling and linking all modules, and finally running and debugging the modules together. **Incremental testing** involves first coding and testing each module (or subprogram) separately and then incorporating each into a correctly working program; each newly formed unit is then tested. It should be obvious that incremental testing is preferable to phased testing, since incremental testing makes it easier to detect which module causes an error in the main unit.

Regardless of what method is used, the program must be tested for correctness. This is normally done through input of data which will produce a predetermined solution. If the expected result is not obtained, then it is an indication that the program is not correct and must be checked. Also, the program must be tested to be sure that in each case of a decision process (IF THEN ELSE), each path produces an acceptable result; if a specified data would produce an error, there must be a warning message before the termination of the program. In other words, wrong input should not cause the program to crash.

There are several questions that arise regarding testing of programs: What should be the durations of the tests? When can a test be considered adequate? Which testing method should be used? There are no clear-cut answers to these issues; the solutions should be guided by at least two factors: cost and the importance of the accuracy of the software. There is more information available about testing; interested readers may consult [7] and [9].

3.7 PROGRAMMING TIPS

There are many books available on computer programming but few that provide quick tips. The book by Nagin et al. [10] is recommended; the partial list provided in this section serves only as an aid. The tips are given in two categories: programming and debugging and testing.

PROGRAMMING TIPS

1. Always make use of flowcharts.

2. Make effective use of subprograms: i.e., modularize your program whenever possible.

3. Use modules that are not extremely long; keep them shorter than one page.

4. Avoid excessive use of GO TOs.

5. Use loop mechanisms effectively. For example, if a loop contains an expression whose values do not change, it may be better to put that expression outside the loop. Consider this portion of a FORTRAN program:

```
      DO 23 K = 1,40
23    AHU(K) = A*B*Z(K)/C
```

It may be better to put it in the form

```
      GEM = A*B/C
      DO 43 K=1,40
43    AHU(K) = GEM*Z(K)
```

In this way the computer does not have to compute the value of GEM each time during the repetitive calculation of the variable AHU.

6. Use comments to make the program readable.

7. Make use of existing libraries. For example, it is unnecessary to develop a square root routine when it already exists.

8. Make use of PRINT statements during the development stage of the program, so that you may observe what is going on. Of course, once the program has proven correct, then remove all the unnecessary PRINT statements.

DEBUGGING AND TESTING TIPS

1. Make use of debugging aids if they exist. For example, "flow trace" will show the path of execution until the error occurred.

2. Hand-test the program before running it. The test should involve a check on:

    a. Input/output formats
    b. Execution and statement rules
    c. Program logic, to see if it corresponds with the flowchart
    d. Proper declaration of data

EXAMPLE 3.1

A small engineering firm is involved in the design of riveted connections. It also does some consulting work for a law firm that handles lawsuits related to injuries due to failures of mechanical parts. The company would like to ascertain, in the shortest possible time, if a connected joint failed because of overstressing. The chief engineer attended a workshop on computer-aided design, and as a result became thrilled with the idea of automating some of the design processes of the firm. As a first step, he wants software that will help the firm in the analysis and design of riveted connections. The software must be very easy to use.

SOLUTION We will apply some of the principles developed in this chapter to design such software. Our first step is to restate the problem.

Problem Statement

The need can be cast in three forms:

1. Given a safe load and the number of rivets to be used, determine the safe nominal diameter of a rivet.

2. Given a safe load and nominal diameter of a rivet, find the smallest number of rivets needed to form the connection.

3. Given the number of rivets used and the nominal diameter of each rivet used, determine the safe load.

ASSUMPTIONS

1. The thickness of the main plate is greater than the thickness of the butt straps (see Figure 3.15).

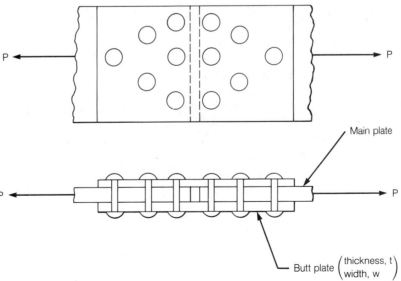

FIGURE 3.15

Sketch for Example 3.1.

2. Each rivet transfers the same amount of load.

3. Plate thickness is always specified based on (1).

4. There is no failure due to edge tearing (a rule of thumb to design against this mode of failure is well known).

5. There are no bending, twisting, or set-up stresses in the rivets.

6. The plate hole is greater than the rivet nominal diameter by a given clearance.

DESIGN EQUATIONS

1. Tension failure mode

$$P = (W - nd)t\sigma_t \tag{1}$$

2. Bearing failure mode

$$P = \sigma_b dtn \tag{2}$$

3. Shearing failure mode

$$P = \frac{\pi d^2 \sigma_s n}{4} \tag{3}$$

where

n = number of rivets
P = allowable load
W = main plate width
t = plate thickness
d = nominal rivet diameter
D = diameter of holes on the plate ($D = d +$ some clearance).
σ_t, σ_b, and σ_s are permissible tensile, bearing, and shearing stresses, respectively.

DESIGN CASES

There are three design cases, according to the problem statement, for which results are required:

1. When the transmitted load and rivet pattern are known and the rivet diameter is desired.

2. When the rivet pattern, as well as the rivet diameter, are known, but the permissible load is sought.

3. When transmitted load and rivet diameter are known, but the number of rivets to be used are unknown.

The results of the initial analysis of our problem are summarized as follows:

1. **Purpose.** To develop a program to analyze a riveted connection.
2. **Data.**
   a. Input: load, number of rivets, or rivet size.
   b. Output: load, number of rivets, or rivet size.
3. **Test cases and expected results.** Provided later.
4. **Flowchart.** All details not shown.

The preceding summary becomes very helpful in the rest of the program design as well as helpful in documenting the software design process.

PROGRAM DESIGN

The design phase of the program involves selection of the appropriate form of data structure, algorithm structure, coding, and testing. The design phase also includes the selection of appropriate programming language. Although FORTRAN has many features in its library functions that are desirable for this problem, BASIC is chosen for its simplicity and its adaptability to interactive conditions, even though it requires more code lines.

The program is developed in three modules, corresponding to each of the three cases developed before.

Module 1 The basic equations used are

$$d_t = \frac{W - P/\sigma_t t}{n} - c \tag{4}$$

$$d_b = \frac{P}{n\sigma_b t} \tag{5}$$

$$d_s = \frac{4P}{\pi\sigma_s nU} \tag{6}$$

where

n = the number of rivets in a half section of the connection.
U = shear term ($U = 1$ for single shear, 2 for double shear, and so on).
c = clearance.
d_t, d_b, d_s are the diameters necessary to guard against tensile, bearing, and shearing failures, respectively. The desired diameter is taken as the minimum diameter that will satisfy the three loading conditions.

Module 2 The equations are the same as (1) through (3). The permissible load is the minimum load predicted using equations (1) through (3).

Module 3 The equations used are

$$n_t = \frac{W}{d+c} - \frac{P}{(d+c)\sigma_t} \qquad (7)$$

$$n_b = \frac{P}{\sigma_b dt} \qquad (8)$$

$$n_s = \frac{4P}{\pi U d^2 \sigma_s} \qquad (9)$$

where n_t, n_b, and n_s are the minimum number of rivets needed to provide the tensile, bearing, and shearing areas respectively.

A stipulation in determining the appropriate number of rivets is that $n_t \geq n_s$. This is necessary, since the number of rivets to withstand tearing must not be smaller than that required to sustain shearing. If $n_t < n_s$, the connection is unsafe and must be redesigned either by increasing plate thickness or increasing the rivet size, or both. The program, however, is designed to do either, but not both.

A flowchart showing the steps necessary to code the program is given in Figure 3.16, but details for coding the various modules are not supplied. A detailed program listing is given in Figure 3.17.

TESTING

The program is tested using problems from each of the three classes. The test problems are:

1. For the problem shown in Figure 3.15, size the rivet if the thickness is 13.5 millimeters and the width is 100 millimeters. The permissible load is 60 kilonewtons.

2. If the width in Figure 3.15 is now 75 millimeters and the nominal diameter of the rivet is 15.5 millimeters, determine the permissible load.

3. For an allowable load of 20 kilonewtons, what should be the minimum number of rivets for the safe operation of a riveted connection?
   For each of the cases given above the following data apply:

   σ_t = 170 megapascals
   σ_b = 387 megapascals
   σ_s = 104 megapascals
   clearance, c, is 1.6 millimeters

The results are shown in Figure 3.17. The reader may verify, through a formal analysis, that the solutions are, in fact, correct. It is important to recognize that the solutions given here represent only one of the many possibilities for the software development of this problem. You may attempt to develop a more efficient program.

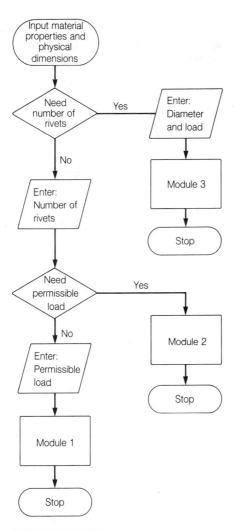

FIGURE 3.16

Partial flowchart for Example 3.1.

CONCLUDING REMARKS

As we have noted, there are two parts to computer-aided design: software and hardware. Hardware components have been discussed in the preceding chapter; in this book we are not concerned with the application packges, since most of them are machine-dependent. This chapter has treated software design, so that the reader can understand the principles involved.

```
100    REM  ***********************************************************
110    REM  *   THIS PROGRAM IS FOR THE DESIGN OF RIVETED JOINTS *
120    REM  *   THREE CASES CAN DESIGNED USED THE PROGRAM:       *
130    REM  *   1 - WHEN THE NUMBER OF RIVETS ARE UNKNOWN         *
140    REM  *   2 - WHEN THE SIZE OF RIVET IS DESIRED             *
150    REM  *   3 - WHEN IT IS DESIRED TO DETERMINE  A SAFE LOAD  *
160    REM  ***********************************************************
170    REM
180    REM  ***********************************************************
190    REM  ***********************************************************
200    REM  * THIS PROGRAM IS DEVELOPED BASED ON THE USUAL       *
210    REM  * ASSUMPTIONS ASSOCIATED WITH RIVETED JOINT DESIGN   *
220    REM  ***********************************************************
230    REM  .........................................................
240       PRINT "ARE YOU USING S.I. UNITS (YES/NO)?"
250       INPUT B$
260      PI = 22/7
270    REM .....ENTER DESIGN INFORMATION.
280       PRINT" ENTER MATERIAL PROPERTIES"
290    PRINT
300       PRINT"***********************************************************"
310       PRINT"*    NOTE:  IF YOU WORKING WITH S.I. UNITS, ALL STRESSES*"
320       PRINT"*             MUST BE ENTERED IN MPa  AND ALL DIMENSIONS  *"
330       PRINT"*             IN MILLIMETERS............................."
332       PRINT"*             IF NOT ENTER STRESSES IN PSI AND DIMENSIONS *"
334       PRINT"*             IN INCHES................................*"
340       PRINT"***********************************************************"
350    INPUT" WHAT IS THE PERMISSIBLE TENSILE STRESS  ?";ST
360       PRINT
370    INPUT" WHAT IS THE PERMISSIBLE BEARING STRESS   ?";SB
380       PRINT
390    INPUT" WHAT IS THE PERMISSIBLE SHEARING STRESS ?";SS
400       PRINT
410    INPUT" ENTER THE THICKNESS OF PLATE - mm OR Inches ";T
420       PRINT
430    INPUT"    WHAT IS THE WIDTH OF THE  PLATE - mm or Inches";W
440       PRINT
450    PRINT" ENTER INFORMATION ON MODE OF SHEAR"
460       PRINT
470     INPUT" -ENTER  1  FOR SINGLE SHEAR, 2 - FOR DOUBLE SHEAR";U
480    PRINT"***********************************************************"
490    PRINT"*                   DESIGN - MENU                        *"
500    PRINT"*                  **************                        *"
510    PRINT"*                  **************                        *"
520    PRINT"*         1 -    SIZING THE RIVET                        *"
530    PRINT"*         2 -    DETERMINING PERMISSIBLE LOAD            *"
540    PRINT"*         3 -    DETERMINING REQUIRED MIN. NO. OF RIVETS *"
550    PRINT"*                                                        *"
560    PRINT"***********************************************************"
570    PRINT
580    INPUT" ENTER YOUR SELECTION; 1/2/3";A$
590    PRINT
600       C = .0625
610       IF A$ = "1" GOTO 680
620       IF A$ =  "2" GOTO 1240
630       IF A$ = "3"   GOTO 1740
640    REM  C IS CLEARANCE  NORMALLY ASSUMED TO BE 1/16 OF AN INCH
650    REM .................................................
660    REM
670    REM .................................................
680    INPUT "WHAT IS THE TOTAL NO. OF RIVETS ON HALF SECTION OF CONNECTIO
690     INPUT "ENTER THE LOAD IN LBS. OR IN NEWTONS";P
700    PC   = P
710    REM ... DESIGNING FOR RIVET SIZE....
720    GOSUB 990
730    REM .................................
740    REM .................................
750 REM
```

FIGURE 3.17

```
760   REM ....SIZE BASED ON BEARING LOAD
770   REM
780   DMOD2=P/(N*SB*T)
790   REM
800   REM ... SIZE BASED ON SHEARING LOAD
810   DMOD3 = SQR(4*P/(SS*N*PI*U))
820 REM
830   IF DMOD2 > DMOD3 THEN DMAX = DMOD2:   GOTO 850
840   DMAX = DMOD3
850    PT = ST*(W - (DMAX + C))*T
860    IF PT > PC GOTO 880
870    DMAX = X
880     IF B$ = "YES" THEN DMAX = DMAX*1000 : GOTO 910
890    PRINT"THE MAXIMUM DIAMETER FOR RIVET IS:  ";DMAX;" IN."
900   GOTO 2000
910    PRINT" THE MINIMUM DIAMETER FOR RIVET IS: ";DMAX;" mm"
920     GOTO 2000
930 REM
940 REM
950   REM ......................................................
960   REM  SUBROUTINE  DETERMINES SIZE OF RIVET BASED
970   REM  ON TENSILE LOAD
980   REM ......................................................
990   PRINT"WHAT IS THE TOTAL NO. OF ROWS?"
1000  INPUT J
1010 IF B$="YES" GOTO 1030
1020  GOTO 1040
1030  GOSUB 2020
1040 FOR L=1 TO J
1050  PRINT "ENTER THE NO. OF RIVETS IN ROW #";L;TAB(34)
1060  INPUT M(L)
1070    IF L > 1 THEN SUM =0 ELSE GOTO 1110
1080    FOR K = 1 TO L-1
1090    SUM = SUM +M(K) : NEXT K
1100    P = P*(N/(N -SUM))
1110   D(L) = ((W - (P/(ST*T)))/M(L)) - C
1120  NEXT L
1130  REM
1140 REM
1150  X = 1E-09
1160  FOR I=1 TO J
1170    IF D(I)>=X GOTO 1190
1180    GOTO 1200
1190  X=D(I)
1200  NEXT I
1210 DMOD1 = X
1220  RETURN
1230  REM .....FINDING PERMISSIBLE LOAD.......
1240  PRINT "WHAT IS THE RIVET DIAMETER - IN. OR MM.?"
1250   INPUT D
1260 INPUT "WHAT IS THE TOTAL NO. OF RIVETS ON HALF SECTION OF CONNECTIO
1270   IF B$= "YES" GOTO 1290
1280   GOTO 1310
1290   GOSUB 2020
1300   PRINT
1310  PRINT "WHAT IS THE TOTAL NO. OF ROWS?"
1320   INPUT J
1330   Y2 = D + C
1340    PRINT " WHAT IS THE NO. OF RIVETS IN THE FIRST ROW?"
1350    FOR I = 1 TO J
1360      IF I = 1  GOTO 1400
1370      IF I= J THEN PRINT "WHAT IS THE NO. OF RIVETS  IN THE LAST ROW
1380      IF I = J GOTO 1400
1390      PRINT "WHAT IS THE NO. OF RIVET IN ROW #";I;TAB(34)
1400      INPUT R(I)
1410      IF I>1 GOTO 1440
1420    PY(I) =  ((W - R(I)*Y2)*T)*ST
```

FIGURE 3.17

(Continued).

```
1430          GOTO 1510
1440          LL =I
1450           SRIVET =0
1460           FOR  JJ = 1 TO LL-1
1470           SRIVET = SRIVET + R(JJ)
1480           NEXT JJ
1490           PM =   ((W - R(I)*Y2))*T*ST
1500         PY(I) = PM*N/(N - SRIVET)
1510          NEXT I
1520      FOR  I= 1 TO J
1530           NEXT I
1540 REM   DETERMINING THE LEAST   TENSILE LOAD
1550    PC = 1E+20
1560    FOR M = 1 TO J
1570    IF PY(M) < PC THEN PC = PY(M)
1580    NEXT M
1590    PT = PC
1600    REM ....BEARING LOAD
1610    PB = SB*D*T*N
1620      REM   ... SHEARING LOAD
1630    PS   =((SS*PI*(D^2)*U)*N)/4
1640    IF PT <   PB THEN PAL = PT ELSE PAL = PB
1650    IF PS < PAL THEN PAL =PS
1660    IF B$ = "YES" GOTO 1690
1670    PRINT "PERMISSIBLE LOAD IN LBS IS:  ";PAL
1680    GOTO 2000
1690    PRINT "PERMISSIBLE LOAD IN NEWTONS IS:   ";PAL
1700    GOTO 2000
1710    REM  ...........................
1720    REM   ... DETERMINING NO. OF RIVETS..
1730    REM  ...............................
1740 PRINT"WHAT IS THE RIVET NOMINAL DIAMETER"
1750 INPUT D
1760  PRINT "WHAT IS THE PERMISSIBLE LOAD?"
1770  INPUT P
1780  IF B$ ="NO" GOTO 1800
1790  GOSUB 2020
1800 Y2 = D+C
1810  N1=  (W/Y2) - P/((Y2)*T*ST)
1820  N2 = P/(D*SB*T)
1830  N3 = 4*P/(U*PI*D^2*SS)
1840  IF N1>N2 THEN N=N1 ELSE N=N2
1850  IF N>=N3 GOTO 1870
1860 N=N3
1870 IF N<=N1 GOTO 1990
1880 PRINT "JOINT IS NOT GOOD (SAFE)"
1890  PRINT"DO YOU WANT TO SELECT ANOTHER RIVET SIZE?"
1900 INPUT C$
1910 IF C$ = "YES" GOTO 1740
1920  PRINT"DO YOU WANT TO INCREASE PLATE THICKNESS?"
1930  INPUT D$
1940  IF D$ = "NO" GOTO 2000
1950 PRINT"WHAT IS THE PLATE THICKNESS?"
1960 INPUT T
1970 GOTO 1810
1980 REM
1990 PRINT "THE MINIMUM NO. OF RIVETS =       ";N
2000 END
2010 REM ... CONVERSION NEEDED FOR S.I. UNITS
2020   C = C* .0254
2030   T =T /1000
2040   D = D/1000
2050   ST = ST*1000000!
2060   SB = SB*1000000!
2070   SS = SS*1000000!
2080     W = W/1000
2090     RETURN
```

F I G U R E 3.17

(Continued).

```
RUN
ARE YOU USING S.I. UNITS (YES/NO)?
? YES
 ENTER MATERIAL PROPERTIES

**********************************************************
*    NOTE:  IF YOU WORKING WITH S.I. UNITS, ALL STRESSES*
*           MUST BE ENTERED IN MPa  AND ALL DIMENSIONS  *
*           IN MILLIMETERS..............................
**********************************************************
 WHAT IS THE PERMISSIBLE TENSILE STRESS  ?? 170

 WHAT IS THE PERMISSIBLE BEARING STRESS  ?? 387

 WHAT IS THE PERMISSIBLE SHEARING STRESS ?? 104

 ENTER THE THICKNESS OF PLATE - mm OR Inches ? 13.5

    WHAT IS THE WIDTH OF THE  PLATE - mm or Inches? 100

 ENTER INFORMATION ON MODE OF SHEAR

 -ENTER  1  FOR SINGLE SHEAR, 2 - FOR DOUBLE SHEAR? 2
**********************************************************
*                 DESIGN - MENU                         *
*                 *************                         *
*                 *************                         *
*       1 -   SIZING THE RIVET                          *
*       2 -    DETERMINING PERMISSIBLE LOAD             *
*       3 -   DETERMINING REQUIRED MIN. NO. OF RIVETS   *
*                                                       *
**********************************************************

 ENTER YOUR SELECTION; 1/2/3? 1

WHAT IS THE TOTAL NO. OF RIVETS ON HALF SECTION OF CONNECTION?? 6
ENTER THE LOAD IN LBS. OR IN NEWTONS? 60E3
WHAT IS THE TOTAL NO. OF ROWS?
? 3
ENTER THE NO. OF RIVETS IN ROW # 1
                                 ? 1
ENTER THE NO. OF RIVETS IN ROW # 2
                                 ? 2
ENTER THE NO. OF RIVETS IN ROW # 3
                                 ? 3
 THE MINIMUM DIAMETER FOR RIVET IS:  12.1183  mm
Ok
RUN
ARE YOU USING S.I. UNITS (YES/NO)?
? YES
 ENTER MATERIAL PROPERTIES

**********************************************************
*    NOTE:  IF YOU WORKING WITH S.I. UNITS, ALL STRESSES*
*           MUST BE ENTERED IN MPa  AND ALL DIMENSIONS  *
*           IN MILLIMETERS..............................
**********************************************************
 WHAT IS THE PERMISSIBLE TENSILE STRESS  ?? 170
```

FIGURE 3.17

(Continued).

To further an understanding of the principles, we turn our attention to the numerical methods needed for computer-aided design. The programming requirements may task the reader; a review of the fundamentals of programming may be necessary before one continues in this book.

REVIEW QUESTIONS

1. Define the following:
   a. Firmware
   b. Software
   c. Array
   d. Records
   e. Files

2. What do the acronyms LIFO and FIFO stand for? To what data structure do they refer?

3. Give six characteristics of a good software.

4. What are the four steps in software design?

5. Why is a flowchart necessary during algorithm design?

6. What is top-down design?

7. What is the ripple effect?

8. What is the difference between DO WHILE and DO constructs?

9. Name two methods of testing a program. Which method is preferable and why?

EXERCISES

1. Develop a software package for the design of thin-walled pressure vessels. The software should be capable of

   Testing if a given design was valid or not.
   Giving the principal normal strains.
   Test your software with the following cases:

   Case 1: Design a cylindrical pressure vessel for the following
   Fluid pressure   = 400 kPa
   Diameter   < 10 m
   Factor of safety   = 3.5
   Material—any class of steel
   Height—600 mm

   (make a detail drawing to help in its fabrication).

   Case 2: Repeat case 1 for a spherical container.

   Case 3: A cylindrical pressure vessel was designed to contain fluid under a pressure of 1.77 MPa. The design specifications are:
   Diameter—160 mm
   Thickness—26 mm
   Material—aluminum UNS A93003-H12

If the design was based on maximum shear stress theory and a factor of 6 was used, is this a safe design?

2. A small company tests failed stepped and straight shafts for a law firm. The company would like you to develop a relatively inexpensive reliable software for its work. The package should be capable of:

(i) Providing the angle of twist if the loading conditions and adequate dimensions are known.

(ii) Predicting the maximum shearing stress.

(iii) Sizing a shaft.

Test your package with the following two problems

a. The gear shown is driven by a 210 kW motor at 20 hertz. Gears 1 and 2 utilize 120 and 90 kW respectively. If the permissible shear stress of the shaft is 49.6 MPa and the angle of twist between the motor and gear 2 is 1 3°, what is the diameter of the shaft? Use Shear modulus of 79.3 GPa.

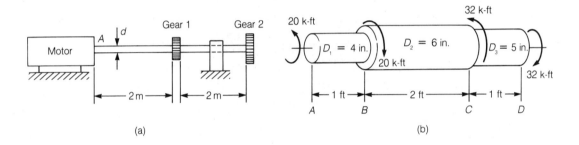

(a)   (b)

b. For the shaft shown determine the maximum shearing stress in each of the three segments. Determine the angle of twist of end D with respect to end A. Use shear modulus of 11.5×10^6 pounds per square inch.

3. A small company manufactures helical compression springs. Because of its size the company can not afford to stock various spring materials. Therefore, all springs are made from one of three classes of spring materials shown in Table 3.2. Also, the ends of the springs it manufactures are either plain, square, plain and ground, or square and ground.

The company periodically gets complaints of failed springs. For this reason the company needs an interactive program that will help it in design of new springs and also aid in determining why a spring failed. Consider yourself as the only design engineer the company has. Develop the necessary software to meet the desired goals. Using the design procedures outlined in this chapter, show (using a flowchart) how the main program interacts with the other modules (subprograms). For maximum effectiveness of the software, the information on the ends and material properties should be a part of the software.

From the nature of the applications of the spring designed by this company, it has been determined that buckling would not occur if

$$\frac{y}{L_f} \leq a \left(\frac{L_f}{D}\right)^b$$

where

a = 19.4681
b = -2.1942
y = deflection
L_f = free length
D = mean diameter

Furthermore, the fundamental critical frequency should be 20 times the operational frequency in order to avoid resonance with harmonics.

The tensile strength of the material given in Table 3.2 may be computed (as suggested in the mechanical design book by [11] Shigley and Mitchell) using

$$S_{ut} = A/d^m$$

where

S_{ut} = tensile strength
d = wire diameter
A, m = constants given in Table 3.2.

Test your program with the following:

a. Design a spring to meet the following specifications:

End configurations : square and ground
Permissible deflection—1.5 inches
Maximum operating load—160 pounds
Loading condition : essentially static

The spring must fit in a space with a diameter of 1.75 inches. The minimum acceptable free length is 4 inches.

b. A failed spring had the following specifications:

End configuration: plain and ground
Wire diameter: 6.199 millimeters
O.D.: 45.500 millimeters
Total number of coils: 12.5
Free length: 320.00 millimeters
Operational speed: 450 revolutions per minute
Life: infinite
Maximum load: 850 newtons
Minimum load: 500 newtons
Material: oil-tempered wire

The spring was designed with 99% reliability and a fatigue safety factor of 1.5.
Speculate on the possible cause of failure.

4. The data

0.261, 1.787, 4.436, 8.120, 10.220, 0.500, 0.003

Material	Size Range, in.	Size Range, mm	Exponent, m	Constant, kpsi	A MPa
Musical wire	0.004–0.250	0.10–6.50	0.146	196	2170
Oil-tempered wire	0.020–0.500	0.50–12	0.186	149	1880
Hard-drawn wire	0.028–0.500	0.70–12	0.192	136	1750

TABLE 3.2.

Properties of available materials.

are to be printed out in the following order:

8.120, 0.261, 0.500, 1.787, 4.436, 0.003, 10.220

Design a linked list for printing out the data, and then write a short program to accomplish this.

REFERENCES

1. Yaohan, Chu. *Software Blueprint and Examples.* Lexington, Mass.: D.C. Heath and Company, 1982.

2. Marca, David. *Applying Software Engineering Principles.* Boston: Little, Brown and Company, 1984.

3. Dodd, G.G. "Elements of Data Management Systems." *Computer Survey* 1, no. 2 (June 1969): 115–35.

4. Thurber, K., and P.C. Patton. *Data Structures and Computer Architecture.* Lexington, Mass.: D.C. Heath and Company, 1977.

5. Ellzey, Roy. *Data Structures for Computer Information Systems.* Chicago: Science Research Associates, 1982.

6. Linger, R.C., H.D. Mills, and B.I. Witt. *Structured Programming Theory and Practice.* Reading, Mass.: Addison-Wesley Publishing Company, 1979.

7. Tassel, D.V. *Program Style, Design, Efficiency, Debugging and Testing.* Englewood Cliffs, N.J.: Prentice- Hall, Inc., 1978.

8. Myers, G.J. *Composite/Structure Design.* New York: Van Nostrand Reinhold Company, 1978.

9. Constantine, L., and E. Yourdon. *Structure Design.* New York: Yourdon Press, 1975.

10. Nagin, P., and H.F. Ledgard. *Basic with Style— Programming Proverbs.* Rochelle Park, N.J.: Hayden Book Company, Inc., 1978.

11. Shigley, J.E. and R. Mitchell, eds. *Handbook of Machine Design,* New York: McGraw Hill, 1986.

CHAPTER 4

Computer Solution of Nonlinear Equations

4.1 INTRODUCTION

One step in an engineering design is the analysis of the problem. Often such analysis will result in certain algebraic equations being formulated. These equations may be higher-degree polynomial or transcendental functions. The analysis is not complete unless the solutions to such equations are obtained. Since these functions are mainly nonlinear, their solutions are obtained via an iterative process. Our focus in this chapter is on the methods for obtaining the required solutions of the higher-order polynomial and transcendental equations.

A transcendental function is defined as a function that cannot be expressed in terms of algebraic operations on polynomials. Simply put, it is a function whose root cannot be determined by a finite number of additions, subtractions, divisions, and multiplications. Transcendental functions include trigonometric, exponential, and logarithmic functions or a combination thereof. Forms of transcendental equations are as follows:

$$x \tan x - x^2 - 1 = 0 \qquad \textbf{(4.1a)}$$

$$e^x - \cos x + 1 = 0 \qquad \textbf{(4.1b)}$$

An example of a higher-order polynomial equation is

$$6x^5 - 3x^4 + 10x^2 - 3x + 1 = 0 \qquad \textbf{(4.2)}$$

It is very difficult, if not impossible, to obtain the analytical solutions of equations (4.1) and (4.2). There are two kinds of information that may be required: The first is to find an approximate real root; the second is to find all possible roots, both real and complex. The second kind of information is more difficult to obtain than the first. Methods for supplying the second information can be found in the books by Gerald et al. [1] and Burden et al. [2].

The determination of an approximate real root is the concern of the present chapter. Equations (4.1) and (4.2) may be solved by a graphical approach, which is tedious and time-consuming. There are, however, more systematic approaches that can be used in the solutions of equations (4.1) and (4.2), and the advent of high-speed computers makes these systematic techniques very appealing. Discussions will be limited to the following techniques:

- The binary search method
- The false position method
- The Newton-Raphson method
- The secant method

4.2   THE BINARY SEARCH METHOD

The binary search method, also known as the bisection or half-search method, utilizes the principle that a continuous function passes through zero when its sign changes from positive to negative or vice versa.

Consider the function plotted in Figure 4.1. Also, consider two points x_1 and x_2 on the graph and note that:

$$f(x_1) < 0 \quad \text{and} \quad f(x_2) > 0$$

To reach point 2 from point 1, one must pass through point 3. At point 3, $f(x) = 0$, which is the required solution. In order to arrive at point 3, we must keep on reducing the distance between point 1 and point 2, only we must remain on opposite sides of point 3. Suppose we chose two points on the same side of point 3; it is obvious that we will keep moving away from point 3 and never reach the required solution. This method is very simple, but the key is that you must choose points on the opposite sides of the solution.

To generalize the procedure for obtaining a solution, let us choose two points (on the opposite sides of the desired solution), x_n and x_{n+1}, and evaluate the functions at x_n and x_{n+1}. Of course, $f(x_n)f(x_{n+1}) < 0$. Next we find the midpoint between x_n and x_{n+1} and designate this point as x_m, hence,

$$x_m = \frac{x_n + x_{n+1}}{2} \tag{4.3}$$

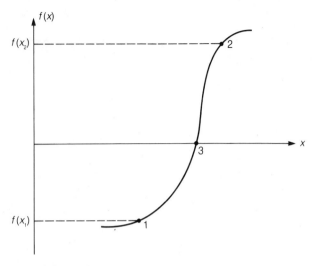

FIGURE 4.1

An illustration of a function that changes sign by passing
through the point $f(x) = 0$.

We now have three points; since we must always work with two points, we
make a test to see which point (x_n, x_{n+1}) should be replaced with x_m. This is done
by examining the value of the product $f(x_n)f(x_m)$ and $f(x_{n+1})f(x_m)$. The point that
gives a positive quantity is replaced by x_m. This process is continued until a value
of x_m is obtained for the $f(x_m)$ that is as close to zero as desired. This value of x_m
is x^*, the required solution. The flowchart for accomplishing this process is
shown in Figure 4.2, and a sample program is listed in Figure 4.3.

It must be noted that if for any reason the given function is discontinuous
between the two initial points, then a false root is obtained.

EXAMPLE 4.1

Find the solution to the equation

$$xe^x - 3 \cos \pi x = 0$$

within a tolerance of 1×10^{-5}

SOLUTION   Although the interval is not specified, we know that a possible solution range is
between 0 and 1.

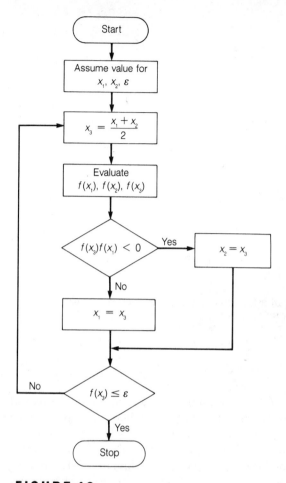

FIGURE 4.2

Binary search method.

Step 1 Chose two points 0.0 and 1.0. Check if $f(0)f(1) < 0$: $f(0) = -3.0$ and $f(1) = 5.71828$, so $f(0)f(1) < 0$. We proceed to step 2.

Step 2 Determine the midpoint using equation (4.3). Decide which point to discard:

$$x_m = \frac{x_n + x_{n+1}}{2}$$

$x_m = 0.5$, and $f(0.5) = 0.8243$. It is obvious that the point $x = 1.0$ will be re-placed by $x = 0.5$, since $f(0.5)f(1) > 0$. Also $f(.5)$ is greater than 1×10^{-5}; hence, the process is continued. Subsequent iterations are given in Table 4.1. The solution after 18 iterations is $x = 0.42943$.

```
***************************************************************
*      THIS PROGRAM USES THE BINARY SEARCH METHOD TO DETERMINE*
*            THE ROOT OF A NONLINEAR EQUATION                 *
* -------------------------------------------------------------
*
*        VARIABLE:
*                   LOWER : = X1
*                   F1 := F(LOWER)
*                   UPPER : = X2
*                   F2: = F(UPPER)
*                   MID : = X3
*                   F3 : = F(MID)
*                   ITER: NO OF ITERATIONS
*                   E: DESIRED ACCURACY
* ..........................................,..................
         REAL LOWER, UPPER, MID, F1, F2, F3, EQN, TOL
         INTEGER ITER
         OPEN(6,FILE='PRN')
*.............................................................
*   DEFINE THE LOWER AND UPPER POINTS
*
         WRITE(6,10)
  10     FORMAT(' ITER',3X,'X1',8X,'X2',8X,'X3',8X,'F1',8X,'F2',
      .  8X,'F3')
         LOWER = 0.0
         UPPER = 1.0
         ITER = 1
         TOL = 1E-5
*
*   EVALUATE THE FUNCTION AT THE LOWER AND UPPER POINTS
*
         F1 = EQN(LOWER)
         F2 = EQN(UPPER)
* .............................................................
*   TEST WHETHER THE ROOT COULD LIE IN THE SELECTED RANGE
*   IF SO CONTINUE ITERATION ELSE PRINT A MESSAGE AND STOP .
*.............................................................
         TEST = F1*F2
         IF(TEST.GT.0.0) THEN
             WRITE(6,20)
  20         FORMAT(' ERROR! : NO SOLUTION IS POSSIBLE IN THE
      .      RANGE SELECTED. THEREFORE SELECT ANOTHRE RANGE ')
                GO TO 100
         END IF
*
  30     CONTINUE
         MID = 0.5*(LOWER + UPPER)
*
*        EVALUATE FUNCTION AT THE MID POINT
*
         F3 = EQN(MID)
         WRITE(6,50)ITER,LOWER,UPPER,MID,F1,F2,F3
  50     FORMAT(1X,I2,6(F10.6))
*
*   TEST WHICH OF THE TWO POINTS (UPPER OR LOWER) TO DISCARD
```

FIGURE 4.3

A sample program for binary search.

```
*
            IF(F3*F1 .LT.0.0) THEN
                 UPPER = MID
                 F2 = F3
            ELSE
                 LOWER = MID
                 F1 = F3
            END IF
*
*   TEST IF  TERMINATION CRITERIA IS SATISFIED.  IF SO OUTPUT
*   THE SOLUTION.  OTHERWISE CONTINUE THE ITERATION.
*
            IF(ABS(F3).LE. TOL) THEN
              WRITE(6,70) MID
 70           FORMAT('THE ROOT OF THE EQUATION IS: ',F10.6)
            ELSE
              ITER = ITER + 1
                 GO TO 30
            END IF
*
 100        CONTINUE
            END
* -----------------------------------------------------------
*   DEFINE THE EQUATION TO BE SOLVED
* -----------------------------------------------------------
            REAL FUNCTION EQN(X)
            REAL X
            EQN = X*EXP(X) - 3.0*COS(22.0*X/7.0)
            RETURN
            END
```

FIGURE 4.3

(Continued).

n	x_n	x_{n+1}	x_m	$f(x_n)$	$f(x_{n+1})$	$f(x_m)$
1	0.00000	1.00000	0.50000	−3.00000	5.71828	0.82436
2	0.00000	0.50000	0.25000	−3.00000	0.82436	−1.80031
3	0.25000	0.50000	0.37500	−1.80031	0.82436	−0.60243
4	0.37500	0.50000	0.43750	−0.60243	0.82436	0.09234
5	0.37500	0.43750	0.40625	−0.60243	0.09234	−0.26100
6	0.40625	0.43750	0.42188	−0.26100	0.09234	−0.08566
7	0.42188	0.43750	0.42969	−0.08566	0.09234	0.00306
8	0.42188	0.42969	0.42579	−0.08566	0.00306	−0.04135
9	0.42579	0.42969	0.42774	−0.04135	0.00306	−0.01914
10	0.42774	0.42969	0.42872	−0.01914	0.00306	−0.00805
11	0.42872	0.42969	0.42921	−0.00804	0.00306	−0.00247
12	0.42921	0.42969	0.42945	−0.00247	0.00306	0.00032
13	0.42921	0.42945	0.42933	−0.00247	0.00032	−0.00104
14	0.42933	0.42945	0.42939	−0.00104	0.00032	−0.00036
15	0.42939	0.42945	0.42942	−0.00036	0.00032	−0.00002
16	0.42942	0.42945	0.42944	−0.00002	0.00032	0.00015
17	0.42942	0.42944	0.42943	−0.00002	0.00150	0.00009
18	0.42942	0.42943	0.42942	0.00002	0.00009	0.00003

TABLE 4.1

4.3   THE FALSE POSITION METHOD

The **method of false position** is an iterative procedure based on linear interpolation. It is similar in principle to the binary search method in that the iteration must commence with two values whose functions are of opposite signs; however, this method is more efficient. The binary search method finds the values for subsequent iterations by taking the average of the previous points, but the false position method establishes the subsequent iterative values by interpolating between the two previous points. Admittedly, the rate of convergence in this method depends on the degree to which the function can be approximated by a straight line in the interval of interest.

Consider Figure 4.4 and two points x_1 and x_2 such that $f(x_1)$ and $f(x_2)$ are of opposite sign. The root of the given function is x^*, since $f(x^*) = 0$. By similar triangles (triangles ABC and ADE), ignoring signs, we have

$$\frac{f(x_1)}{f(x_1) - f(x_2)} = \frac{x_3 - x_1}{x_2 - x_1}$$

$$x_3 = x_1 + \frac{f(x_1)\,(x_2 - x_1)}{f(x_1) - f(x_2)}$$

(4.4)

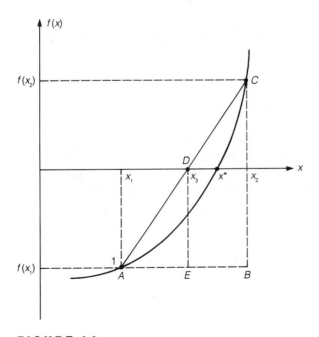

FIGURE 4.4

Illustration for the false position method.

Note that the desired root must lie within the two intervals

$$x_1 < x^* < x_3 \quad \text{or} \quad x_3 < x^* < x_2$$

We now determine which of the two subintervals contains the desired root. As in the binary search method, the interval containing the root is determined by checking the sign of f(x_3) in relation to the other two, f(x_1) and f(x_2). If $f(x_3)f(x_1)$ < 0, then the root lies in the left-hand interval—that is, in the interval x_1 and x_3. In this case, x_2 is now replaced with x_3 for the next iteration. The iterations continue until either f(x_3) is within a specified tolerance or the absolute value of $x_2 - x_1$ is within the tolerance.

For easy computation using a computer, equation (4.4) can be written in a general form:

$$x_{n+2} = x_n + \frac{f(x_n)(x_{n+1} - x_n)}{f(x_n) - f(x_{n+1})} \tag{4.5}$$

The flowchart for executing the false position method is given in Figure 4.5, and a sample program is shown in Figure 4.6.

E X A M P L E 4.2

Repeat Example 4.1 using the method of false position.

SOLUTION   From step 1 of Example 4.1, x_1 and x_2 are chosen as 0.0 and 1.0, respectively.

Step 2   Evaluate $f(x_1)$ and $f(x_2)$: $f(0.0) = -3.00$ and $f(1.0) = 5.7183$. Using equation (4.4), $x_3 = 0.34483$; $f(0.34483) = -0.91839$.

Step 3   Since f(x_3) f(x_2) < 0, we replace x_1 with x_3 and repeat the process. Subsequent iterations are shown in Table 4.2. The solution obtained after four iterations is $x^* = 0.42941$. Note that, using the binary search method, 18 iterations were needed.

n	x_n	x_{n+1}	x_{n+2}	f(x_n)	f(x_{n+1})	f(x_{n+2})
1	0.00000	1.00000	0.34483	−3.00000	−5.71828	−0.91839
2	0.34483	1.00000	0.43549	−0.91839	5.71828	0.06934
3	0.34483	0.43549	0.42913	−0.91839	0.06934	−0.00335
4	0.42913	0.43549	0.42941	−0.00334	0.06934	−0.00001

TABLE 4.2

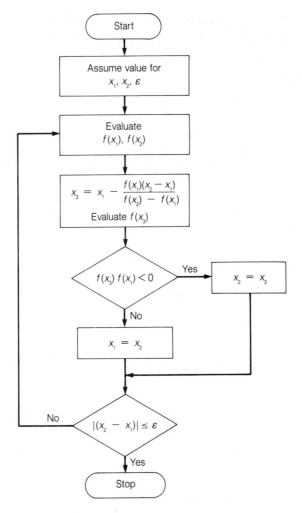

FIGURE 4.5

False position.

4.4 THE NEWTON-RAPHSON METHOD

A method of iteration more powerful and popular than the two previously discussed is called the **Newton-Raphson** (or Newton's) **method.** Unlike the method of false position, which uses interpolation centered on two functions values, this method uses extrapolation based on a line that is tangent to a curve at a point.

Consider the function graphed in Figure 4.7. Also, consider a line drawn tangent to the curve at the point C. The value of x, i.e., x_1, is the initial guess. If

```
***************************************************************
*    THIS PROGRAM USES THE FALSE POSITION METHOD TO DETERMINE*
*          THE ROOT OF A NONLINEAR EQUATION                  *
*    -------------------------------------------------------
*
*         VARIABLE:
*                  LOWER : = X1
*                  F1 := F(LOWER)
*                  UPPER : = X2
*                  F2: = F(UPPER)
*                  MID : = X3
*                  F3 : = F(MID)
*                  ITER: NO OF ITERATIONS
*                  E: DESIRED ACCURACY
* ............................................................
          REAL LOWER, UPPER, MID, F1, F2, F3, EQN, TOL
          INTEGER ITER
          OPEN(6,FILE='PRN')
*...........................................................
*    DEFINE THE LOWER AND UPPER POINTS
*
          WRITE(6,10)
   10     FORMAT(' ITER',3X,'X1',8X,'X2',8X,'X3',8X,'F1',8X,'F2',
        .  8X,'F3')
          LOWER = 0.0
          UPPER = 1.0
          ITER = 1
          TOL = 1E-5
*
*    EVALUATE THE FUNCTION AT THE LOWER AND UPPER POINTS
*
          F1 = EQN(LOWER)
          F2 = EQN(UPPER)
* ..........................................................
*    TEST WHETHER THE ROOT COULD LIE IN THE SELECTED RANGE
*    IF SO CONTINUE ITERATION ELSE PRINT A MESSAGE AND STOP .
*..........................................................
          TEST = F1*F2
          IF(TEST.GT.0.0) THEN
              WRITE(6,20)
   20         FORMAT(' ERROR! : NO SOLUTION IS POSSIBLE IN THE
        .     RANGE SELECTED. THEREFORE SELECT ANOTHRE RANGE ')
                 GO TO 100
          END IF
*
   30     CONTINUE
          MID = LOWER - (F1*(UPPER - LOWER)/(F2 - F1))
*
*    EVALUATE FUNCTION AT THE MID POINT
*
          F3 = EQN(MID)
          WRITE(6,50)ITER,LOWER,UPPER,MID,F1,F2,F3
   50     FORMAT(1X,I2,6(F10.6))
*
*    TEST WHICH OF THE TWO POINTS (UPPER OR LOWER) TO DISCARD
```

FIGURE 4.6

Sample program for method of false position.

```
*
             IF(F3*F1 .LT.0.0) THEN
                  UPPER = MID
                  F2 = F3
             ELSE
                  LOWER = MID
                  F1 = F3
             END IF
*
*     TEST IF  TERMINATION CRITERIA IS SATISFIED.   IF SO OUTPUT
*     THE SOLUTION.   OTHERWISE CONTINUE THE ITERATION.
*
             IF(ABS(F3).LE. TOL) THEN
                WRITE(6,70) MID
   70           FORMAT('THE ROOT OF THE EQUATION IS: ',F10.6)
             ELSE
                 ITER = ITER + 1
                   GO TO 30
             END IF
*
   100     CONTINUE
           END
* ------------------------------------------------------------
*   DEFINE THE EQUATION TO BE SOLVED
* ------------------------------------------------------------
           REAL FUNCTION EQN(X)
           REAL X
           EQN = X*EXP(X) - 3.0*COS(22.0*X/7.0)
           RETURN
           END
```

FIGURE 4.6

(Continued).

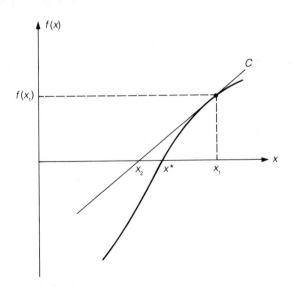

FIGURE 4.7

Illustration for Newton-Raphson method.

we extrapolate along the tangent line to its x-intercept, i.e., x_2, we then use x_2 as our next iteration value. This procedure is continued until either $f(x) = 0$ or until the change in the value of x is within a specified tolerance. A more general approach is developed as follows:

$$\tan x = f'(x_1) = \frac{f(x_1)}{x_1 - x_2}$$

or

$$x_2 = x_1 - \frac{f(x_1)}{f'(x_1)} \qquad \textbf{(4.6)}$$

An iterative scheme fitted for computer application can be set using the form:

$$x_{n+1} = x_n - \frac{f(x_n)}{f'(x_n)} \qquad \textbf{(4.7)}$$

A flowchart for developing a computer program is given in Figure 4.8, and a sample computer program is given in Figure 4.9.

The Newton-Raphson method, though very powerful, still has some drawbacks. If the initial guess is far away from the actual root, the method fails to yield a solution. In addition, if the value of the slope at the initial guess point is zero, the method also fails. The reason is obvious from either equation (4.6) or (4.7).

EXAMPLE 4.3

Repeat Example 4.1 using the Newton-Raphson method.

SOLUTION **Step 1** Let us take our initial guess to be 0.0, i.e., $x_1 = 0.0$. $F'(x) = e^x(1 + x) + 3\pi \sin \pi x$.

Step 2 Evaluate $f(0)$ and $f'(0)$;

$$f(0) = -3.00 \quad \text{and} \quad f'(0) = 1.00$$

Using equation (4.7), $x_2 = 3.0$. At this point notice that the solution is divergent. If we continue, the next point will be 638.271, and so we never reach the solution. What is wrong? Recall that it has been stated that if our initial guess is far from the actual root, no solution can be obtained. Let us return to step 1, only this time let us use an initial guess of 0.5. The process is repeated. The result of subsequent iterations is shown in Table 4.3. The solution obtained after five iterations is $x^* = 0.42941$. This exercise reveals the fact that if the initial guess is

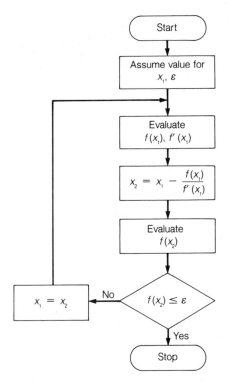

FIGURE 4.8

Newton's method.

```
**************************************************************
*       NEWTON RAPHSON METHOD FOR DETERMINING THE ROOT OF A *
*       NONLINEAR EQUATION.                                  *
**************************************************************
*
* ------------------------------------------------------------
*       VARIABLES:
*               X1: = XOLD
*               X2 := XNEW
*               FXO := VALUE OF THE FUNCTION AT XOLD
*               FXN := FUNCTION EVALUATED AT XNEW
*               FXP := DERIVATIVE OF EQUATION EVALUATED AT
*                      XOLD
*               ITER:= NUMBER OF ITERATIONS
*               TOL:=  DESIRED ACCURACY
* ------------------------------------------------------------
*
        REAL XOLD, XNEW, TOL, FXN, FXP, FXO, DER, EQN
        INTEGER ITER
        OPEN(6,FILE='PRN')
        WRITE(6,5)
```

FIGURE 4.9

Sample program for Newton-Raphson method.

```
    5        FORMAT(' ITER ',3X,' X1',8X,'X2 ',8X,'FX ',8X,'FP')
*
*    ENTER INITIAL STARTING POINT AND REQUIRED ACCURACY
*
         XOLD = 0.5
         TOL = 1E-5
         ITER = 1
*
*    EVALUATE FUNCTION AT XOLD
*
         FXO = EQN(XOLD)
   10    CONTINUE
*
*    EVALUATE THE DERIVATIVE AT THE POINT XOLD
*
         FXP = DER(XOLD)
*
*    DETERMINE AN IMPROVED POINT XNEW
*
*    CHECK THAT FXP IS NOT ZERO.  IF ZERO PRINT AN ERROR MESSAGE
*
         IF(FXP.EQ.0.0) THEN
               WRITE(6,20)
   20          FORMAT(' ERROR! SOLUTION IS DIVERGENT')
               GO TO 50
         ELSE
               XNEW = XOLD - (FXO/FXP)
               FXN =  EQN(XNEW)
         END IF
*
*    TEST FOR TERMINATION CRITERIA
*
         IF(FXN.GT.TOL) THEN
               XOLD = XNEW
               FXO = FXN
               ITER = ITER + 1
               WRITE(6,25)ITER,XOLD,XNEW,FXO,FXP
   25          FORMAT(2X,I2,4(F10.6))
               GO TO 10
         ELSE
               WRITE(6,40) XNEW,ITER
   40          FORMAT(' THE SOLUTION IS:',F10.6,I2)
         END IF
   50    CONTINUE
         END
* ---------------------------------------------------------------
*  DEFINE THE FUNCTION
*---------------------------------------------------------------
         REAL FUNCTION EQN(X)
         REAL X
         EQN = X*EXP(X) - 3*COS(22.0*X/7.0)
         RETURN
         END
* ---------------------------------------------------------------
*      DEFINE THE DERIVATIVE OF THE EQUATION
* ---------------------------------------------------------------
         REAL FUNCTION DER(X)
         REAL X
         DER  = (1 + X)*EXP(X) + (3.0*22.0/7)*SIN(22.0*X/7)
         RETURN
         END
```

FIGURE 4.9

(Continued).

not as close to the actual root, at most no solution is possible, and at best Newton's method becomes more efficient than the binary search method but less efficient than the method of false position.

n	x_n	x_{n+1}	$f(x_n)$	$f'(x_n)$
1	0.50000	0.41520	0.82436	9.72804
2	0.41526	0.43182	−0.16024	9.67759
3	0.43182	0.42897	0.02733	9.57832
4	0.42897	0.42951	−0.00518	9.56292
5	0.42951	0.42941	0.00099	9.56590

TABLE 4.3

4.5 SECANT METHOD

In the previous section we noted that Newton's method fails when the slope at the initial guess point is zero. There is yet another limitation to Newton's method in relation to the slope. In many instances, it may be inconvenient to determine the derivative of a given function, and as such Newton's method becomes difficult to use. A modification of Newton's method that overcomes the problem of finding the derivative of the function is called the **secant method.**

The secant method, being a modification of Newton's method, uses the same equation with little modification. Consider equation (4.7):

$$x_{n+1} = x_n - \frac{f(x_n)}{f'(x_n)} \tag{4.8}$$

If we take two points x_n, x_{n-1} on the slope, we can define the slope as:

$$f'(x_n) = \frac{f(x_n) - f(x_{n-1})}{x_n - x_{n-1}} \tag{4.9}$$

Then

$$x_{n+1} = x_n - \frac{f(x_n)(x_n - x_{n-1})}{f(x_n) - f(x_{n-1})} \tag{4.10}$$

The algorithm for applying equation (4.10) is the same as that of Newton's method, except that the formula for computing x_{n+1} is replaced with equation (4.10). Also, the termination criteria are the same as that of Newton.

APPLICATION

We have studied the techniques for obtaining solutions for equations that would be difficult through any direct method. We now demonstrate how these techniques may be applied in an engineering situation.

Problem Statement 1

Hol-Mac Corporation in Mississippi was requested to mass-produce the piston rods for an air cylinder that would form a part of a braking system for a well-drilling operation. The customer provided the following specifications:

1. The rod is to be made from cold-drawn or hot-rolled steel.

2. Because of space and weight considerations, the relationship between the extended length (L) and the diameter of the rod has been determined to be:

$$L = 12d^{3.5}$$

6 in. $< L <$ 8 in. (see Figure 4.10)

3. The thrust load is to be 20 kips.

Let us design the rod. One important aspect of engineering practice is that the design procedure must be properly documented as well as being systematic. We

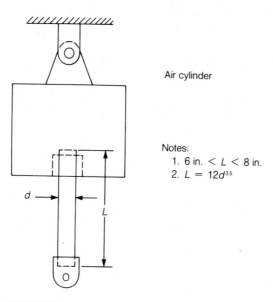

Air cylinder

Notes:
1. 6 in. $< L <$ 8 in.
2. $L = 12d^{35}$

FIGURE 4.10

Cylinder of problem 1.

approach this problem using a format that has been proven very successful for many students in the past. We proceed as follows:

Given: Load $= 20$ kips.

$$L = 12d^{3.5}$$

Material: cold-drawn or hot-rolled steel.

Find: 1. Length (L)

    2. Diameter (d)

REQUIRED EQUATIONS

Johnson's formula for short column design is:

$$P_{cr} = AS_y\,(1 - Q/4r^2) \tag{4.11}$$

Euler's formula is:

$$P_{cr} = \frac{AS_y r^2}{Q} \tag{4.12}$$

where

$$Q = \frac{S_y L^2}{C\,\pi^2 E} \tag{4.13}$$

and

P_{cr} = critical load
A = area of section ($\pi d^2/4$)
L = length of column
C = coefficient of end conditions
E = modulus of elasticity
r = radius of gyration ($\sqrt{I/A}$)
I = moment of inertia

Thus

$$n = \frac{P_{cr}}{P}$$

where

n = factor of safety
P = load

Note that the formulas are from [3].

ASSUMPTION

1. Fixed guided end condition
2. $C = 2.0$
3. Factor of safety $= 2.0$

ANALYSIS

First, simplify Johnson's equation

$$A = \frac{\pi d^2}{4} \tag{4.14}$$

$$r^2 = \frac{I}{A} = \frac{d^2}{16} \tag{4.15}$$

Substituting equations (4.13), (4.14), and (4.15) into equation (4.11) and simplifying, we have

$$P_{cr} = \frac{\pi d^2 S_y}{4}\left(1 - \frac{4S_y L^2}{C\pi^2 E d^2}\right) \tag{4.16}$$

but

$$L = 12 d^{3.5} \tag{4.17}$$

and

$$P_{cr}/P = n \tag{4.18}$$

Substituting equations (4.17) and (4.18) and simplifying gives

$$4Pn = \pi S_y d^2 - \frac{576 S_y^2 d^7}{C\pi E} \tag{4.19}$$

If we let

$$R_1 = \pi S_y$$

$$R_2 = \frac{576 S_y^2}{C\pi E}$$

then

$$4Pn = R_1 d^2 - R_2 d^7 \tag{4.20}$$

Alternatively, we can write

$$f(d) = 0 = R_1 d^2 - R_2 d^7 - 4Pn \qquad \textbf{(4.21)}$$

Similar operations transform equation (4.12) into:

$$Pn = \frac{S_y^2}{16R_2 d^3} \qquad \textbf{(4.22)}$$

At this point we could easily determine the desired diameter using equation (4.22), if we were sure that the piston rod could be treated as a long column. However, we do not know if we have a long column, so we must use either equation (4.20) or (4.22). The criteria for deciding which formula is applicable is that: If $Q/r^2 < 2$, equation (4.20) is used; otherwise use equation (4.22).

If we use equation (4.20), then an iterative process becomes necessary. Ah! We have learned some techniques that can be used to solve equation (4.20). Let us apply the Newton-Raphson method. We have

$$f(d) = 0 = R_1 d^2 - R_2 d^7 - 4Pn \qquad \textbf{(4.21)}$$

and

$$f'(d) = 0 = 2R_1 d - 7R_2 d^6 \qquad \textbf{(4.23)}$$

We can now employ a computer to our advantage. A flowchart for execution of this design process is given in Figure 4.11, the computer program listing is in Figure 4.12, and results are shown in Tables 4.4 and 4.5.

Although this is a very simple design, it demonstrates the need for computer-aided design. The company had available several materials of differing strengths and so had to perform a series of analyses based on each one. Since there were two options available (cold-drawn or hot-rolled), the design was performed based on the materials available. If the techniques that have been discussed in this chapter were not available, Tables 4.5 and 4.6 would be painstaking to generate. On examination of the two tables, the company may decide on the following:

Material: UNS G10450
Rod diameter: 27/32 in.
Rod length: 7.0 in.

Note that we have not examined the economics of manufacturing these rods. It is possible that the solution obtained may be unrealistic even though the specifications of the customer may seem to have been satisfied, or it could be that it is not possible to satisfy the customer's specifications. In that case, the engineer must inform the customer and suggest alternative solutions.

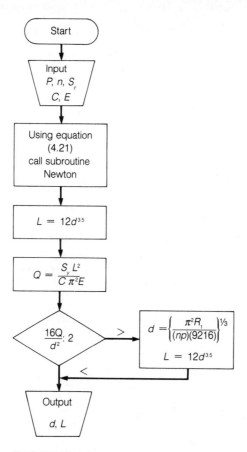

FIGURE 4.11

Flowchart for problem 1.

Problem Statement 2

Design a solid shaft to carry a torsional load of 220 kN-m and an axial load of 300 kN. Using our usual format we have:

Given: Torque $= 220$ kN-m, load $(P) = 300$ kN.

 Find: Diameter D

MATERIAL

Select AISI 1020 CD, yield stress $= 420$ MPa.

ASSUMPTION

Factor of safety $= 2$. Maximum shear stress theory applies.

```
* ****************************************************************
*           PROGRAM FOR THE ROD DESIGN IN CHAPTER 4             *
* ****************************************************************
*
*---------------------------------------------------------------*
* VARIABLES:                                                    *
*         DIA:= Diameter                                        *
*      LENGTH:= Length of the rod                               *
*      YSTRES:= Yield stress                                    *
*           C:= End condition                                   *
*       ELAST:= Modulus of elasticity                           *
*           N:= Factor of safety                                *
*          PI:= A constant                                      *
*        LOAD:= Design load                                     *
*           R:= Product of YSTRES,C, and PI                     *
*                                                               *
*---------------------------------------------------------------*
        REAL C,DIA,E,LENGTH,LOAD,R1,R2,YSTRES,XOLD,XNEW
        INTEGER N
        COMMON/BLOCK1/LOAD,N,PI,R1,R2,XOLD,XNEW,YSTRES
*
        OPEN(6,FILE='PRN')
*...............................................................*
*         INPUT DESIGN DATA                                     *
*...............................................................*
        LOAD = 2E4
        YSTRES = 6.7E4
             C = 2.
             N = 2
            PI = 22./7.
         ELAST = 30E6
            R1 = PI*YSTRES
            R2 = 576.0*YSTRES**2/(C*PI*ELAST)
        CALL RAPHSN
        DIA = XNEW
        LENGTH = 12.*DIA**3.5
        Q = (YSTRES*LENGTH**2)/(C*PI**2*ELAST)
        IF(((16.*Q)/DIA**2).GT.2.) THEN
             WRITE(6,30)
  30         FORMAT(2X,'COLUMN IS EULERS')
*
*             Compute the diameter using Euler's equation
             DIA = (PI**3*C*ELAST/(N*LOAD*9216.0))**.333
             LENGTH = 12.*DIA**3.5
        ELSE
             WRITE(6,40)
  40         FORMAT(2X,'COLUMN IS JOHNSON')
        END IF
*...............................................................*
*         OUTPUT DESIGN INFORMATION                             *
*...............................................................*
        WRITE(6,50)DIA,LENGTH
  50    FORMAT(2X,'THE DIAMETER IS:',E14.7,'THE LENGTH IS:',E14.7)
        END
* ****************************************************************
```

FIGURE 4.12

Main program for problem 1.

Material (UNS)	Yield (kpsi)	Diameter (inches)	Length (inches)
G10100	44	1.7145	79.19962
G10180	60	0.7484	4.35134
G10350	67	0.83571	6.40303
G10400	71	0.83425	6.36039
G10450	77	0.81596	5.88893
G10500	84	0.78754	5.20156

TABLE 4.4

Cold-drawn steel.

Material (UNS)	Yield (kpsi)	Diameter (inches)	Length (inches)
G10100	26	1.7145	79.19962
G10180	32	1.7145	79.19962
G10350	45	1.7145	79.19962
G10400	64	0.8220	6.04353
G10450	69	0.83678	6.43179
G10500	78	0.81213	5.79251

TABLE 4.5

Hot-rolled steel.

EQUATIONS

See Figure 4.13.

$$\sigma_x = \frac{4P}{\pi d^2}$$

$$\tau_{xy} = \frac{16T}{\pi d^3}$$

$$\frac{S_y}{2n} = \left[\left(\frac{\sigma_x}{2} \right)^2 + \tau_{xy}^2 \right]^{1/2}$$

SOLUTION The design equation in terms of the torque (T) and the load (P) becomes

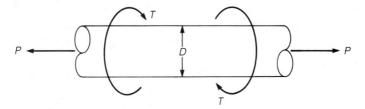

FIGURE 4.13

Sketch for problem 2.

$$\left(\frac{Sy}{2n}\right)^2 = \left(\frac{2P}{\pi d^2}\right)^2 + \left(\frac{16T}{\pi d^3}\right)^2$$

Examination of the design equation indicates that an iterative process is required to obtain the value of the diameter. Using the Newton-Raphson method, a diameter of 220 mm was obtained after 51 iterations. The number of iterations would be different if another starting point were chosen (instead of 21 mm, as was used here).

This simple design problem was included to demonstrate the usefulness of the techniques discussed in this chapter.

EXERCISES

1 Find the root of the function

$$f(x) = 3x^2 - \cos x - e^{-x}$$

first by the method of false position and then using the Newton-Raphson method.
(Ans, 0.6600)

2. Design a piston rod to meet the following specifications:
   (i) The length should not exceed 0.60 m.
   (ii) The rod is to made from either cold-drawn or hot-rolled steel.
   (iii) The diameter is known to be directly proportional to the ninth root of the square of the length. A similar rod is known to have a length of 250 mm and a diameter of 30mm.
   (iv) The rod must support a load of 190 kN (use a factor of safety of 2).

3. A hollow steel shaft is to be designed for power transmission. The power source is 30 Hp and the speed of the shaft is 100 rev/min. The inside diameter of the shaft is 2 in. If the permissible shearing stress is 11,000 psi, what is the thickness of the shaft? (Ans, 0.24 in.)

4. The van der Waals equation of state is given as

$$\left(P + \frac{a}{v^2}\right)(v - b) = RT$$

Determine the specific volume for air under the following conditions: $P = 25.68$ MPa, $T = 270°C$, $a = 172.6$ $(m^3/Kg)^2Pa$, and $b = 1.362$ (10^{-3}) m^3/Kg. Use an R value of 0.287 kJ/kg.°K. (*Caution:* Be careful with the units.)
(Ans, 0.0066 m^3/Kg)

5. Swamee and Jain (Proceedings of the ASCE, *Journal of Hyraulics Division* 102, HY5 (May 1976): 657–664) stated that an initial guess (which is within 1% accuracy) for the friction factor may be obtained by the formula

$$f_o = 0.25 \left[\log \left(\frac{1}{3.7 \ (D/e)} + 5.74/Re^{0.9} \right) \right]^{-2}$$

whereas the Moody chart is based on the formula

$$\frac{1}{f^{1/2}} = -2.0 \log \left(\frac{1}{3.7 \ (D/e)} + \frac{2.51}{Ref^{1/2}} \right)$$

How valid is their formula if $D/e = 850$ and $Re = 1.4 \times 10^{-5}$?

6. Two vertical plates each of area 0.10 m^2 are placed in a room at a temperature of 25°C. One plate is maintained at 160°C. What would be the temperature of the second plate for thermal equilibrium? Consider only radiative and convective heat transfer. Take the emissivity of each plate to be 0.8. The convective heat transfer coefficient may be approximated by the relation

$$h = 1.43(3.330 \ \Delta T)^{0.25}$$

The radiation shape factor between the two plates is 0.65 and between the environment and each of the plates is 0.35.

REFERENCES

1. Gerald, C. F., and P. Wheatley. *Applied Numerical Analysis*. Reading, Mass.: Addison-Wesley Publishing Company, 1983.

2. Burden, R. L., J. D. Faires, and A. C. Reynold. *Numerical Analysis*. Boston, Mass.: Prindle, Weber and Schmidt, 1978.

3. Hindhede, U., J. Zimmerman, R. B. Hopkins, R. Erisman, W. Hull, and J. D. Lang. *Machine Design Fundamentals*. New York: John Wiley & Sons, Inc., 1983.

CHAPTER 5

Basic Computer Graphics

5.1 INTRODUCTION

In this chapter we present the fundamentals of computer graphics. We discuss the necessary geometric transformations that are pertinent to graphical representation of objects. Next the principles of orthographic projections are presented. Finally, brief discussions of clipping and removal of hidden surfaces and hidden lines are presented.

5.2 GEOMETRIC TRANSFORMATIONS

Computer graphics involves generation of images by connecting a defined set of points on the object. Which points on the object that are to be connected depends on how the object is viewed. Consider the experience of photographing a historic building. We know that to get all views, the photographer will keep changing positions. These same views could have been obtained if it were possible to position the camera at a certain location while the building is rotated. You say that is foolish! How can we rotate the building? You are right; we cannot. Therefore, we opt for the more plausible solution, which is positioning the photographer at varying locations. The photographer may also change the extent of the view of the building by either coming close or moving away from the object.

105

These operations are really what we do in computer graphics. Since an object is defined with reference to a coordinate system, we choose to operate on the coordinate system instead of the object. A set of operations on the coordinate system (or the object) that result in a change in location of the coordinate system (or object) is known as a **geometric transformation.**

The three basic geometric transformations encountered in computer graphics and computational geometry are translation, scaling, and rotation. The other geometric transformations encountered are reflection and shearing. Before considering the various geometric transformations, a discussion of the concept of homogeneous coordinates is in order, since this concept is used in presenting the final form of the various transformations.

HOMOGENEOUS COORDINATES

In the graphical representation of objects, it is desirable to be able to manipulate local points or infinitely distant points. The representation of a local point in a Cartesian coordinate is quite simple. It can be represented in two dimensions, for example, by the coordinate (x, y). However, the representation of a point at infinity is usually done with a set of the direction cosines, which is usually not convenient. In order to be able to represent an ordinary point and points at infinity, a set of coordinates $[wx\, wy\, w]$, called **homogeneous coordinates,** are introduced. The name homogeneous simply indicates that the coordinates are of the same dimension.

The introduction of homogeneous coordinates serves a very important purpose. A point in a plane is represented by three coordinates instead of two. Homogeneous coordinates allow some geometric transformations that could otherwise not be performed by matrix operation. For example, as we will see shortly, if we want to obtain a single matrix that is the result of combining some sequence of geometric transformations, it would not be possible because of the rules of multiplication of matrices. Also, the homogeneous coordinates allow us to perform projective transformations. We often use the normalized coordinate system $[x\, y\, 1]$ in our geometric transformations.

TRANSLATION

Translation is the movement of an object from one position to another. Translation is accomplished by adding translation distances such as T_x and T_y to the original coordinates. If (x, y) represents the coordinates of a point, a translation to a new point (x', y') is given by

$$x' = x + T_x, \quad y' = y + T_y \tag{5.1}$$

In matrix notation, using homogeneous coordinates, we have, for two-dimensional translation,

$$[x' \; y' \; 1] \; = \; [x \; y \; 1] \begin{bmatrix} 1 & 0 & 0 \\ 0 & 1 & 0 \\ T_x & T_y & 1 \end{bmatrix} \qquad \textbf{(5.2)}$$

and for three-dimensional translation

$$[x' \; y' \; z' \; 1] \; = \; [x \; y \; z \; 1] \begin{bmatrix} 1 & 0 & 0 & 0 \\ 0 & 1 & 0 & 0 \\ 0 & 0 & 1 & 0 \\ T_x & T_y & T_z & 1 \end{bmatrix} \qquad \textbf{(5.3)}$$

SCALING

Scaling is a geometric transformation that results in either magnification or re-duction of the size of an object. Scaling involves multiplying each of the coordi-nates by scaling factors S_x and S_y. A point (x, y) of an object is scaled to the point (x', y'), where

$$x = xS_x \quad \text{and} \quad y' = yS_y \qquad \textbf{(5.4)}$$

In matrix form we have, for two-dimensional scaling,

$$[x' \; y' \; 1] \; = \; [x \; y \; 1] \begin{bmatrix} S_x & 0 & 0 \\ 0 & S_y & 0 \\ 0 & 0 & 1 \end{bmatrix} \qquad \textbf{(5.5)}$$

and for three-dimensional scaling,

$$[x' \; y' \; z' \; 1] \; = \; [x \; y \; z \; 1] \begin{bmatrix} S_x & 0 & 0 & 0 \\ 0 & S_y & 0 & 0 \\ 0 & 0 & S_z & 0 \\ 0 & 0 & 0 & 1 \end{bmatrix} \qquad \textbf{(5.6)}$$

TWO-DIMENSIONAL ROTATION

A geometric transformation of object points in a circular path through a speci-fied angle is called **rotation**. Consider the vector **A** (see Figure 5.1). Let us rotate it an angle θ in a counterclockwise direction to the point (x', y'). Using dot prod-uct, we can express the points (x, y) and (x', y') as

$$x = \mathbf{A} \cdot \mathbf{i} = |A| \cos \alpha$$
$$y = \mathbf{A} \cdot \mathbf{j} = |A| \cos (90 - \alpha) = |A| \sin \alpha$$

(5.7a)

Similarly

$$x' = \mathbf{A} \cdot \mathbf{i} = A \cos (\alpha + \theta)$$
$$y' = \mathbf{A} \cdot \mathbf{j} = A \sin (\alpha + \theta)$$

(5.7b)

Applying trigonometric identities, equation (5.7b) becomes

$$x' = |A| [\cos \theta \cos \alpha - \sin \theta \sin \alpha]$$
$$y' = |A| [\sin \theta \cos \alpha + \cos \theta \sin \alpha]$$

(5.7c)

Substituting equation (5.7a) into equation (5.7c), we have

$$x' = x\cos \theta - y\sin \theta$$
$$y' = x\sin \theta + y\cos \theta$$

(5.7d)

In matrix notation (using homogeneous coordinate), we have:

$$[x' \, y' \, 1] = [x \, y \, 1] \begin{bmatrix} \cos \theta & \sin \theta & 0 \\ -\sin \theta & \cos \theta & 0 \\ 0 & 0 & 1 \end{bmatrix}$$

(5.8)

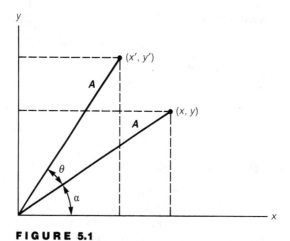

FIGURE 5.1

THREE-DIMENSIONAL ROTATION

Three-dimensional rotation is an extension of two-dimensional rotation. We have derived the rotation about the origin. If now we consider the z axis as the axis of rotation, then no dimensions on the z axis would change. In addition, if we consider the origin as a point on the z axis, then we can apply equation (5.8) to three-dimensional rotation about the z axis by adding a column vector with the z coordinate as unity. Then equation (5.8) modified for rotation about the z axis becomes

$$\mathbf{R}_z = \begin{bmatrix} \cos\theta & \sin\theta & 0 & 0 \\ -\sin\theta & \cos\theta & 0 & 0 \\ 0 & 0 & 1 & 0 \\ 0 & 0 & 0 & 1 \end{bmatrix} \tag{5.9}$$

By a similar operation, the rotation about the x axis is

$$\mathbf{R}_x = \begin{bmatrix} 1 & 0 & 0 & 0 \\ 0 & \cos\theta & \sin\theta & 0 \\ 0 & -\sin\theta & \cos\theta & 0 \\ 0 & 0 & 0 & 1 \end{bmatrix} \tag{5.10}$$

and for the y axis is

$$\mathbf{R}_y = \begin{bmatrix} \cos\theta & 0 & -\sin\theta & 0 \\ 0 & 1 & 0 & 0 \\ \sin\theta & 0 & \cos\theta & 0 \\ 0 & 0 & 0 & 1 \end{bmatrix} \tag{5.11}$$

Sometimes it may become necessary to transform an axis system (for example, the origin of a coordinate system may be translated into a new point). This is accomplished by the use of the inverse of the matrix required to perform the same type of transformation of the points in the coordinate system. For example, the rotation of an axis system about its y axis is performed using

$$\mathbf{R}_{yy} = \begin{bmatrix} \cos\theta & 0 & \sin\theta & 0 \\ 0 & 1 & 0 & 0 \\ -\sin\theta & 0 & \cos\theta & 0 \\ 0 & 0 & 0 & 1 \end{bmatrix} \tag{5.12}$$

The use of the notation $\mathbf{R}_{yy}$ is to show that a coordinate system is rotated instead of a point. Rotation about an arbitrary point is accomplished by a series of transformations. For example, a point (x, y) may be rotated about an arbitrary point

(xa, ya) by first translating it to the origin, then rotating it about the origin, and finally translating it to the former position. The steps involved are as follows.
First, translate (xa, ya) to the origin using

$$\mathbf{T}_0 = \begin{bmatrix} 1 & 0 & 0 \\ 0 & 1 & 0 \\ -xa & -ya & 1 \end{bmatrix}$$

Second, rotate about the origin using

$$\mathbf{R}_0 = \begin{bmatrix} \cos\theta & \sin\theta & 0 \\ -\sin\theta & \cos\theta & 0 \\ 0 & 0 & 1 \end{bmatrix}$$

And finally, translate back to the point (xa, ya) using

$$\mathbf{T}_a = \begin{bmatrix} 1 & 0 & 0 \\ 0 & 1 & 0 \\ xa & ya & 1 \end{bmatrix}$$

The overall transformation matrix is obtained by multiplying all the transformation matrices together to obtain

$$\mathbf{T}_0\mathbf{R}_0\mathbf{T}_a = \begin{bmatrix} \cos\theta & \sin\theta & 0 \\ -\sin\theta & \cos\theta & 0 \\ -xa\cos\theta + ya\sin\theta + xa & -xa\sin\theta - ya\cos\theta + ya & 1 \end{bmatrix}$$
$$= \mathbf{TT}$$

So we can write

$$[x'\ y'\ 1] = [x\ y\ 1]\ \mathbf{TT} \tag{5.13}$$

REFLECTION

Reflection is the reproduction of a mirror image of an object on the opposite side of an axis (for two-dimensions) or on the opposite side of a plane (for three dimensions). It is achieved by the following matrices.
For two-dimensional reflection about the y axis, use

$$\begin{bmatrix} -1 & 0 \\ 0 & 1 \end{bmatrix} \tag{5.14}$$

About x, use

$$\begin{bmatrix} 1 & 0 \\ 0 & -1 \end{bmatrix}$$

(5.15)

About the origin, use

$$\begin{bmatrix} -1 & 0 \\ 0 & -1 \end{bmatrix}$$

(5.16)

For three-dimensional we have the following. About the xy plane,

$$\begin{bmatrix} 1 & 0 & 0 & 0 \\ 0 & 1 & 0 & 0 \\ 0 & 0 & -1 & 0 \\ 0 & 0 & 0 & 1 \end{bmatrix}$$

(5.17)

About the xz plane,

$$\begin{bmatrix} 1 & 0 & 0 & 0 \\ 0 & -1 & 0 & 0 \\ 0 & 0 & 1 & 0 \\ 0 & 0 & 0 & 1 \end{bmatrix}$$

(5.18)

About the yz plane,

$$\begin{bmatrix} -1 & 0 & 0 & 0 \\ 0 & 1 & 0 & 0 \\ 0 & 0 & 1 & 0 \\ 0 & 0 & 0 & 1 \end{bmatrix}$$

(5.19)

5.3 PROJECTIONS

One problem encountered in computer graphics is how to project three-dimensional objects onto a two-dimensional viewing screen. This task is accomplished by two basic methods of projection: **parallel** and **perspective.** In parallel projection, all the points on the object are projected onto the viewing screen along parallel lines, while in perspective projection all the points on the object are projected along lines that converge to a point called the center of projection.

PARALLEL PROJECTION

Parallel projection is of two categories, depending on the orientation of the projection. If the direction of projection is perpendicular to the projection plane, it is known as **orthographic projection.** On the other hand, the case in which the projection plane is not perpendicular to the projection plane is called **oblique projection.**

The geometric transformation equations for achieving an orthographic parallel projection can easily be derived. If we consider the xy plane (i.e., $z = 0$ plane) as the viewing plane, it follows that any point on the object (x, y, z) would be represented by the projection point (xp, yp, zp). Since $z = 0$, then the correspondence is as follows:

$$xp = x$$
$$yp = y \tag{5.20}$$
$$zp = 0$$

The derivation of the transformation equations for achieving oblique projection can be established by considering Figure 5.2. The points B_r and B_o are the orthographic and oblique projections of the point B. The coordinates of the two projected points are related as follows:

$$x_o = x_r + S_1 \tan \varphi \cos \theta$$
$$y_o = y_r + S_1 \tan \varphi \sin \theta \tag{5.21}$$

where S_1 is the distance between the projection (viewing screen) plane and the object, φ is the angle between the oblique projection line and the line normal to the projection plane, and θ is the angle between the line from B_r to B_o and a horizontal line on the projection plane. The subscripts r and o refer to orthographic and oblique, respectively. Noting that S_1 represents the z coordinate and using equation (5.20), we can rewrite equation (5.21) as

$$x_o = x + z \tan \varphi \cos \theta$$
$$y_o = y + z \tan \varphi \sin \theta \tag{5.22}$$

Using homogeneous coordinates, the parallel oblique projection transformation can be represented in matrix form as

$$[x_o \, y_o \, z_o \, 1] = [x \; y \;\; z \;\; 1] \begin{bmatrix} 1 & 0 & 0 & 0 \\ 0 & 1 & 0 & 0 \\ \tan \varphi \cos \theta & \tan \varphi \cos \theta & 0 & 0 \\ 0 & 0 & 0 & 1 \end{bmatrix} \tag{5.23}$$

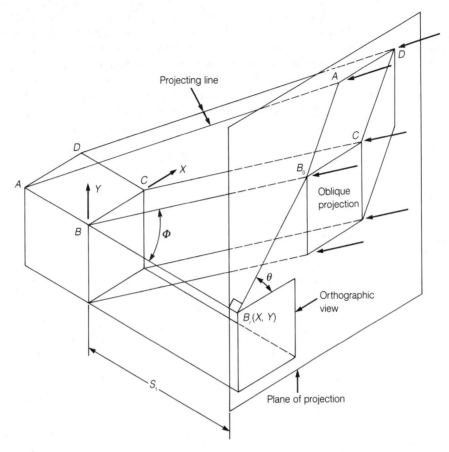

FIGURE 5.2

Oblique projection.

Note that when $\varphi = 45°$, we have the so-called cavalier projection, and if $\varphi = 36.6°$, we have the cabinet projection. Of course, when $\varphi = 0$, equation (5.23) reduces to that of orthographic projection. Therefore, equation (5.23) is a general matrix for parallel projection.

AUXILIARY VIEWS

The orthographic projection discussed in previous section produces principal views. However, the description of the shape of some objects (such as objects with sloping surfaces) cannot be accomplished except by the use of primary auxiliary views. Since primary auxiliary views are forms of orthographic projections, it is fitting that we discuss methods of their creation. We limit our discussion to two approaches.

The first approach consists of treating the observer as being positioned in the negative z axis and looking towards the origin. It is also assumed that the line of sight of the observer is perpendicular to the desired plane of projection. The task then is to move an observer in an imaginary fashion from a given point O in space to a point O' (see Figure 5.3). This is accomplished by two successive rotations. The first is the rotation of the observer around the z axis in a clockwise direction through the angle θ so that the observer is now positioned in the xz plane. The rotation matrix that accomplishes this is given by

$$\mathbf{R}_z = \begin{bmatrix} \cos\theta & -\sin\theta & 0 & 0 \\ \sin\theta & \cos\theta & 0 & 0 \\ 0 & 0 & 1 & 0 \\ 0 & 0 & 0 & 1 \end{bmatrix}$$

The second rotation is about the y axis through an angle of $180° - \varphi$. The rotation matrix is

$$\mathbf{R}_y = \begin{bmatrix} \cos\varphi & 0 & \sin\varphi & 0 \\ 0 & 1 & 0 & 0 \\ -\sin\varphi & 0 & \cos\varphi & 0 \\ 0 & 0 & 0 & 1 \end{bmatrix}$$

The entire process can be represented by the equation

$$\mathbf{M}_p = \mathbf{R}_z \mathbf{R}_y \tag{5.24}$$

where

$$\mathbf{M}_p = \begin{bmatrix} \cos\theta\cos\varphi & -\sin\theta & \cos\theta\sin\varphi & 0 \\ \sin\theta\cos\varphi & \cos\theta & \sin\theta\cos\varphi & 0 \\ -\sin\varphi & 0 & \cos\varphi & 0 \\ 0 & 0 & 0 & 1 \end{bmatrix}$$

A point as seen by the observer is related to the actual object by the use of the following equation:

$$[x_o \, y_o \, z_o \, 1] = [x \; y \; z \; 1] \, \mathbf{M}_p \tag{5.25}$$

The second approach involves the establishing of a folding line in the xy plane and three rotations of the coordinate system (see Figure 5.4). The first is

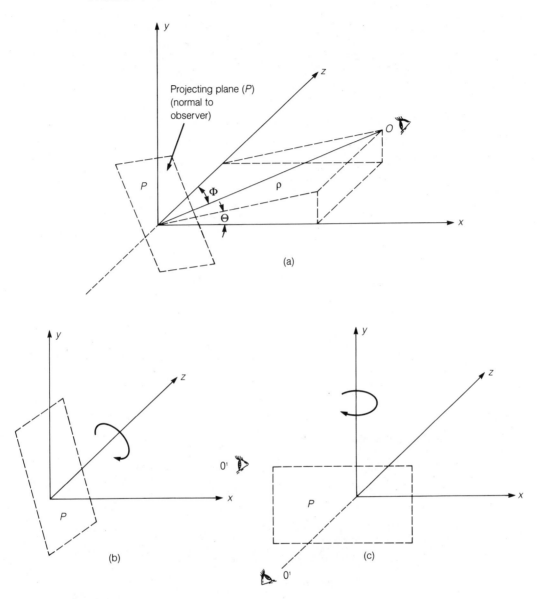

FIGURE 5.3

Creation of auxiliary views by two rotations (first approach).

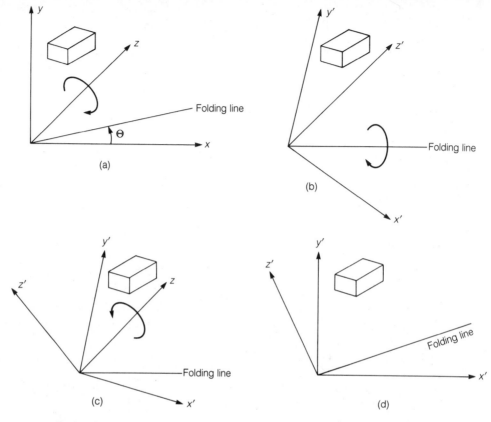

FIGURE 5.4

Alternate approach to creating auxiliary views (three rotations).

about the z axis through an angle of θ in clockwise direction, the second is about the x axis through an angle of 90° in a clockwise direction, and the third is about the z axis through an angle of θ, but this time in the opposite direction. The resulting single matrix from these rotations is

$$M'_p = \begin{bmatrix} \cos^2\theta & \sin\theta\cos\theta & -\sin\theta & 0 \\ \sin\theta\cos\theta & \sin^2\theta & \cos\theta & 0 \\ \sin\theta & \cos\theta & 0 & 0 \\ 0 & 0 & 0 & 1 \end{bmatrix}$$ (5.26)

AXONOMETRIC PROJECTION

The projections discussed so far are useful for a two-dimensional representation of an object. The implication is that at least three views or three projection planes are necessary to describe the shape of an object completely. These views form the conventional engineering drawings used in the machine shop to create the true shape of the object. There are times, however, when it is preferable to present a three-dimensional (pictorial) view of an object. One way to do this is by the use of **axonometric** projection (the others being obliques and perspectives). An axonometric projection is an orthographic projection utilizing only a single projection plane with the object placed in an oblique position relative to the projection plane. The resulting projected image is a three-dimensional view of the object. Axonometric projections are of three main types, depending on the orientation of the axes of the object. If the object is oriented so that at projection all the three axes of the object are equally foreshortened, then the projection is known as **isometric**. However, if only two of the three axes are equally foreshortened, then we have **dimetric** projection. If none of the axes have the same foreshortening, then we have **trimetric** projection.

Axonometric projection is achieved by first rotating the object around the y axis through an angle of θ in clockwise direction (angles are defined as shown in Figure 5.3). The rotation matrix is

$$\mathbf{R}_y = \begin{bmatrix} \cos\theta & 0 & \sin\theta & 0 \\ 0 & 1 & 0 & 0 \\ -\sin\theta & 0 & \cos\theta & 0 \\ 0 & 0 & 0 & 1 \end{bmatrix}$$

Then the object is rotated around the x axis in a clockwise direction through an angle φ using matrix

$$\mathbf{R}_x = \begin{bmatrix} 1 & 0 & 0 & 0 \\ 0 & \cos\varphi & -\sin\varphi & 0 \\ 0 & \sin\varphi & \cos\varphi & 0 \\ 0 & 0 & 0 & 1 \end{bmatrix}$$

The combined operation is

$$\mathbf{M}_a = \begin{bmatrix} \cos\theta & \sin\theta\sin\varphi & -\cos\varphi\sin\theta & 0 \\ 0 & \cos\varphi & -\sin\varphi & 0 \\ -\sin\theta & \sin\theta\sin\varphi & \cos\theta\cos\varphi & 0 \\ 0 & 0 & 0 & 1 \end{bmatrix} \qquad \textbf{(5.27)}$$

An axonometric projection results by the use of the equation

$$[xa \ ya \ za \ 1] = [x \ y \ z \ 1]\mathbf{M}_a \qquad \textbf{(5.28)}$$

where xa, ya, and za are the coordinates of the projected object.

PERSPECTIVE PROJECTION

The method of determining the point on the projection plane corresponding to a point on an object uses very simple geometric relations. Consider Figure 5.5 and the eye of the viewer as the center of projection and the origin of our axis on the projection plane that is $z = 0$.

From similar triangles OAD and OPC,

$$\frac{x_D}{d} = \frac{x}{z + d} \quad \text{and} \quad \frac{y_D}{d} = \frac{y}{z + d} \tag{5.29}$$

Simplifying, we have

$$x_D = \frac{x}{z/d + 1} \quad \text{and} \quad y_D = \frac{y}{z/d + 1} \tag{5.30}$$

Equation (5.30) does not indicate the orientation of the observer. To allow for the orientation of the observer, the point P should be expressed in terms of the coordinate system of the observer. This involves using the substitutions $x = x_o$ and $z_o = z + d$, equation (5.30) becomes

$$x_p = \frac{x_o d}{z_o}$$

$$y_p = \frac{y_o d}{z_o} \tag{5.31}$$

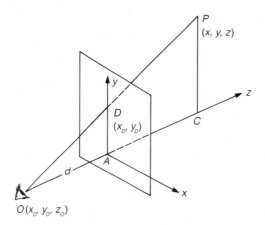

FIGURE 5.5

Geometry for establishing the perspective projection relationship between observer and object.

Equation (5.31) requires that the object in view be defined in terms of the observer's coordinate system. But an object is defined in terms of the standard (world-view) coordinate system; therefore, it becomes necessary to establish a relationship between the eye coordinate and the standard coordinate. The desired relationship is obtained when the z axis of the eye coordinate system can be measured in terms of the standard coordinate (see Figure 5.6). This requires some basic transformations of the coordinate system of the observer. These are a translation to the origin using

$$\mathbf{T}_x = -\rho \sin \varphi \cos \theta, \quad \mathbf{T}_y = -\rho \sin \theta \sin \varphi, \quad \mathbf{T}_z = \rho \cos \varphi$$

a rotation about z_o in a clockwise direction through an angle of $(90 - \theta)$, a rotation about x_o through an angle of $(180 - \varphi)$, and, finally, a reflection about the

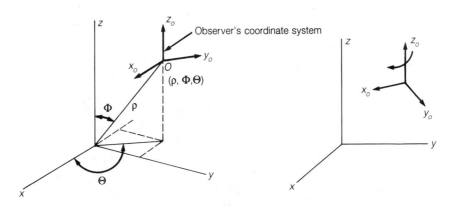

(a) Observer's position in relation to standard coordinate

(b) Rotation about z_o axis

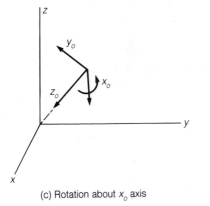

(c) Rotation about x_o axis

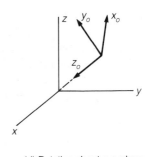

(d) Rotation about $y_o z_o$ plane

FIGURE 5.6

The relationship between the eye coordinate system and standard coordinate system.

$y_o z_o$ plane. A reflection was necessary to convert the observer's coordinate system into a standard left-hand coordinate system. The combined operations result in a single matrix given by

$$M_e = \begin{bmatrix} -\sin\theta & -\cos\theta\cos\varphi & -\cos\theta\sin\varphi & 0 \\ \cos\theta & -\sin\theta\cos\varphi & -\sin\theta\sin\varphi & 0 \\ 0 & \sin\varphi & -\cos\varphi & 0 \\ 0 & 0 & \rho & 1 \end{bmatrix} \qquad \textbf{(5.32)}$$

Thus, the relationship between the observer's coordinate system and the standard coordinate system is

$$[x_o\ y_o\ z_o\ 1] = [x\ y\ z\ 1]M_e \qquad \textbf{(5.33)}$$

5.4 CLIPPING

In many graphics applications, it is desirable to display only a portion of a picture, although the data base may contain the full information for the picture. To do this means that some part of the picture must be erased or eliminated from the display area. The process of cutting off the portion of the picture outside the viewing boundaries is called **clipping.**

Pictures are made up of a collection of points; therefore, one way of performing clipping is to clip each point. Point clipping simply requires the establishment of rectangular boundaries defined by the points $(x_{min},\ y_{min})$ and $(x_{max},\ y_{max})$ (see Figure 5.7). A point $(x,\ y)$ is considered visible if it satisfies the following conditions

$$x_{min} \le x \le x_{max}$$
$$y_{min} \le y \le y_{max} \qquad \textbf{(5.34)}$$

If the point does not satisfy all four inequalities, it is considered invisible and is clipped. For example, in Figure 5.7 the point (x_2, y_2) is invisible because $x_2 > x_{max}$, even though it is true that $y_{min} < y < y_{max}$. Clipping of a picture by clipping each point of the picture is no doubt an inefficient method. There are much better methods of clipping a picture that are based on the concept that a graphical image consists of line segments.

There are many clipping algorithms that have been developed, such as that of Cyrus and Beck [2], but we have chosen to present the efficient line-clipping algorithm developed by Liang and Barsky [3]. The algorithm is based on making use of equation (5.34) and writing the equation of a line between two points (x_1, y_1) and (x_2, y_2) in a parametric form:

$$x = x_1 + \Delta x v$$
$$y = y_1 + \Delta y v \qquad \textbf{(5.35)}$$

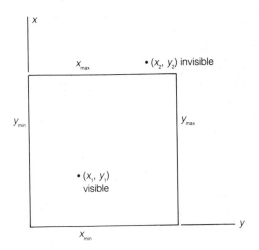

FIGURE 5.7

Definition of boundaries needed for clipping a picture.

where

$$\Delta x = x_2 - x_1$$
$$\Delta y = y_2 - y_1$$
$$0 \leq v \leq 1$$

Substituting equation (5.35) into (5.34) and simplifying results in

$$x_{min} \leq x_1 + \Delta x v \leq x_{max}$$
$$y_{min} \leq y_1 + \Delta y v \leq y_{max}$$

(5.36)

These four inequalities can be expressed as

$$p_j v \leq q_j, \quad j = 1, 2, 3, 4$$

(5.37)

where p and q are defined as

$$
\begin{aligned}
p_1 &= -\Delta x; & q_1 &= x_1 - x_{min} \\
p_2 &= \Delta x; & q_2 &= x_{max} - x_1 \\
p_3 &= -\Delta y; & q_3 &= y_1 - y_{min} \\
p_4 &= \Delta y; & q_4 &= y_{max} - y_1
\end{aligned}
$$

(5.38)

Examination of equation (5.38) reveals three possible conditions for p_j.

CONDITION 1

$$p_j = 0$$

The interpretation of this condition is that the line in question is parallel (since $x = 0$ or $y = 0$) to one of the boundary lines. If, in addition, $q_j < 0$, then the line is outside the display area.

CONDITION 2

$$p_j < 0$$

This situation arises if for a given line, its infinite extension proceeds from the outside to the inside of the infinite extension of the display area.

CONDITION 3

$$p_j > 0$$

This is the reverse of condition 2; that is, the line proceeds from the inside of the display area to the outside.

In equation (5.37) if $p_j \neq 0$, the value of v that corresponds to the point where the infinitely extended line intersects the extension of a boundary line j is

$$v = \frac{q_j}{p_j} \tag{5.39}$$

and the values of v that correspond to the terminals of the visible line segment, denoted by v_1 and v_2, respectively, are given as

$$v_1 = \max \left(\{q_j/p_j \, | \, p_j < 0, \quad j = 1, 2, 3, 4\} \cup \{0\} \right)$$
$$v_2 = \min \left(\{q_j/p_j \, | \, p_j > 0, \quad j = 1, 2, 3, 4\} \cup \{1\} \right) \tag{5.40}$$

Equation (5.40) is used for a visibility test. If $v_1 > v_2$, then the line is completely outside the display area and is rejected.

The algorithm begins with initializing v_1 and v_2 to 0 and 1, respectively. For each defining boundary, the ratio p/q is calculated. If the corresponding $p < 0$, then the ratio is compared with v_2. If it is greater than v_2, the line is rejected; otherwise, it is compared with v_1, and if it is greater than v_1, then we update v_1 with this new value. If the corresponding $p > 0$, then the ratio is compared with v_2. If it is less, it is used to update v_2. If we have the case $p = 0$ and $q < 0$, we reject the line, since it is outside the display area and also parallel to one of the boundary lines. The detail of the algorithm, with a little modification, is given in Figure 5.8, along with a sample program in Figure 5.9.

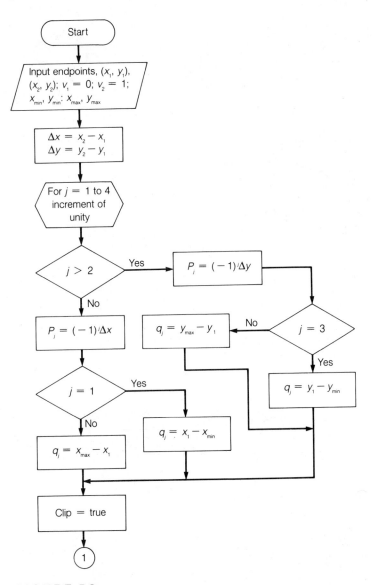

FIGURE 5.8

Flowchart for clipping algorithm.

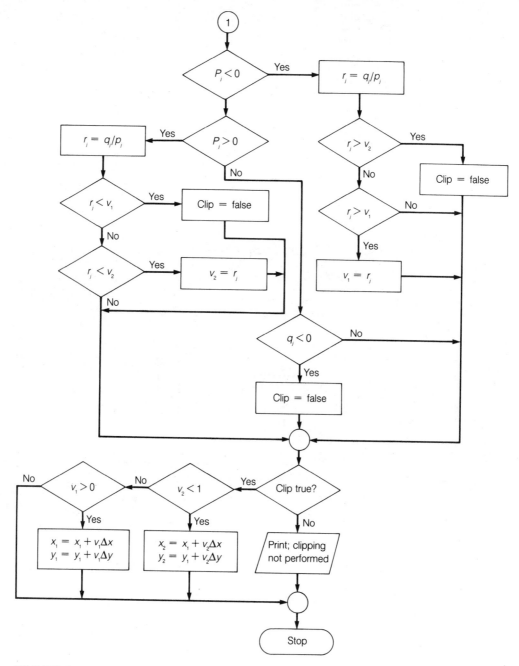

FIGURE 5.8

(Continued).

```
100      '*******************************************************
110      '* THIS PROGRAM IS FOR 2-D LINE CLIPPING. IT IS BASED  *
120      '* ON THE ALGORITHM DEVELOPED BY LIANG AND BARSKY      *
130      '*******************************************************
140      '-----------------------------------------------------
150      '  DEFINE THE COORDINATES OF THE WINDOW IN TERMS OF THE
160      '  LOWER CORNER (XMIN,YMIN) AND UPPER RIGHT HAND CORNER
170      '  (XMAX,YMAX). INITIALIZE THE PARAMETER V1 AND V2 TO
180      '  0 AND 1 RESPECTIVELY.
190      '-----------------------------------------------------
200      READ XMIN,XMAX,YMIN,YMAX,V1,V2
210      DATA 2,4,2,4,0,1
220      '.....................................................
230      ' GIVE THE END POINTS OF THE LINE TO BE CLIPPED,(X1,Y1),
240      ' (X2,Y2).
250      '.....................................................
260      INPUT"STARTING POINT: X1,Y1 ";X1,Y1
270      INPUT"END POINT: X2,Y2";X2,Y2
280      '
290      DELTX = X2 - X1 : DELTY = Y2 - Y1 :A$ ="TRUE"
300      '-----------------------------------------------------
310      ' DETERMINE IF LINE IS WITHIN THE WINDOW USING CLIP SUB-
320      ' ROUTINE. IF A$= FALSE THEN NO CLIPPING OTHER CLIP.
330      '-----------------------------------------------------
340      GOSUB 500
350      IF A$="TRUE" THEN 360 ELSE 430
360      IF V2 < 1 THEN X2 = X1 + V2*DELTX : Y2 = Y1 + V2*DELTY
370      IF V1 > 0 THEN X1 = X1 + V1*DELTX : Y1 = Y1 + V1*DELTY
380      '-----------------------------------------------------
390      ' OUTPUT THE NEW END POINTS OF THE LINE.
400      '-----------------------------------------------------
410      PRINT"X1 =";X1;"Y1=";Y1;"X2 = ";X2;"Y2 = ";Y2
420      PRINT"V1 = ";V1;"V2=";V2
430      IF A$ = "FALSE" THEN PRINT"NO CLIPPING IS PERFORMED"
435      END
440      '-----------------------------------------------------
450      ' SUBROUTINE CLIP.    THIS SUBROUTINE TESTS IF  CLIPPING
460      ' SHOULD BE PERFORMED.  THE PARAMETER V1 AND V2 ARE
470      ' UPDATE SO THAT ON LEAVING CLIP  THE FOLLOWING IS TRUE:
480      ' V1 =MAX({Q(J)/P(J)1 P(J) < 0 ,J=1,2,3,4} U {V1}) AND
490      ' V2 =MIN({Q(J)/P(J)1 P(J) > 0 ,J=1,2,3,4} U {V2})
495      '-----------------------------------------------------
500      FOR J = 1 TO 4
510      IF J < = 2 THEN 520 ELSE 550
520      P(J) = (-1)^J*DELTX
530      IF J = 1 THEN Q(J) = X1 - XMIN ELSE Q(J) = XMAX - X1
540      GOTO 570
550      P(J) = (-1)^J*DELTY
560      IF J = 3 THEN Q(J) = Y1 - YMIN ELSE Q(J) = YMAX - Y1
570      A$ ="TRUE"
580      IF P(J) < 0 THEN 650
590      IF P(J) > 0 THEN 600 ELSE 630
600      R(J) = Q(J)/P(J)
610      IF R(J) < V1 THEN A$ = "FALSE"
620      IF R(J) < V2 THEN V2 = R(J): GOTO 680
630      IF Q(J) < 0 THEN A$ ="FALSE"
640      GOTO 680
650      R(J) = Q(J)/P(J)
660      IF R(J) > V2 THEN A$="FALSE" : GOTO 680
670      IF R(J) > V1 THEN V1 = R(J)
680      PRINT"P =";P(J);"Q=";Q(J);"DELTX = ";DELTX;"DELTY =";DELTY;J
690      NEXT J
700      RETURN
```

FIGURE 5.9

EXAMPLE

Consider the line with the endpoints $(-2, -3)$ and $(4, 6)$. Let $x_{min} = 0 = y_{min}$ and $x_{max} = y_{max} = 1$. Let us test if the line is within the display area.

We have

$$\Delta x = x_2 - x_1 = 6 \quad \text{and} \quad \Delta y = y_2 - y_1 = 9$$

Using equation (5.38)

$$p_1 = -\Delta x = -6; \quad q_1 = x_1 - x_{min} = -2; \quad \frac{q_1}{p_1} = \frac{1}{3}$$

$$p_2 = \Delta x = 6; \quad q_2 = x_{max} - x_1 = 3; \quad \frac{q_2}{p_2} = \frac{1}{2}$$

$$p_3 = -\Delta y = -9; \quad q_3 = y_1 - y_{min} = -3; \quad \frac{q_3}{p_3} = \frac{1}{3}$$

$$p_4 = \Delta y = 9; \quad q_4 = y_{max} - y_1 = 4; \quad \frac{q_4}{p_4} = \frac{4}{9}$$

We compute v_1 and v_2:

$$v_1 = \max \left(\{q_j/p_j \,|\, p_j < 0, \quad j = 1, 2, 3, 4\} \cup \{0\} \right)$$
$$= \max \left(\frac{1}{3}, \frac{1}{3}, 0 \right) = \frac{1}{3}$$
$$v_2 = \min \left(\{q_j/p_j \,|\, p_j > 0, \quad j = 1, 2, 3, 4\} \cup \{1\} \right)$$
$$= \min \left(\frac{1}{2}, \frac{4}{9}, 1 \right) = \frac{4}{9}$$

Since $v_1 < v_2$, there is a visible segment. The endpoints of this line are calculated with equation (5.35) as follows: When $v_1 = 1/3$, the beginning point is $(0, 0)$; for $v_2 = 4/9$, the terminal point is $(2/3, 1)$.

HIDDEN SURFACES AND LINES

In the previous section, we introduced the modeling of three-dimensional objects through the use of projections. Such an approach produces pictures that are defined in terms of lines or edges. If the object is complex, it becomes difficult to differentiate various surfaces. Therefore, to achieve a more realistic picture, the surfaces that are normally hidden from the observer's view must be eliminated.

There are several algorithms available for removal of hidden surfaces, but we discuss only the back-face removal algorithm. The reader who is interested in learning other techniques may consult the references given in Chapter 2 and also at the end of this chapter. Our selection of this algorithm does not imply that it is the best technique available, but it is very simple to implement. In addition, it is easily adaptable for hidden-line removal.

BACK-FACE REMOVAL

The **back-face algorithm** makes use of the concept of cross product and dot product to determine if a face is visible or hidden. Recall from vector calculus (using the right-hand rule) that the cross product of two vectors **u** and **v** yields a third vector **n** that is normal to the plane containing the two vectors; that is

$$\mathbf{n} = \mathbf{u} \times \mathbf{v} \quad \text{(see Figure 5.10)}$$

In addition

$$\mathbf{v} \times \mathbf{u} = -\mathbf{n}$$

Consider a sheet of paper with vertices numbered as shown in Figure 5.11 and a point at the center of the sheet. The vectors **u** and **v** are defined as follows:

$$\mathbf{u} = \mathbf{v}_2 - \mathbf{v}_5$$
$$\mathbf{v} = \mathbf{v}_3 - \mathbf{v}_5$$

where $\mathbf{v}_5$ is a point on the sheet of paper. If we apply the right-hand rule, so that the normal to each side of the sheet would be outward, we note that the face visible to us has the normal defined as

$$\mathbf{n} = \mathbf{u} \times \mathbf{v}$$

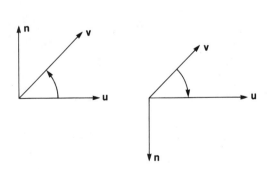

FIGURE 5.10

Dot product of two vectors.

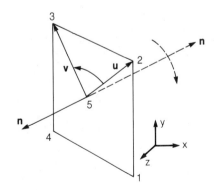

FIGURE 5.11

Differentiating between front- and backsides of a sheet of paper.

For the surface hidden from our view, its normal

$$-\mathbf{n} = \mathbf{v} \times \mathbf{u}$$

In three-dimensional space, the cross product can be fully expanded to yield (in scalar)

$$
\begin{aligned}
n_x &= u_y v_z - u_z v_y \\
n_y &= u_x v_z - u_z v_x \\
n_z &= u_x v_y - u_y v_x
\end{aligned}
\tag{5.41}
$$

To formulate a condition for determining which face is visible, we must define the line-of-sight vector of the observer $\mathbf{s}$ (see Figure 5.12). We now can define the direction for each surface using the dot product; that is

$$\mathbf{s} \cdot \mathbf{n} = |s| \, |n| \cos \theta \tag{5.42}$$

where θ is the angle between the line-of-sight vector and the normal to the surface under consideration. Immediately we note that the dot product is positive and the surface is visible if $0° < \theta < 90°$, and if $90° < \theta < 180°$, then the dot product is negative and the surface is invisible. Therefore, the test for a visible surface is that the dot product be positive.

In general, to test whether a face is a front or back face, we form the cross product of two vectors on the surface to determine the normal to the face; then we determine the dot product of the normal and projection vector, or line-of-sight vector, resulting in the formation of the so-called mixed-triple product. We then can state the condition for a face being visible in a matrix form as follows: If

$$
\begin{vmatrix}
s_x & s_y & s_z \\
u_x & u_y & u_z \\
v_x & v_y & v_z
\end{vmatrix}
> 0
\tag{5.43}
$$

then the face is visible.

The formation of the sight vector for perspective projection can easily be achieved by subtracting the coordinates of a chosen vertex on the surface and the center of projection. The chosen vertex should serve as a reference for defining the two vectors $\mathbf{u}$ and $\mathbf{v}$. In developing a program, it may be necessary to insert a condition to make sure that the three points chosen for the definition of the two vectors do not lie on the same line. In addition, it is necessary to define the two vectors of the given surface so that the normal is directed outward.

HIDDEN-LINE REMOVAL

The back-face removal algorithm is suitable for hidden-line removal. When all the hidden surfaces of an object are identified, then only the edges of the visible surfaces are displayed; in this way, all hidden lines are eliminated. Another approach may be to view hidden-line removal as a form of clipping. In this case, we use the visible surface as the display area (see Figure 5.13) and then clip any portion of a line that lies within the visible surface. This is a simplistic approach. There are more advanced methods for hidden-line removal, but we do not have the space to deal with them. A reader interested in other methods should consult the references cited in Chapter 2.

APPLICATIONS OF THE LINKED LIST

In Chapter 3 we discussed the various data structures that are applicable to computer-aided design. Since then we have made extensive use of one type of data structure, the array. This is the appropriate place to discuss the possible application of linked-list data structure in graphical representation.

We have seen how to identify a hidden surface. The question that arises is, How do we store these surfaces once we have determined which are visible and which are not? A more practical application is the representation of objects where some of the objects are behind each other (see Figure 5.14). To keep the illustration simple, we use surfaces collected as shown in Figure 5.15. We assume that these surfaces are the result of some geometric sorting scheme.

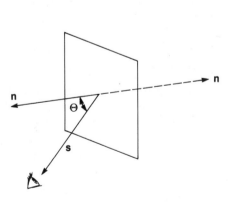

FIGURE 5.12

Establishing visibility test.

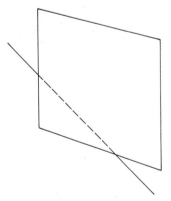

FIGURE 5.13

Hidden-line removal using clipping approach.

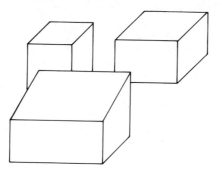

FIGURE 5.14

An example of objects partially obscured by another.

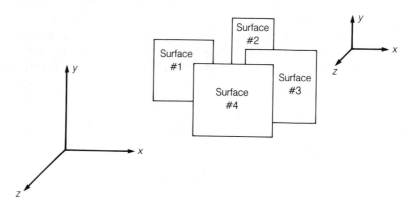

FIGURE 5.15

A collection of surfaces for illustration of the use of linked list data structure.

Suppose that all the data describing each surface are available and it is desired to store these surfaces in the manner shown in Figure 5.15. The best applicable data structure is the linked data structure. Recall that the position of an element in a linked list is determined by a pointer. Let us use an array SURF for the identification of the surfaces. The formation of the linked list requires an array list to hold the lists of the surfaces and a link to hold the pointer (for linking lists). We also need two additional arrays: BEFORE, to hold the pointer that indicates where each list of each surface begins, and AFTER, to indicate how many surfaces lie behind each surface. Let DELTA be a variable used as a pointer to the next free cell in an array.

We start forming the list as follows: Suppose that we start with surface 3 and want to add to its list surface 4. Since surface 4 is before surface 3, we use the index of an unused array cell DELTA to indicate that surface 4 is now before surface 3, as follows:

```
LINK(DELTA) = BEFORE(3)
```

Surface 4 is now added to the list as

```
LIST(DELTA) = 4
```

Then we update the BEFORE array, since the list now starts with the new cell DELTA; this is done using

```
BEFORE(3) = DELTA
```

We must now indicate that surface 4 now has one more surface lying behind it by

```
AFTER(4) = AFTER(4) + 1
```

If we use the variable A to identify a surface that is in front and B to identify a surface that is at the back, a portion of the BASIC program that will produce the desired list is

```
        .
        .
        .
300 LINK(DELTA) = BEFORE(B)
310 LIST(DELTA) = A
320 BEFORE(B) = DELTA
330 AFTER(A) = AFTER(A) + 1
340 DELTA = DELTA + 1
        .
        .
        .
```

CONCLUDING REMARKS

This chapter is by no means an advanced treatment of issues involved in computer graphics. Its purpose of introducing the reader to computer graphics has been served. Advanced topics may be obtained from the references cited.

EXERCISES

1. Write a program that draws any of the principal views of the object shown.

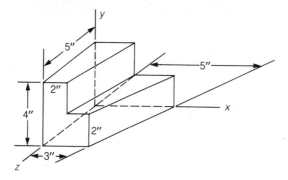

2.   Produce a perspective view of the object shown. Use view angles of $\theta = 63.4°$ and $\varphi = 143.2°$. Vary the values of ρ and D to see their effects on the image produced.

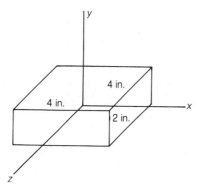

3.   Repeat Exercise 2 but remove all the hidden lines. (*Hint:* Identify each vertex, each edge, and each surface. Test the visibility of each surface. If a surface is visible, then its edges [composing of two vertices each] are visible; otherwise, the edges are invisible).

REFERENCES

1. Myers, R.E. *Microcomputer Graphics for the IBM PC.* Reading, Mass.: Addison-Wesley Publishing Company, 1984.

2. Cyrus, M., and J. Beck. "Generalized Two- and Three-Dimensional Clipping." *Computers and Graphics* 3, no. 1: 23–28.

3. Liang, D., and B. A. Barsky. "A New Concept and Method of Line Clipping." *ACM Transactions on Graphics* 3, no. 1 (January 1984): 1–22.

CHAPTER 6

Computer-Aided Curve and Surface Design

6.1 INTRODUCTION

The purpose of this chapter is to introduce the student to the field of computer-aided geometry design, which, according to Forrest [1], is a subset of computational geometry. Computational geometry is a wide field of study dealing with computer representation and manipulation of shape information. Discussions here are limited to the mathematical methods for defining shaped curves.

Curve design is very useful in the design of ships, cars, aircraft, tools and any other sculptured surfaces. The introduction of numerically controlled machines and high-speed computers has made curve design not only necessary but also highly desirable. It is now possible to store information on curves and shapes in the computer either for visualizing or for producing parts by numerically control tools. The two types of curves discussed in this chapter are the spline (cubic and the B-spline) and the Bezier. For more information in the area of computational geometry, the book by Faux and Pratt [2] should be consulted, along with [3], [4], and [5].

6.2 SPLINES

Consider the data points shown in Figure 6.1. How would one pass a smooth curve through these points? How could one use the computer to generate a smooth curve through these points? This section answers the first question, and subsequent sections answer the second.

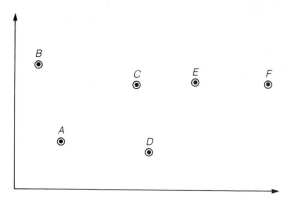

FIGURE 6.1

Illustration of the need for a spline.

The first approach could be to use a french curve; however, this would make it difficult to generate a smooth curve to flow in the *ABCDEF* direction. With a thread, the smooth curve could be generated provided there was a means of pinning the thread at points *A, B, C,* and so on. This second approach is similar to how a loftsperson generates a curve between specified points, except that his or her tool is called a **spline.** A spline is a flexible strip that can be made to go through a set of points in such a way as to produce a smooth curve. The curve is obtained by placing weights, or "ducks," at the various points and forcing the spline around these points (see Figure 6.2). The shape between two points then follows the laws of beam deflection.

FORMS AND PROPERTIES OF SPLINES

There are two major types of splines: cubic and B-spline. The cubic spline is considered first. It is the lowest-order polynomial that allows inflection within a specified segment. In general, a cubic polynomial is of the form

$$f(x) = \sum_{j=0}^{3} a_j x^j \qquad (6.1)$$

Equation (6.1) can used to construct a curve between two given intervals. Suppose a function f is defined between a given set of points $x_0, x_1, \ldots, x_n$ such that $x_0 < x_1 < \cdots < x_n$. It is possible to use equation (6.1) to approximate the function between each two successive points in such a way that the approximating curves would be joined and become a single smooth curve between x_0 and x_n. This single curve, consisting of a set of cubic polynomial arcs joined smoothly end to end, is denoted by S and approximates the original function f. S is said to be a spline function if it satisfies the following conditions:

1. S is a cubic polymonial denoted by S_i in each subinterval $[x_i, x_{i+1}]$ for $i = 0, 1, \ldots, n-1$.

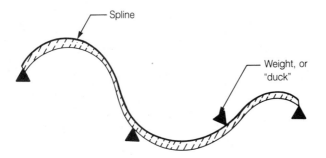

FIGURE 6.2

A physical spline.

2. S and its first and second derivatives are continuous on a set of interval from x_0 to x_n.

These two conditions can be expressed in the interval $[x_o, x_n]$ as:

$$S(x_i) = f(x_i), \quad i = 0, 1, \ldots, n \tag{6.2}$$

$$S_{i+1}(x_{i+1}) = S_i(x_{i+1}), \quad i = 0, 1, \ldots, n - 2 \tag{6.3}$$

$$S'_{i+1}(x_{i+1}) = S'_i(x_{i+1}), \quad i = 0, 1, \ldots, n - 2 \tag{6.4}$$

$$S''_{i+1}(x_{i+1}) = S''_i(x_{i+1}), \quad i = 0, 1, \ldots, n - 2 \tag{6.5}$$

The spline function, being a cubic polynomial, may be represented as

$$S_i(x) = a_{1i} + a_{2i} x + a_{3i} x^2 + a_{4i} x^3, \quad i = 0, 1, 2, \ldots, n - 1 \tag{6.6}$$

To generate a spline requires the determination of the preceding constants to uniquely describe a cubic polymonial at a given set of data points. The method of determining these constants is presented next.

6.3 SPLINE CONSTRUCTION

In the previous section it was stated that the generation of splines requires that the constants in equation (6.6) be determined. To simplify the derivation, equation (6.6) is put in a more convenient form as:

$$S_i(x) = a_i + b_i(x - x_i) + c_i(x - x_i)^2 + d_i(x - x_i)^3 \tag{6.7}$$

Consider Figure 6.3. In the study of spline, the points x_i are known as **knots** and each interval (x_i, x_{i+1}) is called the **span.** If we apply (6.7) to a typical single span of the spline, then at the two end points x_i, x_{i+1} we have

$$S_i(x_i) = a_i + b_i(x_i - x_i) + c_i(x_i - x_i)^2 + d_i(x_i - x_i)^3 = a_i \tag{6.8}$$

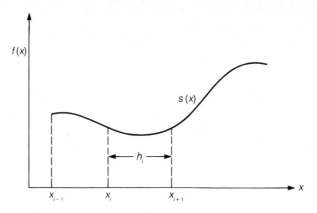

FIGURE 6.3

Illustration of the definition of a spline.

and

$$S_{i+1}(x_{i+1}) = a_i + b_i(x_{i+1} - x_i) + c_i(x_{i+1} - x_i)^2 + d_i(x_{i+1} - x_i)^3 \quad \text{(6.9)}$$

For simplicity let

$$h_i = x_{i+1} - x_i$$

Then

$$S_{i+1}(x_{i+1}) = a_i + b_i h_i + c_i h_i^2 + d_i h_i^3 \quad \text{(6.10)}$$

Differentiation of equation (6.7) gives

$$S_i' = b_i + 2c_i(x - x_i) + 3d_i(x - x_i)^2 \quad \text{(6.11)}$$

$$S_i'' = 2c_i + 6d_i(x - x_i) \quad \text{(6.12)}$$

A spline must satisfy equations (6.2)–(6.5). If we apply equation (6.2) and (6.3), then

$$S_i(x_i) = f(x_i) = a_i$$

$$S_i(x_{i+1}) = S_{i+1}(x_{i+1}) = a_{i+1}$$

From equation (6.10),

$$a_{i+1} = a_i + b_i h_i + c_i h_i^2 + d_i h_i^3 \quad \text{(6.13)}$$

Using equation (6.11) we have

$$S_i'(x_i) = b_i + 2c_i(x_i - x_i) + 3d_i(x_i - x_i)^2 = b_i$$

and

$$S_i'(x_{i+1}) = b_i + 2c_i h_i + 3d_i h_i^2$$

Also,

$$S_{i+1}'(x_{i+1}) = b_{i+1}$$

If we now apply equation (6.4), we have

$$b_{i+1} = b_i + 2c_i h_i + 3d_i h_i^2 \tag{6.14}$$

A similar procedure using equations (6.12) and (6.5) and reasoning similar to the preceding reasoning yields

$$2c_i + 6d_i h_i = 2c_{i+1}$$

or

$$c_{i+1} = c_i + 3d_i h_i \tag{6.15}$$

We have defined the relationships between the various coefficients of S_i in equation (6.7). Solving equation (6.15) for d_i gives:

$$d_i = \frac{c_{i+1} - c_i}{3h_i} \tag{6.16}$$

Substitution of d_i into (6.13) and (6.14) gives

$$a_{i+1} = a_i + b_i h_i + \frac{h_i^2(2c_i + c_{i+1})}{3} \tag{6.17}$$

and

$$b_{i+1} = b_i + h_i(c_i + c_{i+1}) \tag{6.18}$$

Since the values of the a_i's are known, we can solve equation (6.17) for b_i, giving

$$b_i = \frac{(a_{i+1} - a_i)}{h_i} - \frac{h_i(2c_i + c_{i+1})}{3} \tag{6.19}$$

So far we have matched the derivatives of S_i and S_{i+1}, which is a necessary condition for the smoothness of two curves joined at a point. A similar match of derivatives of S_{i-1} and S_i yields

$$b_i = b_{i-1} + h_{i-1}(c_{i-1} + c_i) \tag{6.20}$$

$$b_{i-1} = \frac{a_i - a_{i-1}}{h_{i-1}} - \frac{h_{i-1}(2c_{i-1} + c_i)}{3} \tag{6.21}$$

Substituting equation (6.21) into (6.20) and simplifying gives

$$b_i = \frac{a_i - a_{i-1}}{h_{i-1}} + \frac{h_{i-1}(c_{i-1} + 2c_i)}{3} \tag{6.22}$$

Equating (6.19) and (6.22) and simplifying, we obtain

$$h_{i-1}c_{i-1} + 2(h_{i-1} + h_i)c_i + h_i c_{i+1}$$
$$= 3\left(\frac{a_{i+1} - a_i}{h_i} - \frac{a_i - a_{i-1}}{h_{i-1}}\right), \text{ for } i = 1, 2, \dots, n - 1 \tag{6.23}$$

Note that final equation (6.23) contains the c_i's as the unknown, since the h_i's and a_i's are known. If we can solve for the values of c_i's in equation (6.23), we can determine the rest of the constants, the b_i's and d_i's, by equations (6.16) and (6.19).

Equation (6.23) produces a system of $n - 1$ equations with $n + 1$ unknowns. If we write equation (6.23) in matrix form, we have:

$$
\begin{bmatrix}
h_0 & 2(h_0 + h_1) & h_1 & & 0 & \cdots & \cdots & 0 & \cdots & \cdots & 0 \\
0 & h_1 & 2(h_1 + h_2) & h_2 & & & 0 & & & 0 \\
0 & & & h_{n-3} & 2(h_{n-3} + h_{n-2}) & & h_{n-2} & & & 0 \\
0 & \cdots & 0 & \cdots & 0 & & h_{n-2} & & 2(h_{n-2} + h_{n-1}) & h_{n-1}
\end{bmatrix}
\begin{bmatrix}
c_0 \\
c_1 \\
\vdots \\
\vdots \\
c_{n-1} \\
c_n
\end{bmatrix}
$$

$$
= 3
\begin{bmatrix}
\dfrac{a_2 - a_1}{h_1} - \dfrac{a_1 - a_0}{h_0} \\[2ex]
\dfrac{a_3 - a_2}{h_2} - \dfrac{a_2 - a_1}{h_1} \\[2ex]
\dfrac{a_4 - a_3}{h_3} - \dfrac{a_3 - a_2}{h_2} \\[2ex]
\vdots \\[1ex]
\dfrac{a_n - a_{n-1}}{h_{n-1}} - \dfrac{a_{n-1} - a_{n-2}}{h_{n-2}}
\end{bmatrix}
\tag{6.24}
$$

It is very clear that we would be unable to solve equation (6.24) unless we eliminated two of the unknowns by specifying two additional equations. There are several choices for generating the additional equations (for example, see [6]), but we consider the cases generally called the natural and the clamped splines.

Natural Splines

When the boundary conditions

$$S''(x_0) = S''(x_n) = 0$$

are imposed, the spline generated is called a **natural spline.** This condition is related to zero bending in a spline tool, which no doubt flattens the curve too much at the ends. In this case, we have

$$c_0 = 0$$
$$c_n = 0$$

(6.25)

and the resulting set of equations is solvable. Note that the coefficient matrix is a tridiagonal matrix. Determination of the constants b_i, c_i, ... is done by solving the tridiagonal linear system of equations. For easy computer application, a flowchart (based on [7]) for obtaining the constants using an algorithm for solving a tridiagonal linear system of equations is given in Figure 6.4, and a sample program (in BASIC) is shown in Figure 6.5.

Clamped Splines

When the tangents at both ends of the interval are specified, this boundary condition is known as a *clamped* condition, and the spline is called a **clamped cubic spline.** In our notation these boundary conditions are

$$S'(x_0) = f'(x_0)$$
$$S'(x_n) = f'(x_n)$$

(6.26)

Once more, the resultant equation is solvable. The flowchart for the computer application is given in Figure 6.6, and a sample program is listed in Figure 6.7.

The preceding development has resulted in the determination of the constants that uniquely define the spline function in a given interval. In addition, if we develop a general program to determine the constants quickly, we have indirectly placed a physical spline in the computer. Now we can answer our second question. How can we use the computer to generate smooth curves through a given set of points that we suspect need the use of a spline? By putting all the information necessary to determine the constants of a spline function into the computer, we have precisely answered the question. Of course, generating a smooth curve is a software and hardware function. Once we have developed the

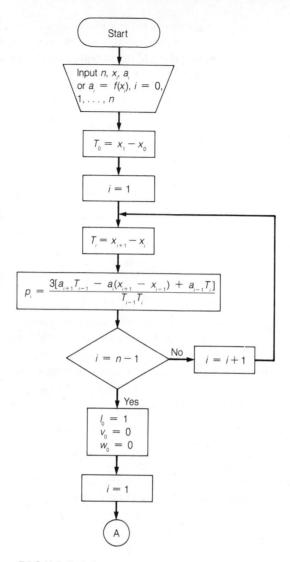

FIGURE 6.4

A flowchart for construction of a cubic spline.

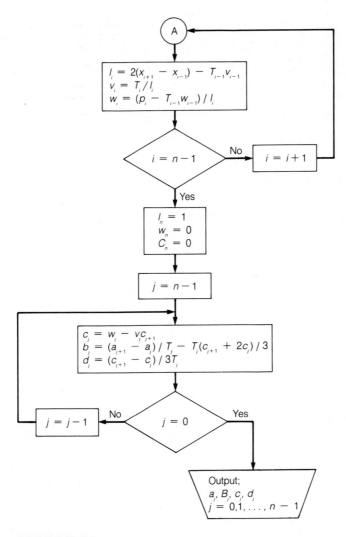

$$l_i = 2(x_{i+1} - x_{i-1}) - T_{i-1}v_{i-1}$$
$$v_i = T_i / l_i$$
$$w_i = (p_i - T_{i-1}w_{i-1}) / l_i$$

$i = n - 1$

No → $i = i + 1$

Yes

$$l_n = 1$$
$$w_n = 0$$
$$C_n = 0$$

$$j = n - 1$$

$$c_j = w_j - v_j c_{j+1}$$
$$b_j = (a_{j+1} - a_j) / T_j - T_j(c_{j+1} + 2c_j) / 3$$
$$d_j = (c_{j+1} - c_j) / 3T_j$$

$j = 0$

No → $j = j - 1$

Yes

Output;
a_j, B_j, c_j, d_j
$j = 0,1, \ldots, n - 1$

FIGURE 6.4

(Continued).

```
10 REM ***********************************************************************
20 REM * THIS PROGRAM CALLED CSPLINE DETERMINES THE COEFFICIENTS OF A *
30 REM * CUBIC SPLINE. THE POLYNOMIAL IS OF THE FORM:                 *
40 REM *                                                              *
50 REM * A(I)+B(I)*(X-X(I))+C(I)*(X-X(I))^2+D(I)*(X-X(I))^3.          *
60 REM *                                                              *
70 REM * THE EXAMPLE USED HERE IS THE COSINE FUNCTION                 *
80 REM ***********************************************************************
90 REM ***********************************************************************
100 DIM Z(100),Y(100),RF(100),P(100)
110   REM ......................................................
120   REM . INPUT THE DATA POINTS X AND Y OR DEFINE FUNCTION      .
130   REM ......................................................
140   DEF FNA(X)=X*COS(22*X^2/7)
150   INPUT "HOW MANY DATA POINTS WILL YOU USE";N
160   PRINT "GET READY TO ENTER THE X VALUES OR THE KNOTS"
170 FOR I=1 TO N
180 PRINT "ENTER X(";I;")"
190   INPUT X(I)
200   NEXT I
210 INPUT "ARE YOU FITTING A FUNCTION (Y/N)";A$
220 IF A$ = "Y" OR A$ ="N" THEN 240
230 PRINT"WRONG RESPONSE TRY AGAIN": GOTO 210
240 IF A$="Y" GOTO 340
250 PRINT"GET READY TO ENTER THE VALUES OF Ys"
260 FOR J=1 TO N
270 PRINT"ENTER Y(";J;")"  : INPUT A(J)
280 NEXT J
290   GOTO 370
300   REM ......................................................
310   REM . SOLVE FOR THE COEFFICIENTS OF THE CUBIC POLYNOMIAL    .
320   REM . THE METHOD USED HERE IS APPLICABLE TO TRI-DIAGONAL MATRIX.
330   REM ......................................................
340   FOR I=1 TO N
350 A(I)=FNA(X(I))
360 NEXT I
370 H(1)=X(2)-X(1)
380 FOR I=2 TO N-1
390 H(I)=X(I+1)-X(I)
400 P(I) = 3*(A(I+1)*H(I-1)-A(I)*(X(I+1)-X(I-1))+A(I-1)*H(I)))/(H(I-1)*H(I))
410 REM
420 NEXT I
430 L(1)=1
440 V(1)=0
450 W(1)=0
460 FOR I=2 TO N-1
470 L(I)=2*(X(I+1)-X(I-1))-H(I-1)*V(I-1)
480 V(I)=H(I)/L(I)
490 W(I)=(P(I)-H(I-1)*W(I-1))/L(I)
500 NEXT I
510 L(N)=1
520 W(N)=0
530 C(N)=0
540 FOR J =N-1 TO 1 STEP -1
550 C(J) = W(J)-V(J)*C(J+1)
```

F I G U R E   6.5

A sample program for a natural cubic spline.

```
560 B(J) = ((A(J+1)-A(J))/H(J))-H(J)*(C(J+1)+2*C(J))/3
570 D(J) = (C(J+1)-C(J))/(3*H(J))
580 NEXT J
590  REM ...............................................
600  REM .          OUTPUT THE COEFFICIENTS A,B,C AND D         .
610  REM ...............................................
620 PRINT "  J";TAB(20);"A";TAB(28);"B";TAB(36);"C";TAB(44);"D"
630 FOR J = 1 TO N-1
640 PRINT J,:PRINT USING "##.##### ";A(J);B(J);C(J);D(J)
650 NEXT J
660 INPUT"DO YOU WANT TO PLOT THE FITTED FUNCTION (Y/N)";B$
670 IF B$ = "N" THEN 970
680 REM ...............................................
690 REM .                                                     .
700 REM . GENERATION OF THE POINTS NEEDED TO PLOT CURVE        .
710 REM . USE FIVE POINTS IN EACH INTERVAL I.E. M = 5          .
720 REM ...............................................
730 M=5
740 K=1
750 FOR I=1 TO N-1
760 G=(X(I+1)-X(I))/M
770 Z(K) = X(I)
780 P(K)=A(I)+B(I)*(Z(K)-X(I))+C(I)*((Z(K)-X(I))^2)+D(I)*((Z(K)-X(I))^3)
790 REM ...RF(K) IS THE REAL VALUE OF THE FUNCTION  BEING FITTED .
800 IF A$ = "Y" THEN RF(K) = FNA(Z(K))
810 REM
820 Z(K+1) = Z(K)+G
830 K=K+1
840 IF Z(K)> X(I+1) GOTO 860
850 GOTO 780
860 NEXT I
870 REM ...............................................
880 REM . PLOT CURVE TO THE SCREEN                            .
890 REM ...............................................
900 SCREEN 2 : KEY OFF : WINDOW (-2,-2) - (2,2)
910 PSET (Z(1),P(1))
920 FOR I = 2 TO K
930 LINE - (Z(I),P(I)) : NEXT I
940  REM ...............................................
950  REM . CALCULATION OF THE AREA UNDER THE CURVE FITTED.
960  REM ...............................................
970  INPUT"DO YOU WANT THE AREA UNDER THE CURVE (Y/N)";C$
980  IF C$ ="N" THEN 1080
990  A1 = 0 : A2 =0: A3 =0: A4 = 0
1000  FOR I = 1 TO N-1
1010   A1 = A1 + H(I)^4*D(I)
1020   A2 = A2 + H(I)^3*C(I)
1030   A3 = A3 + H(I)^2*B(I)
1040   A4 = A4 + H(I)*A(I)
1050   NEXT I
1060   AREA = A1/4 + A2/3 +A3/2 + A4
1070   PRINT"AREA UNDER THE CURVE = ";AREA; "SQ.UNITS"
1080 END
```

F I G U R E 6.5

(Continued).

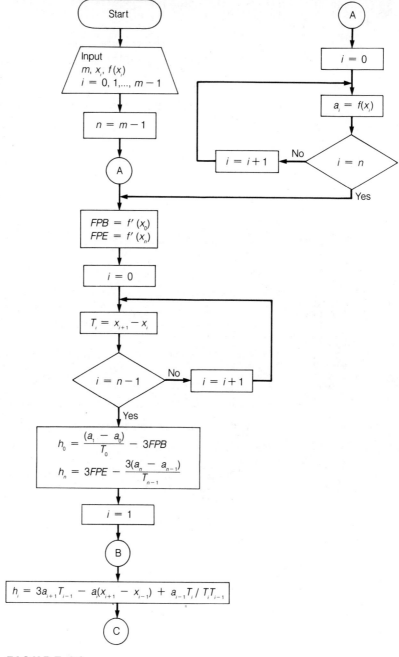

FIGURE 6.6

A flowchart for a clamped cubic spline.

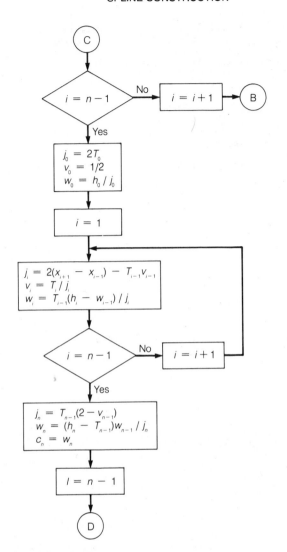
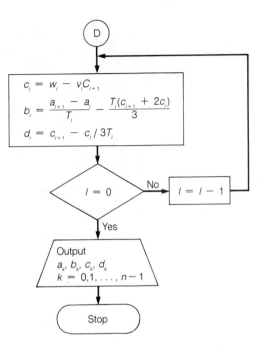

FIGURE 6.6

(Continued).

```
10    REM  ***********************************************************
20    REM  *   THIS PROGRAM GENERATES THE COEFFICIENTS FOR THE   CLAMPED
30    REM  *   CUBIC SPLINE OF THE FORM:
40    REM  *    A(I) + B(I)*(X - X(I)) + C(I)*(X -X(I))^2 + D(I)*(X-X(I))^3
50    REM  ***********************************************************
60    REM  ---------------------------------------------------------------
70    REM   DEFINE THE FUNCTION IF KNOWN.
80    REM  ---------------------------------------------------------------
90    DEF FNX(X) =X*COS(22*X^2/7)
100   REM  ---------------------------------------------------------------
110   REM       DEFINE THE FIRST DERIVATIVE OF THE FUNCTION WITH RESPECT
120   REM       TO THE INDEPENDENT VARIABLE.
130   REM  ---------------------------------------------------------------
140   DEF FNP(X)  = COS(22*X^2/7) -(44*X/7)*SIN(22*X^2/7)
150   REM
160   REM .... ENTER THE VALUES OF THE INDEPENDENT VARIABLE (I.E. X(I))..
170   INPUT "ENTER THE TOTAL NO. OF DATA POINTS";M
180   N = M-1
190   FOR K = 0 TO N
200    PRINT "ENTER X(";K;")"
210    INPUT X(K): NEXT K
220    INPUT "IS THE FUNCTION KNOWN (Y/N)";A$
230    IF A$ = "Y" GOTO 350
240   REM ...............................................................
250   REM . ENTER THE DEPENDENT VARIABLES FOR THE CASE THAT THE .
260   REM . THE FUNCTION IS NOT KNOWN              .
270   REM ...............................................................
280   FOR K = 0 TO N
290   PRINT "ENTER F(";K;")"
300   INPUT F(K): A(K) = F(K) : NEXT K
310    PRINT"ENTER THE VALUES OF THE DERIVATIVE OF THE FUNCTION"
320    PRINT"AT THE INITIAL AND END POINTS,FPB AND FBE"
330    INPUT "FPB,FPE";FPB,FPE
340    GOTO 380
350    FOR I= 0 TO N
360    A(I) = FNX(X(I)): NEXT I
370   FPB= FNP(X(0)): FPE = FNP(X(N))
380     FOR I = 0 TO N-1
390       T(I) = X(I+1) - X(I): NEXT I
400     H(0)  =  3*(A(1)-A(0))/(3*T(0))- 3*FPB
410     H(N) = 3*FPE - 3*(A(N)-A(N-1))/T(N-1)
420     FOR  I = 1 TO N-1
430     H(I) = 3*(A(I+1)*T(I-1) - A(I)*(X(I+1)-X(I-1))+A(I-1)*T(I))/T(I-1)*T(I)
440   NEXT I
450   REM ...............................................................
460   REM .LINE 340 THRU 450 USES THE ALGORITHM FOR SOLVING A    .
470   REM .   TRIDIAGONAL SYSTEM OF LINEAR EQUATIONS            .
480   REM ...............................................................
490     J(0) = 2*T(0): V(0)=.5  : W(0) = H(0)/J(0)
500     FOR I = 1 TO N-1
510     J(I) = 2 *(X(I+1) - X(I-1)) - T(I-1)*V(I-1)
520     V(I) = T(I)/J(I): W(I) = (H(I)-W(I-1)*T(I-1))/J(I)
530   NEXT I
540   J(N) = T(N-1)*(2 - V(N-1))
550   W(N) =   (H(N) - T(N-1)*W(N-1))/J(N): C(N) = W(N)
560   REM ...............................................................
570   REM  DETERMINATION OF THE COEFFICIENTS             .
580   REM ...............................................................
590    FOR  L = N-1 TO 0 STEP -1
600   REM ...............................................................
610   REM . COMPUTING  THE C'S                    .
620   REM ...............................................................
630    C(L) = W(L) - V(L)*C(L+1)
640   REM ...............................................................
```

FIGURE 6.7

Sample program for a clamped cubic spline.

```
650    REM . COMPUTING   THE  B'S                                     .
660    REM ..............................................................
670      B(L) = (A(L+1) - A(L))/T(L) - T(L)*(C(L+1)+2*C(L))/3
680    REM ..............................................................
690    REM . COMPUTING   THE  D'S                                     .
700    REM ..............................................................
710      D(L) = (C(L+1) - C(L))/(3*T(L))
720       NEXT L
730    REM *********************************************************
740    REM .OUTPUT THE A'S, B'S, C'S, AND THE D'S                   .
750    REM *********************************************************
760      PRINT "J";TAB(20);"A";TAB(28);"B";TAB(36);"C";TAB(44);"D"
770      FOR I = 0 TO N-1
780      PRINT I,:PRINT USING "##.#### ";A(I);B(I);C(I);D(I)
790      NEXT I
800      END
```

FIGURE 6.7

(Continued).

spline subroutine, we can then enlist the aid of such software packages as Plot 10 (Tektronix software for plotting graphs) and a plotter. Alternatively, we can use any personal computer with graphics capability to plot the curve. And, if the program is written in BASIC or any higher language, we can obtain hard copy using such plotters as HP 7475A.

It should be realized that when we use an interactive computer graphics system, a spline subroutine is part of the software package. The inclusion of the spline subroutine in the software package of a CAD system has made it unnecessary to use the physical spline in the design process. In fact, the author prefers to think of computer-aided drafting as a replacement for the drafting tools with various software packages in a CAD system.

EXAMPLE 6.1

Approximate the function $f(x) = x \cos \pi x^2$ using the natural spline. Use the knot vector $[0.0 \ 0.25 \ 0.5 \ 0.75 \ 1.0]^T$.

SOLUTION The cubic spline approximation is of the form

$$S(x) = a_i + b_i(x - x_i) + c_i(x - x_i)^2 + d_i(x - x_i)^3$$

Using equation (6.23) with $n = 4$, we have

$$h_0 c_0 + 2(h_0 + h_1)c_1 + h_1 c_2 = 3\left(\frac{a_2 - a_1}{h_1} - \frac{a_1 - a_0}{h_0}\right)$$

$$h_1 c_1 + 2(h_2 + h_1)c_2 + h_2 c_3 = 3\left(\frac{a_3 - a_2}{h_2} - \frac{a_2 - a_1}{h_1}\right)$$

$$h_2 c_2 + 2(h_3 + h_2)c_2 + h_3 c_4 = 3\left(\frac{a_4 - a_3}{h_3} - \frac{a_3 - a_2}{h_2}\right)$$

i	x_i	a_i	b_i	c_i	d_i
0	0.0000	0.0000	0.9788	0.0000	0.0309
1	0.2500	0.2451	0.9846	0.0232	-8.9192
2	0.5000	0.3534	-0.6761	-6.6662	-5.4632
3	0.7500	-0.1468	-2.9846	-2.5680	3.4239
4	1.0000	—	—	—	—

TABLE 6.1

x	$f(x)$	$S(x)$
0.1	0.0995	0.0979
0.2	0.1984	0.1960
0.3	0.2881	0.2934
0.4	0.3505	0.3350
0.5	0.3534	0.3534
0.6	0.2552	0.2246
0.7	0.0215	-0.0047
0.8	-0.3412	-0.3020
0.9	-0.7448	-0.6408
1.0	-1.0000	-1.0000

TABLE 6.2

Since the step size is constant (0.25) and for natural splines, $c_0 = c_4 = 0$ and $a_i = f(x_i)$ for $i = 0, 1,..., 4$, we have (in matrix form)

$$\begin{bmatrix} 1.0 & 0.25 & 0.0 \\ 0.25 & 1.0 & 0.25 \\ 0.0 & 0.25 & 1.0 \end{bmatrix} \begin{bmatrix} c_1 \\ c_2 \\ c_3 \end{bmatrix} = \begin{bmatrix} -1.6428 \\ -7.2972 \\ -4.2468 \end{bmatrix}$$

The values of c_1, c_2, and c_3 can easily be determined, and consequently b_i's and d_i's can be found. However, the algorithm given in Figure 6.4 was used. The results obtained are shown in Table 6.1.

Table 6.2 is given as a means of comparing how good the fit is.

6.4 PARAMETRIC CURVES

The curve-generation method described in the last section is actually an interpolation technique. This technique is quite useful for data points that are axis-dependent and single-valued—that is, for a set of data (x_i, y_i) of the form

$$y_i = f(x_i)$$

This explicit form of representation of a curve is limited in application. It cannot be used to represent multivalued curves or closed curves as may be required in geometric modeling. To overcome this limitation, implicit curve representation of the form

$$f(x_i, y_i) = 0$$

has been used. Both of these representations form the basis of the so-called nonparametric curves. In the design of physical objects whose surfaces are to be represented by several intersecting curves, it is important that the shape of a solid object does not change when it is rotated. This means that the curves used should be invariant under the rotation of the coordinate system and the shape of the curve should depend not on the position of the data points relative to some particular axis but rather on the relative position of the data points with each other. Immediately, we see a problem. The implicit and explicit forms just described are axis-dependent; therefore, they are unsuitable when shape design is of primary interest.

For shape descriptions, the curve is better represented in a parametric form. In parametric form the two variables x and y are themselves represented as a function of a third parameter such as t, which varies along the length of the curve. Equations of the form

$$x = x(t)$$
$$y = y(t)$$

are known as **parametric equations.** When we use this form, a point on the curve, $P(t)$, is represented by

$$P(t) = [x(t)\ y(t)]$$

The parametric curve representation overcomes some of the problems of the nonparametric form. For example, in using the nonparametric form, equal increments in x do not necessarily result in uniform distribution of points along the length of the curve, a problem not found with the parametric form. In addition, in the nonparametric form if an endpoint has a vertical slope relative to the chosen coordinate system, then the application of slope conditions at the endpoints becomes very difficult, if not impossible. However, the parametric representation does not have this problem.

Now that we have seen the importance of parametric representation, we are ready to examine other curve-design methods that use parametric representation.

6.5 PARAMETRIC CUBIC CURVES

In practice, many people design curves as combinations of segments of other smaller curves. The form that is very useful in this approach is the parametric cubic curve. This is a third-order polynomial of a given parameter, say t. Its representation in vector form is

$$P(t) = \mathbf{a}t^3 + \mathbf{b}t^2 + \mathbf{c}t + \mathbf{d}, \ t \in [0, 1] \tag{6.27}$$

where $P(t)$ is the position vector of any point on the curve and the constants determine the given point.

Examination of equation (6.27) reveals that we need 4 (or 12 in three-dimensional space) boundary conditions to determine the constants. One possible form for the boundary conditions is to specify the endpoints of the curve and two tangent vectors at the endpoints. The curve resulting from this set of boundary conditions is known as the **Hermite** curve. Applying these boundary conditions to equation (6.27) and using $P'(t)$ for dP/dt, we have

$$
\begin{aligned}
P(0) &= \mathbf{d} \\
P(1) &= \mathbf{a} + \mathbf{b} + \mathbf{c} + \mathbf{d} \\
P'(0) &= \mathbf{c} \\
P'(1) &= 3\mathbf{a} + 2\mathbf{b} + \mathbf{c}
\end{aligned}
\tag{6.28}
$$

Solving these four equations and substituting into equation (6.27) gives, upon simplifying,

$$
\begin{aligned}
P(t) = (2t^3 - 3t^2 + 1)P(0) + (-2t^3 + 3t^2)P(1) \\
+ (t^3 - 2t^2 + t)P'(0) + (t^3 - t^2)P'(1)
\end{aligned}
\tag{6.29}
$$

For simplification, let

$$
\begin{aligned}
G_1(t) &= 2t^3 - 3t^2 + 1 \\
G_2(t) &= -2t^3 + 3t^2 \\
G_3(t) &= t^3 - 2t^2 + t \\
G_4(t) &= t^3 - t^2
\end{aligned}
\tag{6.30}
$$

If we denote the $P(t)$ as P and $P(0)$ and $P(1)$ as P_0 and P_1, respectively, then equation (6.30) can be represented in matrix form as

$$P = [G_1 \ G_2 \ G_3 \ G_4] \ [P_0 \ P_1 \ P_0' \ P_1']^T \tag{6.31}$$

The G terms are called **blending functions**, since they control the contribution of the endpoints and the tangent vectors to the shape of the curve. The **P** terms (column vectors) are called the *geometric coefficients* of the parametric cubic curve. We can also represent the G terms using matrix notation as

$$G = [t^3 \ t^2 \ t \ 1] \begin{bmatrix} 2 & -2 & 1 & 1 \\ -3 & 3 & -2 & -1 \\ 0 & 0 & 1 & 0 \\ 1 & 0 & 0 & 0 \end{bmatrix} \tag{6.32}$$

This 4×4 matrix is popularly known as the **universal transformation matrix,** denoted by **M**. If we also denote the geometric coefficient vector as **C** and the row vector of t's as **T**, then the parametric cubic equation is represented as

$$P(t) = TMC, \ t\epsilon[0, 1] \tag{6.33}$$

6.6 BEZIER CURVE

In Section 6.3, we studied a method of generating a curve that passes through every data point in a given interval. In reality, the use of a cubic spline is a curve-fitting technique, meaning the designer does not have control over the shapes of the curve, since they are uniquely defined within a specified interval. Therefore, when we wish to design curves in which the designer has control of the shapes, we must resort to another technique, the Bezier curve, which was introduced by the Frenchman P.E. Bezier.

The Bezier technique is very attractive because it allows for aesthetics in design and for styling. The designer is able to conform to a desired style or shape simply by controlling the input parameters. Other attractive features of the Bezier curves are:

1. The shape of the Bezier curve is determined by vertices of a polygon resulting from the input data points. The curve not only passes through the first and last vertices of the polygon but also is tangent to the polygon at these points, as shown in Figure 6.8. Of course, the curve can, with special manipulation, be made to pass through another single point within the polygon called the **generating polygon.** The curve lies within the convex of the generating polygon; this property is generally referred to as the **convex hull property.**

2. The degree of a Bezier polynomial is determined by the number of data points within a specified span. If there are n data points within a span, the corresponding degree of the resulting Bezier polynomial is $(n - 1)$. It follows that the degree and hence the shape of the curve can be changed simply by adding or removing data points within the span (see Figure 6.9). It is this feature that makes this technique very suitable for interactive curve

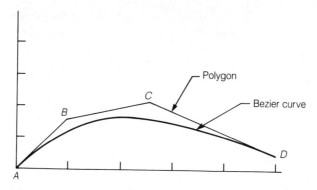

FIGURE 6.8

A typical Bezier curve.

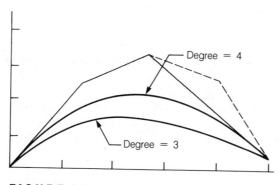

FIGURE 6.9

Altering the shape of a Bezier curve by altering its degree.

design. It must, however, be noted that the control of the shape of the curve is global, which means that one portion of the shape of the curve can not be altered without affecting the entire shape of the curve.

3. The curve never oscillates widely away from the defining points of the generating polygon; this property is called **variation diminishing.**

4. The computational requirement of a Bezier curve is less than that of the cubic spline curve. The Bezier curve requires that a single equation be developed for each variable; the spline requires that a separate equation be written for each pair of points.

The ease with which the curve is generated can be seen by examining the mathematical representation of the Bezier curve. The curve is based on the Bernstein polynomial. A detailed discussion of the mathematical development of the curve can be found in [8] and [9]. The Bernstein polynomials $(B_i^n(t))$ of degree n are defined by

$$B_i^n(t) = \binom{n}{i}(1 - t)^{n-i}t^i, \; i = 0, 1, \ldots, n$$

where t is a parameter. The Bernstein polynomial has some important properties that make it suitable as the basis for the Bezier technique:

1. Positivity, which is mathematically represented as

$$B_i^n(t) \geq 0 \; \text{ for } t \in [0, 1]$$

It is this property that allows the Bezier curve to possess the convex hull property.

2. Partition of unity, represented in the form

$$\sum_{i=0}^{n} B_i(t) = 1$$

This property allows the relationship between the Bezier curve and the defining polygon to be maintained under geometric transformation.

Using the Berstein polynomial as the basis, the Bezier curve is defined as

$$P(t) = \sum_{i=0}^{n} P_i B_{i,n}(t)$$

More formally, the points on the Bezier curve are generally calculated using the equation

$$P(t) = \sum_{i=0}^{n} \frac{P_i \, n! t^i (1 - t)^{n-i}}{i!(n - i)!} \tag{6.34}$$

where

$P(t)$ = Bezier control points
P_i = specified data points
n = total number of data points less one
t = chosen increment, usually between 0 and 1, i.e., $0 \leq t \leq 1$.

Equation (6.34) is applicable to both two-dimensional and three-dimensional curves. If we apply equation (6.34) to two-dimensional curves, plotting in xy-coordinates, equation (6.34) can be recast as

$$X(t) = \sum_{i=0}^{n} \frac{x_i n! t^i (1 - t)^{n-i}}{i!(n - i)!} \tag{6.35}$$

and

$$Y(t) = \sum_{i=0}^{n} \frac{y_i n! t^i (1 - t)^{n-i}}{i!(n - i)!} \tag{6.36}$$

where

$x_i, y_i,$ = coordinates of the data points
$X(t), Y(t),$ = control points

For three-dimensional curve plotting, all we need is to include the z axis and express (6.34) as

$$Z(t) = \sum_{i=0}^{n} \frac{z_i n! t^i (1 - t)^{n-i}}{i!(n - i)!} \tag{6.37}$$

The three-dimensional plotting requires a three-dimensional plotter; therefore, we illustrate the method using two-dimensional curve plotting.

Before illustrating the Bezier curve-generation technique, we need to make an important observation concerning equation (6.34). The value obtained using equation (6.34) depends on the value assigned to t. If it is 0, then $p(t) = 0$. If we increase the value of t, $P(t)$ increases; as we increase t, $P(t)$ reaches a maximum, after which an increase in t leads to a decrease in $P(t)$. The maximum value of equation (6.34) is obtained when $t = i/n$. Knowing that the maximum occurs at $t = i/n$ is very useful in controlling the shape of the curve. It is important to realize that the intermediate points actually control the shape of the curve.

EXAMPLE 6.2

Generate a Bezier curve using position vectors (1, 0), (3, 2), (4, 1), (3, −1), (4, −2), and (5, −1).

SOLUTION   There are six data points, so $n = 5$. The generation of control points requires the expansion of equations (6.35) and (6.36). Because of space limitation we show only a few of the terms involved in the expansion of equations (6.35) and (6.36):

$$X(t) = (1 - t)^5 x_0 + 5t(1 - t)^4 x_1 + \cdots + t^5 x_5$$

and

$$Y(t) = (1 - t)^5 y_0 + 5t(1 - t)^4 y_1 + \cdots + t^5 y_5$$

The point $(1, 0)$ is taken as the starting point, i.e., $x_0 = 1$ and $y_0 = 0$. Starting with $t = 0$ and incrementing with 0.1, the various values of $X(t)$ and $Y(t)$ are calculated using a simple program (Figure 6.10). The values of $X(t)$ and $Y(t)$ obtained are listed in Table 6.3, and the points are plotted in Figure 6.11. Note that the control points pass through the initial and final points, as they should.

```
10    REM*********************************************************
20    REM* THIS PROGRAM GENERATES THE POINTS FOR BEZIER CURVE      *
30    REM*********************************************************
40    INPUT"DO YOU WANT A HARD COPY (Y/N)";H$
50    IF H$ = "Y" OR H$ = "N" THEN 70
60    PRINT"WRONG RESPONSE, TRY AGAIN": GOTO 40
70    IF H$ = "N" THEN 140
80    REM ...................................................
90    REM .   THE OPEN STATEMENT IS FOR HP PLOTTER 7475A       .
100   REM ...................................................
110   OPEN "COM2:9600,S,7,1,RS,CS65535,DS,CD" AS #1
120   PRINT #1, "IN;SP3;"
130   PRINT #1, "IN;IP4000,3000,5000,4000;SP2;SC0,1,0,1;"
140   KEY OFF: SCREEN 2: CLS
150   WINDOW (-4,-3) - (4,3)
160   DIM X(30),X1(20),Y(30),Y1(20)
170   REM ------------------------------------------------------
180   REM     ENTER THE NUMBER OF POINTS FOR THE GENERATING POLYGON
190   REM ------------------------------------------------------
200   PRINT "WHAT IS THE TOTAL NO. OF POINTS"
210   INPUT M
220   N=M-1
230   REM ------------------------------------------------------
240   REM     ENTER THE  DATA POINTS
250   REM ------------------------------------------------------
260   PRINT "ENTER THE X AND Y COORDINATES"
270   FOR J=0 TO N
280   PRINT"X(";J;")";"=" : INPUT X1(J)
290   PRINT"Y(";J;")";"=" : INPUT Y1(J)
300   NEXT J
310   REM ------------------------------------------------------
320   REM          DRAW THE  GENERATING POLYGON
330   REM ------------------------------------------------------
340   PSET(X1(0),Y1(0)) : IF H$ = "N" THEN 360
350    PRINT #1, "PA";X1(0);Y1(0)
360    FOR I = 0 TO N
370    LINE - (X1(I),Y1(I)) : IF H$ = "N" THEN 390
380    PRINT #1, "PAPD";X1(I);Y1(I)
390    NEXT I
400   REM ------------------------------------------------------
410   REM  RESET THE PEN TO THE INITIAL DATA POINT
420   REM ------------------------------------------------------
430   PSET(X1(0),Y1(0)) : IF H$ = "N" THEN 480
440    PRINT #1, "PAPU";X1(0);Y1(0)
450   REM ------------------------------------------------------
```

FIGURE 6.10

A sample program for the Bezier method.

```
460   REM      SET THE DESIRED INCREMENT FOR T
470   REM  -------------------------------------------------------------
480 INPUT "WHAT INCREMENT OF T DO YOU WANT ";DT
490   REM  -------------------------------------------------------------
500   REM  -------------------------------------------------------------
510   REM      GENERATE THE CONTROL POINTS
520   REM  -------------------------------------------------------------
530   L =1 : F = N
540   REM  -------------------------------------------------------------
550   REM      GO TO THE SUBROUTINE FOR GENERATING FACTORIAL
560   REM  -------------------------------------------------------------
570 GOSUB 920
580 NF=FACT
590 K=1/DT
600 FOR J=0 TO K
610 T=J*DT
620 SUM1=0
630 SUM2=0
640 FOR I=0 TO N
650 F=I
660 GOSUB 920
670 FI=FACT
680 F=N-I
690 GOSUB 920
700 NI=FACT
710   REM  -------------------------------------------------
720   REM      TYPE THE BEZIER EQUATION
730   REM  -------------------------------------------------
740 C=NF*(T^I)*((1-T)^(N-I))/(FI*NI)
750 SUM1=SUM1+X1(I)*C
760 SUM2=SUM2+Y1(I)*C
770 NEXT I
780 X(L)=SUM1
790 Y(L)=SUM2
800   REM  ==================================================
810   REM  PLOT THE CURVE DESIGNED. PLOTTER IS HP 7475A.
820   REM  ==================================================
830 LINE - (X(L),Y(L)) : IF H$ = "N" THEN 850
840   PRINT #1, "PAPD";X(L);Y(L)
850 L=L+1
860 NEXT J  : IF H$ = "N" THEN 880
870   PRINT #1, "PAPU";X(L);Y(L)
880 END
890   REM  ...........................................................
900   REM @ SUBROUTINE FACTORIAL                                     @
910   REM  ...........................................................
920 IF F<=0 GOTO 980
930 FACT=F
940 FOR F=F-1 TO 1 STEP -1
950 FACT=FACT*F
960 NEXT F
970 GOTO 990
980 FACT=1
990 RETURN
```

FIGURE 6.10
_____

(Continued).

t	X(t)	Y(t)
0.0	1.0000	0.0000
0.1	1.8724	0.7200
0.2	2.5565	0.9597
0.3	3.0058	0.8376
0.4	3.2874	0.4694
0.5	3.4688	−0.0313
0.6	3.6246	−0.5578
0.7	3.8237	−1.0081
0.8	4.1152	−1.2877
0.9	4.5171	−1.3105
1.0	5.0000	−1.0000

TABLE 6.3

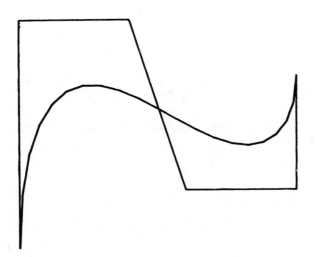

FIGURE 6.11

Bezier curve for Example 6.2.

6.7 COMPOSITE BEZIER CURVES

In constructing the Bezier curve shown in Figure 6.11, we used a polygon with six controlling points. We could have obtained the same result if we viewed the curve as consisting of two different curves generated with two different controlling polygons. This approach is the use of **composite curves**. In practice it is the cubic Bezier form that is utilized. The cubic Bezier curve is derived by expansion of equation (6.34) and it is of the form

$$P(t) = (1 - t)^3 P_0 + 3t(1 - t)^2 P_1 + 3t^2(1 - t)P_2 + t^3 P_3 \tag{6.38}$$

Or

$$P(t) = TM_b C_b \tag{6.39}$$

where

$$M_b = \begin{bmatrix} -1 & 3 & -3 & 1 \\ 3 & -6 & 3 & 0 \\ -3 & 3 & 0 & 0 \\ 1 & 0 & 0 & 0 \end{bmatrix}$$

and

$$C_b = [P_0\ P_1\ P_2\ P_3]^T$$

The use of composite curves demands that at the point where the ends of the curves are joined:

1. The curve be continuous.
2. The curves have a common tangent line. Of course, the tangent vectors need not be equal.
3. There be curvature continuity. This requires the centers of curvature of the two curves to coincide and the curvature vectors at the common point be of the same direction.

These requirements can be expressed as (see Figure 6.12)

$$P^{(i)}(1) = P^{(i+1)}(0) \tag{6.40}$$
$$P'^{(i)}(1) = b_1 P'^{(i+1)}(0) \tag{6.41}$$
$$P''^{(i)}(1) = b_2 P''^{(i+1)}(0) \tag{6.42}$$

Differentiating equation (6.38) and evaluating at $t = 0$ and $t = 1$ we have

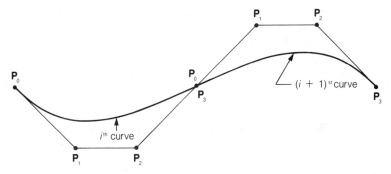

FIGURE 6.12

Composite Bezier curve.

$$P'(0) = 3(P_1 - P_0)$$
$$P'(1) = 3(P_3 - P_0)$$
$$P''(0) = 6(P_0 - 2P_1 + P_2)$$ (6.43)
$$P''(1) = 6(P_1 - 2P_2 + P_3)$$

By applying equations (6.40) through (6.43) to both curves and letting $c_1 = 1/b_1$ and $c_2 = 1/b_2$, we have the following:

$$P_0^{i+1} = P_3^i$$ (6.44)
$$P_1^{i+1} = c_1(P_3^i - P_2^i) + P_3^i$$ (6.45)
$$P_2^{i+1} = (2c_1 + c_2 + 1) P_3^i - 2(c_2 + c_1)P_2^i + c_2 P_1^i$$ (6.46)

Equations (6.44) through (6.46) establish the relationship between the controlling points of composite curves. The constants c_1 and c_2 are additional shape-controlling parameters.

B-SPLINE

In the previous section we noted the superiority of the Bezier curve over the cubic spline in curve design, especially when styling and aesthetics are of primary concern. In spite of its obvious superiority and flexibility, the Bezier method has two main flaws. First, the order of the curve cannot be changed without altering the number of vertices of the generating polygon, which implies that a smooth curve cannot be obtained without changing the number of vertices. Secondly, it is not possible to make any local changes in the curve without affecting the entire curve. This can be a serious handicap in some design situations. These two flaws exist because the Bezier curve is an extension of the Bernstein polynomial [9].

A curve generation technique that overcomes these two inherent flaws of the Bezier curve method is the B-spline method. The theory of the B-spline was first introduced in 1946 [10] and since then has received the attention of several authors [11], [12], [13], and [14]. The ensuing discussions are based primarily on the works of [12] and [14].

FORM AND GENERATION OF THE B-SPLINE

The representation of the B-spline of order k (degree $k - 1$) assumes that a given set of knots $x_1, x_2, \ldots, x_{n-1}$ and the interpolating points $t_1, t_2, \ldots, t_m$ of a given function $f(x)$ are strictly ordered such that

$$t_1 < t_2 < \cdots < t_m$$

and

$$t_1 < x_1 < x_2 < \cdots x_{n-1} < t_m \tag{6.47}$$

Since the function f is to be interpolated by the spline function s of order k, then

$$s(t_i) = f(t_i) \quad i = 1, 2, \ldots, m$$

For a unique solution of the preceding equation, the parameters k, n, m must satisfy the relation

$$m = n + k - 1 \tag{6.48}$$

In addition, the condition

$$t_1 < x_1 < t_{1+k}$$
$$t_2 < x_2 < t_{2+k}$$
$$\cdot$$
$$\cdot \tag{6.49}$$
$$\cdot$$
$$t_{n-1} < x_{n-1} < t_m$$

must be satisfied.

If equations (6.47) through (6.49) are satisfied, then a B-spline is represented as

$$B(x) = \sum_{i=1}^{m} c_i M_{ki}(x) \tag{6.50}$$

where

$$c_i = \text{constant}$$
$$M_{k,i}(x) = \text{the B-spline of order } k, \text{ defined upon some specified knots } x_{i-k},$$
$$x_{i-k+1}, \ldots, x_i$$

The term $M_{k,i}$ deals with the subject of divided difference. Since a detailed discussion of the divided difference is outside the scope of this text, only the property of $M_{k,i}$ is given. It has the property

$$M_{k,i}(x) \begin{array}{c} > \\ = \end{array} \begin{cases} 0, & x_{i-k} < x < x_i \\ 0, & x < x_{i-k}, x > x_i \end{cases} \tag{6.51}$$

A reader interested in the subject of the divided difference should see [15].

The B-spline curve, being a piecewise polynomial curve, is useful not only for curve design but also for curve interpolation. Equations (6.50) and (6.51) are not the most convenient form for use in either operation. Therefore, a more useful parametric form is defined as follows:

$$P(u) = \sum_{i=0}^{n} P_i N_{i,k}(u) \tag{6.52}$$

where

$$P(u) = \text{a point on the B-spline curve}$$
$$P_i = n + 1 \text{ control points, or the so-called de Boor points}$$
$$N_{i,k} = \text{the normalized B-spline of order } k.$$

The normalized B-splines are blending functions similar to the blending function of the Bezier curve. Like the Bernstein polynomial, the basis of the B-spline curve possesses the following properties:

1. Positivity:

$$N_{i,k}(u) > 0$$

2. Partition of unity:

$$\sum_{i=1} N_i(u) = 1$$

The implications of these properties are the same as described for the Bezier curve in Section 6.6. However, the normalized B-spline blending functions are different in that they possess additional properties:

3. Local support:

$$N_{i,k} = 0 \quad \text{if } u \notin [t_i, t_{i-k+1}]$$

It is this property that gives the B-spline curves an added advantage over the Bezier curves. The local support properties imply that a change in the control points will affect only a limited part of the B-spline curve.

4. Recursion: The curves are recursively defined as follows:

$$N_{i,1} = \begin{cases} 1 & \text{if } t_i \leq u \leq t_{i+1} \\ 0 & \text{otherwise} \end{cases}$$

$$N_{i,k}(u) = \frac{(u - t_i)N_{i,k-1}(u)}{t_{i+k-1} - t_i} + \frac{(t_{i+k} - u)N_{i+1,k-1}(u)}{t_{i+k} - t_{i+1}} \qquad \text{(6.53)}$$

Examination of equation (6.53) reveals that the computation of $N_{i,k}(u)$ requires the generation of the knot sequence $\{t\}$ from the specified simple knots $(x_1, x_2, \ldots, x_n)$ according to the following:

$$\begin{aligned} t_1 &= t_2 = \cdots = t_k = x_1 \\ t_{m+1} &= t_{m+2} = \cdots = T_{m+k} = x_n \\ t_{k+i} &= x_{i+1}, \quad i = 1, 2, \ldots, n - 2 \end{aligned} \qquad \text{(6.54)}$$

Equation (6.54) assumes that the knot values are known, but in more general cases they are not known. In this case the knot sequence must be carefully selected. The choice of the knot values, t_i, depends on whether the uniform nonperiodic B-spline or the uniform periodic B-spline (periodic because the blending function repeats itself over successive intervals of the parametric variable) is used. For example, in the design of open curves (see Figure 6.13), the nonperiodic B-spline is used and the knot values are chosen as follows:

$$t_i = \begin{cases} 0 & \text{if } i < k \\ i - k + 1 & \text{if } k \leq i \leq n \\ n - k + 2 & \text{if } i > n, \ 0 \leq i \leq n + k \end{cases} \qquad \text{(6.55)}$$

Also, the range of the parameter u is $0 < u < n - k + 2$. On the other hand, if a closed curve (see Figure 6.14) is to be designed, the periodic B-spline is more suitable, and the knot values may be chosen by

$$t_i = i \qquad \text{(6.56)}$$

The use of equation (6.56) requires that the normalized B-spline be defined as:

$$N_{i,k}(u) = N_{0,k}(u - i + n + 1) \mod (n + 1) \qquad \text{(6.57)}$$

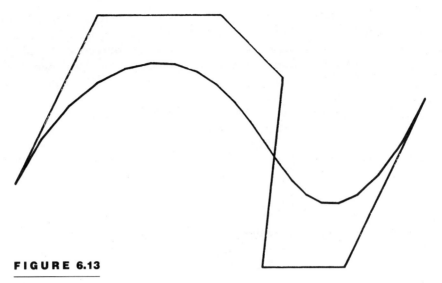

FIGURE 6.13

Open B-spline curve.

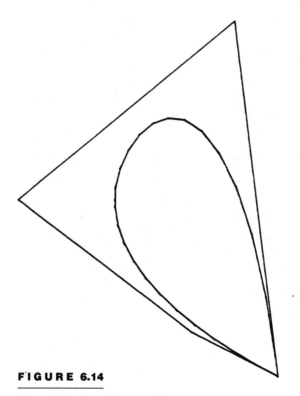

FIGURE 6.14

Closed B-spline curve.

The operator "mod" stands for modulo; it is a remainder operator. For example, 19 mod 4 is 3, since 19 divided by 4 gives 4, remainder 3.

The shape of the B-spline curve can be altered by changing the order of the spline. However, there are cases when it is desirable to model sharp corners (or fillets); in this situation, multiple coincident control points (a condition often described as multiplicity of control points) may be used. The multiplicity of points has the effect of pulling the curve closer to the point.

As mentioned previously, one other use of the B-spline is for curve interpolation of a set of given points $[v_i, P(v_i)]$. The form used is

$$P(v_i) = \sum_{i=1}^{n} c_i N_{i,k}(v) \tag{6.58}$$

or, in matrix notation,

$$[N]\ [C]\ =\ P \tag{6.59}$$

Expansion of equation (6.58) or (6.59) will yield a system of n linear equations. The solution of such a system will yield the values of c_i, which are the unknowns, since $P(v_i)$ are known and $N_{i,k}$ can be determined.

A flowchart for generating both the knot values and the B-splines for various values of u is given in Figure 6.15, and a sample program (in BASIC) is shown in Figure 6.16.

In practice many designers prefer the use of the cubic form of the B-spline. This form is given by

$$P_i(t)\ =\ TM_s C_i \tag{6.60}$$

where

$$M_s = \frac{1}{6} \begin{bmatrix} -1 & 3 & -3 & 1 \\ 3 & -6 & 3 & 0 \\ -3 & 0 & 3 & 0 \\ 1 & 4 & 1 & 0 \end{bmatrix}$$

and

$$C_i\ =\ [P_{i-1}\ P_i\ P_{i+1}\ P_{i+2}]^T, \quad 1 \le i \le n - 2$$

Detailed treatment of this form may be obtained from [18].

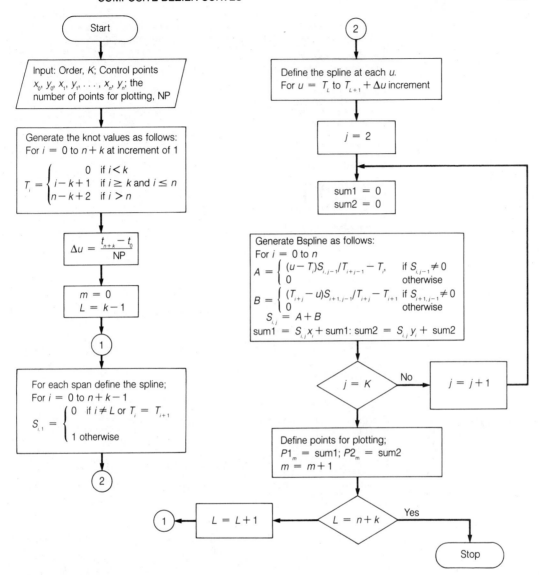

FIGURE 6.15

A flowchart for B-spline generation.

```
10    '   ***************************************************
20    '   *    THIS PROGRAM USES THE BSPLINE TECHNIQUE FOR     *
30    '   *             FOR CURVE DESIGN                        *
40    '   ***************************************************
50        DIM P1(200),P2(200)
60        KEY OFF : SCREEN 2 : CLS
70        WINDOW (-5,-5) - (5,5)
80        INPUT"THE ORDER OF THE BSPLINE IS";K
90        INPUT"THE NUMBER OF CONTROL POINTS IS";N1 : N = N1 - 1
100        FOR J = 0 TO N
110        PRINT"ENTER THE X AND Y CORDINATES OF CONTROL POINT";J;"X,Y"
120        INPUT X(J),Y(J) : NEXT J
130   '.................................................
140   ' PLOT THE CONTROLLING POLYGON TO THE SCREEN         .
150   '.................................................
160       PSET(X(0),Y(0))
170       FOR J = 0 TO N
180       LINE -(X(J),Y(J)) : NEXT J : PSET (X(0),Y(0))
190       ' -------------------------------------------
200       ' GENERATE THE VALUE OF THE KNOTS T().
210       FOR I = 0 TO N + K
220       IF I < K THEN T(I) = 0
230       IF I > = K AND  I < = N THEN T(I) = I - K + 1
240       IF I > N THEN T(I) = N - K + 2
250       NEXT I
260       ' DEFINE THE NUMBER OF POINTS FOR PLOT CURVE
270       INPUT"HOW MANY POINTS DO YOU WISH TO USE FOR PLOTTING";NP
280       'SET THE INCREMENT FOR THE PARAMETER U AS TMAX - TMIN/NP
290       '
300       DELTAU =(T(N+K)   - T(0))/NP
310       'DETERMINE THE NORMALIZED SPLINE AT EACH U AND IN EACH
320       ' KNOT SPAN.
330       FOR L = K-1 TO N + K
340       'DEFINE THE BSPLINE IN EACH SPAN
350       FOR I = 0 TO N + K -1
360         IF I < > L THEN 390
370         IF T(I) = T(I+1) THEN 390
380         S(I,1) = 1 : GOTO 400
390         S(I,1) = 0
400       NEXT I
410       'DEFINE UMIN AND UMAX
420       UMIN = T(L) : UMAX = T(L+1) - DELTAU
430           FOR U = UMIN TO UMAX STEP DELTAU
440       ' CALCULATE THE POINT CORRESPONDING TO U ON THE CURVE
450               FOR J = 2 TO K
460                 SUM1 = 0 : SUM2 = 0  : SS =0
470       GOSUB 700
480   '               FOR I = 0 TO N
490   '                 SUM1 = SUM1 + N(I,J)*X(I)
500   '                 SUM2 = SUM2 + N(I,J)*Y(I)
510   '               NEXT I
520           NEXT J
530   '   IF SS = 0 THEN 560
540               P1(M)  = SUM1 : P2(M) = SUM2
550       M = M + 1
560           NEXT U
570       IF L = N + K THEN P1(M) = X(N) :  P2(M) = Y(N)
580       NEXT L
590   '.................................................
600   ' PLOT THE CURVE TO  THE SCREEN                      .
610   '.................................................
```

FIGURE 6.16

A sample program for B-spline generation.

```
620        PSET (X(0),Y(0))
630 FOR M = 1 TO NP
640        X1 = P1(M) : Y1 = P2(M)
650        LINE - (X1,Y1)
660            NEXT M
670        END
680        ' SUBROUTINE GENERATES THE BSPLINE
690        '
700        FOR I = 0 TO N
710 '      IF U < T(L) AND U > T(L+1) THEN S(I,J) = 0 : GOTO 680
720        IF S(I,J-1) <> 0 THEN 740
730        A = 0 : GOTO 750
740        A = ((U - T(I))*S(I,J-1))/(T(I+J-1) - T(I))
750        IF S(I+1,J-1) <>0 THEN 770
760        B = 0 : GOTO 780
770        B = (T(I+J) - U)*S(I+1,J-1)/(T(I+J) - T(I+1))
780        S(I,J) = A + B
790        SS = SS + S(I,J)
800                   SUM1 = SUM1 + S(I,J)*X(I)
810                   SUM2 = SUM2 + S(I,J)*Y(I)
820 '      PRINT"S(";I;J;")=";S(I,J);"U = ";U,
830        NEXT I
840        RETURN
```

FIGURE 6.16

(Continued).

EXAMPLE 6.3

Use the B-spline of order 3 to approximate the function $f(x) = x \cos x^2$. Use the knot vector $[0\ 0.25\ 0.5\ 0.75\ 1]^T$.

SOLUTION

$$n = 4, \quad k = 3, \quad \mathbf{x} = [0\ \ 0.25\ \ 0.5\ \ 0.75\ \ 1]^T$$

This being a case of curve fitting, we apply equations (6.54) and (6.58). Using the given information, we generate the knot sequence t as follows:

$$t_1 = t_2 = t_3 = 0.0$$

With

$$m = n + k - 1 = 6$$
$$t_7 = t_8 = t_9 = 1.0$$

and

$$t_4 = 0.25, \quad t_5 = 0.5, \quad t_6 = 0.75$$

If we choose $v = 0, 0.2, 0.4, 0.6, 0.8, 1$ and expand equation (6.58), we have

$$\begin{bmatrix} N_{31}(0) & N_{32}(0) & N_{33}(0) & N_{34}(0) & N_{35}(0) & N_{36}(0) \\ N_{31}(0.2) & N_{32}(0.2) & N_{33}(0.2) & N_{34}(0.2) & N_{35}(0.2) & N_{36}(0.2) \\ N_{31}(0.4) & N_{32}(0.4) & N_{33}(0.4) & N_{34}(0.4) & N_{35}(0.4) & N_{36}(0.4) \\ N_{31}(0.6) & N_{32}(0.6) & N_{33}(0.6) & N_{34}(0.6) & N_{35}(0.6) & N_{36}(0.6) \\ N_{31}(0.8) & N_{32}(0.8) & N_{33}(0.8) & N_{34}(0.8) & N_{35}(0.8) & N_{36}(0.8) \\ N_{31}(1.0) & N_{32}(1.0) & N_{33}(1.0) & N_{34}(1.0) & N_{35}(1.0) & N_{36}(1.0) \end{bmatrix} \begin{bmatrix} c_1 \\ c_2 \\ c_3 \\ c_4 \\ c_5 \\ c_6 \end{bmatrix}$$

$$= [f(0) \ f(0.2) \ f(0.4) \ f(0.6) \ f(0.8) \ f(1.0)]^T$$

To determine the c's requires the evaluation of the normalized B-splines. This can be obtained by repeated application of equation (6.53). However, it is more convenient to use the algorithm described previously. The computer results for the B-spline are given in Table 6.4.

The c's are determined using the method of matrix inversion, and they have the values $c_1 = 0$, $c_2 = 0.1185$, $c_3 = 0.3830$, $c_4 = 0.3199$, $c_5 = 0.6306$, and $c_6 = -1.0000$. Having determined the c's, the fitting is complete. As a means of comparison, the fitted value and the exact value of the function are given in Table 6.5. Note that the calculated values are obtained using equation (6.58).

E X A M P L E 6.4

Design a curve using the characteristic polygon with the points (0, 0), (1, 2), (2, 2), (3, 1), (4, 1), (5, −1), and (6, 1). Use the B-spline technique.

SOLUTION   This is a case of curve design, so equation (6.52) is utilized. Since we need the co-ordinates, we recast equation (6.52) in a more convenient form, giving

$$X(s_j) = \sum_{i=1}^{n} x_i N_{ik}(s_j)$$

$$Y(s_j) = \sum_{i=1}^{n} y_i N_{ik}(s_j) \quad j = 1, 2, \ldots, M_1$$

where M_1 = total number of points desired. We shall use B-splines of varying order (k). Using the algorithm for determining B-splines and $M_1 = 20$ with $k = 6$, the coordinates are determined for various values of s. A sample output is shown in Table 6.6. The curves for various values of k (order) are shown in Figure 6.17. For comparison, Figure 6.18 (based on Bezier method) is given. Note that the curve with $k = n$ in Figure 6.17 is the same as Figure 6.18. This is to be expected, since the B-spline reduces to Bezier basis when $k = n$. Figures 6.19 and

t	N_{31}	N_{32}	N_{33}	N_{34}	N_{35}	N_{36}
0.0	1.0000	0.0000	0.0000	0.0000	0.0000	0.0000
0.2	0.0400	0.6400	0.3200	0.0000	0.0000	0.0000
0.4	0.0000	0.0800	0.7400	0.1800	0.0000	0.0000
0.6	0.0000	0.0000	0.1800	0.7400	0.0800	0.0000
0.8	0.0000	0.0000	0.0000	0.3200	0.6400	0.0400
1.0	0.0000	0.0000	0.0000	0.0000	0.0000	1.0000

TABLE 6.4

t	Calculated	$f(x)$
0.0	0.00000	0.00000
0.2	0.19842	0.19842
0.4	0.35048	0.35048
0.6	0.25522	0.25522
0.8	−0.341209	−0.34121
1.0	−1.000000	−1.00000

TABLE 6.5

s	$X(s)$	$Y(s)$
0.0	0.0000	0.0000
0.5	0.8750	1.5000
1.0	1.5000	2.0000
1.5	2.0000	1.8750
2.0	2.5000	1.5000
2.5	3.0000	0.8750
3.0	3.5000	0.0000
3.5	4.0000	−0.7500
4.0	4.5000	−1.0000
4.5	5.1250	−0.5000
5.0	6.0000	1.0000

TABLE 6.6

6.20 are curves designed with more than ten control points using both Bezier and B-spline techniques. Note how the curve is more closely approximated by B-spline of order 5.

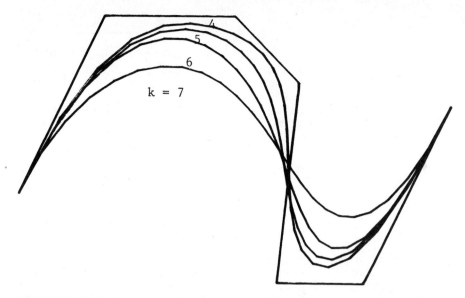

FIGURE 6.17

B-spline curves of various orders for Example 6.4.

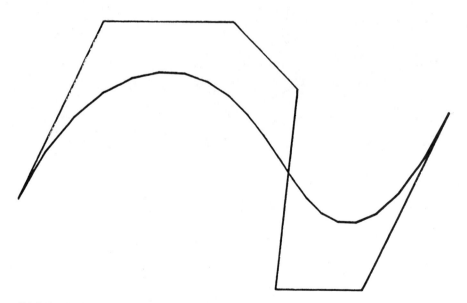

FIGURE 6.18

Bezier curve for the same control points as Figure 6.17.

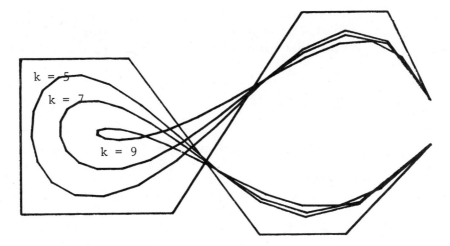

FIGURE 6.19

B-spline curve design with ten control points.

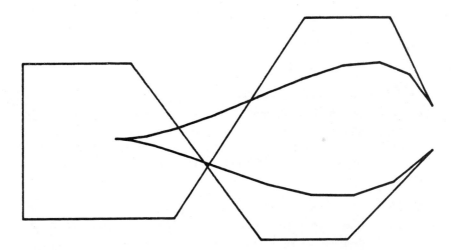

FIGURE 6.20

Bezier curve design with ten control points. (Note the superiority of the B-spline in Figure 6.19.)

Before leaving this section, we need to summarize the differences between B-spline curves and Bezier curves. B-spline curves allow for local control, whereas Bezier curves do not. Any change in any part of the Bezier curve affects the entire curve. B-splines allow for easy modeling of shape corners or edges, but

Bezier curves allow no such shape modeling. The shapes of B-spline curves are affected by a multiplicity of control points, whereas Bezier curves are not really affected, although they allow the use of multiple control points.

6.9 APPLICATION

As you read through the examples given in the preceeding sections, you may have been wondering how one really applies these methods and if these methods are really useful. The Bezier method has been successfully applied by the Association Renault-Peugeot. The application of the curve-design techniques discussed in this chapter is really an iterative process. The designer would normally sketch the desired curve and then specify the vertices of a polygon that he or she hopes would approximate the curve in question. The first approximate curve will give the designer an idea of what steps to take in order to obtain the desired shape and a given aesthetic condition. In the case of the Bezier, polygon vertices may be deleted, added, or moved, whereas in that of B-spline, vertices may be added or moved or the order may be altered. Although this method is iterative, it has been observed that an acceptable curve can be obtained in about four iterations.

Perhaps the best application of the techniques described in this chapter is in the area of computer-aided surface design, which is introduced next.

SURFACE DESIGN

The purpose of this section is to briefly acquaint the reader with the rapidly advancing field of computer-aided surface design. We define a few relevant terms and cite useful papers that may be consulted for further study.

A **surface,** in its basic form, can be defined as a graph of an equation in three variables. A surface S may be represented in the form

$$f(x, y, z) = 0 \tag{6.61}$$

where x, y, z are the Cartesian coordinates in space. It is also the locus of a point in space that moves with two degrees of freedom. For computer-aided design of surfaces, the parametric form

$$x = x(u, v), \quad y = y(u, v), \quad z = z(u, v) \tag{6.62}$$

where u and v are some independent parameters, is very effective. For example, a Bezier surface can be generated for a region bounded by four curves (see Figure 6.21) by

$$\mathbf{B}(u, v) = \sum_{i=0}^{m} \sum_{j=0}^{n} P_{i,j} C_{i,m}(u) C_{j,n}(v) \tag{6.63}$$

where $P_{i,j}$ specify the $(m+1)$ by $(n+1)$ control points. $\mathbf{B}(u,v)$ is the surface point vector $[x(u,v) \quad y(u,v) \quad z(u,v)]$,

$$C_{i,m}(u) = \frac{m!u^i(1-u)^{m-i}}{i!(m-i)!}$$

and

$$C_{j,n}(v) = \frac{n!v^i(1-v)^{n-i}}{i!(n-i)!}$$

In practice it is rare for a large surface to be constructed by only one equation. The most widely used approach is to build a complex surface by adjoining many small ones, called **patches** (see Figure 6.22). Coon [3] pioneered this concept. A surface may also be formed by an infinite family of straight lines; this results in a **ruled surface** (Figure 6.23). An application of this technique can be found in [17]. Yet another technique of surface design, which is especially useful in the design of aircraft fuselage or surfaces stretching in one direction, is the **lofting technique.** This involves the blending of a set of defined cross sections by means of a number of longitudinal curves; its application may be found in [18].

The mathematical developments of the aforementioned techniques are outside the scope of this text; the interested reader should consult [2], [3], [15], [16], [19], and [20].

SURFACE REPRESENTATION

Regardless of the method of surface generation applied, the surface must be displayed on a two-dimensional screen or on a plotter. This requires the surface to

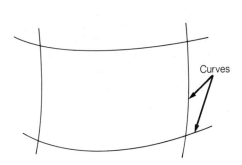

FIGURE 6.21

Boundary curves of a surface.

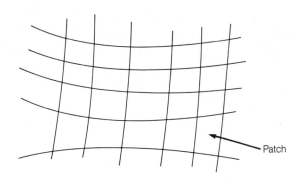

FIGURE 6.22

Surface construction using patches.

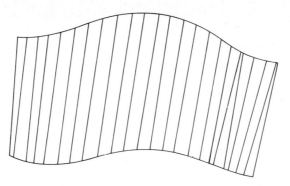

FIGURE 6.23

A typical ruled surface.

be orthographically projected to the screen or the plotter. To understand the process, consider an algebraic surface of the form given by equation (6.61). Generally, the intersection of two surfaces is a curve. Using this fact we can intersect a surface with either the coordinate planes (projection planes) or planes parallel to the coordinate planes. The resulting series of curves define the surface on the various planes (see Figure 6.24). The same result is achieved if we project the surface to the planes instead of intersecting the surface with coordinate planes. Therefore, a surface is produced by the method of perspective projection discussed in Chapter 5. The surface can be presented as a series of curves for either a constant x or a constant y, producing longitudinal curves or latitudinal curves, as shown in Figure 6.25. Alternatively, the longitudinal curves and the latitudinal curves may be crossed to form the surface (see Figure 6.26).

During the course of projection, some of the curve segments may be hidden and should be eliminated for more pleasing representation. The simplest method of doing this is to define the minimum and maximum values of the variable x as x_o and x_n and for y as y_o and y_m. It is such that $x_o < x_n$ and $y_o < y_m$. Suppose it is desired to project along the curve of constant y. Projection should proceed from the point on the surface defined by $z = f(x_n, y_m)$. Initially, this projected point is set as y_{max}, and it forms the upper visible boundary point. Similarly, the lower visible boundary point y_{min} is defined as the projection of the point $z = f(x_o, y_m)$. The projection proceeds from a point removed from x_n by a selected step size until the point $x = x_o$ is reached. The visibility test is as follows: If the projected point is above y_{max}, the line from y_{max} to the given point is visible; hence, it is drawn and the new point replaces y_{max}. If the point is below y_{min}, it is also visible and y_{min} is replaced by the new point. The process is repeated for the next constant y curve until the plotting of the surface is complete.

The process just described was used in producing Figures 6.25 and 6.26. A complete listing of the program is given in Figure 6.27.

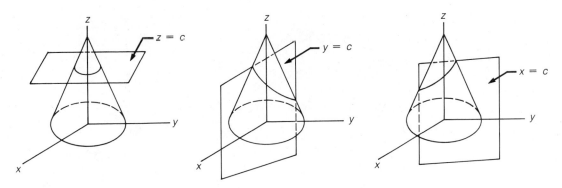

FIGURE 6.24

Intersection of a cone by various coordinate planes.

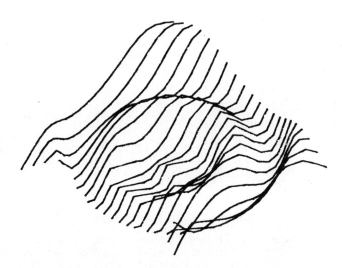

FIGURE 6.25

First approach for plotting a surface (Surface: $f(x,y) = \sin\sqrt{x^2 + y^2} - 1.5 \cos\sqrt{x^2 + y^2}$).

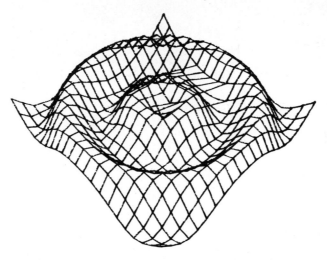

FIGURE 6.26

A second approach for plotting a surface ($f(x,y) = \sin\sqrt{x^2 + y^2} - 1.5\cos\sqrt{x^2 + y^2}$).

```
10    '*******************************************************
20    '*     THIS PROGRAM IS FOR PLOTTING AN ALGEBRAIC       *
30    '*     SURFACE.   IT CAN BE MODIFIED TO PLOT ANY SURFACE*
40    '*                                                     *
50    '*******************************************************
60    ' . . . . . . . . . . . . . . . . . . . . . . . . . . . . . . .
70    ' .  THE FOLLOWING STATEMENT APPLIES TO HP PLOTTER    .
80    ' .  HP MODEL 7475A                                   .
90    ' . . . . . . . . . . . . . . . . . . . . . . . . . . . . . . .
100       OPEN "COM2:9600,S,7,1,RS,CS65535,DS,CD" AS #1
110       PRINT #1, "IN;IP4000,3000,5000,4000;SP1;SC0,4,0,4;"
120       SCREEN 2 : KEY OFF
130       WINDOW (-10,-10) - (10,10)
140   '. . . . . . . . . . . . . . . . . . . . . . . . . . . . . . .
150       PI = 22/7
160       INPUT"ENTER RADIUS, RHO";RHO : PRINT
170       CLS
180       PRINT " D IS THE DISTANCE BETWEEN OBSERVER ": PRINT
190       PRINT "  AND THE DISPLAY PLANE OR THE SCREEN":PRINT
200       INPUT"ENTER THE PARAMETER D";D
210       INPUT"ENTER THETA,PHI (IN DEG)";THETA,PHI
220   '   CONVERSION OF ANGLES TO RADIAN
230       THETA = THETA*PI/180 :   PHI = PHI*PI/180
240   '   COMPUTE THE ANGLES NEEDED FOR TRANSFORMATIONS
250       STHETA = SIN(THETA) : CTHETA = COS(THETA)
260       SPHI = SIN(PHI)   : CPHI = COS(PHI)
270       CLS
```

FIGURE 6.27

A sample program for plotting a surface.

```
280      SIZE = 1  : EP = 1/2
290      YBOT =-10: YTOP = 10
300      XBOT =-10: XTOP = 10
310      DEF FNA(X,Y) =SIN((X^2 + Y^2)^EP)-COS((X^2+Y^2)^EP)*1.5
320      FOR Y = YBOT TO YTOP STEP SIZE
330      X = XTOP
340      Z = FNA(XTOP,Y) : GOSUB 740  : YMAX = YD
350      X = XBOT
360      Z = FNA(XBOT,Y) : GOSUB 740  : YMIN = YD
370      FLAG = 0
380      FOR X = XTOP TO XBOT STEP - SIZE
390    ' TEST VISIBILITY
400      Z = FNA(X,Y) : GOSUB 740
410      IF YD > = YMAX THEN HIDE = 1 : YMAX = YD :GOTO 440
420      IF YD < = YMIN THEN HIDE = 1 : YMIN = YD :GOTO 440
430      HIDE = 0
440      IF HIDE = 0 THEN 510
450      IF FLAG = 0 THEN PSET (XD,YD)
460      LINE - (XD,YD)
470    ' SCALE FOR PLOTTER
480      XD = INT(XD*10000)/10000 : YD = INT(YD*50)/50
490      IF FLAG = 0 THEN PRINT #1, "PAPU";XD;YD : FLAG = 1
500      PRINT #1, "PAPD";XD;YD
510      NEXT X
520      PRINT #1, "PAPU";XD;YD
530      NEXT Y
540      INPUT"DO YOU WANT CROSSWIRES (Y/N)";A$
550    ' REVERSE PLOTTING DIRECTION
560      IF A$ ="Y" THEN 570 ELSE 700
570      FOR X = XBOT TO XTOP STEP SIZE
580      FLAG = 0
590      FOR Y = YTOP TO YBOT STEP - SIZE
600      Z = FNA(X,Y) : GOSUB 740
610      IF FLAG = 0 THEN PSET (XD,YD)
620      LINE - (XD,YD)
630    ' SCALE FOR PLOTTER
640      XD = INT(XD*10000)/10000 : YD = INT(YD*50)/50
650      IF FLAG = 0 THEN PRINT #1, "PAPU";XD;YD : FLAG = 1
660      PRINT #1, "PAPD";XD;YD
670      NEXT Y
680      PRINT #1, "PAPU";XD;YD
690      NEXT X
700      END
710    '   PERSPECTIVE PROJ. SUBROUTINE
720    ' DETERMINATION OF OBSERVER'S COORDINATES
730    '
740      XO = - X*STHETA + Y*CTHETA
750      YO = -X*CTHETA*CPHI - Y*STHETA*CPHI + Z*SPHI
760      ZO = - X*SPHI*CTHETA - Y*STHETA*SPHI - Z*CPHI + RHO
770    ' DETERMINATION OF DISPLAY COORDINATES
780    '
790      XD =  D*XO/ZO
800      YD =  D*YO/ZO
810    RETURN
```

F I G U R E 6.27

(Continued).

EXERCISES

1. Using the definition of spline (equation 6.7), show that the integral of the function $f(x)$ can be approximated as

$$\int f(x)\ dx \ = \ \sum_{i=1}^{n} a_i h_i + 0.5 \ \sum_{i=1}^{n} b_i h_i^2 + 0.333 \ \sum_{i=1}^{n} c_i h_i^3 + 0.25 \ \sum_{i=1}^{n} d_i h_i^4$$

where

$$h_i = x_{i+1} - x_i$$

2. The data shown represent measurements of a clay model of a portion of a proposed car body (all dimensions in feet).

x	0.0	0.2	0.4	0.6	1.0	1.5	2.0	2.4	3.0	3.4	4.0	4.5	4.7
y	1.0	1.1	1.38	1.4	1.6	1.8	1.81	2.2	2.4	2.6	2.8	2.82	2.81
x	5.0	5.2	5.4	6.0	6.4	7.0	8.0	8.5	9.0	9.4	10.0		
y	2.8	2.81	2.79	2.7	2.5	2.2	1.75	1.7	1.6	1.5	0.0		

Using the given information, draw the outline of the car body. If the average width of the car is 4 ft, what is the volume of this portion of the car?

3. The characteristic polygon for a Bezier curve is given by the following points

$$(0, 3), \ (1, 4), \ (2, 1.5), \ (3, 3), \ (3.2, 0.4), \ (5, 1)$$

Draw the corresponding Bezier curve.

4. Model the sole of the shoe shown in Figure 6.28. (*Hint:* To construct the initial polygon, bear in mind the convex hull property. Three or more iterations may be necessary.)

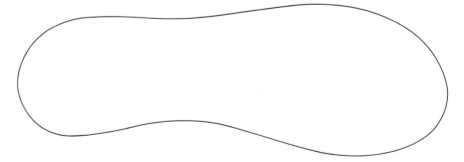

FIGURE 6.28

Shoe sole for Exercise 4.

5. Using the same characteristic polygon as in Exercise 4, draw the corresponding B-spline curve for orders of 7, 5, 3, and 2. What did you observe? Attempt an explanation.

6. Plot the surface represented by the equation $x^2 - 3y^2 + z^2 = 2$. (Try various viewpoints; see Chapter 5).

7. Rotate and translate the surface of Exercise 6 as follows: 63.7° about the x axis, $T_x = T_y = 2T_z = 3$.

REFERENCES

1. Forrest, A. R. "Computational Geometry—Achievements and Problems." In *Computer Aided Geometric Design*. Ed. R. E. Barnhill, and R. F. Riesenfeld. New York: Academic Press, 1974.

2. Faux, I. D. and M. J. Pratt. *Computational Geometry for Design and Manufacture*. New York: Halsted Press; John Wiley & Sons, Inc., 1979.

3. Coons, S. A. "Surfaces for Computer Aided Design of Space Forms. M.I.T." Project MAC TR-41, June 1967.

4. Coons, S. A. "Surfaces for Computer Aided Design of Space Figures." M.I.T. Project MAC, Memo MAC-M-255, January 1964.

5. Forrest, A. R. "Computational Geometry." *Proceedings of the Royal Society of London* A. 321 (1971): 187–95.

6. Gerald, C. F. and P. O. Wheatley. *Applied Numerical Analysis*. Reading, Mass.: Addison-Wesley Publishing Co., 1984.

7. Burden, R. L., J. D. Faires, and A. C. Reynolds. *Numerical Analysis*. Boston: Prindle, Weber & Schmidt, 1978.

8. Bezier, P. *Numerical Control—Mathematics and Applications*. New York: John Wiley & Sons, Inc. 1972.

9. Gordon, W. J. and R. F. Riesenfeld. "Bernstein-Bezier Methods for the Computer Aided Design of Free-forms and Curves and Surfaces." *Journal of the Association for Computing Machinery* 21, no. 2 (April 1974): 293–310.

10. Schoenberg, I. J. "Contribution to the problem of approximation of equidistant data by analytic functions." *Quarterly of Applied Mathematics* 4 (1946): 45–99.

11. Cox, M. J. "The Numerical Evaluation of B-splines." *Journal of the Institute of Mathematics and Its Applications* 10 (1972): 134–49.

12. Cox, M. J. "An Algorithm for Spline Interpolation." *Journal of the Institute of Mathematics and Its Applications* 15 (1975): 95–108.

13. De Boor, Carl. "On calculating with B-splines." *Journal of Approximation Theory* 6 (1972): 50–56.

14. De Boor, Carl. "Package for Calculating with B- splines." *SIAM Journal on Numerical Analysis* 14, no. 3 (June 1977): 441–72.

15. Hildebrand, F. B. *Introduction to Numerical Analysis*. 2d ed. New York: McGraw-Hill Book Co., 1974.

16. Mortenson, M. E. *Geometric Modeling*, New York: John Wiley & Sons, Inc., 1985.

17. Ravani, B. and Y. J. Chen. "Computer-Aided Design and Machining of Composite Rules Surfaces." ASME Paper 85-DET-58, 1985.

18. Razavi, S. E. and D. A. Milner. "Design and Manufacturing of Free-Form Surfaces by Cross-Sectional Approach." *Journal of Manufacturing Systems* 2, no. 1 (1983): 69–77.

19. G. Loi, W., *Interactive Computer Graphics.* Englewood Cliffs, N.J.: Prentice-Hall, Inc., 1978.

20. Bezier, P. "Mathematical and Practical Possibilities of UNISURF." In *Computer Aided Geometric Design.* Ed. R. E. Barnhill and R. F. Riesenfeld. New York: Academic Press, 1974.

CHAPTER 7

Single-Variable Optimization

7.1 INTRODUCTION

In an industrial setting, many problems arise that require making the best possible decision. For example, a manufacturing manager may be required to allocate resources among several operations in order to increase the overall efficiency of a manufacturing process or may be required to plan and schedule the various operations efficiently in order to reduce costs. Similarly, an engineer may be required to design new, more efficient, and less expensive systems or may be required to improve the performance of an existing system.

These problems become more complex when the manager or the engineer is faced with several alternatives. He or she must, however, select the one most likely to produce the desired result, which may be either the greatest profit or the highest performance. The question that arises is: How can such a choice be made? The answer is, through an optimization technique. This chapter discusses the basic principles of optimization and the method of its application when only one variable is concerned. The next chapter examines the techniques involved when there are several variables.

7.2 ELEMENTS OF OPTIMIZATION

Optimization may be defined as a mathematical process of obtaining the set of conditions required to produce the maximum or the minimum value of a function. Of course, it would be ideal to obtain the perfect solution to a design situation. But because we must always work within the constraints of the time and funds available, we can only hope for the best solution possible. It must also be remembered that optimization is simply a technique that aids in decision making but does not replace sound judgment and technical know-how.

DESIGN VARIABLES

An engineering optimization model consists of parameters whose numerical values are to be determined in order to achieve an optimum design. These parameters are called **design variables.** They include such things as size or weight or the number of teeth in a gear, coils in a spring, or tubes in a heat exchanger. In short, they represent any number of variables that may be required to quantify or completely describe an engineering system. The number of variables depends upon the type of design involved. Of course, as this number increases, so does the complexity of the solution to the design problem.

OBJECTIVE FUNCTION

The process of selecting the "best solution" from various possible solutions must be based on a prescribed criterion, which is the **objective function.** For the purpose of optimization, we define the objective function as a mathematical equation that embodies the design variables to be minimized or maximized. It can be given in the form

$$D = f(x_1, x_2, \ldots, x_n)$$
(7.1)

D is used here to show that a desired effect is to be achieved.

The function of an engineering design objective may be to maximize the life and the efficiency of a mechanical element such as a gear-set; it could be to reduce an undesirable condition, such as minimizing the weight of a machine element. The choice of the objective function is crucial. Different functions produce different optima. Therefore, the choice of the objective function is one of the most important steps in an optimization process. In cases when a company's policy is clear, it may be easy to decide what the objective is. However, in instances where there is no defined policy, it may not be easy. As an illustration, suppose one is called upon to set up a CAD/CAM laboratory from scratch. There are several issues to be raised, such as how to determine the size of the laboratory, how to minimize the cost, and how to maximize the number of workstations. Any of these could become the objective; the result would depend upon which objective is chosen. For example, if one chooses to maximize the number of workstations, the results would be quite different than if the choice were to minimize the cost. An example for minimizing the cost is given in [1]. This illustration demonstrates the need for careful choice of the objective function.

There are cases in which it is possible to have only one objective function and other cases in which several may be required. Sometimes these objective functions may conflict. For example, suppose that a car manufacturer sets up four objectives: to minimize the cost, to minimize the weight, to maximize the strength, and to maximize the size of the car. Obviously, it would be very difficult to maximize the size and minimize the weight at the same time. Therefore, in cases of two or more possible objective functions, the designer must set up priorities and assign weighting values to each objective function. By examining these, he or she can reach a single objective function. If one must deal with multiobjective functions, a good starting point will be to consult the book by Osyczka [2].

CONSTRAINTS

In many engineering situations, the designer is often not free to do what he or she chooses, for any of several reasons. For example, in the design of thermal systems requiring high temperature conditions, a designer is limited because there are few materials that are able to withstand high temperatures; in fact, for very high temperatures, suitable materials have not as yet been developed. Another source of restrictions are economic considerations. The engineer/designer must learn to operate within such restrictions; in the field of optimization, these are termed **constraints.**

Optimization constraints are the restrictions or conditions that must be satisfied before the numerical values of the design variable can represent a feasible solution to a given problem. Generally, there are two types of constraints: *internal* and *external.*

External constraints are those uncontrollable restrictions or specifications imposed upon a system by an outside agency and therefore not under the direct control of the designer. Typical examples of external constraints may be the laws and regulations set by governmental agencies, such as materials that are allowable for house construction. Availability of raw materials may also be an external constraint.

Internal constraints are those imposed by the designer. They require physical understanding of the system or an engineering background. Such constraints may arise from the fundamental laws of conservation of mass, momentum, and energy. Other constraints may arise from mathematical expressions. For example, the design of a helical spring may require a restrictive expression relating the volume, the number of coils (N), the mean spring diameter (D), and the wire diameter (d) as

$$V = \frac{\pi^2 d^2 D^2 N}{4} \tag{7.2}$$

Additional restrictions may be placed on the ratio D/d (also called the **spring index**) so it will lie within a prescribed range.

Mathematically, constraints can be written either in the form of an equality; such as

$$g_i = g_i(x_i) = 0 \quad i = 1, 2, \ldots, n \tag{7.3}$$

or in the form of an inequality; such as

$$g_j = g_j(x_j) \geq 0 \quad j = 1, 2, \ldots, n \tag{7.4}$$

7.3 MINIMIZATION AND MAXIMIZATION

In most optimization problems, the objective is to find a minimum. Of course, a maximization problem can be converted to a minimization by changing the sign of the objective function; that is:

$$\text{maximize } D(x) = -\text{minimize } [-D(x)] \tag{7.5}$$

The maximizing of a function in a design situation requires the definition of certain terms.

DESIGN SPACE

The total region, or domain, defined by all the design variables in the objective function is called the **design space.** This is normally limited by constraints; otherwise, we might have unbounded design space for which no feasible solution may exist. So the use of constraints is especially useful in restricting the region in which to search for the desired minimum or maximum design variables.

LOCAL AND GLOBAL MAXIMUM

Consider the function shown in Figure 7.1; it is certain that

$$f(D) > f(C) > f(B) > f(A) \tag{7.6}$$

The point A is the highest point in its immediate vicinity, yet it is the least of the four points. This illustrates the concept of *local* and *global* maximum.

The point in the design space that is higher than all other points within its immediate vicinity is therefore the **local maximum,** whereas the highest of all local maxima is called the **global maximum.**

The topic of maximum and minimum of functions is covered in differential calculus. There it is taught that a necessary condition for a local maximum or minimum of a function $f(x)$ at a point $x = x_0$ is that

$$f'(x_0) = 0 \tag{7.7}$$

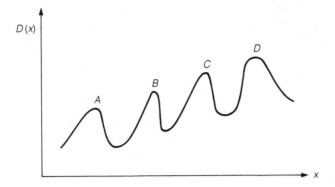

FIGURE 7.1

Illustration of local and global maximum.

If, in addition,

$$f''(x_0) < 0 \qquad \textbf{(7.8)}$$

then $f(x)$ has a local maximum at $x = x_0$. However, if instead

$$f''(x_0) > 0 \qquad \textbf{(7.9)}$$

then $f(x)$ has a local minimum at $x = x_0$. In optimization, it is really difficult to say whether the maximum obtained is global or local. In fact, all one can say is that the maximum is a local maximum in the search region. From Figure 7.1, it is obvious that a function may contain several local maxima, and one of these maxima is the global maximum. To determine the global maximum in a design space requires the evaluation of all the local maxima. In the rest of this book, the term maximum (or minimum) will refer to the local maximum (or minimum).

7.4 CLASSIFICATION OF OPTIMIZATION PROBLEMS

There are many approaches to optimization techniques; see, for example, Chapter 7 of [3]. To determine the appropriate optimization algorithm needed to solve any optimization problem, the problem must be categorized. Generally, optimization problems can be classified into four categories.

Category 1

Problems in category 1 are classified according to the type of constraints. If the problem is stated with some constraints, we have a **constrained optimization** problem. If, however, the problem is stated without constraints, then we have **unconstrained optimization.** In the latter case, the only requirement is to find the values of the design variables that maximize or minimize the objective function.

Category 2

Problems in category 2 are classified according to the number of independent design variables. If the objective function is a function of one variable and unconstrained, the problem is said to be a **single-variable** optimization. If, however, it is a function of two or more variables, it is called a **multi-variable** optimization.

Category 3

Problems in category 3 are classified according to whether they are time-dependent or not. If they are not time-independent, they are called static optimization. If the problems are time-dependent, they are said to be dynamic optimization.

Category 4

Problems in category 4 are classified according to the type of data available. If the data are known with certainty, the problems are said to be **deterministic optimization.** If the data are not known with certainty, the problems are called stochastic **optimization** problems.

7.5 SEARCH METHODS FOR UNCONSTRAINED OPTIMIZATION

Perhaps the easiest way to find the minimum (maximum) of an objective function is by graphical means, but graphing is time-consuming, tedious, and limited to two-dimensional problems. The advent of computers has made graphical techniques undesirable. Another method is the use of differential calculus (see [4] for further discussion). However, if the objective function $D(x)$ is not differentiable or if the derivatives are discontinuous, finding solutions becomes very difficult. This difficulty is overcome by using what are termed **search methods.** Search methods can be unsatisfactory, since there is no one systematic procedure that is followed; however, if other methods of optimization fail, a search method must be applied.

The so-called direct search method is a method based on evaluating $D(x)$ at a sequence of points $x_1, x_2, \ldots, x_n$ and comparing values in order to reach the optimal solution x^*. The search method for single variables is considered in the remainder of this chapter; the multivariable search is examined in the next chapter.

The single-variable direct search method is performed using two types of techniques: the less efficient, such as the *exhaustive (total) search;* and the more efficient, such as the *golden section* and the *Fibonacci*. Further discussions are limited to the more efficient techniques. The book by Shoup [5] can be consulted for further discussion on the total search method. More information on other search techniques, such as the *Davis, Swann,* and *Campey method,* can be obtained from a book by Adby and Dempster [6].

7.6 PRINCIPLES OF SINGLE-VARIABLE SEARCH TECHNIQUES

The more efficient techniques in a single-variable search method are applicable to the **unimodal functions.** A function $f(x)$ is said to be unimodal in an interval if it increases monotonically to a maximum x^* and thereafter decreases monotonically. Simply put, a unimodal function is one that possesses one hump (or one depression) within a defined interval (see Figure 7.2). In Figure 7.2, note that in the interval $0 < x < x_2$, the function monotonically decreases to point 1 and then increases monotonically to point 2. Note that points 3 and 5 are global maxima within their respective intervals.

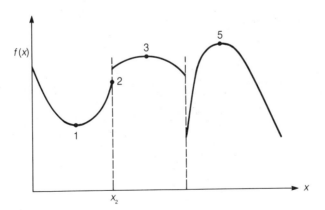

FIGURE 7.2

Illustration of unimodal functions.

To illustrate the principles of search techniques, we restrict our illustration to unimodal functions. Consider two points x_1 and x_2 on the interval $[a, b]$, at which the objective function is to be evaluated. Since we want to confine our search in the region $[a, b]$, this bounded region, called the **initial interval of uncertainty**, is shown in Figure 7.3. Also shown in Figure 7.3 is $D(x_1)$ and $D(x_2)$. Suppose that we are seeking a maximum. We compare the two functions $D(x_1)$ and $D(x_2)$. Since $D(x_2) > D(x_1)$, we discard the region between point a and x_1. The solution, x^*, must lie between x_1 and b. Next, we must determine how to select the next point for evaluation and comparison. There are several possible methods used to decide where to place the next point. One method is to divide the interval into two parts and place two points equidistant from the center of the new interval. This process of comparing the evaluated functions is continued until we obtain an interval of uncertainty that is the same value as our specified tolerance, say ε, after n evaluations. The other methods are the subjects of subsequent sections.

It is important to realize that this process could not have been performed if the function were not unimodal within the intervals $[a, b]$. As an illustration, consider Figure 7.4 in which we take two points, x_1 and x_2. Again, we note that $D(x_2) > D(x_1)$, but discarding the region to the left of x_1 will lead to only a local maximum in the region between x_1 and the point c. There is no means of ever attaining the global maximum located between a and x_1 because the function is not unimodal in the interval $[a, b]$.

The process of "zeroing in" on the actual solution of an objective function can be improved by the use of the techniques described in the next section.

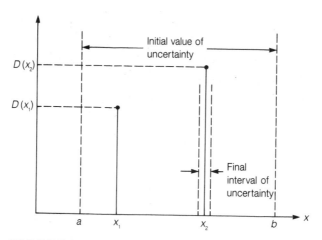

FIGURE 7.3

Illustration of definitions used in a search method.

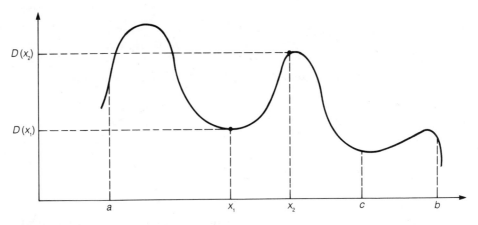

FIGURE 7.4

IIllustration of the importance of unimodality in the objective function.

7.7 GOLDEN SECTION SEARCH

The **golden section search method** is based on what is called the golden section rule. This rule deals with the division of an interval into two unequal parts such that the ratio of the smaller to the larger interval is equal to the ratio of the larger to the whole. Consider Figure 7.5. The golden section rule states that

$$\frac{R_2}{R_1} = \frac{R_1}{R} \qquad \qquad \textbf{(7.10)}$$

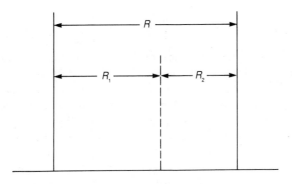

FIGURE 7.5

Golden section rule.

but

$$R = R_1 + R_2 \qquad\qquad \textbf{(7.11)}$$

Combining equations (7.10) and (7.11) and simplifying gives

$$\left(\frac{R_2}{R_1}\right)^2 + \frac{R_2}{R_1} = 1 \qquad\qquad \textbf{(7.12)}$$

Let $K = R_2/R_1$; then

$$K^2 + K = 1 \qquad\qquad \textbf{(7.13)}$$

The positive solution to equation (7.13) is $K = 0.6180$. If the golden section rule is applied in a search, the interval of uncertainty is reduced by the value of $K = 0.6180$. By repeated applications of the rule, the interval of uncertainty after n evaluations is related to the initial value of uncertainty by the equation

$$I_n = I_0(0.6180)^{n-1} \qquad\qquad \textbf{(7.14)}$$

where

I_n = interval of uncertainty after n evaluations
I_0 = initial interval of uncertainty
n = number of evaluations

The golden section search method is illustrated in Figure 7.6.

Let the boundaries of the region of search be denoted b_l for the lower boundary and b_u for the upper boundary. It follows that the interval for the search I is given as

$$I = b_u - b_l \qquad\qquad \textbf{(7.15)}$$

The question then is where to place the first point. Using the golden section rule, the point must be placed then at point x_u, such that $x_u = 0.6180I$. Since a search method involves comparison of two values, another point is required. This second point must be placed such that the interval of uncertainty is the same from either end (see Figure 7.6), so we place the point at x_l, which is also $0.6180I$ but from the upper boundary. The function can be evaluated at the two points. Then we make a comparison to see if $D(x_l) > D(x_u)$ (for minimization). If this is the case, then we confine our search to the region right of $x = x_l$; otherwise we confine our search to the left of $x = x_u$. A new interval of uncertainty is defined, using the same approach as in the first case. The process of evaluation is continued until an interval of uncertainty is obtained that is equal to the desired tolerance.

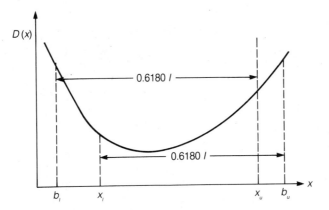

FIGURE 7.6

Illustration of golden section search method.

Before we give a step-by-step procedure for conducting the golden section search technique, note from Figure 7.6 that

$$x_l = b_u - KI \qquad \text{(7.16)}$$
$$x_u = b_l + KI \qquad \text{(7.17)}$$

where

$$K = 0.6180$$

The steps for finding a minimum of a function, using the golden section rule, are as follows.

Step 1 Input $b_{l,1}$, $b_{u,1}$, K, function f, and tolerance ε.

Step 2 Define the two initial points for evaluating the functions using equations (7.16) and (7.17); that is:

$$x_{l,1} = b_{u,1} - KI, \qquad \text{(7.18)}$$
$$x_{u,1} = b_{l,1} + KI, \qquad \text{(7.19)}$$

(Note $I_1 = b_{u,1} - b_{l,1}$.) Set $n = 1$.

Step 3 Make a comparison of the values to determine the interval that contains the desired minimum. If $f(x_{l,n}) \leq f(x_{u,n})$, set

$$b_{l,n+1} = b_{l,n} \qquad \text{(7.20)}$$

$$b_{u,n+1} = x_{u,n} \tag{7.21}$$

$$I_{n+1} = b_{u,n+1} - b_{l,n+1} \tag{7.22}$$

$$x_{l,n+1} = b_{u,n+1} - KI_{n+1} \tag{7.23}$$

$$x_{u,n+1} = x_{l,n} \tag{7.24}$$

Go to step 5. Otherwise, go to step 4.

Step 4 Set

$$b_{l,n+1} = x_{l,n} \tag{7.25}$$

$$b_{u,n+1} = b_{u,n} \tag{7.26}$$

$$I_{n+1} = b_{u,n+1} - b_{l,n+1} \tag{7.27}$$

$$x_{l,n+1} = x_{u,n} \tag{7.28}$$

$$x_{u,n+1} = b_{l,n+1} + KI_{n+1} \tag{7.29}$$

Step 5 Test to see if a satisfactory level of tolerance has been achieved. Set

$$\text{TEST} = b_{u,n} - b_{l,n}.$$

If TEST $\leq \varepsilon$, go to step 6. Otherwise set $n = n + 1$ and return to step 3.

Step 6 Output the solution as follows: Find value $x^* = \min\{x_{l,n}, x_{u,n}\}$ and $f_{\min} = \min\{f(x_{l,n}), f(x_{u,n})\}$. The preceding steps can be used for finding the maximum by modifying the test condition in step 3. A flowchart based on these steps is given in Figure 7.7. A sample program is given in Figure 7.8.

EXAMPLE 7.1

Determine the maximum value of the function of $f(x) = x \cos \pi x^2$ in the interval $[0.0, 0.7]$. Use $\varepsilon = 1 \times 10^{-4}$.

SOLUTION   **Step 1**

$$b_{l,1} = 0.0$$
$$b_{u,1} = 0.7$$
$$I_l = 0.7$$
$$f(x) = x \cos \pi x^2$$
$$\varepsilon = 1 \times 10^{-4}$$

This input satisfies step 1.

Step 2 Define the two initial points, using equations (7.16) and (7.17)

$$xl_1 = 0.7 - (0.6180)(0.7) = 0.2674$$
$$xu_1 = 0.0 + (0.6180)(0.7) = 0.4326$$

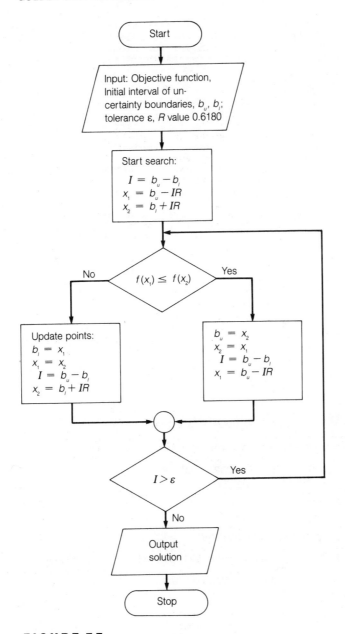

FIGURE 7.7

Flowchart for the golden section method.

```
****************************************************************
*    This Program uses the Gold section technique to determine  *
*    the maximum of a unimodal function.                        *
****************************************************************
*
*---------------------------------------------------------------*
*    Variables:                                                  *
*              blower:= the lower boundary of the search region  *
*              bupper:= the upper boundary of the search region  *
*              xlower:= the lower starting point for each search *
*              xupper:= the upper starting point for each search *
*              lfun : = value of objective function evaluated at *
*                       xlower.                                   *
*              ufun : = value of objective function evaluated at *
*                 j : = counter                                  *
*              x2, x1:= final search values.                     *
*              xmin : = result of search                         *
*              interv:= interval of uncertainty                  *
*              ointer:= original interval of uncertainty         *
*                   R:= golden ratio (0.6180)                    *
*                   E:= termination criterion                    *
*---------------------------------------------------------------*
          REAL INTERV,XLOWER,XUPPER,BLOWER,BUPPER,EVA,LFUN,UFUN
*...............................................................*
*    Define the upper and lower boundaries, the number of iterat-*
*    erations,N, and the interval of search.                    *
*...............................................................*
*    Define the objective function                              *
*...............................................................*
          EVA(X) = X*COS(X**2*22.0/7.0)
          OPEN(6,FILE='PRN')
          BLOWER = 0.0
          BUPPER = 0.7
          E = 1.E-04
          R = 0.6180
          J = 1
          INTERV = BUPPER - BLOWER
*...............................................................*
*  Define two points for starting the search.                  *
*...............................................................*
          XLOWER = BUPPER - INTERV*R
          XUPPER = BLOWER + INTERV*R
*...............................................................*
*  Evaluate the objective function at these two points.        *
*...............................................................*
          LFUN = EVA(XLOWER)
          UFUN = EVA(XUPPER)
*...............................................................*
*    Determine which interval contains the optimum             *
*...............................................................*
 40       IF(-LFUN.LE.-UFUN) THEN
*                                  discard the region to the right *
*                                  of xupper.                      *
                    BUPPER = XUPPER
                    XUPPER = XLOWER
                    INTERV = BUPPER - BLOWER
                    XLOWER = BUPPER - INTERV*R
                    UFUN   = LFUN
                    LFUN   = EVA(XLOWER)
```

F I G U R E 7.8

A sample program for the golden section method.

```
            IF(INTERV.GT.E) THEN
*                           continue the search
                J = J + 1
                GO TO 40
            END IF
      ELSE
*           discard the region to  the left of xlower.
            BLOWER = XLOWER
            XLOWER = XUPPER
            INTERV = BUPPER - BLOWER
            XUPPER = BLOWER + INTERV*R
            LFUN =   UFUN
            UFUN   = EVA(XUPPER)
            IF(INTERV.GT.E) THEN
*                           continue the search
                J = J + 1
                GO TO 40
            END IF
      END IF
*  Define the final solution
*
*
            X1 = XLOWER
            X2 = XLOWER
*    Define the solution as the bigger of x1 and x2.
*
            XMAX = AMAX1(X1,X2)
            FOPT = EVA(XMAX)
*    Output the solution
*
            WRITE(6,100)XMAX,FOPT,J
  100       FORMAT(3X,'THE MAXIMUM VALUE OF DESIGN VARIABLE IS:',/30X,
      .     E14.7,/3X,'THE OPTIMUM SOLUTION IS:',/30X,E14.7,/3X,
      .     'AFTER ',I3,' ITERATION(S)')
            END
```

FIGURE 7.8

(Continued).

Step 3 Determine the interval that contains the maximum:

$$f(0.26740) = 0.2606$$
$$f(0.4326) = 0.3600$$

Since $f(0.4326) > f(0.2674)$, the region of interest must lie between $x_{l,1}$ and $b_{u,1}$. We go to step 4 and update as follows.

Step 4 Set

$$b_{l,2} = x_{l,1} = 0.2674$$
$$b_{u,2} = b_{u,1} = 0.7$$
$$I_2 = 0.4326$$
$$x_{l,2} = x_{u,1} = 0.4326$$
$$x_{u,2} = b_{l,2} + KI_2 = 0.5347$$

ITER	b_i	b_u	x_i	x_u	$f(x_i)$	$f(x_u)$	I
1	.000000	.700000	.267400	.432600	.260676	.359906	.700000
2	.267400	.700000	.432600	.534747	.359906	.332943	.432600
3	.267400	.534747	.369527	.432600	.336017	.359906	.267347
4	.369527	.534747	.432600	.471633	.359906	.361001	.165220
5	.432600	.534747	.471633	.495727	.361001	.355079	.102147
6	.432600	.495727	.456714	.471633	.362040	.361001	.063127
7	.432600	.471633	.447510	.456714	.361757	.362040	.039033
8	.447510	.471633	.456714	.462418	.362040	.361867	.024122
9	.447510	.462418	.453205	.456714	.362013	.362040	.014908
10	.453205	.462418	.456714	.458899	.362040	.362006	.009213
11	.453205	.458899	.455380	.456714	.362041	.362040	.005694
12	.453205	.456714	.454546	.455380	.362035	.362041	.003509
13	.454546	.456714	.455380	.455886	.362041	.362042	.002169
14	.455380	.456714	.455886	.456205	.362042	.362042	.001334
15	.455380	.456205	.455695	.455886	.362042	.362042	.000825
16	.455695	.456205	.455886	.456010	.362042	.362042	.000510
17	.455695	.456010	.455815	.455886	.362042	.362042	.000315
18	.455815	.456010	.455886	.455936	.362042	.362042	.000195
19	.455886	.456010	.455936	.455963	.362042	.362042	.000124

TABLE 7.1

Iteration results of Example 7.1.

Step 5 Test whether the tolerance is satisfied. $|0.7| > \varepsilon$, so we increase n to 2 and return to step 3. The results for subsequent iterations are given in Table 7.1. The final solution after 19 iterations is:

$$x^* = 0.4560 \text{ and } f_{max} = 0.3620.$$

7.8 FIBONACCI SEARCH METHOD

The efficient **Fibonacci search method** is characterized by the fact that at the end of each iteration, at least one of the previous points will be contained in the new region of search. In addition, the intervals are irregularly spaced, which leads to a faster rate of convergence to the desired solutions. The method that converges more quickly than any other single variable search technique is the Fibonacci technique.

The Fibonacci search method is based on the Fibonacci number theory developed in the thirteenth century. In general terms, the Fibonacci number can be obtained from the Fibonacci series, given by the expression

$$F_k = \frac{(\sqrt{5} + 1)^{k+1} + (-1)^k(\sqrt{5} - 1)^{k+1}}{\sqrt{5} \ \ 2^{k+1}}$$

(7.30)

Using equation (7.30), it is easy to see that

$$F_0 = 1$$
$$F_1 = 1 \qquad \qquad \textbf{(7.31)}$$

However, a more useful formula for generating the Fibonacci number is

$$F_k = F_{k-2} + F_{k-1} \text{ for } k \geq 2 \qquad \qquad \textbf{(7.32)}$$

By the use of equations (7.29) and (7.30), a set of Fibonacci numbers can be generated. Table 7.2 shows some numbers in the Fibonacci series.

The Fibonacci method is very similar to the golden section search method. For example, note that for a very large value of k, the ratio of two consecutive Fibonacci numbers is the same as the golden section ratio from equation (7.30):

$$\lim_{k \to \infty} \frac{F_k}{F_{k+1}} = \frac{\sqrt{5} - 1}{2}$$

The simple exercise just given suggests that the final interval of uncertainty for a Fibonacci method is smaller than that of the golden section method. In [6], it is demonstrated that the final interval of uncertainty for Fibonacci is 17% smaller than that of the golden section.

The Fibonacci method does, however, have a drawback: It requires that the number of function evaluations be specified in advance, so that the position of the first two evaluations can be determined. This drawback is not a serious one, since it is easy to determine the number of evaluations required for a given resolution or accuracy. If the desired resolution is designated ε, then:

$$\varepsilon = \frac{1}{F_k} \qquad \qquad \textbf{(7.33)}$$

As an illustration of the method of determining the number of evaluations, suppose a resolution of 0.001 is required. Then

$$\varepsilon \leq \frac{1}{F_k}$$

or

$$F_k \geq 1000.0$$

From Table 7.2, $F_{16} = 1597 > 1000$. Therefore, 16 evaluations are needed. Table 7.3 is provided as an aid in determining the number of evaluations, n, needed.

K	F_K
0	1
1	1
2	2
3	3
4	5
5	8
6	13
7	21
8	34
9	55
10	89
11	144
12	233
13	377
14	610
15	987
16	1,597
17	2,584
18	4,181
19	6,765
20	10,946
21	17,711
22	28,657
23	46,368
24	75,025
25	121,393

TABLE 7.2

Fibonacci numbers.

The procedure for applying this technique is the same as for the golden search method. The only modification required is to replace equations (7.16) and (7.17) with the following:

$$x_l = b_u - \frac{F_{n-1}}{F_n} I \qquad (7.34)$$

$$x_u = b_l + \frac{F_{n-1}}{F_n} I \qquad (7.35)$$

$$b_{l,j+1} = x_{l,j}$$

$$b_{u,j+1} = b_{u,j}$$

$$x_{l,j+1} = x_{u,j}$$

$$x_{u,j+1} = b_{l,j+1} + \frac{F_{n-j-1}}{F_{n-j}} (b_{u,j+1} - b_{l,j+1})$$

Tolerance	Number of Evaluations
0.00001	25
0.00002	24
0.00005	22
0.0001	20
0.0002	19
0.0005	17
0.001	16
0.002	14
0.005	12
0.01	11
0.02	9
0.05	7
0.1	6

TABLE 7.3

Number of iterations for a given tolerance for the Fibonacci method.

and

$$F_{l,j+1} = F_{u,j}$$
$$F_{u,j+1} = f(x_{u,j+1})$$

Alternatively, if the solution is to lie in the right interval, the following equations apply:

$$b_{l,j+1} = x_{l,j}$$
$$b_{u,j+1} = b_{u,j}$$
$$x_{l,j+1} = x_{u,j}$$
$$x_{l,j+1} = b_{u,j+1} - \frac{F_{n-j-1}}{F_{n-j}}(b_{u,j+1} - b_{l,j+1})$$

and

$$F_{u,j+1} = F_{l,j}$$
$$F_{l,j+1} = f(x_{l,j+1})$$

Every other step is identical. The flowchart for the Fibonacci method is, however, repeated for simplicity (see Figures 7.9 and 7.10). A detailed study of this method can be found in [4] and [7].

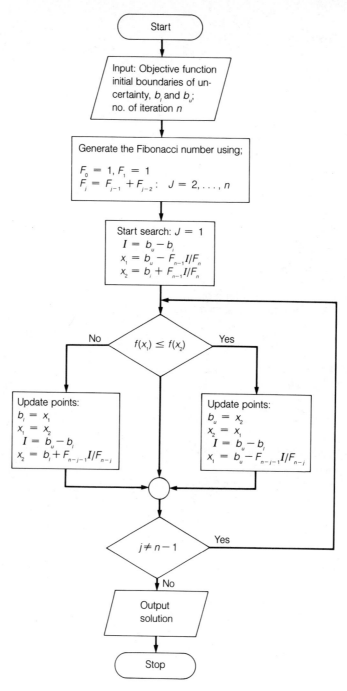

FIGURE 7.9

```
***************************************************************
*    This Program uses the Fibonacci technique to determine the  *
*    the maximum of a unimodal function.                         *
***************************************************************
*
*-------------------------------------------------------------*
*   Variables:                                                    *
*            blower:= the lower boundary of the search region   *
*            bupper:= the upper boundary of the search region   *
*            xlower:= the lower starting point for each search  *
*            xupper:= the upper starting point for each search  *
*            fib  : = fibonacci number                          *
*            lfun : = value of objective function evaluated at  *
*                     xlower.                                     *
*            ufun : = value of objective function evaluated at  *
*               j : = counter to check when to terminate search *
*            x2, x1:= final search values.                       *
*            xmin : = result of search                          *
*            interv:= interval of uncertainty                   *
*            ointer:= original interval of uncertainty          *
*-------------------------------------------------------------*
           REAL FIB(25)
           REAL INTERV,XLOWER,XUPPER,BLOWER,BUPPER,EVA,LFUN,UFUN
*.............................................................*
*   Define the upper and lower boundaries, the number of iterat-*
*   erations,N, and the interval of search.                      *
*.............................................................*
*    Define the objective function                              *
*.............................................................*
           EVA(X) = X*COS(X**2*22.0/7.0)
           OPEN(6,FILE='PRN')
           BLOWER = 0.0
           BUPPER = 0.7
           N = 18
           J = 1
           OINTER = BUPPER - BLOWER
           INTERV = OINTER
*.............................................................*
*   Generate the Fibonacci numbers                              *
*.............................................................*
           CALL FIBNUM(FIB,N)
*.............................................................*
*   Define two points for starting the search.                  *
*.............................................................*
           XLOWER = BUPPER - (FIB(N-1)/FIB(N))*INTERV
           XUPPER = BLOWER + (FIB(N-1)/FIB(N))*INTERV
*.............................................................*
*   Evaluate the objective function at these two points.        *
*.............................................................*
           LFUN = EVA(XLOWER)
           UFUN = EVA(XUPPER)
*.............................................................*
*    Determine which interval contains the optimum             *
*.............................................................*
  40       IF(-LFUN.LE.-UFUN) THEN
```

FIGURE 7.10

A sample program using the Fibonacci method.

```
*                                                discard the region to the right *
*                                                of xupper.                      *
                        BUPPER = XUPPER
                        XUPPER = XLOWER
                        INTERV = BUPPER - BLOWER
                        XLOWER = BUPPER - (FIB(N-J-1)/FIB(N-J))*INTERV
                        UFUN   = LFUN
                        LFUN   = EVA(XLOWER)
                        IF(J.NE.(N-1)) THEN
*                                                continue the search
                            J = J + 1
                            GO TO 40
                        END IF
            ELSE
*                       discard the region to  the left of xlower.
                        BLOWER = XLOWER
                        XLOWER = XUPPER
                        INTERV = BUPPER - BLOWER
                        XUPPER = BLOWER + (FIB(N-J-1)/FIB(N-J))*INTERV
                        LFUN =   UFUN
                        UFUN   = EVA(XUPPER)
                        IF(J.NE.(N-1)) THEN
*                                                continue the search
                            J = J + 1
                            GO TO 40
                        END IF
            END IF
*   Define the final solution
*
            FINTER = OINTER/FIB(N)
*
            X1 = XLOWER + FINTER
            X2 = XLOWER - FINTER
*   Define the solution as the bigger of x1 and x2.
*
            XMAX = AMAX1(X1,X2)
            FOPT = EVA(XMAX)
*   Output the solution
*
            WRITE(6,100)XMAX,FOPT
    100     FORMAT(3X,'THE MAXIMUM VALUE OF DESIGN VARIABLE IS:',/30X,
         .  E14.7,/3X,'THE OPTIMUM SOLUTION IS:',/30X,E14.7)
            END
*-----------------------------------------------------------------*
*   This subroutine generates the Fibonacci numbers               *
*-----------------------------------------------------------------*
            SUBROUTINE FIBNUM(F,N)
            REAL F(N)
            F(0) = 1.
            F(1) = 1.
            DO 5 I = 2,N
            F(I) = F(I-1) + F(I-2)
    5       CONTINUE
            RETURN
            END
```

F I G U R E 7.10

(Continued).

E X A M P L E 7.2

Repeat Example 7.1 using the Fibonacci method.

SOLUTION The problem requires the solution to be obtained within an accuracy of 1×10^{-4}. We must determine the number of function evaluations required by using equation (7.33); $F_k = 10,000$. Using Table 7.2, the nearest Fibonacci number is 10,946.0; therefore, we need 20 evaluations (the same value could be obtained from Table 7.3).

Step 1 Specify the function, and the lower and the upper bounds.

$$f(x) = x \cos \pi x^2$$
$$b_l = 0.0 \quad \text{and} \quad b_u = .7$$

Set the iteration counter, j, to 1.

Step 2 Generate Fibonacci numbers up to F_{20} using equation (7.32).

Step 3 Determine the first two points at which the function may be evaluated, using equations (7.34) and (7.35). For the first iteration, x_l and x_u are obtained as:

$$x_{l,1} = 0.7 - \left(\frac{6765}{10,946}\right)(0.7)$$

$$= 0.2673.$$

A similar operation yields $x_{u,1} = 0.4326$.

Step 4 Determine which interval to discard by evaluating the function at the two initial values of x_l and x_u.

$$F_l = f(0.2673) = 0.26063$$
$$F_u = f(.4326) = 0.35996$$

Since $F_u > F_l$, the search is confined to the region right of x_l. Therefore, proceed to step 5.

Step 5 Update the boundaries and obtain the points necessary for the next iteration. Using equations (7.16) to (7.29), obtain

$$b_{l,2} = 0.2673 \qquad b_{u,2} = 0.7$$
$$x_{l,2} = 0.4326 \qquad x_{u,2} = 0.5348$$
$$F_{l,2} = 0.3360 \qquad F_{u,2} = 0.3599$$

Step 6 Increase j to 2. Check if $j = n - 1$; if so, end the search. At this point note that $j < 19$; therefore, return to step 4 and repeat the process. The result of subsequent iterations is shown in Table 7.4. The final solution is $x^* = 0.4561$ and $f_{max} = 0.36220$.

REMARKS

The output becomes the larger of the two values:

$$x_{l,n-1} + \frac{b_{u,1} - b_{l,1}}{F_n}$$

or

$$x_{l,n-1} - \frac{b_{u,1} - b_{l,1}}{F_n}$$

This illustration applies to the case of maximization. For minimization, the same procedure is followed, with minor modification at step 4.

j	$x_l(j)$	$x_u(j)$	$b_l(j)$	$b_u(j)$	$F(x_l)$	$F(x_u)$	$I(j)$
1	0.5348	0.4326	0.7000	0.2674	0.3600	0.3333	0.7000
2	0.4326	0.3695	0.5348	0.2674	0.3361	0.3600	0.4326
3	0.4716	0.4326	0.5348	0.3695	0.3600	0.3612	0.2674
4	0.4957	0.4716	0.5348	0.4326	0.3612	0.3553	0.1652
5	0.4716	0.4567	0.4957	0.4326	0.3622	0.3612	0.1021
6	0.4567	0.4475	0.4716	0.4326	0.3619	0.3622	0.0631
7	0.4624	0.4567	0.4716	0.4475	0.3622	0.3620	0.0390
8	0.4567	0.4532	0.4624	0.4475	0.3622	0.3622	0.0241
9	0.4589	0.4567	0.4624	0.4532	0.3622	0.3622	0.0149
10	0.4567	0.4554	0.4589	0.4532	0.3622	0.3622	0.0092
11	0.4576	0.4567	0.4589	0.4554	0.3622	0.3622	0.0057
12	0.4567	0.4562	0.4576	0.4554	0.3622	0.3622	0.0035
13	0.4562	0.4559	0.4567	0.4554	0.3622	0.3622	0.0022
14	0.4564	0.4562	0.4567	0.4559	0.3622	0.3622	0.0013
15	0.4562	0.4561	0.4564	0.4559	0.3622	0.3622	0.0008
16	0.4563	0.4562	0.4564	0.4561	0.3622	0.3622	0.0005
17	0.4562	0.4562	0.4563	0.4561	0.3622	0.3622	0.0003
18	0.4562	0.4561	0.4562	0.4561	0.3622	0.3622	0.0002
19	0.4561	0.4561	0.4562	0.4561	0.3622	0.3622	0.0001

TABLE 7.4

APPLICATION
Problem Statement

A company desires to mass produce helical springs for a customer. Because the customer buys the springs from another manufacturer at $10 per spring, this company must make them available for less than $10. The would-be customer provides the following specifications:

Spring material: steel $(G = 79.3 \text{ GPa})$
Load requirement: must support 2 KN
Wire size: 7 mm
Permissible deflection: 160 mm
Permissible shear stress: 752 MPa

The company has conducted a study that shows that the cost of material and labor is related to the spring index by the following expression:

$$C_s = 0.007C^2\cos(0.125C^2)$$

where

C_s = cost (in dollars) per unit coil
C = spring index

Because the company is desperate for customers, the manager has committed the company. Now the engineers must develop a design that will lead to a spring costing less than $10.

SOLUTION   **Given:**

Material: steel $(G = 79.3 \text{ GPa})$
Load (P):   2 kN
Wire size (d):   7 mm
Deflection (y):   160 mm

Find: Spring index (C) and number of active coils (n) for minimum cost.

Equations:

$$\tau = \frac{8KPC}{\pi d^2} \qquad\qquad \textbf{(7.36)}$$

$$K = \frac{4C - 1}{4C - 1} + \frac{0.615}{C} \tag{7.37}$$

$$n = \frac{yGd}{8PC^3} \tag{7.38}$$

where

τ = shear stress

K = Wahl correction factor

n = number of active coils

ANALYSIS

From equation (7.36) we have

$$d = \left(\frac{8KPC}{\pi\tau}\right)^{0.5} \tag{7.39}$$

Substituting equations (7.37) and (7.38) into (7.39) and simplifying gives

$$n = \frac{yG[C(4C - 1) + 2.46(C - 1)]^{0.5}}{(8\pi\tau\,P)^{0.5}\,4C^6(C - 1)}$$

The total cost C_T for a spring of n active coils is then

$$C_T = \frac{yG[C(4C - 1) + 2.46(C - 1)]^{0.5}(0.007C^2\cos(0.125C^2)}{(8\pi\tau P)^{0.5}4C^6(C - 1)} \tag{7.40}$$

With the analysis complete, equation (7.40) must now be optimized for the optimum value of C for a minimum cost. To use either of the two methods described in this chapter, we must provide an interval for a search for the solution. For good spring design, C is usually between 5 and 12, so the search is limited to this region.

The search is conducted using the Fibonacci method. The computer output is as follows:

$$
\begin{aligned}
C_T &= 6.973215 \\
\text{number of active coils} &= 17.12532 \\
\text{spring index} &= 7.062886
\end{aligned}
$$

Based on this result, the engineering group may recommend

$$
\begin{aligned}
\text{total number of coils} &= 18 \quad \text{(assuming squared ends)} \\
\text{spring index} &= 7
\end{aligned}
$$

$$\begin{aligned}
\text{wire diameter} &= 7 \text{ mm} \\
\text{solid height} &= 126 \text{ mm} \\
\text{outside diameter} &= 56 \text{ mm} \\
\text{minimum cost} &= \$6.00
\end{aligned}$$

REMARKS

The preceding design would have been very painstaking without an optimization technique and the computer.

EXERCISES

1. Maximize the function $f(x) = x^3 + 6x^2 - 4x - 8$. Search for the solution in the range $-2 \le x \le 2$.

2. What is the minimum value of the function

$$y = x^2(e^{-x} + \cos\pi x)$$

in the following intervals?
   a. $1.75 \le x \le 3.25$
   b. $3.5 \le x \le 5.25$

   Is the solution you obtained the true minimum? If not, why is your solution not correct, and what should be the correct one? (*Hint:* Examine the interval $3.75 \le x \le 5.25$.)

3. Maximize the function

$$y = (0.92 - 0.4 \sin \theta)^2 + (0.34 + 0.4 \cos \theta)^2$$

   Use the Fibonacci method and a tolerance of 1×10^{-6}. Does the selection of interval of search affect the maximum obtained?

4. It is desired to fabricate a V-shaped watering trough by joining four pieces of metal of uniform thickness. Formulate the objective function in terms of the missing dimension for a maximum volume. What is the value of the missing dimension? Using differential calculus or any other similar method, verify your solution. ($w = 710$ mm)

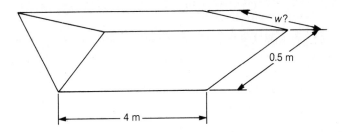

5. A jib crane was designed to transport a maximum load of 15 kN. The I-beam has a mass of 400 kg. The crane is installed in a machine shop, as shown in the figure below, but it was realized that the designer had underestimated the reaction supported by

the pin at A. The design can be made safe by constraining the jib's movement. At what distance, L, must the constraint be placed? ($L = 2.25$ m)

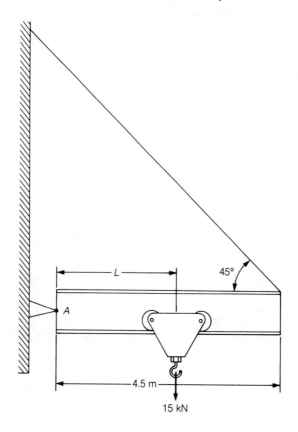

REFERENCES

1. Onwubiko, C. "Mathematical Model for Setting Up a CAD/CAM Laboratory." Annual Central Texas Engineering Conference, CAD/CAM, University of Texas at Austin, July 19–21, 1984.

2. Osyczka, A. *Multicriterion Optimization in Engineering.* New York: Halsted Press, John Wiley & Sons, Inc., 1984.

3. Stoecker, W. F. *Design of Thermal Systems.* New York: McGraw-Hill Book Co., 1980.

4. Beveridge, G. S., and R. S. Schechter, *Optimization: Theory and Practice.* New York: McGraw-Hill Book Co., 1970.

5. Shoup, T. E. *A Practical Guide to Computer Methods for Engineers.* Englewood Cliffs, N.J.: Prentice-Hall, Inc. 1979.

6. Adby, P. R., and Dempster, M. A. H, *Introduction to Optimization Methods.* New York: Halsted Press, John Wiley & Sons, Inc., 1974.

7. Walsh, G. R. *Methods of Optimization,* New York; John Wiley & Sons, Inc., 1975.

Multivariable Optimization

8.1   INTRODUCTION

In the previous chapter we examined the search methods for single-variable functions. The methods examined were found to be very efficient for the unimodal functions. However, in practice, many engineering-type problems cannot be modeled with unimodal functions. In addition, design decisions involve many variables. These factors make even the powerful Fibonacci search method unusable. Therefore, we must look for other techniques to handle functions of several variables, or multidimensional problems.

Traditionally, multivariable optimization methods are classified into two main categories: search methods and gradient methods. The search methods utilize function evaluations and comparisons similar to the single-variable search method. The gradient methods employ, in addition, mathematical principles involving such presumptions as the function possessing continuous partial derivatives with respect to each of the independent variables. In this chapter, we devote more attention to search methods, and we give a brief treatment of gradient methods.

8.2   PRINCIPLES OF SEARCH IN *N* DIMENSIONS

In the single-variable search methods, the problem of where to place the initial and subsequent points during the search is resolved using the golden section rule or the Fibonacci number theory. In the multidimensional search, there is no such easy solution. Two important questions that are raised in the multivariable search method are: Where should the search begin and in what direction should the search commence? and what must be the distance of the movement in the chosen direction?

A multidimensional search, in principle, begins with the selection of an initial point x_0, called the base point. Then the objective function is evaluated at this initial base point. Using a suitable method (the method is dependent on the algorithm selected), a second feasible point is chosen. The objective function is again evaluated at that second point. If the second point leads to an improvement in the objective function, the first initial base point is abandoned, and the second point becomes the new base point from which the search continues. This process of locating base points is continued until the extremum is obtained.

The movement from one point to another presents a great challenge. Should one move in all the n dimensions at one time? If so, how can this be achieved? Attempting to move in all the n dimensions simultaneously would be equal to the experience of trying to walk by moving two legs simultaneously. To walk, one takes one step at a time; similarly, the best method of advancing from one point to another is to go in one direction at a time. This simply means that one variable is changed at a time, while the other $n - 1$ variables are held constant. This reduces the objective function to a function of one variable. By using the one-dimensional search, the extremum is found, and the next variable is selected. The procedure is repeated from the new point until there is no change in the objective function. This process can be visualized by referring to Figure 8.1. The base point is x_0; x_1 is kept constant, and the search is conducted in the x_2 direction reaching point 1, at which x_2 is kept constant and the search conducted along the x_1 direction until point 2 is reached. Point 2 is now the new base point for conducting the next series of the search. The procedure is repeated until the minimum is located, as shown. This search process described so far is sometimes called the **method of sectioning.**

The method of sectioning works well for simple functions but becomes very inefficient or even ineffective in the case of complex nonlinear functions. We therefore focus our attention on methods that are more practical. In the subsequent sections, we discuss in detail the following direct search methods:

1. Hooke and Jeeves pattern search method

2. Powell's conjugate direction method

8.3   HOOKE AND JEEVES METHOD

One of the most widely used direct search techniques is that developed in 1961 by Hooke and Jeeves [1]; this method, generally known as the **pattern search,**

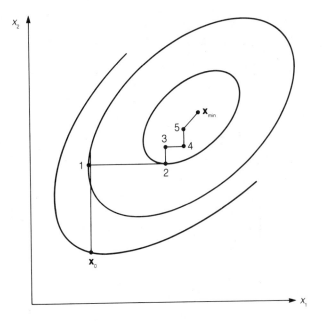

FIGURE 8.1

Illustration of principles of multivariable search (specific method of sectioning).

is based on a sequence of exploratory and pattern moves, starting at an initial base point.

A step size for each variable is selected. A local exploration commences with the evaluation of the objective function at a feasible initial base point, $x_0 = (x_1, x_2, \ldots, x_n)$, and two other points removed from it by the step size of the search variable. If one of the points results in a decrease in the objective function (for the case of minimization), a success is said to result, and the particular point that produced the success is called a temporary base point, x_0'. If neither of the two points produces a success, the step size for that variable is reduced by half, and the exploration is repeated. Figure 8.2 illustrates the local exploration for the two-dimensional case.

The search begins at the base point x_0 with a step size of $\pm h$. An exploration search is carried out on x_1. Suppose that the point $x_1 - h$ produces a success; this point becomes a temporary base. An exploration search is then performed on x_2 using x_0 as the base point. If a success results, then a new temporary base point is established and identified as x_1. With establishment of this new base point, the exploration is stopped and a pattern move is carried out.

The pattern move is a way to accelerate the search process by using greater step sizes. The original and the most recently established base points create a pattern that is used to locate the first pattern point, designated x_{p1}. The direction of the pattern move is represented by a line passing through the original point

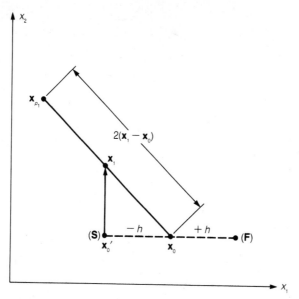

FIGURE 8.2

Local exploration for the Hooke and Jeeves method.

$(\mathbf{x}_0)$ and the newest base point $(\mathbf{x}_1)$. The pattern base point $(\mathbf{x}_{p1})$ is obtained by doubling the distance from $\mathbf{x}_0$ to $\mathbf{x}_1$; that is the same as subtracting the original base point from twice the newest base point. This is expressed as:

$$\mathbf{x}_{p,1} = \mathbf{x}_0 + 2(\mathbf{x}_1 - \mathbf{x}_0) \qquad (8.1)$$

or

$$\mathbf{x}_{p,1} = 2\mathbf{x}_1 - \mathbf{x}_0 \qquad (8.2)$$

To move to this new pattern point, we must be assured that such a move will result in a success. The objective function is evaluated at the pattern point $(\mathbf{x}_{p1})$. If this results in an improvement of the objective, then we make the pattern move to the pattern point $(\mathbf{x}_{p1})$. From this pattern point, the process of the local exploration is repeated. However, if there has been no improvement in the objective function—that is, if failure has resulted—then the pattern move to point $\mathbf{x}_{p1}$ is discontinued. Instead, local exploration is conducted using the base point $\mathbf{x}_1$. This alternation between local exploration and the pattern move is continued until the step size is reduced to the specified resolution and the search is terminated. A detailed algorithm for minimization, using the Hooke and Jeeves method, is given next.

Step 1 Input initial base point (starting point) x_b, step size, **h**, and termination criterion ε.

Step 2 Conduct a local exploration about the base point; denote the resulting point by x_t.

Step 3 Is x_t a better point than x_b?
- **a.** Yes: Go to step 5.
- **b.** No: Go to step 4.

Step 4 Is termination criterion satisfied?
- **a.** Yes: Stop; x_t approximates the optimum solution.
- **b.** No: Reduce step size by a half and return to step 2.

Step 5 Accelerate search by making a pattern move to the point x_p defined by

$$x_p = 2x_t - x_b$$

Step 6 Conduct a local exploration using the point x_p and designate the resultant new point of the exploration as x_p'.

Step 7 Is x_p' a better point than x_t?
- **a.** Yes: Set

$$x_b = x_t$$
$$x_t = x_p'$$

Go to step 5.
- **b.** No: Set

$$x_b = x_t$$

Go to step 4.

The algorithm for the local exploration is as follows.

Step 1 Save the starting point x_b as x_e and denote the step size as h. Set $i = 1$.

Step 2 Is $f(x_b) \leq f(x_b + hu_i)$? Note that **u** is a unit vector that defines the positive direction for each of the variables.
- **a.** Yes: Is $f(x_b) > f(x_b - hu_i)$?
  - (i) Yes: Set $x_b = x_b - hu_i$. Go to step 3.
  - (ii) No: Go to step 3.
- **b.** No: Set $x_b = x_b + hu_i$. Go to step 3.

Step 3 Have all the variables been explored (i.e., $i = n$)?
- **a.** Yes: Terminate exploration.
- **b.** No: Explore the next variable, i.e., set $i = i + 1$. Go to step 2.

A flowchart for easy programming is given in Figure 8.3 and a sample program is given in Figure 8.4.

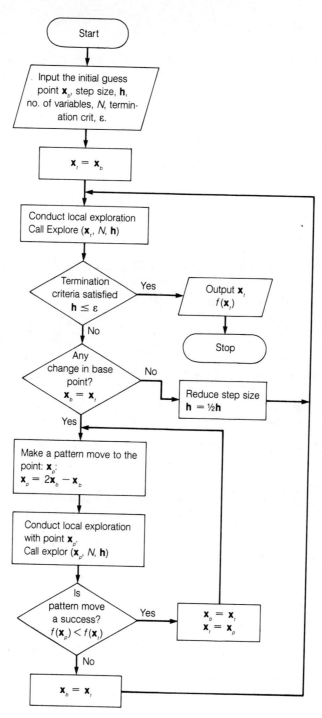

FIGURE 8.3

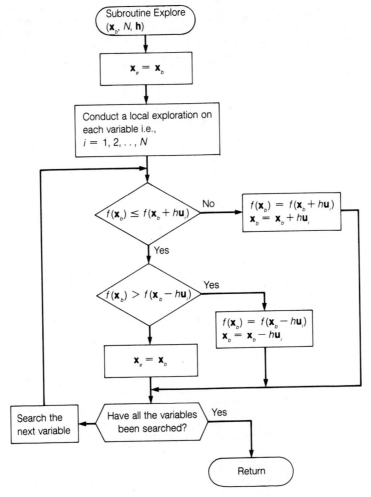

Note: $\mathbf{u}$ = directional unit vector.

FIGURE 8.3

(Continued).

```
*****************************************************************
*    THIS PROGRAM USES HOOKES AND JEEVES SEARCH METHOD          *
*    TO OPTIMIZE A GIVEN FUNCTION.   IT CAN BE USED FOR CONS-   *
*    TRAINED OPTIMIZATION.                                      *
*                                                              *
*****************************************************************
*
* .............................................................*
* VARIABLES:                                                    *
*        xbase:=   the value of the design variables for each   *
*                  iteration.  Initial guess is entered as  a   *
*                  xbase point.                                 *
*        xtemp:=   the value of design variable at intermediate *
*                  steps.                                       *
*        xpatn:=   the value of design variable for pattern     *
*                  search.                                      *
*        step: =   step size for each iteration.               *
*        iter: =   no. of iterations                           *
*        Tol : =   termination criteria                        *
*          N : =   no of design variables                      *
*          yes: =  variable for testing if xtemp is not same   *
*                  xbase.                                       *
*        Term:=    termination condition set to zero at start   *
*                  and set to 1 if satisfied                   *
*        Xmin:=  min.value of  design variable.                 *
*        Xmax:=  max.value of  design variable.                 *
*        constr:= variable that sets the type of optimization  *
*                  Set to 1 if constrained else set to zero     *
*..............................................................*
*
          REAL XBASE(5),XTEMP(5),XPATN(5),STEP(5),XMIN(5),
     .    XMAX(5)
          REAL TOL
          INTEGER ITER,N,YES,TERM,CONSTR
          OPEN(6,FILE='PRN')
*
*   STEP 1:
*    Input the initial guess point, step size, and tolerance
* .............................................................
*
          WRITE(6,3)
    3     FORMAT(2X,'ITER',4X,'XB',8X,'XT',8X,'XP',6X,'F(XB)',
     .    5X,'F(XB+H)',5X,'F(XB-H)',4X,'STEP')
          N = 2
          DO 5 I = 1,N
          XBASE(I) = 2.0
          STEP(I) =  0.5
    5     CONTINUE
          TOL = 1.0E-4
          ITER = 1
          TERM = 0
          CONSTR = 0
          IF(CONSTR.EQ.0) THEN
             DO 7 I = 1,N
             XMAX(I) = 0.0
```

FIGURE 8.4
_____

A sample program for the Hooke and Jeeves method.

```
                    XMIN(I) = 0.0
    7            CONTINUE
             END IF
*
*    STEP 2:
*    Set the base point to the temporary point xtemp and conduct
*    a local exploration using subroutine explor.
*    ....................................................................
*
   10        DO 15 I = 1,N
             XTEMP(I) = XBASE(I)
   15        CONTINUE
   18        CALL EXPLOR(XTEMP,STEP,XMAX,XMIN,N,CONSTR,ITER)
*
*    STEP 3:
*    Test to determine if the termination criteria has been
*    satisfied.  If so stop. Otherwise, continue search.
*    ....................................................................
*
             DO 20 I = 1,N
             IF(STEP(I).LE.TOL) THEN
*                          Set term = 1 for output of solution

             TERM = 1
             END IF
   20        CONTINUE
*
             IF((TERM.EQ.0).AND.(ITER.EQ.1)) THEN
*                          The initial guess is not good
                 WRITE(6,21)
   21            FORMAT('  THE INITIAL GUESS IS NOT A GOOD ONE
                 TRY ANOTHER')
                 GO TO 300
             END IF
*
             IF(TERM.EQ.1)THEN
*                          output the solution
             OPTIMI = EVA(XTEMP,N)
             WRITE(6,22)
   22        FORMAT(2X,' THE SOLUTION OF THE OPTIMIZATION IS:')
             WRITE(6,23)(I,XTEMP(I), I = 1,N)
   23        FORMAT(2('    X(',I2,') = ',F10.6))
             WRITE(6,25)OPTIMI,ITER
   25        FORMAT('  THE OPTIMUM VALUE OF THE FUNCTION IS:'/
    .        20X,E14.7,'    NO.OF ITERATIONS =',I3)
             GO TO 300
             END IF
*
*    STEP 4:
*    Determine if the new point is different from the starting
*    base point.  If so make a pattern move. Otherwise, reduce
*    step size and repeat local exploration.
*    ....................................................................
*
             YES = 0
```

FIGURE 8.4

(Continued).

```
             DO 35 I = 1,N
             IF(XBASE(I).NE.XTEMP(I)) THEN
                    YES = 1
             END IF
  35         CONTINUE
  70         IF(YES.EQ.1) THEN
  *                                                STEP 5:
  *                                      Make a pattern move to
  *      the point  defined by 2*xtemp - xbase.
  *

             DO 80  I = 1,N
             XPATN(I) = 2*XTEMP(I) - XBASE(I)
             WRITE(6,82)XPATN(I)
  *
  *    If problem is constrained then test that constraints are
  *    not violated.
  *

             IF(CONSTR.EQ.1)THEN
                    CALL CONSTN(XPATN,I,XMAX,XMIN,N)
             END IF
  *
  80          CONTINUE
  82          FORMAT(26X,F9.6)
  *
  *  STEP 6:
  *    Conduct a local exploration using the newly defined point
  *    xpatn.
  *

             CALL EXPLOR(XPATN,STEP,XMAX,XMIN,N,CONSTR,ITER)
             DO 84 I = 1,N
             WRITE(6,86)ITER,XPATN(I),STEP(I)
  84          CONTINUE
  86          FORMAT(2X,I3,22X,F9.6,28X,F7.6)
  *
  *  STEP 7:
  *    Test if pattern move is a success . If so establish a new
  *    base point.  Otherwise abandon the temporary base point
  *    and repeat local exploration.
  *

             FXTEMP = EVA(XTEMP,N)
             FXPATN = EVA(XPATN,N)
                IF(FXPATN.LT.FXTEMP) THEN
                       DO 100 I = 1,N
                       XBASE(I) = XTEMP(I)
                       XTEMP(I) = XPATN(I)
  100                  CONTINUE
                       GO TO 70
                ELSE
                       DO 110 I = 1,N
                       XBASE(I) = XTEMP(I)
  110                  CONTINUE
                       GO TO 18
                END IF
         ELSE
             DO 45 I = 1,N
```

FIGURE 8.4

(Continued).

```
                          STEP(I) = 0.5*STEP(I)
    45                    CONTINUE
                          GO TO 18
              END IF
*
   300        CONTINUE
              END
```
* ....
*   SUBROUTINE EXPLOR IS FOR LOCAL EXPLORATION.
*
* ....
*
```
              SUBROUTINE EXPLOR(EBASE,ESTEP,EMAX,EMIN,N,ECONS,ITER)
              REAL EBASE(5),ETEMP(5),ESTEP(5),EMAX(5),EMIN(5)
              REAL FO,FF,FB
              INTEGER ITER,ECONS,N
```
*
*   Set the base point to a temporary point.
*
```
              DO 200 I = 1,N
              ETEMP(I) = EBASE(I)
   200        CONTINUE
```
*
*   Evaluate the objective function at the base point
*
```
              FO = EVA(ETEMP,N)
```
*   Evaluate the objective function at a point a step from
*   the base point.
*
```
              DO 210 I = 1,N
              EBASE(I) = ETEMP(I) + ESTEP(I)
```
*
*   If problem is constrained then test that constraints are
*   not violated.
*
```
              IF(ECONS.EQ.1)THEN
                     CALL CONSTN(EBASE,I,EMAX,EMIN,N)
              END IF
```
*
```
              FF = EVA(EBASE,N)
```
*
*...
*   Test if the new point is better than the original point.
*
```
              WRITE(6,212)ITER,EBASE(I),FO,FF,ESTEP(I)
   212        FORMAT(2X,I3,2X,F9.6,20X,F9.6,1X,F9.6,15X,F7.5)
              IF(FO.LE.FF) THEN
```
*   take a step in the reverse direction.
*   and re-evaluate the objective function
*
```
                  EBASE(I) = ETEMP(I) - ESTEP(I)
```
*
*   If problem is constrained then test that constraints are
*   not violated.
*

FIGURE 8.4
_____

(Continued).

```
            IF(ECONS.EQ.1)THEN
                CALL CONSTN(EBASE,I,EMAX,EMIN,N)
            END IF
                FB = EVA(EBASE,N)
            WRITE(6,214)ITER,EBASE(I),FO,FB,ESTEP(I)
  214       FORMAT(2X,I3,2X,F9.6,20X,F9.6,10X,F9.6,3X,F7.6)
*
*   Test if new point is a better point.
*
            IF(FO.GT.FB) THEN
*                         take the new point as a base point
*                         for the variable being considered.
*
                 FO = FB
            ELSE
*                still retain the old base point
*
                 EBASE(I) = ETEMP(I)
            END IF
        ELSE IF(FO.GT.FF) THEN
*                         take point as better than base pt.
*
                 FO = FF
        ELSE
*                exploration is a failure retain the base point.
*
                 EBASE(I) = ETEMP(I)
        END IF
  210   CONTINUE
        DO 250 I = 1 ,N
        WRITE(6,252)ITER,EBASE(I),ESTEP(I)
  250   CONTINUE
  252   FORMAT(2X,I3,11X,F9.6,40X,F7.6)
        ITER = ITER + 1
        RETURN
        END
*
*.................................................................
*   Begin testing for constraints using subroutine CONSTN.
*.................................................................
        SUBROUTINE CONSTN(CBASE,J,CMAX,CMIN,N)
            REAL CBASE(N),CMAX(N),CMIN(N)
            IF(CBASE(J).GT.CMAX(J))THEN
*                         adjust the base point accordingly
                 CBASE(J) = CMAX(J)
            END IF
*
            IF(CBASE(J).LT.CMIN(J))THEN
                 CBASE(J) = CMIN(J)
            END IF
            RETURN
            END
*
*   Define the objective function
*
```

FIGURE 8.4

(Continued).

```
REAL FUNCTION EVA(D,N)
REAL D(5)
INTEGER N
EVA = D(1)**2*D(2) + D(1)*D(2)**2 - 3*D(1)*D(2)
RETURN
END
```

FIGURE 8.4

(Continued).

E X A M P L E   8.1

Find the minimum of the function

$$f(x_1, x_2) = x_1^2 x_2 + x_1 x_2^2 - 3x_1 x_2$$

starting at the point (2, 2) with a stopping criteria of $\varepsilon = \frac{1}{8}$. Use the Hooke and Jeeves pattern search.

Given: $x_0 = (2, 2)$, $h_0 = (0.5, 0.5)$ $\varepsilon = \frac{1}{8}$

SOLUTION We denote success with S and failure with F.

Step 1 We begin our search by first conducting a local exploration. The initial base point $x_0 = (2, 2)$. We make local exploration on x_1, keep x_2 constant by evaluating $f(2, 2)$, $f(x_1 + h, x_2)$ and $f(x_1 - h, x_2)$

$$f(2, 2) = 4.0$$

$$f(2.5, 2) = 7.5 \quad \text{(F)}$$

$$f(1.5, 2) = 1.5 \quad \text{(S)}$$

Since $f(2.5, 2) > f(2, 2)$ and $f(1.5, 2) < f(2, 2)$, the temporary base point $x_0^t = (1.5, 2)$. Next we conduct a local exporation on x_2 by evaluating $f(x_1, x_2 + h)$ and $f(x_1, x_2 - h)$:

$$f(1.5, 2.5) = 3.75 \quad \text{(F)}$$

$$f(1.5, 1.5) = 0.00 \quad \text{(S)}$$

Since $f(1.5, 1.5 < f(1.5, 2)$ our new base point $x_1 = (1.5, 1.5)$.

Step 2 We want to make a pattern search. The pattern point is determined by

$$x_{p,1} = 2x_1 - x_o = (1, 1)$$

We evaluate $f(\mathbf{x}_{p,1})$; that is, $f(1, 1) = -1.0$.

Since $f(\mathbf{x}_{p,1}) < f(\mathbf{x}_1)$, we make a pattern move to $\mathbf{x}_{p,1}$. For the next cycle of iteration $\mathbf{x}_2 = \mathbf{x}_{p,1} = (1, 1)$.

We conduct a local exploration on $\mathbf{x}_1$ starting at a base point $\mathbf{x}_2$:

$$f(1, 1) = -1.0$$

$$f(1.5, 1) = -0.7499 \quad \textbf{(F)}$$

$$f(0.5, 1) = -0.75 \quad \textbf{(F)}$$

Both $f(1.5, 1)$ and $f(0.5, 1)$ are greater than $f(1, 1)$; therefore, there is no improvement in the function. We must return to the base point $\mathbf{x}_2$ and explore on $\mathbf{x}_2$:

$$f(1, 1.5) = -0.7499 \quad \textbf{(F)}$$

$$f(1, 0.5) = -0.75 \quad \textbf{(F)}$$

Again, there is no improvement on the function, and the step size is greater than the desired accuracy. We reduce the step size and repeat our exploration from the base point $\mathbf{x}_2$. The new step size is given as

$$\mathbf{h}_2 = 0.5\mathbf{h}_0 = (0.25, 0.25)$$

Conducting local exploration on $\mathbf{x}_1$ gives:

$$f(1, 1) = -1$$

$$f(1.25, 1) = -0.9375 \quad \textbf{(F)}$$

$$f(0.75, 1) = -0.9375 \quad \textbf{(F)}$$

and local exploration on $\mathbf{x}_2$ results:

$$f(1, 1.25) = -0.9375 \quad \textbf{(F)}$$

$$f(1, 0.75) = -0.9375 \quad \textbf{(F)}$$

Exploration results in failure in both $\mathbf{x}_1$ and $\mathbf{x}_2$, so we reduce the step size by half and repeat our local exploration. Exploring on $\mathbf{x}_1$, the step size now being 0.125 results in

$$f(1, 1) = -1.0$$

$$f(1.125, 1) = -0.98447 \quad \textbf{(F)}$$

$$f(.875, 1) = -0.9844 \quad \textbf{(F)}$$

Exploring on x_2 gives

$$f(1, 1.25) = -0.9844 \quad \text{(F)}$$
$$f(1, 0.875) = -0.9844 \quad \text{(F)}$$

Once more, failure results, since no improvement is realized in the function, and the step size is equal to the desire tolerance. The search terminates, giving the following:

$$x_1 = 1.0$$
$$x_2 = 1.0$$
$$f_{\min} = -1.0$$

With differential calculus, the solution obtained can be shown to be correct.

8.4 POWELL'S METHOD

In 1964, Powell [2] presented a very powerful method of multivariable optimization. **Powell's conjugate direction method,** which is an extension of the pattern search, is based on the concept of conjugate directions. In theory, the method will find the minimum of a quadratic function in a finite number of steps. Since this method involves minimizing a given function along a defined line, we examine it in detail, using Powell's algorithm.

POWELL'S METHOD OF QUADRATIC INTERPOLATION

Effective use of Powell's method of optimization requires that the minimum of a quadratic function be determined. We therefore examine Powell's algorithm in this section, and in the section dealing with gradient methods we simply apply the result of this section. The ensuing discussion is based primarily on the original work by Powell.

Suppose that it is desired to minimize a function $f(\mathbf{x})$ along a line $\mathbf{x} = \mathbf{x}_1 + \lambda \mathbf{d}$, where $\mathbf{x}_1$ is the current point and $\mathbf{d}$ is a given search direction. Powell's. method consists of finding a quadratic function $f(\lambda)$ that has the same values as $f(\mathbf{x}_1 + \lambda \mathbf{d})$ for three current values of λ. The value of λ that minimizes $f(\lambda)$ replaces one of the three current values of λ. This process is continued in each iteration process until a prescribed accuracy is achieved.

Let the three points on the line $\mathbf{x}_1 + \lambda \mathbf{d}$ be $\mathbf{x}_1 + a\mathbf{d}$, $\mathbf{x}_1 + b\mathbf{d}$, and $\mathbf{x}_1 + c\mathbf{d}$; furthermore, let the values of the function at the three points be defined as follows:

$$f_a = f(\mathbf{x}_1 + a\mathbf{d}) \tag{8.3}$$

$$f_b = f(\mathbf{x}_1 + b\mathbf{d}) \tag{8.4}$$

$$f_c = f(\mathbf{x}_1 + c\mathbf{d}) \tag{8.5}$$

Assume that the quadratic function is of the form

$$f(\lambda) = f_0 + f_1\lambda + f_2\lambda^2 \tag{8.6}$$

Then

$$f_a = f(a) = f_0 + f_1 a + f_2 a^2 \tag{8.7}$$

$$f_b = f(b) = f_0 + f_1 b + f_2 b^2 \tag{8.8}$$

$$f_c = f(c) = f_0 + f_1 c + f_2 c^2 \tag{8.9}$$

Equations (8.7) through (8.9) consist of three simultaneous equations that can easily be solved, giving:

$$f_0 = \frac{bc(c - b)f_a + ac(a - c)f_b + ab(b - a)f_c}{(a - b)(b - c)(c - a)} \tag{8.10}$$

$$f_1 = \frac{(b^2 - c^2)f_a + (c^2 - a^2)f_b + (a^2 - b^2)f_c}{(a - b)(b - c)(c - a)} \tag{8.11}$$

$$f_2 = \frac{(c - b)f_a + (a - c)f_b + (b - a)f_c}{(a - b)(b - c)(c - a)} \tag{8.12}$$

Differentiating equation (8.6) with respect to λ and setting the derivative equal to zero reveals that the critical point is at

$$\lambda = -\frac{f_1}{2f_2}$$

and it is the minimum value if $f_2 > 0$. If we define the minimum λ as λ_m, using equations (8.11) and (8.12) gives

$$\lambda_m = \frac{0.5[(b^2 - c^2)f_a + (c^2 - a^2)f_b + (a^2 - b^2)f_c]}{(b - c)f_a + (c - a)f_b + (a - b)f_c} \tag{8.13}$$

and $f(\lambda)$ has a minimum if

$$\frac{(b - c)f_a + (c - a)f_b + (a - b)f_c}{(a - b)(b - c)(c - a)} < 0 \tag{8.14}$$

Having found the minimum value λ_m, with an initial point x_1 and a direction of search d, minimizing a function $f(x)$ along a line $x = x_1 + \lambda d$ by Powell's algorithm involves the following steps.

Step 1 Select a step length defined as $h|d| - h$ (a scalar). The vector d, a direction vector, is not necessarily a unit vector, although the use of unit vectors is highly desirable. Set a maximum permissible step size, M. Set the allowable tolerance ε. Select an appropriate starting point x_1.

Step 2 Evaluate the function at two points x_1 and $x_1 + hd$.

Step 3 Perform a test; if $f(x_1) < f(x_1 + hd)$ then evaluate $f(x_1 - hd)$; otherwise go to step 4. The three points are now x_1, $x_1 + hd$, and $x_1 - hd$. Set $a = 0$, $b = h$, and $c = -h$; go to step 5.

Step 4 Evaluate $f(x_1 + 2hd)$; the three points on the line $x = x_1 + \lambda d$ are now x_1, $x_1 + hd$, and $x_1 + 2hd$. Set $a = 0$, $b = h$, and $c = 2h$.

Step 5 Find the turning point λ_m using equation (8.13)

Step 6 Test to determine which point to discard or if a minimum value has been attained. If the turning point is a maximum (i.e., if equation 8.14 > 0) or if the turning point is a minimum and the nearest of the three points from the turning point is at a distance greater than the permissible maximum step M, then go to step 8. Otherwise go to step 7.

Step 7 Test if the difference between the nearest of the three points from the turning point is at a distance less than or equal to the specified tolerance. If so, go to step 9. Otherwise, discard the point with the maximum function value and replace it with the turning point. Of course, the point with maximum function should not be discarded if doing so would result in the loss in the bracket of the minimum. Return to step 5.

Step 8 Discard one of the three current points, according to whether the turning point is a minimum or a maximum.

   a. If the turning point is a minimum, take a step of Md from the nearest of the three points. Replace a, b, or c with M, depending on which corresponds to the discarded point. Return to step 5.

   b. If the turning point is a maximum, then take a step of Md from the point farthest from the turning point. Replace a, b, or c with M, depending on which corresponds to the discarded point. Return to step 5.

Step 9 Output the result of the search as $x = x_1 + \lambda_m d$.

It is of interest to note that if an equal step is taken from either side of the origin, say $b = 0$, $a = -1$, $c = 1$, then equation (8.13) reduces to

$$\lambda_m = \frac{f_a - f_c}{2(f_a - 2f_b + f_c)} \tag{8.15}$$

and from equations (8.3) through (8.5), (8.6) through (8.9), and (8.15)

$$f(\lambda_m) = f_b - \frac{(f_a - f_c)^2}{8(f_a - 2f_b + f_c)} \tag{8.16}$$

In order to reduce the number of function evaluations in the Powell technique, the second derivative;

$$\frac{\delta^2}{\delta^2\lambda} \ \{f(\mathbf{x}_1 + \lambda\mathbf{d})\}$$

is predicted using

$$D = 2f_2 = \frac{2[(c - b)f_a + (a - c)f_b + (b - a)f_c]}{(a - b)\ (b - c)\ c - a)} \tag{8.17}$$

Subtracting equation (8.8) from (8.7), we obtain

$$f_a - f_b = f_1(a - b) + f_2(a^2 - b^2) \tag{8.18}$$

Using equation (8.18) and the fact that

$$\lambda_m = \frac{f_1}{2f_2}$$

equation (8.18) becomes

$$\lambda_m = 0.5(a + b) - \frac{(f_a - f_b)}{D\ (a - b)} \tag{8.19}$$

Equation (8.19) can be used for the second and subsequent searches, the next time a minimum is sought in the same direction **d**.

A flowchart for quadratic interpolation based on Powell's method is given in Figure 8.5, and a sample program is listed in Figure 8.6.

Although we have given a flowchart based on Powell's method, this chart must be used with caution. Powell's method does not always converge to the minimum of a quadratic in a finite number of steps. Realizing this problem, Powell proposed a modification to his original algorithm. Zangwill [3] also suggested a modification to Powell's algorithm to alleviate the problem of linear dependence, which is the reason for not obtaining convergence in a finite number of iterations. However, the method suggested by Powell is preferable to that of Zangwill. Further information on the problem of linear dependence and how to avoid it can be obtained from books by Brent [4] and by Jacoby et al. [5].

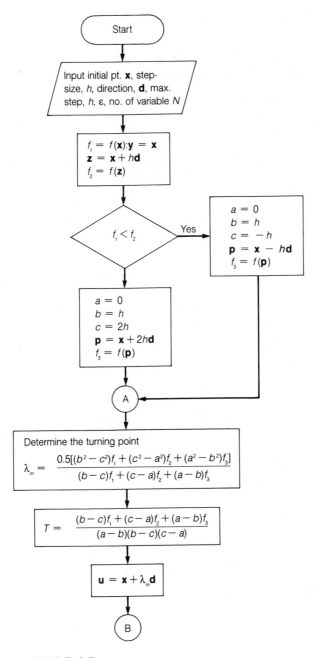

FIGURE 8.5

A flowchart for Powell's line search.

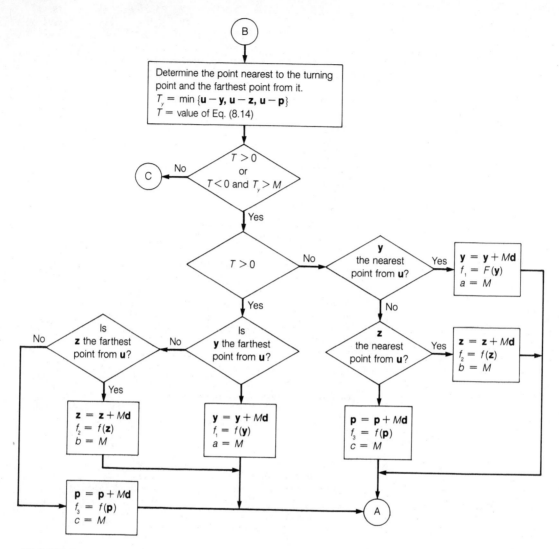

FIGURE 8.5

(Continued).

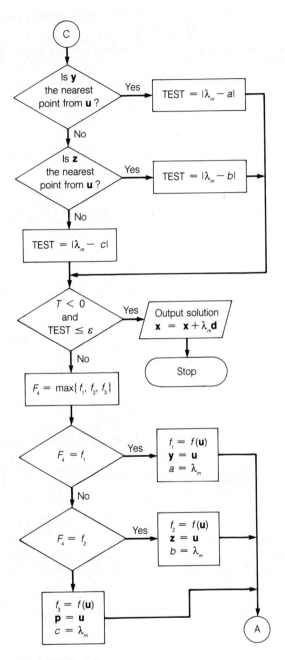

FIGURE 8.5

(Continued).

```
********************************************************************
*              POWELL'S LINEAR SEARCH                             *
*    This program  uses Powell's method of line search           *
*    to determine the minimum of a function in a given           *
*    direction.                                                  *
*                                                                *
********************************************************************
*                                                                *
* --------------------------------------------------------------*
*    VARIABLES:                                                  *
*                x :=   design variables                         *
*                xo:=   temporary replacement for x              *
*                y :=   base point for each iteration cycle      *
*                h :=   step size                                *
*                dr,ds:= search direction                        *
*                z := a point step size away from y              *
*                u : = the turning point                         *
*                p := a point 2*step size away from y            *
*                f1:= value of objective function at pt. y       *
*                f2:= value of objective function at pt. z       *
*                f3:= value of objective function at pt. p       *
*                a,b,c := replacement values for step sizes      *
*                ql:=  the turning point                         *
*                fq:=  value of objective function at ql         *
*                s1,s2,s3 : = distances from y,z,p to ql         *
*                ty := min(s1,s2,s3)                             *
*                tl := max(s1,s2,s3)                             *
*                t2 := test for min. or. max of function at u    *
*                m:= maximum step to be taken in any direction   *
*                l := counter for no. of function evaluations    *
*                iter:= no. of iteration cycles                  *
*                object: = objective function                   *
*                tol:= termination criteria                      *
*                                                                *
* --------------------------------------------------------------
*                          MODULE 2                              *
* --------------------------------------------------------------*
        REAL X(10),XO(10),Z(10),U(10),Y(10),DS(10),DR(10,10),
   .    P(10)
        REAL A,B,C,F1,F2,F3,F4,FQ,H,QL,T2,G,M
        REAL T1,TY,S1,S2,S3,NUM1,NUM2,NUM3,TOL,LS,DSS
        INTEGER L,N
        COMMON X,XO,Z,U,DS,DR,P,A,B,C,F1,F2,F3,FQ,H,QL,T2,
   .    N,M,G,TY,Y,F4,T1,S1,S2,S3,L
*................................................................
*    Enter data
*
        TOL = .001
*
*   Begin search along each direction
*
*
*    Establish that the chosen step size is appropriate.
*    If the step size is so big then use the smallest value
```

FIGURE 8.6

A sample program for Powell's line search.

```
*       of the size direction.
*
              LS = 1.0E10
              DO 3 I = 1,N
                  DSS = ABS(DS(I))
                      IF(DSS.NE.0.0) THEN
                                  IF(DSS.LT.LS) THEN
                                      LS = DSS
                                  ELSE
                                      CONTINUE
                                  END IF
                      ELSE
                                  CONTINUE
                      END IF
3             CONTINUE
              IF(LS.LT.H) THEN
                  H = LS
              ELSE
                  CONTINUE
              END IF
*       End procedure for checking appropriateness of step size.
*
*       STEPS 1 AND 2:
*                   Set the initial point x equal to xo and the
*                   search direction dr to ds. Establish the base
*                   point y.  Evaluate objective function at a point
*                   a step size H from y.
* ................................................................
*
5             CONTINUE
                  DO 10 I = 1,N
                      XO(I) = X(I)
                      Y(I) = X(I)
                      Z(I) = XO(I) + H*DS(I)
10                CONTINUE
              F1 = EVA(Y,N)
              F2 = EVA(Z,N)
*
* ................................................................
*
*       STEP 3:
*                   Perform a test to  determine if the point at 2*step
*                   size away from the base point or a point a step size
*                   in the reverse direction should be selected as the
*                   third point.
* ................................................................
              IF(F1.LT.F2) THEN
                  DO 15 I = 1,N
                      P(I) = XO(I) - H*DS(I)
15                CONTINUE
                  A = 0.0
                  B = H
                  C = - H
                  GO TO 25
              ELSE
                  DO 20 I = 1,N
```

F I G U R E 8.6

(Continued).

```
                          P(I) = XO(I) + 2*H*DS(I)
   20         CONTINUE
              A = 0.0
              B = H
              C = 2*H
          END IF
*
   25       CONTINUE
            F3 = EVA(P,N)
*.............................................................
*       STEP 4:
*           Determine the turning point using the three points
*           obtained above(steps 2 and 3).
*.............................................................
   27       CONTINUE
            NUM1 = 0.5*((B*B - C*C)*F1 + (C*C -A*A)*F2 + (A*A - B*
        .      B)*F3)
            NUM2 = ((B - C)*F1 + (C - A)*F2 + (A - B)*F3)
            NUM3 = (A - B)*(B - C)*(C - A)
*
*       Check and see if the chosen direction contains a minimum
*       if not print an error message.  Otherwise determine the
*       turning point.
*
            IF((NUM2.EQ.0.0). OR. (NUM3.EQ.0.0)) THEN
                     WRITE(6,30)J
   30                FORMAT('FAILURE IN DIRECTION',I2)
                     GO TO 90
            ELSE
                     QL = NUM1/NUM2
                     G = QL
                     T2 = NUM2/NUM3
            END IF
*
*     Determine the distance between each of the three points and
*     turning point.
*
            S1 = 0.0
            S2 = 0.0
            S3 = 0.0
            DO 35 I = 1,N
                U(I) = XO(I) + QL*DS(I)
                S1 = S1 + (U(I) - Y(I))**2
                S2 = S2 + (U(I) - Z(I))**2
                S3 = S3 + (U(I) - P(I))**2
   35       CONTINUE
            S1 = S1**0.5
            S2 = S2**0.5
            S3 = S3**0.5
*
*     Evaluate the objective function at the turning point.
*
            FQ = EVA(U,N)
*
*     Determine which of the three points that is nearest to
```

FIGURE 8.6

(Continued).

```
*       the turning point and save the shortest distance as TY.
*
        TY = AMIN1(S1,S2,S3)
*
*   Determine the point furthest from the turning point and
*   save it as T1.
*
        T1 = AMAX1(S1,S2,S3)
*
* ...............................................................
*       STEPS 5 AND 6:
*   Determine if any of the selected three points should be
*   replaced with the turning point or if termination criteria
*   has been satisfied. Check if in calculating the turning pt.
*   a step greater than M (max. allowable) has been taken.
* ...............................................................
*
        IF((T2.GT.0.0).OR.((T2.LT.0.0).AND.(TY.GT.M))) THEN
                CALL TEST1
                L = L + 1
                GO TO 27
        ELSE
                IF(TY.EQ.S1) THEN
                        TEST = ABS(QL - A)
                ELSE IF(TY.EQ.S2) THEN
                        TEST = ABS(QL - B)
                ELSE
                        TEST = ABS(QL - C)
                END IF
        END IF
*
*   If the turning point is a minimum and the termination cri-
*   teria is met then compute the new value of x in the given
*   search direction.  Otherwise continue the search.
*
        IF((T2.LT.0.0).AND.(TEST.LE.TOL)) THEN
                GO TO 60
        ELSE
*               Determine the highest function value
*
                F4 = AMAX1(F1,F2,F3)
                CALL TEST3
                L = L + 1
                GO TO 27
        END IF
60      CONTINUE
*
        IF(TEST.EQ.ABS(QL - A)) THEN
                QL = 0.5*(QL + A)
        ELSE IF(TEST.EQ.ABS(QL - B)) THEN
                QL = 0.5*(QL + B)
        ELSE
                QL = 0.5*(QL + C)
        END IF
*
```

F I G U R E 8.6

(Continued).

```
*     Determine a new point which is the minimum in the given
*     search direction.
*
          DO 67 I = 1,N
             XO(I) = XO(I) + QL*DS(I)
              X(I) = XO(I)
  67      CONTINUE
*
          FOPT = EVA(XO,N)
*
*     Output result of search
*
          DO 83 I = 1,N
             WRITE(6,87)I,XO(I)
  83      CONTINUE
  87      FORMAT(3X,'X(',I2,') = ',F10.6)
          WRITE(6,89)FOPT
  89      FORMAT(5X,'THE MINIMUM VALUE OF OBJECTIVE FUNCTION
      .   IS:   ',E14.7)
  90      RETURN
          END
          SUBROUTINE TEST1
*
* ------------------------------------------------------------
*              MODULE 3
*     This subroutine determines from which point the maximum
*     allowable step should be taken.
* ------------------------------------------------------------
*
          REAL X(10),XO(10),Z(10),U(10),Y(10),DS(10),DR(10,10),
      .   P(10)
          REAL A,B,C,F1,F2,F3,F4,FQ,H,QL,T2,G,M
          REAL T1,TY,S1,S2,S3,NUM1,NUM2,NUM3,TOL,LS,DSS
          INTEGER L,N
          COMMON X,XO,Z,U,DS,DR,P,A,B,C,F1,F2,F3,FQ,H,QL,T2,
      .   N,M,G,TY,Y,F4,T1,S1,S2,S3
*
          IF(T2.GT.0.0) THEN
                CALL TEST2
*
          ELSE IF(TY.EQ.S1) THEN
*                           Take the max. step from pt. Y
                A = M
                DO 75 I = 1,N
                   Y(I) = Y(I) + M*DS(I)
  75            CONTINUE
                F1 = EVA(Y,N)
          ELSE IF(TY.EQ.S2) THEN
*                           Take the max. step from pt Z
                B = M
                DO 80 I = 1,N
                   Z(I) = Z(I) + M*DS(I)
  80            CONTINUE
                F2 = EVA(Z,N)
          ELSE
```

FIGURE 8.6

(Continued).

```
*                           Take the max. step from pt. P.
                        C = M
                        DO 85 I = 1,N
                           P(I) = P(I) + M*DS(I)
     85                 CONTINUE
                        F3 = EVA(P,N)
              END IF
                        RETURN
              END
              SUBROUTINE TEST2
*  ..................................................................
*  This subroutine determines from which point to take the
*  the maximum allowable step since the turning point is a
*   maximum.
*  ..................................................................
              REAL X(10),XO(10),Z(10),U(10),Y(10),DS(10),DR(10,10),
     .  P(10)
              REAL A,B,C,F1,F2,F3,F4,FQ,H,QL,T2,G,M
              REAL T1,TY,S1,S2,S3,NUM1,NUM2,NUM3,TOL,LS,DSS
              INTEGER L,N
              COMMON X,XO,Z,U,DS,DR,P,A,B,C,F1,F2,F3,FQ,H,QL,T2,
     .  N,M,G,TY,Y,F4,T1,S1,S2,S3
              IF(T1.EQ.S1) THEN
*                           Take the max. step from pt. Y.
                A = M
                DO 92 I = 1,N
                   Y(I) = Y(I) + M*DS(I)
     92         CONTINUE
                F1 = EVA(Y,N)
              ELSE IF(T1.EQ.S2) THEN
*                           Take the max. step from pt Z.
                B  = M
                DO 95 I = 1,N
                Z(I) = Z(I) + M*DS(I)
     95         CONTINUE
                F2 = EVA(Z,N)
              ELSE
*                     Take the max. step from pt P.
                C = M
                DO 100 I = 1,N
                P(I) = P(I) + M*DS(I)
    100         CONTINUE
                F3 = EVA(P,N)
              END IF
                RETURN
              END
              SUBROUTINE TEST3
*
* ..................................................................
*  This subroutine determines which point is to be replaced
*  with the turning point.
* ..................................................................
*
              REAL X(10),XO(10),Z(10),U(10),Y(10),DS(10),DR(10,10),
     .  P(10)
```

FIGURE 8.6

(Continued).

```
      REAL A,B,C,F1,F2,F3,F4,FQ,H,QL,T2,G,M
      REAL T1,TY,S1,S2,S3,NUM1,NUM2,NUM3,TOL,LS,DSS
      INTEGER L,N
      COMMON X,XO,Z,U,DS,DR,P,A,B,C,F1,F2,F3,FQ,H,QL,T2,
     N,M,G,TY,Y,F4,T1
      IF(T2.GT.0.0) THEN
          CONTINUE
      ELSE
          CALL TEST4
      END IF
      IF(F4.EQ.F1) THEN
*                        Replace pt. Y with the turning pt.
       F1 = FQ
       A = QL
       DO 120 I = 1,N
          Y(I) = U(I)
  120     CONTINUE
      ELSE IF(F4.EQ.F2) THEN
*                        Replace pt. Z with the turning pt.
       F2 = FQ
       B = QL
       DO 125 I = 1,N
        Z(I) = U(I)
  125     CONTINUE
      ELSE
*                Replace point P with the turning point
       F3 = FQ
       C = QL
       DO 130 I = 1,N
        P(I) = U(I)
  130     CONTINUE
      END IF
      RETURN
      END
      SUBROUTINE TEST4
* ...................................................
* Subroutine checks if the barracket in the minimum is lost
* by discarding the point with maximum function
* ...................................................
*
      REAL X(10),XO(10),Z(10),U(10),Y(10),DS(10),DR(10,10),
     . P(10)
      REAL A,B,C,F1,F2,F3,F4,FQ,H,QL,T2,G,M
      REAL T1,TY,S1,S2,S3,NUM1,NUM2,NUM3,TOL,LS,DSS
      INTEGER L,N
      COMMON X,XO,Z,U,DS,DR,P,A,B,C,F1,F2,F3,FQ,H,QL,T2,
     . N,M,G,TY,Y,F4,T1
      IF(F4.EQ.F1) THEN
            IF(((B - G)*(G - A)).GT.0.0) THEN
              IF(((B - G)*(G - C)).GT.0.0) THEN
                IF(F2.GT.F3) THEN
                    F4 = F2
                ELSE
                    F4 = F3
                END IF
```

F I G U R E   8.6

(Continued).

```
                               ELSE
                                       F4 = F3
                               END IF
                       ELSE
*                              Discard point corresponding to A.
                               F4 = F1
                       END IF
*
*

               ELSE IF(F4.EQ.F2) THEN
                     IF(((A - G)*(G - B)).GT.0.0) THEN
                         IF(((A - G)*(G - C)).GT.0.0) THEN
                               IF(F1.GT.F3) THEN
                                  F4 = F1
                               ELSE
                                     F4 = F3
                               END IF
                         ELSE
                               F4 = F3
                         END IF
                     ELSE
*                              Discard the point corresponding to B.
                               F4 = F2
                     END IF
               ELSE
*
                     IF(F4.EQ.F3) THEN
                         IF(((A - G)*(G - C)).GT.0.0) THEN
                             IF(((A - G)*(G - B)).GT.0.0) THEN
                                   IF(F1.GT.F2) THEN
                                        F4 = F1
                                   ELSE
                                        F4 = F2
                                   END IF
                             ELSE
                                     F4 = F2
                             END IF
                         ELSE
*                              Discard the point corresponding to C.
                                   F4 = F3
                         END IF
                     END IF
               END IF
       END IF
               RETURN
       END
*
*...........................................................
*    Define the objective function
*...........................................................
*
       REAL FUNCTION EVA(R,N)
*
       REAL R(10)
       INTEGER N
*
```

FIGURE 8.6

(Continued).

$$\text{EVA} = R(1)**2*R(2) + R(1)*R(2)**2 - 3*R(1)*R(2)$$
$$\text{RETURN}$$
$$\text{END}$$

FIGURE 8.6

(Continued).

There is another method, developed by Davidon [6], of finding the minimum along a line. This method employs two points on the given line and the value of the directional derivatives of the objective function along the same line and at the same two points. This method is very useful if the evaluation of the derivatives of the function does not present undue difficulties.

E X A M P L E 8.2

Find the minimum value of $x_1^2 x_2 + x_1 x_2^2 - 3x_1 x_2$ using the starting point $\mathbf{x}_0 = [0.5, 0.5]$. Use $M = h = 1$ and $\varepsilon = 1 \times 10^{-4}$.

SOLUTION Let us begin the search by first seeking the minimum along the first direction, i.e., along the x_1 axis.

Step 1 Determine the step length and the search direction.

$$\text{step length} = h|\mathbf{d}| = [1.0 \quad 0.0]^T$$

Step 2 Evaluate the function at two points, $\mathbf{x}_0$ and $\mathbf{x}_0 + (h\mathbf{d})$

$$f_1 = f(0.5, 0.5) = -0.5$$
$$f_2 = f(1.5, 0.5) = -0.75$$

Steps 3 and 4 Perform a test: Since $f_1 > f_2$ we evaluate the function at the point $\mathbf{x}_0 + 2(h\mathbf{d})$:

$$f_3 = f(2.5, 0.5) = 0.0$$

Then

$$a = 0, \ b = h = 1.0, \ \text{and} \ \ c = 2h = 2.0$$

Therefore, the three points through which the quadratic function is being fitted are (0.5, 0.5), (1.5, 0.5), and (2.5, 0.5)

Step 5 Determine the turning point, using equation (8.13): Let $T =$ the value of equation (8.14). With $a = 0, b = 1, c = 2, f_1 = -0.5, f_2 = -0.75$, and $f_3 = 0$, we obtain $\lambda_m = 0.75$ and $T = -0.5$.

Step 6 Since $T = -0.5$ we know that the turning point is a minimum; therefore, we proceed to step 7.

Step 7 The nearest point to the turning point is (1.5, 0.5) and $|b - \lambda_m| = 0.25 > 0.001$. Therefore, we should discard the point with the largest value of the function. This point is (2.5, 0.5), but discarding it will lead to a loss of the bracket in the minimum. Instead, we discard the point (0.5, 0.5) and replace it with the turning point (1.25, 0.5). We return to step 5 to find another turning point. Repeating the entire process, we found a minimum point of (1.25, 0.5). Next we searched in the direction of $[0 \ 1]^T$ for a minimum point of (1.25, 0.875). The solution obtained is

$$\mathbf{x}^* = (1.25, 0.875) \text{ and } f_{\min} = -0.95703.$$

8.5 GRADIENT METHODS

The gradient methods for optimization of unconstrained problems are based on the fact that the fastest way of finding an extreme is to move along the gradient, which is a vector of directional derivative of a given function. The gradient methods differ from other search methods in the amount of computational work involved. In a search method, for example, only the evaluations of the objective functions are required, whereas some of the gradient methods may also require the evaluation of the derivatives of the objective functions. This drawback notwithstanding, the overall computational efficiency of some of the gradient methods is higher than some of the search methods, since application of the gradient methods leads to convergence in relatively fewer steps.

The gradient methods can generally be classified in two categories:

1. Those requiring the evaluation of derivatives of the objective functions. This would include such methods as the Davidon-Fletcher-Powell method [7] and the Fletcher-Reeves method [8].

2. Those not requiring the evaluation of derivatives. One of the most popular methods in this class is Powell's method. This class is preferred when the evaluation of the derivative of the function is extremely difficult, either because such an evaluation would be very time-consuming and probably inaccurate, or because no analytic expression can be found for the derivative.

In the next two sections, we briefly discuss the Fletcher-Reeves method and the Powell method. There are several reasons for treating these two methods. Firstly, both of these methods depend on the properties of conjugate directions. Although we have not treated the properties associated with the conjugate direction methods in this book, Powell's quadratic interpolation algorithm already discussed is based on the properties of conjugate direction. Further information on the topic can be found in a book by Murray [9]. Secondly, these two methods make use of the two routines given in Section 8.4. And thirdly, both methods have been demonstrated to be efficient in practice.

8.6 POWELL'S SEARCH METHOD

In Section 8.4, we discussed Powell's method for linear interpolation. Powell's method is a modification of a quadratic convergent method developed by Smith [10]. Of course, these methods, because they make use of some properties of conjugate directions, are able to converge to a solution in a finite number of steps for a positive definite quadratic function.

The application of Powell's initial algorithm to nonquadratic functions is plagued with serious defects. It fails to function if the directions of search are linearly dependent. This would easily be the case for nonquadratic functions and also for quadratic functions if the step size is zero. In addition, if the step size is very small, the next direction of search is very likely going to be colinear with the previous direction of search, creating the problem of linear dependence. Figure 8.7 illustrates the case in point. Note that linear dependence occurs if points 1 and 2 are close—that is, if $h = 0$. Powell modified his algorithm to avoid these difficulties while retaining the feature of quadratic convergence. This modification is a criterion for deciding whether to commence the search in a new direction or to reuse the old direction in the search process. The modified algorithm is given here.

Step 1 Define resolution ε, the initial base point $\mathbf{x}$, the function $D(\mathbf{x})$, and a direction of search $\mathbf{s}$. The direction of search should be defined to be parallel to the coordinate axes comprising the design space, i.e.,

$$s_{i,j} = \begin{cases} 1 & \text{if } i = j, \; i = 1, 2, \ldots, n \\ 0 & \text{otherwise}, j = 1, 2, \ldots, n \end{cases}$$

Step 2

a. Evaluate $D_1 = D(\mathbf{x})$. Save the starting point as $\mathbf{x}_b$, i.e.,

$$\mathbf{x}_b = \mathbf{x} \text{ and also set } F_0 = D_1.$$

b. Using Powell's method of quadratic interpolation, find the minimum along each direction $j = 1, 2, \ldots, n$ and $s_{i,j}, i = 1, 2, \ldots, n$. Set the minimum value of the objective function obtained in each direction as F_j. Let the resulting point after the nth direction be $\mathbf{x}$.

c. Determine the point $\mathbf{v}$ given by

$$\mathbf{v} = 2\mathbf{x} - \mathbf{x}_b$$

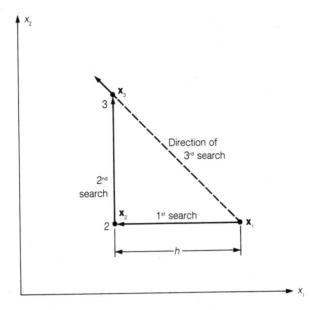

FIGURE 8.7

Illustration of problem of linear depending in Powell's method. (Note linear dependence can be experienced if h is very small, i.e., $\mathbf{x}_2 \approx \mathbf{x}_1$.)

Evaluate the objective function at two points $\mathbf{x}$ and $\mathbf{v}$ and designate the values D_2 and D_3, respectively—that is,

$$D_2 = D(\mathbf{x})$$
$$D_3 = D(\mathbf{v})$$

Step 3 Determine the direction that produced the maximum change in the objective function and denote the maximum function change as Δ, i.e.,

$$\Delta = \max\{F_{j-1} - F_j\}, \quad j = 1, 2, \ldots, n$$

and let this direction be *JC.*

Step 4 Determine if the search is to be continued in the old direction, a new direction is to be introduced, or termination criteria have been achieved, as follows. If

$$(D_1 - 2D_2 + D_3)(D_1 - D_2 - \Delta)^2 < \frac{\Delta(D_1 - D_3)^2}{2}$$

or

$$D_3 < D_1$$

then go to step 5, otherwise go to step 6.

Step 5 If $JC < n$, form a new direction of search, as follows:

$$s_{i,j} = s_{i,j+1}, \quad j = JC, JC + 1, \ldots, n - 1, i = 1, 2, \ldots, n$$

Otherwise continue.

Form a new search direction as follows:

$$s_{i,n} = \frac{\mathbf{x} - \mathbf{x}_b}{|\mathbf{x} - \mathbf{x}_b|}, i = 1, 2, \ldots, n$$

Note that the new direction $s_{i,n}$ has been normalized. Conduct a linear search using the newly formed direction. Again, denote the result of the search as $\mathbf{x}$ and $D_2 = D(\mathbf{x})$. If $D_3 < D_2$ (i.e., point $\mathbf{v}$ is a better point than $\mathbf{x}$) then replace $\mathbf{x}$ with $\mathbf{v}$. Go to step 7.

Step 6 If $D_2 \geq D_3$, then replace $\mathbf{x}$ with $\mathbf{v}$. Go to step 7.

Step 7 Check for termination criteria.

If $|\mathbf{x} - \mathbf{x}_b| \leq \varepsilon$, then go to step 8. Otherwise take the step size for the next line search as $0.4 \, (|D_1 - D_2|)^{1/2}$. Of course, the step size should be adjusted if it is greater than the maximum allowable step size as set in the line-search algorithm. Return to step 2.

Step 8 Output the result of search $\mathbf{x}$.

A flowchart using this Powell's modified algorithm is shown in Figure 8.8. A sample program is also presented in Figure 8.9.

In some cases the algorithm may terminate the search prematurely; to avoid such an occurrence, Powell has suggested a termination criteria. The details of this can be found in Powell's original paper or in the book by Jacoby et al. [5].

EXAMPLE 8.3

Find the minimum of Example 8.2, using the same starting point and a termination criterion of 1×10^{-6}

SOLUTION   **Step 1**   We begin our search by defining the initial search vector

$$s_1 = [1 \ 0]^T \quad \text{and} \quad s_2 = [0 \ 1]^T$$

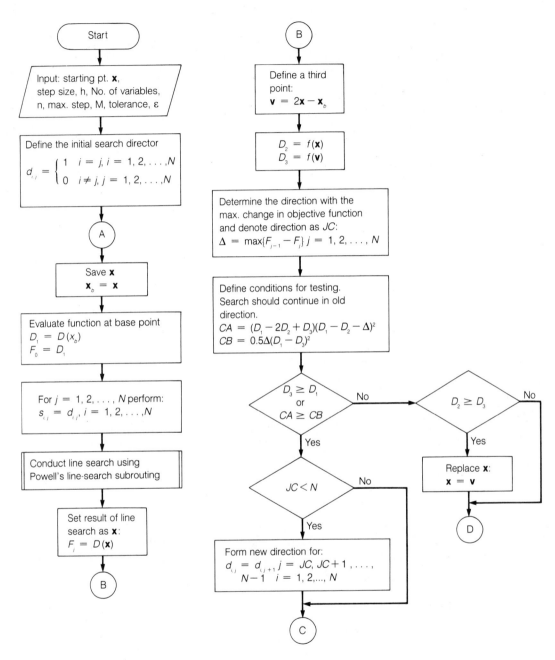

FIGURE 8.8

Flowchart for Powell's multivariable search.

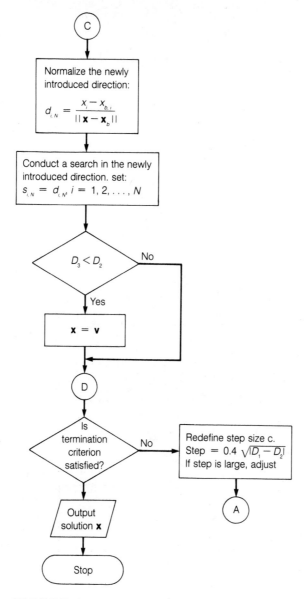

FIGURE 8.8

(Continued).

```
****************************************************************
*  This program uses Powell's modified algorithm to determine *
*  the minimum of a given function.                           *
****************************************************************
* ===========================================================*
*  Note:  To use this program you must use the appropriate    *
*         COMMON or CALL statements to communicate between    *
*         this main program and the Line search program       *
* ===========================================================*
*                                                             *
*-------------------------------------------------------------*
*                                                             *
*  Variables:                                                 *
*       x :=  A vector of design variables [x1,x2,..xN].      *
*     xo,xs := variables that replace the base point  for     *
*             each iteration.                                 *
*   xa,xb,xc : = variables to replace the base point if ult-  *
*             imate convergence test is to be applied.        *
*      v :=  a third point in the direction of the base       *
*             pt. and the final point for each iteration.     *
*     ds :=  direction of search in each iteration cylce.     *
*     dr :=  unit direction vector for the N-dimensional      *
*             space.                                          *
*    f():=  the value of the minimum value of the obj-        *
*             ctive function in each direction.               *
*      h:=  step size.                                        *
*    del:=  the max. change in funtion between direct-        *
*             ctions.                                         *
*   Pass:=  variable set to 1 if ultimate convergence         *
*             test is not required and to 2 if required.      *
*   Trip:=  variable set to 1 to show ultimate converg.       *
*             test is applied. Its value is changed inter-    *
*             nally to 2 when the ultimate converg. is        *
*             applied.                                        *
*  check:=  variable to check when termination criteria       *
*             has been satisfied.                             *
*   acc:=  desired tolerance.                                 *
*    dd:=  for normalizing search direction.                  *
*   iter:= counter                                            *
*-------------------------------------------------------------*
*
        REAL X(10),XO(10),DS(10),DR(10,10),XA(10),XB(10),
    .   XC(10),XS(10),F(10),V(10)
        REAL Y1,Y2,Y3,H,ACC,CA,CB,DEL,DD
        INTEGER CHECK,ITER,JC,L,N,N1,PASS,SCALE,TRIP
        COMMON X,XO,DS,DR,H,N,L
        COMMON/FTEST/XS,Y1,Y2,ACC,CHECK
*
*  Set termination criteria, convergence type, initial iter-  *
*  aration.                                                    *
*
        PASS = 1
        TRIP = 1
        ITER = 0
          L  = 0
        N = 2
```

FIGURE 8.9

A sample program for Powell's multivariable search.

```
          M = 1.0
          H = 1.0
          X(1) =   0.5
          X(2) =   0.50
          ACC = 1E-6
*
*     Define the initial search direction as the unit in each of
*     N - directions.
*
          OPEN(6,FILE='PRN')
          DO 1 J = 1,N
          DO 1 I = 1,N
          IF(I.EQ.J) THEN
             DR(I,J) = 1.0
          ELSE
             DR(I,J) = 0.0
          END IF
1         CONTINUE
4         ITER = ITER + 1
             L = L + 1
*     Save the base point as xs
*
          DO 6 I = 1,N
             XS(I) = X(I)
6         CONTINUE
          Y1 = EVA(X,N)
          F(0) = Y1
*
*     Begin search in each of the given direction.   Redefine    *
*     the search direction for each variable as DS.              *
*
          DO 12 J = 1,N
             DO 8 I = 1,N
             DS(I) = DR(I,J)
8            CONTINUE
*     Call a line search subroutine                              *
*
             CALL SEARCH
*     Evaluate the function value in each direction and save      *
*     as F(j).  This will be used to determine the direction     *
*     that produced maximum function change                      *
*
          F(J) = EVA(X,N)
12        CONTINUE
*     Define a third point  v.                                    *
*
          DO 14 I = 1,N
             V(I) = 2*X(I) - XS(I)
14        CONTINUE
*
*     Evaluate the function at two points                         *
*
          Y2 = EVA(X,N)
          Y3 = EVA(V,N)
*
```

FIGURE 8.9

(Continued).

```
*        Determine the direction that produced the maximum change *
*        in the objective function.  Denote this direction as JC  *
*        and the maximum change as DEL.                           *
              DEL = - 1.0E-20
              DO 16 I = I,N
              DLT = F(I-1) - F(I)
                  IF(DEL.LE.DLT) THEN
                      DEL = DLT
                      JC = I
                  END IF
   16         CONTINUE
*
*        Test if new dirction of search is to be defined or if     *
*        the search is to be continued in the old search direc-    *
*        tion.                                                     *
*
              CA = (Y1 - 2*Y2 + Y3)*((Y1 - Y2 - DEL)**2)
              CB = 0.5*DEL*((Y1 - Y3)**2)
              IF((Y3.LT.Y1).OR.(CA.LT.CB)) THEN
*                                          Define a new search
*                                          direction.
                  DD = 0.0
                  DO 18 I = 1,N
                  DD = (X(I) - XS(I))**2 + DD
   18             CONTINUE
                  DD = DD**0.5
                  IF(JC.LT.N) THEN
*                                Generate linearly independent     *
*                                direction as suggested by Powell   *
                      N1 = N - 1
                      DO 22 J = JC,N1
                          DO 22 I = 1,N
                          DR(I,J) = DR(I,J+1)
   22                 CONTINUE
                  END IF
*
*        Normalize the newly created search direction .            *
*
                  DO 24 I = 1,N
                  DR(I,N) = (X(I) - XS(I))/DD
   24             CONTINUE
                  SCALE = 1
*
                  DO 28 I = 1,N
                  DS(I) = DR(I,N)
   28             CONTINUE
                  L = L + 1
                  CALL SEARCH
                  Y2 = EVA(X,N)
*        Check if the point v is a better point than x.            *
*
                  IF(Y3.LT.Y2) THEN
*                                 Replace pt. x with pt. v          *
                      DO 26 I = 1,N
                      X(I) = V(I)
```

FIGURE 8.9

(Continued).

```
     26                          CONTINUE
                                 Y2 = Y3
                        END IF
*
*
*          Conduct another search in the newly defined direction    *
*
                        GO TO 34
              ELSE
*                         A New direction should not be defined      *
*          Again check if point v is better than pt. x               *
*
                        IF(Y2. GE. Y3) THEN
*                                          Replace pt.x with pt. v    *
*
                        DO 32 I = 1,N
                        X(I) = V(I)
     32                 CONTINUE
                        Y2 = Y3
                   END IF
              END IF
*
*    Test if termination criteria is satisfied                       *
*
     34       CALL TERMIN
              IF(CHECK.GT.0) THEN
*                             Redefine the step size.                 *
                   H = 0.4*(ABS(Y1-Y2))**.5
                        IF((H.EQ.0.0).OR.(H.GT.M)) THEN
                                          Modify H.  *
                             H = .1*M
                        END IF
                        GO TO 4
              END IF
              IF(PASS.EQ.1) THEN
              GO TO 35
*
*
              END IF
*
              IF(TRIP.NE.2) THEN
*                        Increase the value of x by ten times
*                        the accuracy desired and repeat search. *
                   TRIP = 2
                   DO 44 I = 1,N
                   XA(I)   = X(I)
                   X(I)   =  X(I) + 10.0*ACC
     44            CONTINUE
                   Y11 = Y2
                   GO TO 4
              END IF
              Y12 = Y2
              DD = 0.0
                 DO  46 I = 1,N
                 XB(I) = X(I)
                 DS(I) = XA(I) - XB(I)
```

FIGURE 8.9

(Continued).

```
                     DD    =   DS(I)**2 + DD
    46           CONTINUE
             DD = DD**0.5
             IF(DD.NE.0.0) THEN
    *                       Normalize the search direction.
                     DO 48 I = 1,N
                     DS(I) = DS(I)/DD
    48           CONTINUE
             CALL SEARCH
             Y1 = Y11
             CALL TERMIN
             IF(CHECK.GT.0) THEN
    *
                         Y1 = Y12
                         CALL TERMIN
    *
                             DO 52 I = 1,N
                             DR(I,I) = (XA(I) - XB(I))/DD
    52                   CONTINUE
                         GO TO 4
                     END IF
             END IF
    35       CONTINUE
    *
             DO 36 I = 1,N
             WRITE(6,38)I,X(I)
    36       CONTINUE
    38       FORMAT(3X,'X(',I2,') = ',F10.8)
             WRITE(6,42)F(N),ITER,L
    42       FORMAT(3X,'FMIN =',E14.7,'NO.OF ITERATIONS =',I3,'NO.
      .      OF FUNCTION EVALUATIONS = ',I3)
    530      END
    *---------------------------------------------------------------*
    *                     Termination subroutine                    *
    *  -------------------------------------------------------------*
    *
             SUBROUTINE TERMIN
             REAL X(10),XS(10)
             REAL Y1,Y2,ACC
             INTEGER CHECK
             COMMON X
             COMMON/FTEST/XS,Y1,Y2,ACC,CHECK
    *
             CHECK = 1
             WRITE(6,341)Y1,Y2,ACC
    341      FORMAT(2X,'Y1 =',E14.7,'Y2 = ',E14.7,'ACC =', E14.8)
             IF((ABS(Y1) - ACC).GT.0.0) THEN
                     IF((ABS((Y1 - Y2)/Y1) - ACC).LE.0.0) THEN
                         GO TO 57
                     ELSE
                         GO TO 77
                     END IF
             ELSE
                     IF((ABS(Y1 - Y2) - ACC).LE.0.0) THEN
                         GO TO 57
```

FIGURE 8.9

(Continued).

```
                          ELSE
                                     GO TO 77
                    END IF
                          END IF
57                  DO 59 I = 1,N
                    WRITE(6,343)XS(I),X(I)
343                 FORMAT(4X,'XS =',E14.7,'X = ',E14.7)
                    IF((ABS(XS(I)) - ACC).GT.0.0) THEN
                        IF((ABS((XS(I) - X(I))/XS(I)) - ACC).LE.0.0) THEN
                              GO TO 59
                        ELSE
                              GO TO 77
                        END IF
                    ELSE
                        IF((ABS(XS(I) - X(I)) - ACC).LE.0.0) THEN
                              GO TO 59
                        ELSE
                              GO TO 77
                        END IF
                    END IF
59                  CONTINUE
                    CHECK = -1
77                  RETURN
                    END
*
*.....................................................................
*       Define the objective function
*.....................................................................
*
                    REAL FUNCTION EVA(R,N)
*
                    REAL R(10)
                    INTEGER N
*
                    EVA = R(1)**2*R(2) +  R(1)*R(2)**2 - 3*R(1)*R(2)
                    RETURN
                    END
```

FIGURE 8.9

(Continued).

Step 2 Save the starting point for each iteration cycle.

$$\mathbf{x}_b = \mathbf{x} = [0.5\ 0.5]^T; \quad F_0 = D_1 = D(\mathbf{x}_b) = -0.5$$

A line search in the direction of $\mathbf{s}_1$ yields

$$\mathbf{x} = [1.25\ 0.5]^T; \quad F_1 = D(\mathbf{x}) = -0.78125$$

A line search in the direction of $\mathbf{s}_2$ gives

$$\mathbf{x} = [1.25\ 0.875]^T; \quad F_2 = D(\mathbf{x}) = -0.95703$$

We now define the third point $\mathbf{v}$

$$\mathbf{v} = 2\mathbf{x} - \mathbf{x}_b = [2.00 \; 1.25]^T$$
$$D_2 = D(\mathbf{x}) = -0.95703 \quad \text{and} \quad D_3 = D(\mathbf{v}) = 0.625$$

Step 3 Now we determine the direction that produced the greatest function change and the magnitude of the change

$$\Delta = \max\{-0.5 - (-0.78125), -0.78125 - (-0.95703)\}$$
$$\Delta = 0.28125, \quad JC = 1$$

Step 4 We note that

$$(D_1 - 2D_2 + D_3)(D_1 - D_2 - \Delta)^2 = 0.06301$$

and

$$0.5\Delta (D_1 - D_3)^2 = 0.17798$$

Since $D_3 > D_1$, we use the old direction. We proceed to step 6.

Step 6 Since $D_2 < D_3$ we go to step 7.

Step 7 Noting that the termination criterion has not been satisfied, we return to step 2 for subsequent iterations, the results of which are shown in Table 8.1. The final solution is $\mathbf{x} = [1 \; 1]^T$ and the minimum value of function is -1.000.

Iter	s	x
1	$[1 \; 0]^T$	$[1.25 \; 0.5]^T$
	$[0 \; 1]^T$	$[1.25 \; 0.875]^T$
2	$[1 \; 0]^T$	$[1.0625 \; 0.875]^T$
	$[0 \; 1]^T$	$[1.0625 \; 0.9687]^T$
	$[-0.8944 \; 0.4472]^T$	$[1.0019 \; 0.99991]^T$
3	$[1 \; 0]^T$	$[1.0625 \; 0.9688]^T$
	$[-0.8944 \; 0.4472]^T$	$[0.9999 \; 1.00004]^T$
4	$[1 \; 0]^T$	$[0.9999 \; 1.00001]^T$
	$[-0.8944 \; 0.4472]^T$	$[0.9999 \; 1.0000]^T$
	$[0.89438 \; 0.4475]^T$	$[1.0001 \; 0.99999]^T$
5	$[-0.8944 \; 0.4472]^T$	$[1.0000 \; 0.99999]^T$
	$[0.8943 \; -0.4475]^T$	$[1.0000 \; 0.99999]^T$

TABLE 8.1

Result of the iteration for Example 8.3.

THE FLETCHER-REEVES METHOD

The Powell's method, discussed previously, is considered by many as a search method. However, since the gradient method brings the idea of direction of fastest improvement, we deem it necessary to include it among the gradient techniques, in keeping with the discussions in the section on gradient methods.

The Fletcher-Reeves method is in every sense of the word a gradient method of optimization. This method is based on an orthogonization process that generates a sequence of mutually conjugate directions for a search process. A current gradient direction of search, $\mathbf{d}^k$, is computed using

$$\mathbf{d}^k = -\mathbf{g}_k + \frac{\mathbf{g}_k^2 d^{k-1}}{\mathbf{g}_{k-1}^2} \tag{8.20}$$

where

$$g = \left(\frac{\delta F}{\delta x_1}, \frac{\delta F}{\delta x_2}, \ldots, \frac{\delta F}{\delta x_n} \right)$$

This optimization process involves the following basic steps:

Step 1 Evaluate the objective function at an initial (or starting point), $\mathbf{x}^k$.

Step 2 Compute the current gradient direction using equation (8.20).

Step 3 Perform a search in the computed gradient direction, using Powell's method of quadratic interpolation or an equivalent technique, for the determination of the minimum of a function along a given direction.

Step 4 Evaluate the objective function at the point $\mathbf{x}^{k+1}$ resulting from step 3. If $|f(\mathbf{x}^k) - k(\mathbf{x}^{k+1})|$ is less than or equal to a specified tolerance, the process is terminated; otherwise, return to step 2.

Sometimes the computation of the gradient of an objective function may pose some difficulty, and in this case, the gradient may be computed using a numerical method.

APPLICATION

We now demonstrate how the techniques learned in this section may be utilized in an engineering practice. We do this with the problem given next.

Problem Statement 1

Datum Corporation is responsible for furnishing the cylinder barrels of motorcycles to a motorcycle manufacturer. The motorcycle company complains that some of the packings of the cylinder fail because not enough heat is dissipated to the environment. The company therefore, suggests that the cylinder be completely redesigned with fins to enhance heat transfer. Further, the company stipulates the following (see Figure 8.10):

1. The fins must be equally spaced.

2. $t \le 10$ mm

3. $D \le 100$ mm

4. $H \le 300$ mm

5. $T_s = 217°C$

In addition, Datum engineers apply the following:

1. The number of annular fins (rectangular profile) cannot exceed 10.

2. $L \le 25$ mm.

3. Fin efficiency (η_f) of 95% is desired.

REQUIREMENT

Find the optimal design parameters for optimal heat transfer.

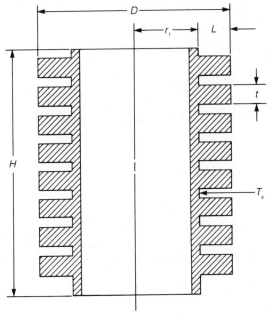

Notes:
1. All dimensions are in millimeters.
2. Material is aluminum.

FIGURE 8.10

For Problem Statement 1.

SOLUTION   **Given:** Convection coefficient of 45 W/m²·K, $T_s = 490$ K.

Find: t, D, L, N, and H for maximum heat transfer.

ASSUMPTIONS

1. Steady-state conditions.
2. No internal heat generation.
3. One-dimensional radial conduction in fins.
4. Constant properties and uniform convection coefficient over outer surface.
5. Negligible radiation effects.

ANALYSIS

By energy balance we have

$$q_{\text{total}} = q_{\text{fin}} + q_p$$

where

q_{total} = total heat transferred to the environment

q_{fin} = heat transferred by the fins

q_p = heat transferred by the exposed surface of the cylinder

We can further express q_{fin} and q_p as [11]:

$$q_{\text{fin}} = 2\pi N\eta_f [(r_1 + L + \frac{t}{2})^2 - r_1^2] (T_s - T_o)$$

and

$$q_p = 2\pi r_1 h (H - Nt) (T_s - T_o)$$

where

$$T_o = \text{surrounding temperature taken as } 27°C$$

Then

$$q_{\text{total}} = 2\pi h \{N\eta_f [(r_1 + L + \frac{t}{2})^2 - r_1^2] + (H - Nt)r_1\}(T_s - T_o)$$

For optimization purposes, the objective function is then the last equation. The maximum heat transfer can be achieved when the maximum values of the design parameters have been obtained. The optimization process is conducted using the Hooke and Jeeves search method. Note that this method, as discussed earlier, is applicable to unconstrained optimization; therefore, the technique is modified for application in constrained optimization. The modification involves consideration of any exploratory search or pattern move that takes a given variable outside the constrained region as a failure. The results of the optimization are as follows:

$$N = 6.0$$
$$H = 130 \text{ mm}$$
$$r_1 = 46 \text{ mm}$$
$$L = 14 \text{ mm}$$
$$t = 9 \text{ mm}$$
$$q_{\text{total}} = 814.00 \text{ W}$$

Recall from Chapter 7 that the design parameters are local rather than global. With the determination of these design variables, the design is now completed.

Problem Statement 2

Suppose we wish to design a 10-kN crane hook. We want to design the hook for a minimum of internal stress. Furthermore, let us assume that the cross section of the hook is trapezoidal (see Figure 8.11) and a factor of safety of 3 is applicable.

SOLUTION   **Given:** A 10-kN force and trapezoidal cross section.

Find: Values of a, b, h, and r_i for minimum stress.

ASSUMPTIONS

Factor of safety = 3; negligible radial stress.

Design equations: Axial stress, $\sigma_x = P/A$. Bending stress is

1. Inner fiber: $\sigma_i = M(r_n - r_i)/Aer_i$
2. Outer fiber: $\sigma_o = M(r_o - r_n)/Aer_i$

where

σ = flexural stress

M = moment

e = distance from the center of gravity axis to the neutral axis

r_n = radius of curvature of the neutral axis

The subscripts i and o refer to inner and outer fibers.

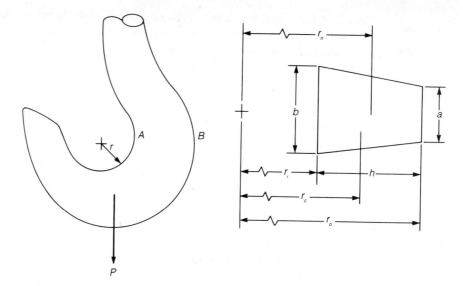

FIGURE 8.11

Sketch for Problem Statement 2.

ANALYSIS

For a trapezoidal cross section we have

$$r_n = b - a + \frac{(br_o - ar_i)(\ln r_o/r_i)}{h}$$

$$r = r_i + \frac{h(b + 2a)}{3(a + b)}$$

$$\text{Area, } A = \frac{(a + b)h}{2}$$

From Figure 8.12 we have

$$M = Pr$$

$$\sigma_A = \frac{Pr(r_n - r_i)}{A(r - r_n)r_i} + \frac{P}{A}$$

$$\sigma_B = \frac{-Pr(r_o - r_i)}{A(r - r_n)r_i} + \frac{P}{A}$$

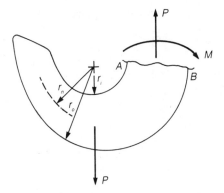

FIGURE 8.12

Free-body diagram for Problem Statement 2.

Experience has shown that the stress in the inside fiber is usually greater than the stress on the outside fiber; for this reason the first equation (for the stress at A) becomes our objective function.

Again, we use the Hooke and Jeeves method for optimization, and the results obtained are as follows:

$$a = 15.6 \text{ mm}$$
$$b = 29.4 \text{ mm}$$
$$h = 45.0 \text{ mm}$$
$$r_i = 35.6 \text{ mm}$$

Minimum stress at A is 3.0 MPa.

The preceding information on the stress may help in selecting the appropriate material for the hook.

CONCLUDING REMARKS

The last two chapters of this book serve to introduce the student to the area of engineering design optimization. Further studies of this subject, especially constrained optimization, may be obtained from [12] and [13].

EXERCISES

1. Find the maximum value of the function

$$f(\mathbf{x}) = 5x_1^2 x_2 + 2x_2^2 x_1 - 30x_1 x_2$$

Use the Hooke and Jeeves algorithm, a starting point of $(1, 1)$, and a step size of unity.

(*Answer:* $\mathbf{x} = [2\ 5]^T, f(\mathbf{x}) = -100$)

2. Repeat Exercise 1 using Powell's algorithm. Select your own starting point.

3. Using Powell's algorithm, find the minimum of Rosenbrock's function

$$f(\mathbf{x}) = 100(x_2 - x_1^2)^2 + (1 - x_1)^2$$

Use the starting point $(1, -1)$, an initial step size of 0.4, an allowable maximum step in any direction of 0.6, and a tolerance of 1×10^{-10}.

4. A metal box is to be designed for storage of waste materials. The profit to be made from constructing the box is Cx_3 dollars. The average of the three dimensions is 4 m. For a maximum profit, what should be the dimensions? Take C to be $0.10/m^3$.

(*Answer:* $x_1 = 6$ m, $x_2 = 3$ m)

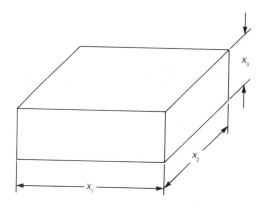

REFERENCES

1. Hooke, R., and T. A. Jeeves. "'Direct Search' Solution of Numerical and Statistical Problems." *Journal of the Association for Computing Machinery* 8 (1961): 212–29.

2. Powell, M. J. D. "An Efficient Method of Finding the Minimum of a Function of Several Variables Without Calculating Derivatives." *Computer Journal* 7 (1964): 155–62.

3. Zangwill, W. I. "Minimizing a Function Without Calculating Derivatives." *Computer Journal* 10: 293–96.

4. Brent, R. P., *Algorithms for Minimization Without Calculating Derivatives*. Englewood Cliffs, N.J.: Prentice-Hall, Inc., 1973.

5. Jacoby, S. L., J. S. Kowalik, and J. T. Pizzo. *Iterative Methods for Nonlinear Optimization Problems*. Englewood Cliffs, N.J.: Prentice-Hall, Inc., 1972.

6. Davidon, W. C. "Variable Metric Method for Minimization." A. E. C. R&D Report ANL-5990 (rev.), Argon National Laboratory, 1959.

7. Fletcher, R., and M. J. D. Powell. "A Rapidly Convergent Descent Method for Minimization." *Computer Journal* 6 (1963): 163–68.

8. Fletcher, R., and C. M. Reeves. "Function Minimization by Conjugate Gradients." *Computer Journal* 7 (1964): 149–54.

9. Murray, W., ed. *Numerical Methods for Unconstrained Optimization*, London: Academic Press, 1972.

10. Smith, C. S. "The Automatic Computation of Maximum Likelihood." N. C. B. Scientific Dept., Report No. SC-846/MR/40, 1962.

11. Kern, D. Q., and Kraus, A. D., *Extended Surface Heat Transfer*. New York: McGraw-Hill Book Co., 1972.

12. Reklaitis, G. V., A. Ravindran, and K. M. Ragsdell. *Engineering Optimization—Methods and Application.* New York: John Wiley & Sons, Inc. 1983.

13. Pike, R. W. *Optimization for Engineering Systems.* New York: Van Nostrand Reinhold Co., 1986.

Johnson's Method of Optimum Design

9.1   INTRODUCTION

In Chapters 7 and 8 we examined the techniques for optimizing both single-variable and multivariable functions. Sometimes these methods fail to yield solutions. For example, if we try applying the Fibonacci method to a given function without first ascertaining the function to be unimodal, no solution may be obtained. An example of a problem where the Davidon-Fletcher-Powell method fails to yield a result is given by Ellis [1]. Therefore, it is desirable that we have a means of knowing beforehand whether a particular method will yield a solution.

An optimization technique that gives an insight into the nature of the problem and the expected solutions is the method of **optimum design.** This method, developed by Professor R. C. Johnson, has been applied effectively to obtain quickly, without employing the usual trial-and-error methods, solutions of many mechanical design problems. The success of this method in circumventing the problems encountered in many optimization techniques lies in the fact that it combines mathematical and graphical methods to present a clear view of the problem.

The purpose of this chapter, based primarily on a book by Johnson [2], is to introduce the reader to this method of optimization. A detailed study of the method can be obtained by consulting [2]. Because this method is more applicable to mechanical systems design than thermal systems design, it is necessary to examine design equations and define those terms that are applicable to Johnson's method.

261

9.2 IMPORTANCE OF EQUATIONS IN MECHANICAL DESIGN

The design of machine elements is based on several fundmental equations, to which engineering students are usually first exposed in solid mechanics courses. Some useful examples from such courses are summarized as follows.

1. Normal stress equation

$$\sigma = \frac{P}{A} \tag{9.1}$$

where

σ = normal stress
P = force normal to the area
A = area

2. Flexural equation

$$\sigma = \frac{Mc}{I} \tag{9.2}$$

where

σ = flexural stress
M = moment
I = moment of inertia
c = distance from the neutral axis

3. Torsional stress equation

$$\tau = \frac{Tc}{J} \tag{9.3}$$

where

τ = torsional stress
T = torque
J = polar moment of inertia

These equations are applied in the design of mechanical elements. For example, the design of a helical spring is based on:

$$\tau = \frac{8PD\,(1 + 0.5/C)}{\pi d^3} \tag{9.4}$$

or

$$y = \frac{8PD^3N}{Gd^4} \tag{9.5}$$

where

P = force exerted by the spring
D = mean diameter
d = diameter of the wire
C = spring index
G = modulus of rigidity
y = deflection
N = number of active coils

Equation (9.5) is used to calculate the deflection. Depending on the application, deflection may be a desired or an undesired effect. Closer examination of the preceding equations reveals that each is a function of either a geometrical term or a material property. It follows that parameters involved in mechanical design can be classified, according to Johnson, into three groups:

1. Functional requirement parameters

2. Material parameters

3. Geometrical parameters

Generally, these groups must be kept in mind during a design process, but they become even more important in the application of Johnson's method of optimum design. For example, it may become necessary to vary the geometrical or material parameters to see the effect they will produce in the design objective.

Changing of geometrical parameters may be easily done as long as no constraint is violated. However, the variations of material parameters must be carefully considered. For example, if the yield strength of a material is specified, one cannot arbitrarily change the modulus of rigidity or elasticity, since each is uniquely defined for a given material. Of course, the functional requirements parameters are usually specified prior to the design and in such cases are considered to be independent of the two other groups. Although the functional requirement parameters are considered independent of the geometrical parameters, the geometrical parameters are dependent on the functional requirement, since the choice of the geometrical parameters must be related to the desirable functional requirement.

9.3 BASIC DEFINITIONS

To understand and be able to apply Johnson's method of optimization requires knowing his definitions of terms, as summarized here.

PRIMARY DESIGN EQUATION

The **primary design equation** (PDE), essentially the same as the objective function discussed in Chapter 7, is simply the expression of the optimization quantity in terms of the three types of design parameters. The equation is of the form:

$$\text{PDE} \;=\; f\left\{ \begin{pmatrix} \text{functional} \\ \text{requirement} \\ \text{parameters} \end{pmatrix}, \; \begin{pmatrix} \text{material} \\ \text{parameter} \end{pmatrix}, \; \begin{pmatrix} \text{geometrical} \\ \text{parameter} \end{pmatrix} \right\} \tag{9.6}$$

As an illustration, suppose we want to minimize the cost of manufacturing a cylinder and the cost C_1 is specified per unit length for different materials. To reduce the total cost C_T, we may want to use the shortest possible length. In this case we can write the primary design equation as:

$$C_T = C_1 L$$

where

C_T = total cost
C_1 = cost per unit length
L = length required

SUBSIDIARY DESIGN EQUATION

Any design equation other than that of the primary is called a **subsidiary design equation** (SDE). Such an equation expresses the functional requirements in terms of the parameters in the PDE. An SDE is either stated directly or implied; in mechanical design, stress equations are often implied.

SDEs can be illustrated by referring to the previous problem of minimizing the cost of manufacturing a cylinder. Suppose it is known that for the cylinder to function properly, it must hold a certain amount of hydraulic fluid; then a subsidiary equation may be required. In this instance we can write:

$$V = \pi D^2 \, \frac{L}{4} \tag{9.7}$$

where

V = volume of the cylinder
D = inside diameter of the cylinder
L = length of the cylinder

It is important that the SDE be considered in the use of Johnson's optimum method. Otherwise, application of the method becomes very difficult.

LIMIT EQUATION

The constraints on optimization discussed in Chapter 7 are applicable to the method of optimum design. On mechanical elements, they are imposed by the strength of the material as well as by geometrical parameters. Furthermore, there are geometrical constraints due to space limitations and availability of standard sizes of components. An equation that expresses the constraints in the design process, using Johnson's method, is called a **limit equation** (LE).

9.4 GENERAL FORM OF JOHNSON'S METHOD OF OPTIMUM DESIGN

Johnson's method of optimum design follows a certain format. Based on the above definition, the problem for optimizations is of the following form:
Optimize

$$D = g_1 (x_1, x_2, \ldots, x_n) \qquad \text{(PDE)} \qquad\qquad \textbf{(9.8)}$$

related by

$$Q = g_2 (x_1, x_2, \ldots, x_n) \qquad \text{(SDE)} \qquad\qquad \textbf{(9.9)}$$

constrained as

$$x_{1min} \leq x_1 \leq x_{1max}$$

$$x_{2min} \leq x_2 \leq x_{2max} \qquad \text{(LE)} \qquad\qquad \textbf{(9.10)}$$

$$\cdot \qquad\qquad \cdot \qquad\qquad \cdot$$
$$\cdot \qquad\qquad \cdot \qquad\qquad \cdot$$
$$\cdot \qquad\qquad \cdot \qquad\qquad \cdot$$

$$x_{nmin} \leq x_n \leq x_{nmax}$$

Most problems that can be solved using Johnson's method of optimum design may be in the form described by equations (9.8) through (9.10). It is not uncommon to find more than two equations that could be the PDE. Of course, it is more common to find several equations functioning as SDEs. The limit equation is essential in establishing regions containing feasible solutions.

9.5 GENERAL PROCEDURE OF JOHNSON'S METHOD OF OPTIMUM DESIGN

The method of applying Johnson's method is explained in detail in Chapter 6 of his book [2]; the steps involved are summarized here. There are basically five steps; we have condensed them to four.

INITIAL FORMULATION

The first step in Johnson's method of optimal design is to state the problem in terms of the primary design equation, the subsidiary equations, and the limit equations (Section 9.4). For simplicity, we will call these initial formulation equations the **primitive form.** This step demands the identification of the types of variables involved; Johnson gives two types. The first is the **constrained parameter,** and the number of such is designated by n_c. This has a direct constraint imposed on it by the limit equation in the primitive form. The second type is termed the **free variable,** and the number of such is designated n_f. It has no direct constraint imposed on it by the limit equation and does not include the optimization variable, D. The total number of variables n_T in the primitive form is then given as:

$$n_T = n_c + n_f \tag{9.11}$$

where

n_T = total number of variables
n_c = number of constrained variables
n_f = number of free variables

FINAL FORMULATION

Often the primitive form is complex or not properly organized in a way that is suitable for Johnson's method; further simplification is then required. This then is the second step, transforming the initial system of equations; it is called the **final formulation.**

This transformation may require two basic processes, reduction and organization. In the first, by a combination process, the free variables in the primitive form are eliminated. (Thus the number of equations in the resulting final form are normally less than those in the primitive form by the original number of free variables.) The elimination process requires a great deal of care and experience for proper reduction into forms suitable for the variation study that follows. Often, an organization process becomes necessary, requiring further mathematical manipulation.

The steps described in the previous paragraph are not necessary in all cases. If the problem is very simple, there may not be any need for reduction or reorganization of the initial formulation. However, the transformation process is vital in many more complicated problems in order properly to relate the primary design equation to the subsidiary design equations.

Going from the primitive-form equation system to the final-form equation system is usually very difficult for the novice. The degree of difficulty increases as one proceeds from what Johnson calls the case of normal specifications (i.e., the case when the number of free variables, n_f, is greater than or equal to the number of subsidiary equations, N_s) through the case of redundant specifications (i.e., $n_f < N_s$) to the case of incompatible specifications. Problems with incompatible specifications are those for which no solution that satisfies all the constraints and specifications exists. Herein lies the beauty of this method, for it would alert the designer that inconsistent specifications have been given. Besides, it would give an insight as to which constraint needs modification in order for a solution to be obtained. Again, the reader is referred to [2, Chapter 6] for details of these techniques.

VARIATION STUDY

After one obtains the final formulation for the problem under consideration, the next step is to conduct a **variation study** to determine how the objective function is affected by the variables. This involves the use of sketched graphs, called **variation diagrams** by Johnson. A plot of the objective functions is made against each variable in the final formulation, taking into consideration the various constraints. If the problem is such that it contains one related variable in the final formulation, a two-dimensional variation diagram is used; if the problem contains two related variables, a three-dimensional diagram may be used. (Johnson provides a detailed method of applying his three-dimensional variation diagram in [3].)

The variation diagram is the heart of Johnson's method, and it is the feature that makes it unique. Its main function is to aid in the extraction from the design space of the optimum design. The variation diagram has several attractive features, such as the ability to indicate the global extremum, a position not easily identified by any other optimization technique. Generally, the variation diagram reveals all potential points that could yield an optimum design. Perhaps one of its most unique functions is to reveal the course of action to be taken to improve a design, a course that may simply be modification of the constraints. This involves modifying the boundary values that most affect the optimization quantity.

In addition to the preceding, this diagram does what most optimization techniques are not able to do: It indicates when no solution is feasible; in cases of incompatible specifications, this is when there is no region of acceptable design because of the relationships of the constraints. Since the variation study is such an important step, the reader is advised to consult [1] and [3] and Johnson's book for further illustration.

EXECUTION AND EVALUATION OF RESULT

Implementing Johnson's method with a high-speed computer requires the construction of a flowchart. The steps given by Johnson for constructing a flowchart are:

1. Input the limiting values of the variables and any other material property.

2. Using results from the variation diagram, eliminate regions that contain no feasible solution for each variable.

3. Select the best point from all the potential points that would lead to optimum design. This selection is based on comparing the various points with each other, which is easily done by the use of the variation diagram.

4. With the optimum design obtained from step 3, determine whether the point has satisfied significant criteria, e.g., an acceptable deflection in a shaft.

The fourth step is actually an evaluation process. The optimum design is carefully examined to see if the performance of the design meets every expectation, including those factors that were ignored in the initial formulation stage. An optimum design is considered if the performance level is acceptable. If it is judged that an optimum design has not been reached, we must return to the first step of Johnson's method, which is the initial formulation. But before returning to that step, we obtain information from the variation diagram as to where modification is needed to obtain an improved solution.

SUMMARY OF
METHOD OF OPTIMUM DESIGN

Following our discussion of the method of optimum design, we now present in a logical manner a detailed procedure for problem solving.

Step 1 Perform the initial formulation of the problem deriving the PDE, SDE, and LE.

Step 2 Identify and record the number of:
  a. Free variables, n_f
  b. Constrained variables, n_c

    c. Total variables, n_T
    d. Subsidiary equations, N_s

Step 3 If $n_f < N_s$ go to step 5; otherwise go to step 4

Step 4 This is the case of normal specification. Therefore:
    a. Reduce the primitive equation system to a final equation system. The PDE should be expressed in terms of the independent variables.
    b. Conduct the variational study. Identify the points of optimum solution on the variational diagram. At this stage observe how an improvement in design objective may be achieved, if desired.
    c. Construct flowchart, apply numerical values, and execute the resultant program.
    d. Evaluate the results. If satisfactory, end; otherwise return to step 4(b).

Step 5 This is the case of redundant specifications. Proceed as follows:
    a. Reduce and transform the primitive equation system to final equation system.
    b. Do a variation study. Note on the variation diagram the potential points for optimum design.
    c. Construct the flowchart, apply numerical values, and execute the resultant program.
    d. Evaluate the result. If the solution is possible, then stop; otherwise go to step 5(e).
    e. Review variational study. If the constraints or specification cannot be altered, then no solution is possible. Then stop, otherwise modify the appropriate constraints or specifications and return to step 5(c).

The whole process of Johnson's method can be better understood by studying the example that follows.

EXAMPLE 9.1

A track field is to be fenced as shown in Figure 9.1. A specific length of material is to be used. We wish to maximize the area by finding the best values of the radius (r) and the distance between the two sections of the semicircles (x).

SOLUTION The initial formulation equations are as follows:

Primitive design equation (PDE):

$$A = \pi r^2 + 2rx \tag{9.12}$$

Primitive subsidiary design equation (PSDE):

$$L = 2\pi r + 2x \tag{9.13}$$

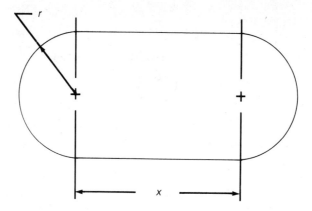

FIGURE 9.1

Track field for Example 9.1.

Primitive limit equations (PLE):

$$r \leq r_{max} \tag{9.14}$$

Specified values are L and r_{max}.

FINAL FORMULATIONS (FF)

There are two variables, x and r (not counting the optimization quantity A). The number of free variables is 1 (i.e., $n_f = 1$, for the variable x) and the number of subsidiary equations is $N_s = 1$. Since $n_f = N_s$ we have the case of normal specification.

We now eliminate the free variable in the PDE. We have

$$x = \frac{(L - 2\pi r)}{2} \tag{9.15}$$

Hence

$$A = rL - \pi r^2 \tag{9.16}$$

Next we investigate the variation of A with the independent variable, r, in (9.16). We have

$$\frac{dA}{dr} = L - 2\pi r \tag{9.17}$$

and

$$\frac{d^2A}{dr^2} = -2\pi \qquad (9.18)$$

Obviously the maximum value of A is obtained when $r = L/2\pi$. Our next step is to sketch the variation diagram, as shown in Figure 9.2. From Figure 9.2 note that there are two possible solutions, depending on the value of r_{max}. If $r_{max} < L/2\pi$, the optimum solution is $r = r_{max}$. If, however, $r_{max} > L/2\pi$, then the optimum solution is $r = L/2\pi$. To help extract the optimum solution for various specified values of L and r_{max}, a flowchart is given in Figure 9.3.

EXAMPLE 9.2

Suppose we wish to design a noncircular tube (for application, say, in an aircraft industry) to resist a given torque. Because of a weight consideration, a thin-walled tube of a specified length is to be used. Furthermore, we have a list of materials (see Table 9.1) from which to select for use in fabricating the tube.

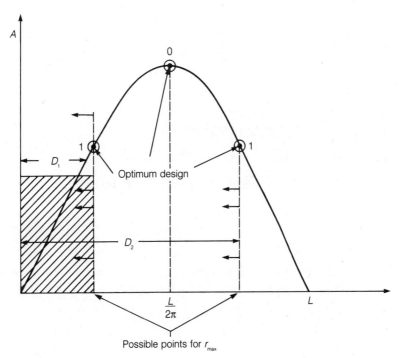

FIGURE 9.2

Variation of A as a function of radius.
(a) The distance designated as D_1 is the region of feasible design if r_{max} is to the left of point O.
(b) D_2 is the region of feasible design if r_{max} is to the right of point O.

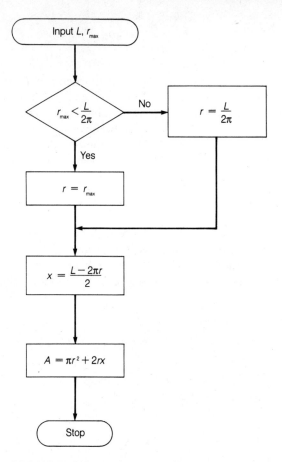

FIGURE 9.3

Flowchart for obtaining optimum area for Example 9.1.

SOLUTION   Our objective is to find a beam of minimum weight. For a specified length, the weight of the tube with a rectangular section (Figure 9.4) is

$$W = \gamma L[2t(b + h) - 4t^2] \qquad \textbf{(9.19)}$$

We know from [4] that the torque and the thickness are related by the equation

$$\tau = \frac{T}{2bht} \qquad \textbf{(9.20)}$$

Material	Yield Stress (MPa)	Unit Weight (kN/m³)
Aluminum		
2014 -T4	290	26.67
6061 -T6	276	26.85
Magnesium Alloy		
AM 100 A	152	17.81
Red Brass (CD)	496	85.76
Steel		
AISI 1010 HR	179	77.27
AISI 4140 HR	434	77.27

TABLE 9.1

Materials for Example 9.2.

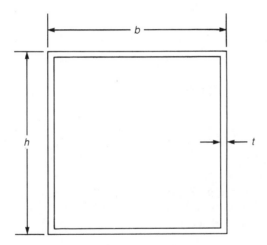

FIGURE 9.4

Rectangular cross section of the tube in Example 9.2.

where

T = torque
γ = unit weight
τ = shearing stress
t = thickness
W = weight of the tube

For manufacturing considerations, we assume that the thickness of the tube is the thickness of the sheet from which the tube is to be fabricated; hence, a thickness (t_s) is specified. Using the maximum shear stress theory, we know that

$$\tau_{max} \leq \frac{S_y}{2N} \tag{9.21}$$

where

S_y = yield strength of material
N = factor of safety

We know that the shear stress in the tube cannot exceed the maximum permissible shear stress. In addition, suppose that one of the dimensions of the tube, say h, cannot exceed a specified value. Then the primitive (or initial formulation) equations for the problem are as follows:

PRIMITIVE FORMULATION

$$W = L[2t(b + h) - 4t^2] \quad \text{(PDE)} \tag{9.22}$$

$$\tau = T/2bht \quad \text{(PSDE)} \tag{9.23}$$

$$\tau \leq \tau_{max} = \frac{S_y}{2N} \tag{9.24}$$

$$h_{min} \leq h \leq h_{max}; \quad t = t_s \quad \text{(PLE)}$$

Specified: L, S_y, N, T

Find: Values of h, t, and b that minimize the weight W.
Examination of the primitive equations indicates that we have the case of normal specification, since the only free variable is b, $n_f = 1$ and we have one subsidiary equations N_s.

From the primitive (initial) formulation, we immediately know that the maximum permissible value of t is t_s. Also, we can replace τ with $\tau_{max} = S_y/2N$. We can eliminate t using equation (9.23) to obtain $t = T/2bh\tau$. Therefore, our final formulation equations are:

$$W = \gamma L \left[\frac{2TN(b + h)}{bhS_y} - 4\left(\frac{TN}{bhS_y}\right)^2 \right] \tag{9.25}$$

$$t = \frac{TN}{bhS_y} \tag{9.26}$$

Our next step, of course, is the variation study and the resultant variations diagrams. To conduct the variation study we examine how W varies with b and h. Let $K = TN/S_y$; then

$$W = 2\gamma LK \left[\frac{b + h}{bh} - \frac{2K}{(bh)^2} \right]$$

$$\frac{dW}{dh} = \frac{2bK\gamma L}{(bh)^3} \, [4K - b^2h]$$

We note that the minimum value of W occurs when $h = 4K/b^2$ and that as the height increases, the width, b, decreases. The variation diagram is shown in Figure 9.5. The optimum solution is at point O, and the region of feasible solution lies to the right of the line $h = 4TN/b^2S_y$. The flowchart necessary for extracting the optimum solution for different materials is shown in Figure 9.6, and the

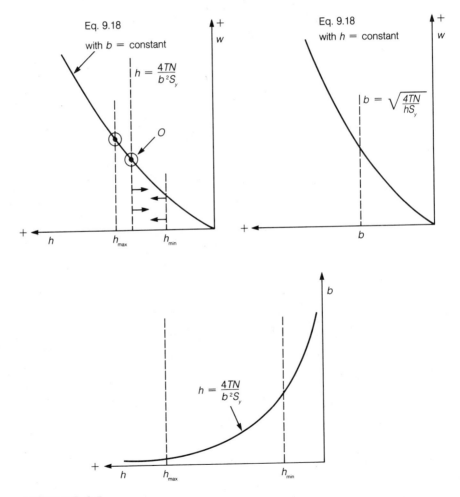

FIGURE 9.5

Variation diagram for Example 9.2.

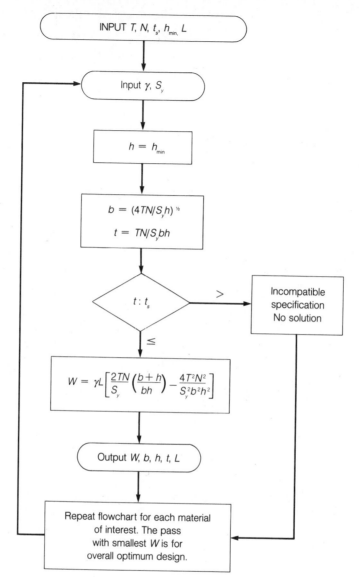

The flowchart contains the following elements:

INPUT T, N, t_s, h_{min}, L

Input γ, S_y

$h = h_{min}$

$b = (4TN/S_y h)^{1/2}$
$t = TN/S_y bh$

$t : t_s$

$>$ Incompatible specification No solution

$\leq$

$W = \gamma L \left[\dfrac{2TN}{S_y} \left(\dfrac{b+h}{bh} \right) - \dfrac{4T^2N^2}{S_y^2 b^2 h^2} \right]$

Output W, b, h, t, L

Repeat flowchart for each material of interest. The pass with smallest W is for overall optimum design.

FIGURE 9.6

Flowchart for Example 9.2.

computer program based on the flowchart is given in Figure 9.7. For numerical values, a torque of 2500 N·m and a minimum height of 50 mm and thickness of 10 mm are used. The result of the optimum design is shown in Table 9.2.

```
10    REM   ------------------------------------------------------
20    REM   THIS PROGRAM USES JOHNSON'S METHOD OF OPTIMUM DESIGN
30    REM   TO DETERMINE THE MINIMUM WEIGHT OF A GIVEN LENGTH OF
40    REM   OF A TUBE REQUIRED TO RESIST A GIVEN TORQUE
50    REM   ------------------------------------------------------
60     PRINT "ENTER THE DESIGN INFORMATION "
70     PRINT"ENTER TORQUE IN N-M"
80     INPUT T
90     PRINT "WHAT IS THE FACTOR OF SAFETY?"
100       INPUT N
110    REM   ------------------------------------------------------
120    REM    INPUT THE   SOME PERTINENT PARAMETERS
130    REM    ------------------------------------------------------
140    REM
150    PRINT "ENTER THE THICKNESS, LENGTH, MIN. HEIGHT - IN mm"
160       INPUT X,L,Y
170     TS = X : HMIN = Y: P = 1E+30 :   C =1000:.V = .001 : G = 2*V
180   REM ------------------------------------------------------------
190    REM  P IS FOR PURPOSE OF DETERMINING MINIMUM VALUE OF WIGHT
200   REM ------------------------------------------------------------
210     H =HMIN
220     PRINT " HOW MANY TYPES OF MATERIAL DO YOU WISH TO CONSIDER?"
230        INPUT M
240      FOR I = 1 TO M
250      PRINT "ENTER THE YIELD STRENGTH (IN MPa) OF MATERIAL #";I;
260         INPUT SY
270       PRINT
280      PRINT"ENTER THE SPECIFIC WEIGHT IN N/M**3"
290          INPUT S
300        Z = 4*T*N/(SY*H*C) : PRINT ;Z;
310        B = SQR(4*T*N/(SY*H*C))
320        U = B*C
330        TC = T*N/(SY*U*H)
340  IF TC>TS THEN PRINT"I.S., NO SOLUTION FOR SY =";SY;"MPa": GOTO 490
350     W  = S*L*((G*T*N/SY)*((U+H)/(U*H))  - (4*T^2*N^2/(SY^2*U^2*H^2))
360        W = W/C
370  REM
380      PRINT" FOR MATERIAL WITH YIELD STRENGTH OF ";SY;"MPa"
390     PRINT
400      PRINT " VALUES OF THE DESIGN VARIABLES ARE:"
410     PRINT
420      PRINT " WIDTH =";U;"mm";"   HEIGHT =";H;"mm";"   THICKNESS =";TS;"m
430     PRINT
440     PRINT"THE OPTIMUM WEIGHT = ";W;" KN ";"FOR THE GIVEN LENGTH OF";L;
450     PRINT
460      IF W < P THEN P =W: SM = SY : A = U : GOTO 490
470  PRINT
480  PRINT
490        PRINT
500        NEXT I
510    PRINT
520    REM   ------------------------------------------------------
530    REM OUTPUT THE RESULT OF THE OPTIMUM DESIGN
540    REM   ------------------------------------------------------
550     PRINT" THE OPTIMUM SOLUTION IS FOR THE MATERIAL WITH YEILD STRENG
560    PRINT
570   PRINT " THE DESIGN SPECIFICATIONS ARE: "
580     PRINT
590        PRINT "WIDTH =";A;"mm";"HEIGHT =";H;"mm      THICKNESS =";TS; "mm"
600     PRINT
610     PRINT"THE OPTIMUM WEIGHT = ";P;" KN";" FOR A SPECIFIED LENGTH OF";
620     END
```

FIGURE 9.7

Material I.D.	Yield Stress (MPa)	Width (mm)	Weight (N)
Aluminum			
2014-T4	290	37.1391	33.9590
6061-T6	276	38.0695	35.2823
Magnesium Alloy			
AM 100 A	152	51.2989	34.5579
Red Brass (CD)	496	28.3981	78.1758
Steel			
AISI 1010 HR	179	47.2719	134.4853
AISI 4140 HR	434	30.3588	76.4498

TABLE 9.2

Results of design for Example 9.2.

Examination of Table 9.2 reveals that the optimum solution is for aluminum 2014-T4. Final specification then is as follows:

$$\text{Tube length (specified)} = 1000 \text{ mm}$$
$$\text{Thickness} = 10 \text{ mm}$$
$$\text{Width} = 37.2 \text{ mm}$$
$$\text{Height} = 50 \text{ mm}$$

for a minimum weight of 34 N.

All our illustrations for Johnson's method of optimum design have involved those of compatible specifications. For examples dealing with incompatible specifications, Johnson's book may be consulted. A problem with two PDEs is given in [5].

Finally, it must be realized that the approach presented in this chapter is time-consuming and for many design variables the derivation of the final formulation system equations can be very complicated. However, because of the advantages mentioned previously, this method should be mastered by a designer who wishes to utilize optimization techniques.

EXERCISES

1. A farmer wants to put up a chicken fence from a roll of chicken wire with a total length of 350 m. The fence is to be rectangular in shape with a maximum width of 80 m. For a maximum area, what should be the size of the fence? Show the point of optimum solution on the variation diagram. If the maximum width is changed to 100 m does the area change? (Area = 7600 m²)

2. A piston rod is to be designed for a thrust load of 16 kN. The permissible minimum length is 300 mm. The material (steel) in stock is given in Table 9.3. Design the rod for a minimum weight. The minimum diameter is 5 mm and the maximum diameter is 100 mm. Use a factor of safety of 1.5.

Material UNS No.	Yield Stress (MPa)
G10100 HR	207
G10180 HR	331
G10150 CD	565
G87400 HR	338
G10400 CD	407

TABLE 9.3

(*Hint:* Model the piston as a short column with end effect $= 2.0$)

REFERENCES

1. Ellis, J. "Johnson's Method of Optimum Design Applied to a Problem with Simple Functional Relationships." *Computer Aided Design* 8, no.1 (January 1976): 9–12.

2. Johnson, R. C. *Optimum Design of Mechanical Elements.* New York: John Wiley & Sons, Inc., 1980.

3. Johnson, R. C. "Three-Dimensional Variation Diagrams for Control Calculations in Optimum Design." *Journal of Engineering for Industry* (August 1967): 391–98.

4. Bauld, Nelson, Jr. *Mechanics of Materials.* Monterey, Calif.: Brooks/Cole Publishing Co., 1982.

5. Onwubiko, C. "Piston Rods Design Using Johnson's Method of Optimum Design." *Journal of Mechanisms, Transmissions, and Automation and Design* 110 (September 1988): 362–65.

Introduction to the Finite Element Method

10.1 INTRODUCTION

In Chapter 4 we examined the numerical methods for the solutions of nonlinear algebraic equations. It may seem that most of the design problems can be modeled to permit the use of the methods of Chapter 4. However, modeling of engineering systems often leads to ordinary or partial differential equations. A design is incomplete until the solutions of the resulting differential equations are obtained. Because most engineering applications may require complicated geometries, loadings, and irregular boundary conditions, it is not always possible to obtain analytical solutions to the resulting differential equations. Therefore, we must again resort to numerical methods. One of the numerical methods that is gaining popularity is the **finite element method.**

An interesting aspect of finite element method is that problem formulation using this approach results in a system of simultaneous algebraic equations instead of a system of differential equations. The algebraic equations result because a system or a body is modeled by subdividing it into smaller units or elements (hence the name finite element), which are interconnected.

There are several situations that require the use of this technique. Since this treatment is meant to be very elementary, we only mention some of the situations warranting the use of this technique. These include (but are not exclusively limited to):

1. The modeling of irregularly shaped bodies
2. Stress analysis of bodies composed of several different materials

3. The modeling of bodies with nonlinear behavior, large deformations, and nonlinear materials

4. Any modeling situation that results in ordinary or partial differential equation with boundary conditions that involve derivatives

10.2 MATRIX ALGEBRA

Before demonstrating the use of finite element method, we need to review some of the pertinent matrix operations that are helpful in the finite element method.

A **matrix** is a rectangular array of numbers with m rows and n columns; it is written:

$$\mathbf{A} = \begin{bmatrix} a_{11} & a_{12} & \cdots & a_{1n} \\ a_{21} & a_{22} & \cdots & a_{2n} \\ & & & \\ \cdot & \cdot & & \cdot \\ \cdot & \cdot & & \cdot \\ \cdot & \cdot & & \cdot \\ a_{m1} & a_{m2} & \cdots & a_{mn} \end{bmatrix}$$

(10.1)

The numbers a_{ij} of the array $\mathbf{A}$ are called **elements**, or **entries**. To avoid any confusion we use the term entries. A matrix with one row is called a **row vector** and a matrix with one column is known as **column vector**. A matrix with m rows and n columns is said to be a matrix of **order (m, n)**, or an **m × n** matrix. If $n = m$, the matrix is a square matrix.

BASIC DEFINITIONS AND OPERATIONS

Equality of Matrices

Two matrices $\mathbf{A}$ and $\mathbf{B}$ are equal if

$$a_{ij} = b_{ij}$$

Addition and Multiplication of Matrices

The addition of two matrices of equal order is a third matrix of the same order, i.e.,

$$\mathbf{A} + \mathbf{B} = \mathbf{C}$$

where $\mathbf{A} = [a_{ij}]$, $\mathbf{B} = [b_{ij}]$, and $\mathbf{C} = [c_{ij}]$, $i = 1, 2, \ldots, m$ and $j = 1, 2, \ldots, n$. If for the two matrices $\mathbf{A}$ and $\mathbf{B}$, the number of columns n of $\mathbf{A}$ is equal to the number of rows m of **B**, we have a conformable matrix, and then we can perform the following:

$$C = AB$$

or

$$c_{ij} = \sum_{k=1}^{n} a_{ik} b_{kj} \qquad \textbf{(10.2)}$$

Identity Matrix

A matrix whose diagonal entries are all unity is called an **identity matrix**, i.e.,

$$A = I$$

if

$$a_{ij} = \begin{cases} 1 & i = j \\ 0 & i \neq j \end{cases}$$

The Transpose of a Matrix

The **transpose** of a matrix **A**, designated by A^T, is the matrix obtained by interchanging the rows and columns of the **A** matrix. For example, the transpose of

$$\begin{bmatrix} 3 & 4 & 6 \\ 2 & 1 & 7 \end{bmatrix} \quad \text{is} \quad \begin{bmatrix} 3 & 2 \\ 4 & 1 \\ 6 & 7 \end{bmatrix}$$

DETERMINANTS

A determinant is a square array of entries that can be reduced to a single value by certain operations. For example, if **A** is a 3×3 matrix, then the determinant, denoted by **A**, is

$$|A| = \begin{vmatrix} a_{11} & a_{12} & a_{13} \\ a_{21} & a_{22} & a_{23} \\ a_{31} & a_{32} & a_{33} \end{vmatrix} \qquad \textbf{(10.3)}$$

where

$$\begin{vmatrix} a_{11} & a_{12} & a_{13} \\ a_{21} & a_{22} & a_{23} \\ a_{31} & a_{32} & a_{33} \end{vmatrix} = a_{11} \begin{vmatrix} a_{22} & a_{23} \\ a_{32} & a_{33} \end{vmatrix} - a_{12} \begin{vmatrix} a_{21} & a_{23} \\ a_{31} & a_{33} \end{vmatrix} + a_{13} \begin{vmatrix} a_{21} & a_{22} \\ a_{31} & a_{32} \end{vmatrix} \qquad \textbf{(10.4)}$$

In general, the determinant of a square matrix A is given by

$$|A| = \sum_{i=1}^{n} a_{ij}A_{ij} \qquad j = 1, 2, \ldots, n \qquad (10.5)$$

where A_{ij} (known as the cofactor) is obtained from

$$A_{ij} = (-1)^{i+j}M_{ij} \qquad (10.6)$$

and M_{ij} is the determinant of a submatrix obtained by deleting the ith row and jth column. For example, the determinant of the 3×3 matrix

$$\begin{bmatrix} 2 & 0 & 6 \\ 8 & 10 & 12 \\ 14 & 16 & 18 \end{bmatrix}$$

is

$$|A| = 2 \begin{vmatrix} 10 & 12 \\ 16 & 18 \end{vmatrix} - 0 \begin{vmatrix} 8 & 12 \\ 14 & 18 \end{vmatrix} + 6 \begin{vmatrix} 8 & 10 \\ 14 & 16 \end{vmatrix}$$

$$= 2(180 - 192) - 0(144 - 168) + 6(128 - 140) = -96$$

If the determinant of a matrix is zero, then the matrix is said to be singular; otherwise it is nonsingular. For a nonsingular matrix the inverse is defined as:

$$AA^{-1} = A^{-1}A = I \qquad (10.7)$$

The inverse is normally obtained by performing row operations on the original matrix. The operation consists of multiplying or dividing any row by a selected number and then multiplying any row by a number and adding it to another row. Consider the following matrix:

$$\begin{bmatrix} 1 & 2 & -1 \\ 1 & 0 & 0 \\ 1 & 1 & 1 \end{bmatrix}$$

To find the inverse we:

Add an identity matrix to the original matrix to form

$$\begin{bmatrix} 1 & 2 & -1 & \vdots & 1 & 0 & 0 \\ 1 & 0 & 0 & \vdots & 0 & 1 & 0 \\ 1 & 1 & 1 & \vdots & 0 & 0 & 1 \end{bmatrix}$$

Multiply row 1 by -1 and add the result to both rows 2 and 3 to get

$$\begin{bmatrix} 1 & 2 & -1 & 1 & 0 & 0 \\ 0 & -2 & 1 & -1 & 1 & 0 \\ 0 & -1 & 2 & -1 & 0 & 1 \end{bmatrix}$$

Divide row 2 by -2, and the new matrix becomes

$$\begin{bmatrix} 1 & 2 & -1 & 1 & 0 & 0 \\ 0 & 1 & -\frac{1}{2} & \frac{1}{2} & -\frac{1}{2} & 0 \\ 0 & -1 & 2 & -1 & 0 & 1 \end{bmatrix}$$

Multiply row 2 by -2 and add the result to row 1. Also add row 2 to row 3 and get

$$\begin{bmatrix} 1 & 0 & 0 & 0 & 1 & 0 \\ 0 & 1 & -\frac{1}{2} & \frac{1}{2} & -\frac{1}{2} & 0 \\ 0 & 0 & \frac{3}{2} & -\frac{1}{2} & -\frac{1}{2} & 1 \end{bmatrix}$$

Multiply row 3 by $\frac{2}{3}$; the new matrix is now

$$\begin{bmatrix} 1 & 0 & 0 & 0 & 1 & 0 \\ 0 & 1 & -\frac{1}{2} & \frac{1}{2} & -\frac{1}{2} & 0 \\ 0 & 0 & 1 & -\frac{1}{3} & -\frac{1}{3} & \frac{2}{3} \end{bmatrix}$$

Multiply row 3 by $\frac{1}{2}$ and add to row 2 to give the final matrix:

$$\begin{bmatrix} 1 & 0 & 0 & 0 & 1 & 0 \\ 0 & 1 & 0 & \frac{1}{3} & -\frac{2}{3} & \frac{1}{3} \\ 0 & 0 & 1 & -\frac{1}{3} & -\frac{1}{3} & \frac{2}{3} \end{bmatrix}$$

Note the position of the identity matrix to be sure we have actually inverted the original matrix. The inverse of the original matrix is

$$\begin{bmatrix} 0 & 1 & 0 \\ \frac{1}{3} & -\frac{2}{3} & \frac{1}{3} \\ -\frac{1}{3} & -\frac{1}{3} & \frac{2}{3} \end{bmatrix}$$

We have demonstrated one method of determining the inverse of a matrix. However, there is a special type of matrix whose inverse is very easy to determine; this is called the orthogonal matrix. An orthogonal matrix is one with the following property:

$$\mathbf{A}^T\mathbf{A} = \mathbf{A}\mathbf{A}^T = \mathbf{I} \tag{10.8}$$

The inverse of an orthogonal matrix is simply the transpose of the matrix, i.e.,

$$\mathbf{A}^{-1} = \mathbf{A}^T \tag{10.9}$$

10.3 FINITE ELEMENT ANALYSIS PROCEDURES

The objective of this chapter is to introduce the finite element method; therefore, we present a simplified approach to the finite element analysis procedure. It is not our intention to give elaborate mathematical treatment to the subject. Such detailed treatments are outside our perimeter; however, we have included many references ([1] through [6]) that could be consulted for detailed treatment of the subject.

Finite element analysis can be viewed as a four-step process:

Step 1 The first step involves the division of the continuum (body) into elements (with identifiable nodes). The elements (which are finite in number) can, in theory, be many shapes and sizes (see Figure 10.1), but the elements must be interconnected at nodes located either at the element's corners or on the boundaries. The number of elements used or the shape of the elements depends on the particular problem. However, to decide which shape and size of elements to use requires the analyst to possess a sound understanding of the physical model and the finite element procedure. For example, if one is modeling a plate with a hole in the middle, an understanding of stress analysis is very helpful. The analyst would realize that the largest stresses are to be expected near the hole. In this case the analyst may decide to use smaller-sized elements near the hole for greater accuracy in the prediction of the stresses near the hole.

Examination of Figure 10.1 leads to the conclusion that the partitioning of the continuum into finite elements can be very tedious and time-consuming, especially for complex systems. However, we can use the graphical abilities of many CAD systems to ease the problem of creating the elements. The term **preprocessor** describes the programs that are useful in the partitioning of the system into finite elements.

Step 2 The second step establishes the properties of each element. One of the most important properties to be established is the relationship between the generalized forces (or any potential) and the displacements. This can be represented as:

$$\mathbf{F} = \mathbf{G}\mathbf{u}$$

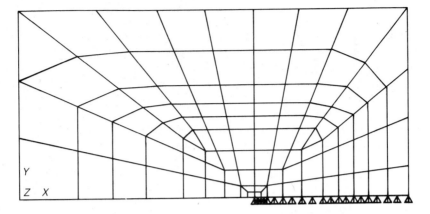

FIGURE 10.1

Finite element model of different shapes. (This was used for the study of crack growth rate.)

Here F represents an applied force or any driving potential such as heat flux and **u** represents the displacement (or nodal temperature) variations within each node. The form **G** is a matrix derived by either the application of minimum potential energy principle or virtual work for stress analysis, or it can represent element conduction matrix for thermal analysis.

Step 3 Calculate the local stiffness matrix **G**.

Step 4 Assemble local **G** into a global **G**. Then solve the resultant system of equations and interpret the result.

Having presented this simplified approach to finite element analysis, we can now demonstrate the procedure by using the **direct-stiffness method.** Because our objective is to introduce the reader to this field, we keep the illustrations simple; however, other approaches to finite element analysis and complex examples are obtainable from the given references.

10.4 ONE-DIMENSIONAL MODEL

To illustrate the principle of the finite element method we analyze an axially loaded member, shown in Figure 10.2. We consider the member to comprise three elements and four nodes. The nodes are to be understood as the points of connection between adjacent elements or the points needed to assemble the elements. Our interest is on the displacement of each node.

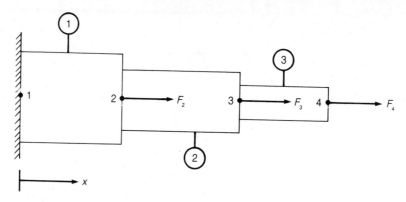

FIGURE 10.2

Axially loaded member.

There are certain assumptions made in this analysis:

1. The forces are applied at the nodes.
2. The nodes are capable of only linear displacements in the horizontal direction.
3. Each node has one degree of freedom (see assumption 2). The degree of freedom is the number of independent displacement/rotations (usually three rotations and three displacements) that a node can exercise.
4. The nodal forces and displacements are considered positive if they are directed to the right. With these assumptions we now apply these steps.

Consider the first element (see Figure 10.3) with forces f_1 and f_2 applied at each node and with displacements of u_1 and u_2, respectively. We use the notation f_{ij} to represent the force on the ith element and jth node. From elementary strength of material we know that the displacement, δ, can be written as

$$\delta = \frac{FL}{AE} = \frac{F}{k} \tag{10.10}$$

where k is the stiffness (AE/L).

From equation (10.10)

$$\begin{aligned} f_{11} &= k_1\delta \\ f_{12} &= k_1\delta \end{aligned} \tag{10.11}$$

But $\delta = u_2 - u_1$ and by the equilibrium of element 1, we have

$$\begin{aligned} f_{11} &= k_1(u_1 - u_2) \\ f_{12} &= -k_1(u_1 - u_2) \end{aligned} \tag{10.12}$$

FIGURE 10.3

A typical one-dimensional element.

In matrix form equation (10.12) becomes

$$\begin{bmatrix} f_{11} \\ f_{12} \end{bmatrix} = \begin{bmatrix} k_1 & -k_1 \\ -k_1 & k_1 \end{bmatrix} \begin{bmatrix} u_1 \\ u_2 \end{bmatrix} \tag{10.13}$$

Following similar treatment for element 2,

$$\begin{bmatrix} f_{22} \\ f_{23} \end{bmatrix} = \begin{bmatrix} k_2 & -k_2 \\ -k_2 & k_2 \end{bmatrix} \begin{bmatrix} u_2 \\ u_3 \end{bmatrix} \tag{10.14}$$

It follows that for the ith element,

$$\begin{bmatrix} f_{ii} \\ f_{ii+1} \end{bmatrix} = \begin{bmatrix} k_i & -k_i \\ -k_i & k_i \end{bmatrix} \begin{bmatrix} u_i \\ u_{i+1} \end{bmatrix} \tag{10.15}$$

If there are n elements, then we have n separate matrix equations of the form given in equation (10.15). The next step in our procedure for finite element analysis involves assembling the elements.

A simple way of understanding how to assemble the elements is to consider the total force at each node due to external forces. Let the sum of the forces be denoted by R_i, $i = 1, 2, \ldots, n$. For node 1 we have only one force; hence $R_1 = f_{11}$. But for the other nodes, we have $R_2 = f_{12} + f_{22}, \ldots, R_4 = f_{34}$ (see Figure 10.4). By the application of equation (10.15), we have:

$$\begin{aligned} R_1 &= f_{11} = k_1(u_1 - u_2) \\ R_2 &= f_{12} + f_{22} = -k_1 u_1 + (k_1 + k_2)u_2 - k_2 u_3 \\ R_3 &= f_{23} + f_{33} = -k_2 u_2 + (k_2 + k_3)u_3 - k_3 u_4 \\ R_4 &= f_{34} = -k_3 u_3 + k_3 u_4 \end{aligned} \tag{10.16}$$

The system of equation (10.16) may be represented in matrix form as:

$$\begin{bmatrix} R_1 \\ R_2 \\ R_3 \\ R_4 \end{bmatrix} = \begin{bmatrix} k_1 & -k_1 & 0 & 0 \\ -k_1 & k_1 + k_2 & -k_2 & 0 \\ 0 & -k_2 & k_2 + k_3 & -k_3 \\ 0 & 0 & -k_3 & k_3 \end{bmatrix} \begin{bmatrix} u_1 \\ u_2 \\ u_3 \\ u_4 \end{bmatrix} \tag{10.17a}$$

FIGURE 10.4

The sum of forces at each node. (Note R_1, R_2 etc. $\equiv F_1$, F_2 F_3 of Figure 10.2.)

In compact form:

$$[R] = [k][u] \tag{10.17b}$$

where $[R]$ is the force matrix of external forces at the nodes, $[k]$ matrix is the stiffness matrix, and $[u]$ is the displacement matrix. Observe that $[k]$ is singular and consequently has no inverse. The implication is that equation (10.17) cannot be solved until some boundary conditions are applied that would lead to another matrix whose stiffness matrix is nonsingular.

The next step in our approach to finite element analysis is to solve equation (10.17). This requires that either the force matrix or some boundary conditions be known. For our example, $u_1 = 0$. This helps us to eliminate column 1 of the stiffness matrix, since it is associated with u_1. Similarly, we eliminate row 1; the final matrix is:

$$\begin{bmatrix} R_2 \\ R_3 \\ R_4 \end{bmatrix} = \begin{bmatrix} k_1 + k_2 & -k_2 & 0 \\ -k_2 & k_2 + k_3 & -k_3 \\ 0 & -k_3 & k_3 \end{bmatrix} \begin{bmatrix} u_2 \\ u_3 \\ u_4 \end{bmatrix} \tag{10.18}$$

Equation (10.18) can readily be solved directly or by one of the several standard computer subroutines. The value of R_1 can be determined from equation (10.16) once u_2 is known. Also, the stress and strain in each element may be determined by the standard procedure of strength of materials. For example, the strain, ε_x, and the stress, σ_x, for the ith element can be expressed as

$$\varepsilon_{x,i} = \frac{u_i - u_{i+1}}{x_{i+1} - x_i}$$

and

$$\sigma_{x,i} = E_i \varepsilon_{x,i} \tag{10.19}$$

E X A M P L E 10.1

For the axially loaded member shown, determine the nodal displacements (see Figure 10.5).

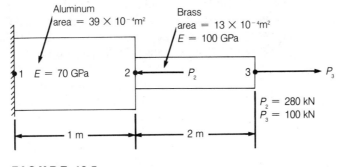

FIGURE 10.5

SOLUTION Using the numbering system of the problem, there are two elements and three nodes. By application of equations (10.13), (10.15), and (10.16), we have:

$$\begin{bmatrix} R_1 \\ R_2 \\ R_3 \end{bmatrix} = \begin{bmatrix} k_1 & -k_1 & 0 \\ -k_2 & k_1 + k_2 & -k_2 \\ 0 & -k_2 & k_2 \end{bmatrix} \begin{bmatrix} u_1 \\ u_2 \\ u_3 \end{bmatrix}$$

From the boundary condition, $u_1 = 0$; therefore, by eliminating the first row and the first column we have:

$$\begin{bmatrix} R_2 \\ R_3 \end{bmatrix} = \begin{bmatrix} k_1 + k_2 & -k_2 \\ -k_2 & k_2 \end{bmatrix} \begin{bmatrix} u_2 \\ u_3 \end{bmatrix}$$

Since $k = AE/L$, $k_1 = 2.73 \times 10^8$, and $k_2 = 1.3 \times 10^8$, then

$$10^{16} \begin{bmatrix} 4.03 & -1.3 \\ -1.3 & 1.3 \end{bmatrix} \begin{bmatrix} u_2 \\ u_3 \end{bmatrix} = \begin{bmatrix} -280 \times 10^3 \\ 1 \times 10^5 \end{bmatrix}$$

Solving, we obtain $u_2 = 0.00066$ m and $u_3 = 0.00011$ m. Note that the reaction at the wall can be obtained as:

$$R_1 = -k_1 u_2 = 180 \text{ kN}$$

The reader should verify that the reaction is indeed correct.

10.5 FINITE ELEMENT ANALYSIS OF PLANE TRUSSES

In this section we illustrate the use of finite element method in the analysis of plane trusses. A plane truss is a framework (structure) composed of bar members, all lying in a plane and connected at their ends by frictionless pins. In the analysis of a truss, we assume that the bar elements are two force members with the forces directed along the axis of the bar element. The implication is that the bar elements do not support any shear load. This assumption is integral to our truss analysis by the finite element method.

We begin by considering a two-force member shown in Figure 10.6. The bar is arbitrarily oriented to the xy axis. The xy axis is called the **global coordinate system.** We define a second coordinate axis, $x'y'$, which is called a **local coordinate system.** Note that one of the axes of the local coordinate system is parallel to the axis of the bar element. The use of the local coordinate system allows us to apply the results of the previous section directly to the bar element with reference to the local coordinate system (i.e., $x'y'$ axis). Since a truss consists of several members and, therefore, several local coordinate systems, we measure the displacement of each joint with reference to the global coordinate system. This requires the establishment of the relationship between the local and global coordinates. From Chapter 5:

$$x = x'\cos \theta - y'\sin \theta$$
$$y = x'\sin \theta + y'\cos \theta$$

(10.20)

or, in matrix form,

$$[x \quad y]^T = [A][x' \quad y']^T$$

(10.21)

where

$$[A] = \begin{bmatrix} \cos \theta & -\sin \theta \\ \sin \theta & \cos \theta \end{bmatrix}$$

We can now express the displacements at the two nodes of the bar element (using equation (10.20)) relative to the global coordinates as:

$$u_{1x} = u_{1x'}\cos \theta - u_{1y'}\sin \theta$$
$$u_{2x} = u_{2x'}\sin \theta + u_{2y'}\cos \theta$$

(10.22)

or, in matrix form,

$$[u_{1x} \quad u_{2x}]^T = [A_1][u_{1x'} \quad u_{1y'} \quad u_{2x'} \quad u_{2y'}]^T$$

where

$$[A_1] = \begin{bmatrix} \cos \theta & -\sin \theta & 0 & 0 \\ 0 & 0 & \sin \theta & \cos \theta \end{bmatrix}$$

(10.23)

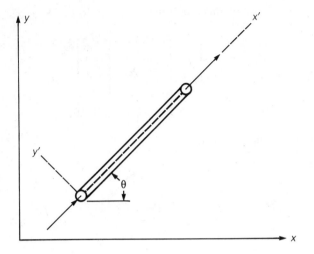

FIGURE 10.6

A two-force member at an orientation of θ^a measured positive in counterclockwise direction.

Suppose that we want to express the local displacements in terms of the global coordinates. We must find the inverse of $[A_1]$, which is not a square matrix. Therefore, we modify equation (10.23) as:

$$
\begin{bmatrix} u_{1x} \\ u_{1y} \\ u_{2x} \\ u_{2y} \end{bmatrix} = [A_2] \begin{bmatrix} u_{1x'} \\ u_{1y'} \\ u_{2x'} \\ u_{2y'} \end{bmatrix}
$$

where

$$
[A_2] = \begin{bmatrix} \cos \theta & -\sin \theta & 0 & 0 \\ \sin \theta & \cos \theta & 0 & 0 \\ 0 & 0 & \cos \theta & -\sin \theta \\ 0 & 0 & \sin \theta & \cos \theta \end{bmatrix}
\qquad \textbf{(10.24)}
$$

or, in compact form,

$$
[\mathbf{u}]_{xy} = [A_2][\mathbf{u}]_{x'y'}
\qquad \textbf{(10.25)}
$$

We can also perform similar operations on the forces F_1 and F_2 as:

$$\begin{bmatrix} F_{1x} \\ F_{1y} \\ F_{2x} \\ F_{2y} \end{bmatrix} = [A_2] \begin{bmatrix} F_{1x'} \\ F_{1y'} \\ F_{2x'} \\ F_{2y'} \end{bmatrix} \tag{10.26}$$

or, in a more compact form,

$$[\mathbf{F}]_{xy} = [A_2][\mathbf{F}]_{x'y'} \tag{10.27}$$

Recall that we assumed no shear force, i.e.,

$$F_{1y} = F_{2y} = 0$$

However, if we incorporate this in the expansion of equation (10.15) and drop the subscript on the stiffness, we have:

$$\begin{bmatrix} F_{1x'} \\ F_{1y'} \\ F_{2x'} \\ F_{2y'} \end{bmatrix} = k \begin{bmatrix} 1 & 0 & -1 & 0 \\ 0 & 0 & 0 & 0 \\ -1 & 0 & 1 & 0 \\ 0 & 0 & 0 & 0 \end{bmatrix} \begin{bmatrix} u_{1x'} \\ u_{1y'} \\ u_{2x'} \\ u_{2y'} \end{bmatrix} \tag{10.28}$$

or, in compact form,

$$[\mathbf{F}]_{x'y'} = [k][\mathbf{u}]_{x'y'} \tag{10.29}$$

Substituting equation (10.29) into (10.27) gives

$$[\mathbf{F}]_{xy} = [A_2][k]_{x'y'}[u]_{x'y'} \tag{10.30}$$

From equation (10.25) we have

$$[\mathbf{u}]_{x'y'} = [A]^{-1}[u]_{xy}$$

Since $[A_2]$ is an orthogonal matrix, then

$$[\mathbf{u}]_{x'y'} = [A]^T[\mathbf{u}]_{xy}$$

Substitution of this into equation (10.30) yields

$$[\mathbf{F}]_{xy} = [A_2][k]_{x'y'}[A_2]^T[\mathbf{u}]_{xy} \tag{10.31}$$

The relationship between the stiffness matrix of the local and global coordinates is

$$[k]_{xy} = [A_2][k]_{x'y'}[A_2]^T \qquad \textbf{(10.32)}$$

Using $[k]_{x'y'}$ from equation (10.29) and combining it with equations (10.24) and (10.32), the global stiffness matrix can be expressed as

$$[k] = k \begin{bmatrix} \cos^2\theta & \cos\theta\sin\theta & -\cos^2\theta & -\cos\theta\sin\theta \\ \cos\theta\sin\theta & \sin^2\theta & -\cos\theta\sin\theta & -\sin^2\theta \\ -\cos^2\theta & -\cos\theta\sin\theta & \cos^2\theta & \cos\theta\sin\theta \\ -\cos\theta\sin\theta & -\sin^2\theta & \cos\theta\sin\theta & \sin^2\theta \end{bmatrix} \qquad \textbf{(10.33)}$$

ASSEMBLING THE ELEMENT STIFFNESS MATRICES

To obtain an expression of the form given in equation (10.18), it is necessary to assemble all the stiffness matrices so the displacement and/or forces acting on the truss members may be solved for. The method of assembling can be tedious and complex, but we present, in a simplified form, the **stiffness method**. The steps involved in the formation of the total stiffness matrix are:

1. Number the global nodes of the truss from 1 to n (number of nodes) and the elements from 1 to NE. Since each element has two nodes, assign two numbers, 1 and 2, to identify the nodes of each element. For example, element two, local node (LN) 1 can be written as $LN_{2,1}$.

2. Assign local identifying numbers to the displacements of each node as:

Local Node	1	2
Node displacements	$u_{1x}\ u_{1y}$	$u_{2x}\ u_{2y}$
Identifying number	1 2	3 4

3. Establish the equivalence between each local number (LN) and its corresponding global node (GN) number as

$$GN_{e,j} = LN_{e,j}, \quad \begin{aligned} e &= 1, 2, \ldots, NE \\ j &= 1, 2 \end{aligned}$$

4. Assign the global identification numbers to the displacement (v) of each node using the relationship

$$GDI(v_{x,i}) = 2i - 1$$
$$GDI(v_{y,i}) = 2i, \quad i = 1, 2, \ldots, n$$

where GDI stands for global displacement identification.

5. Initialize the global stiffness (GK) as

$$GK_{i,j} = 0, \quad j = 1, 2, \ldots, 2n$$
$$i = 1, 2, \ldots, 2n$$

6. Add the entries in each local stiffness matrix to the entry in the global stiffness having the same displacement as the local stiffness matrix. This procedure is illustrated in the example that follows. Because this process requires tracking which local node corresponds to a global node, the computer program shown in Figure 10.7 has proven successful in the assembling of the global stiffness matrix.

```
10      ' ********************************************************
20      ' * THIS PGROGRAM CALLED GSTIFF IS FOR THE FORMATION OF*
30      ' * THE GLOBAL STIFFNESS FROM EACH ELEMENT.            *
40      ' * IT IS LIMITED TO 2-DEGREES OF FREEDOM.             *
50      ' ********************************************************
60         INPUT "THE NO. OF ELEMENTS";NE
70         INPUT "THE NO. OF NODES";N  : NN = 2*N
80         DIM LK(NE,4,4),KG(NN,NN),LNN(NE,2),NDX(NE,N),NDY(NE,N),GDX(N),GD
90      ' DOF IS THE DEGREE OF FREEDOM.
100        DOF = 2 : NDEG  = 2*DOF
110        FOR E = 1 TO NE
120        FOR J = 1 TO DOF
130        PRINT"FOR ELEMENT #";E,"LOCAL NODE";J
140        INPUT"THE GLOBAL NODE NUMBER=";LNN(E,J)
150        NEXT J  : NEXT E
160      ' GENERATE THE STIFFNESS MATRIX FOR EACH ELEMENT
170        FOR E = 1 TO NE
180        PRINT "WHAT IS THE ORIENTATION OF ELEMENT #";E
190        INPUT "ANGLE (DEG) = ";ANGLE
200      ANGLE = ANGLE*(22/(7*180))
210      PRINT"FOR ELEMENT";E
220      INPUT"THE MODULUS OF ELASTICITY IS";EM
230      PRINT"THE AREA OF ELEMENT";E
240      INPUT AM
250      PRINT"THE LENGTH OF ELEMENT ";E
260      INPUT LM
270      KE = AM*EM/LM
280      C2 = (COS(ANGLE))^2 : S2 = (SIN(ANGLE))^2 :  CS = COS(ANGLE)*SIN
290      FOR I = 1 TO NDEG
300         IF I = 1 OR I = 3 THEN LK(E,I,I) = C2 ELSE LK(E,I,I) = S2
310      LK(E,I,I) = LK(E,I,I)*KE
320      PRINT"LK=";LK(E,I,I)
330      NEXT I
340      LK(E,2,1) = CS*KE      :  LK(E,1,2) =   CS*KE
350      LK(E,3,1) = -C2*KE     :  LK(E,1,3) =  -C2*KE
360      LK(E,3,2) = -CS*KE     :  LK(E,2,3) =  -CS*KE
370      LK(E,4,1) = -CS*KE     :  LK(E,1,4) =  -CS*KE
380      LK(E,4,2) = -S2*KE     :  LK(E,2,4) =  -S2*KE
390      LK(E,4,3) =  CS*KE     :  LK(E,3,4) =   CS*KE
400      FOR I = 1 TO 4
410      FOR J = 1 TO 4
420      PRINT"LK(",E,I,J,")=";LK(E,I,J),
```

FIGURE 10.7

Program for the assembling of the element stiffness matrix.

```
430     NEXT J: NEXT I
440     NEXT E
450     ' ASSIGN LOCAL DISPLACEMENT NUMBER
460     FOR E = 1 TO NE
470     M = 1
480     FOR I = 1 TO 2
490     NDX(E,LNN(E,I)) = M  :  M = M + 1
500     NDY(E,LNN(E,I)) = M  :  M = M + 1 : NEXT I
510     NEXT E
520     'ESTABLISH EQUIVALENCE BETWEEN EACH LOCAL NODE AND GLOBAL NODE
530     FOR E = 1 TO NE
540     FOR J = 1 TO DOF
550     GN(E,J) = LNN(E,J)   : NEXT J : NEXT E
560     ' ASSIGN GLOBAL DISPLACEMENT NUMBER
570     FOR I = 1 TO N
580     GDX(I) = 2*I - 1
590     GDY(I) = 2*I   : NEXT I
600     'FORM THE GLOBAL STIFFNESS CONSTANT
610     FOR E = 1 TO NE
620     A = GN(E,1) : B = GN(E,2)
630     FOR J = 1 TO NDEG
640     IF J = 2 THEN 730
650     IF J = 3 THEN 790
660     IF J = 4 THEN 850
670     J1  = GDX(A)
680     KG(J1,GDX(A)) = KG(J1,GDX(A)) + LK(E,J,1)
690     KG(J1,GDY(A)) = KG(J1,GDY(A)) + LK(E,J,2)
700     KG(J1,GDX(B)) = KG(J1,GDX(B)) + LK(E,J,3)
710     KG(J1,GDY(B)) = KG(J1,GDY(B)) + LK(E,J,4)
720     GOTO 900
730     J2  = GDY(A)
740     KG(J2,GDX(A)) = KG(J2,GDX(A)) + LK(E,J,1)
750     KG(J2,GDY(A)) = KG(J2,GDY(A)) + LK(E,J,2)
760     KG(J2,GDX(B)) = KG(J2,GDX(B)) + LK(E,J,3)
770     KG(J2,GDY(B)) = KG(J2,GDY(B)) + LK(E,J,4)
780     GOTO 900
790     J3  = GDX(B)
800     KG(J3,GDX(A)) = KG(J3,GDX(A)) + LK(E,J,1)
810     KG(J3,GDY(A)) = KG(J3,GDY(A)) + LK(E,J,2)
820     KG(J3,GDX(B)) = KG(J3,GDX(B)) + LK(E,J,3)
830     KG(J3,GDY(B)) = KG(J3,GDY(B)) + LK(E,J,4)
840     GOTO 900
850     J4  = GDY(B)
860     KG(J4,GDX(A)) = KG(J4,GDX(A)) + LK(E,J,1)
870     KG(J4,GDY(A)) = KG(J4,GDY(A)) + LK(E,J,2)
880     KG(J4,GDX(B)) = KG(J4,GDX(B)) + LK(E,J,3)
890     KG(J4,GDY(B)) = KG(J4,GDY(B)) + LK(E,J,4)
900     NEXT J  : NEXT E
910     FOR I = 1 TO NN
920     FOR J = 1 TO NN
930     PRINT"KG(";I;J;")=";KG(I,J),
940     NEXT J
950     NEXT I
960     END
```

FIGURE 10.7

(Continued).

E X A M P L E   10.2

For the truss shown in Figure 10.8, determine the displacement of point 3 and the forces in each member of the truss. This information is supplied:

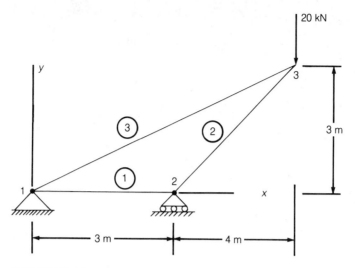

FIGURE 10.8

Truss for example 10.2.

Member	Area (x 10⁴m²)
1–2	6
1–3	15.23
2–3	10

All members are made of steel ($E = 210$ GPa).

SOLUTION   First, establish the global coordinates for the truss as in Figure 10.8 and then identify the various elements (see Figure 10.9). Next, establish the various local coordinates (Figure 10.9). We arbitrarily designate member 1–2 as element 1 (e_1), member 2–3 as element 2 (e_2), and member 1–3 as element 3 (e_3).

Second, establish the global stiffness matrix for each element. For element 1, $\sin \theta_1 = 0$ and $\cos \theta_1 = 1$; therefore, by equation (10.33) we have

$$[k_1]_{xy} = k_1 \begin{bmatrix} 1 & 0 & -1 & 0 \\ 0 & 0 & 0 & 0 \\ -1 & 0 & 1 & 0 \\ 0 & 0 & 0 & 0 \end{bmatrix}$$

For element 2, $\cos \theta_2 = 0.8$ and $\sin \theta_2 = .6$; we have

$$[k_2]_{xy} = k_2 \begin{bmatrix} 0.64 & 0.48 & -0.64 & -0.48 \\ 0.48 & 0.36 & -0.48 & -0.36 \\ -0.64 & -0.48 & 0.64 & 0.48 \\ -0.48 & -0.36 & 0.48 & 0.36 \end{bmatrix}$$

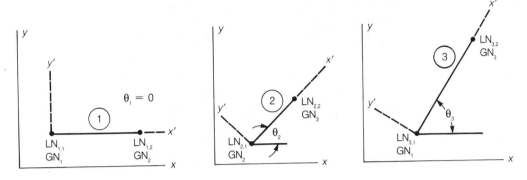

FIGURE 10.9

Identification of the elements of example Problem 10.2. (LN = local node and GN = global number)

For element 3, $\theta = 23.19°$, $\cos \theta = 0.919$, and $\sin \theta = 0.3938$; hence

$$[k_3]_{xy} = k_3 \begin{bmatrix} 0.845 & 0.362 & -0.845 & -0.362 \\ 0.362 & 0.155 & -0.362 & -0.155 \\ -0.845 & -0.362 & 0.845 & 0.362 \\ -0.362 & -0.155 & 0.362 & 0.155 \end{bmatrix}$$

Third, calculate and assemble the element stiffness matrices to obtain the global system stiffness matrix. Here we will adopt the steps previously given. For typical analysis we select element 2. Using step 2 on page 295, and since there are two displacements at each node, we have

Local Node	1		2	
Node displacement	u_{1x}	u_{1y}	u_{2x}	u_{2y}
Identifying number	1	2	3	4

From step 3 we establish the correspondence between the local nodes (LN) and global nodes (GN) as:

e/j	1	2	Element
$GN_{e,j}$ 1	1	2	1
2	2	3	2
3	1	2	3
Local node	1	2	

Next, we assign global identification numbers (GDI) to the displacement (v) of each node:

Node (i)	$v_{x,i}$	$v_{y,i}$	$GDI(v_{x,i})$	$GDI(v_{y,i})$
1	1	1	1	2
2	2	2	3	4
3	3	3	5	6

Using the displacement number, we establish the equivalence between the entries in each element (note that the circled numbers refer to the global system matrix). For element 1 we have

$$
\begin{array}{cc}
 & \begin{array}{cccc} ① & ② & ③ & ④ \\ 1 & 2 & 3 & 4 \end{array} \\
\begin{array}{cc} ① & 1 \\ ② & 2 \\ ③ & 3 \\ ④ & 4 \end{array} &
\left[\begin{array}{cccc}
1 & 0 & -1 & 0 \\
0 & 0 & 0 & 0 \\
-1 & 0 & 1 & 0 \\
0 & 0 & 0 & 0
\end{array}\right] k_1
\end{array}
\quad \leftarrow \text{GDI} \\ \leftarrow \text{LN}
$$

For element 2 we have

$$
\begin{array}{cc}
 & \begin{array}{cccc} ③ & ④ & ⑤ & ⑥ \\ 1 & 2 & 3 & 4 \end{array} \\
\begin{array}{cc} ③ & 1 \\ ④ & 2 \\ ⑤ & 3 \\ ⑥ & 4 \end{array} &
\left[\begin{array}{cccc}
0.64 & 0.48 & -0.64 & -0.48 \\
0.48 & 0.36 & -0.48 & -0.36 \\
-0.64 & -0.48 & 0.64 & 0.48 \\
-0.48 & -0.36 & 0.48 & 0.36
\end{array}\right] k_2
\end{array}
\quad \leftarrow \text{GDI} \\ \leftarrow \text{LN}
$$

and for element 3 we have

$$
\begin{array}{cc}
 & \begin{array}{cccc} ① & ② & ⑤ & ⑥ \\ 1 & 2 & 3 & 4 \end{array} \\
\begin{array}{cc} ① & 1 \\ ② & 2 \\ ⑤ & 3 \\ ⑥ & 4 \end{array} &
\left[\begin{array}{cccc}
0.845 & 0.362 & -0.845 & -0.362 \\
0.362 & 0.155 & -0.362 & -0.155 \\
-0.845 & -0.362 & 0.845 & 0.362 \\
-0.362 & -0.155 & 0.362 & 0.155
\end{array}\right] k_3
\end{array}
\quad \leftarrow \text{GDI} \\ \leftarrow \text{LN}
$$

We can form the global stiffness matrix by adding corresponding entries from each element stiffness matrix. For example, the global stiffness matrix entry (5, 5) is the sum of entry (3, 3) from element stiffness matrix 2 and entry (3, 3) from element 3. With $k = AE/L$, the global matrix is

$$
[\mathbf{k}] = c
\left[\begin{array}{cccccc}
1.845 & 0.362 & -1 & 0 & -0.845 & -0.362 \\
0.362 & 0.155 & 0 & 0 & -0.362 & -0.155 \\
-1 & 0 & 1.640 & 0.480 & -0.640 & -0.480 \\
0 & 0 & 0.480 & 0.360 & -0.480 & -0.360 \\
-0.845 & -0.362 & -0.640 & -0.480 & 1.485 & 0.842 \\
-0.362 & -0.155 & -0.480 & -0.360 & 0.842 & 0.515
\end{array}\right]
$$

where

$$c = 42 \times 10^6$$

Next we form the force and displacement vectors as:

$$[\mathbf{R}] = \begin{bmatrix} R_{1x} \\ R_{1y} \\ R_{2x} \\ R_{2y} \\ R_{3x} \\ R_{3y} \end{bmatrix} \qquad [\mathbf{u}] = \begin{bmatrix} u_{1x} \\ u_{1y} \\ u_{2x} \\ u_{2y} \\ u_{3x} \\ u_{3y} \end{bmatrix}$$

The final system of equations can be written in vector form:

$$[\mathbf{R}] = [\mathbf{k}][\mathbf{u}].$$

From the truss, $R_{3x} = 0$ and $R_{3y} = 20$ kN. The following boundary conditions apply:

$$u_{1x} = u_{1y} = u_{2x} = u_{2y} = 0$$

Then the final system of equations in matrix form is

$$\begin{bmatrix} R_{1x} \\ R_{1y} \\ R_{2x} \\ R_{2y} \\ R_{3x} \\ R_{3y} \end{bmatrix}$$

$$= c \begin{bmatrix} 1.845 & 0.362 & -1 & 0 & -0.845 & -0.362 \\ 0.362 & 0.155 & 0 & 0 & -0.362 & -0.155 \\ -1 & 0 & 1.640 & 0.480 & -0.640 & -0.480 \\ 0 & 0 & 0.480 & 0.360 & -0.480 & -0.360 \\ -0.845 & -0.362 & -0.640 & -0.480 & 1.485 & 0.842 \\ -0.362 & -0.155 & -0.480 & -0.360 & 0.842 & 0.515 \end{bmatrix} \begin{bmatrix} 0 \\ 0 \\ 0 \\ 0 \\ u_{3x} \\ u_{3y} \end{bmatrix}$$

$$(10.34)$$

Since the first four entries of the displacement vector are zeros, we eliminate the first four rows and columns to form

$$\begin{bmatrix} 0 \\ 20{,}000 \end{bmatrix} = 42 \times 10^6 \begin{bmatrix} 1.485 & 0.842 \\ 0.842 & 0.515 \end{bmatrix} \begin{bmatrix} u_{3x} \\ u_{3y} \end{bmatrix}$$

Solving the resulting system of equations, we obtain

$$u_{3x} = -0.007184 \text{ m} \quad \text{and} \quad u_{3y} = 0.01267 \text{ m}$$

By backward substitution in equation (10.34) we can determine the reactions as $R_{1x} = 62.3$ kN, $R_{1y} = 26.7$ kN, $R_{2x} = -62.3$ kN, and $R_{2y} = -46.7$ kN. Note that equilibrium is satisfied, so the sum of the external forces must be equal to zero.

To determine the forces in each member we make use of equation (10.24)—that is,

$$
\begin{bmatrix} u_{1x'} \\ u_{1y'} \\ u_{2x'} \\ u_{2y'} \end{bmatrix} = [A_2]^{-1} \begin{bmatrix} u_{1x} \\ u_{1y} \\ u_{2x} \\ u_{2y} \end{bmatrix}
$$

For element (2)

$$
\begin{bmatrix} u_{1x'} \\ u_{1y'} \\ u_{2x'} \\ u_{2y'} \end{bmatrix} = \begin{bmatrix} 0.8 & 0.6 & 0 & 0 \\ -0.6 & 0.8 & 0 & 0 \\ 0 & 0 & 0.8 & 0.6 \\ 0 & 0 & -0.6 & 0.8 \end{bmatrix} \begin{bmatrix} -0.007184 \\ 0.01267 \\ 0 \\ 0 \end{bmatrix}
$$

from which we have $u_{1x'} = 0.00185$. Using the relationship between the deformation and force,

$$F = \frac{AEu_{1x'}}{L}$$

The force on member 2–3 is 77.90 kN. You may now show that the force in member 1–3 is -67.62 kN and that of member 1–2 is 62.3 kN.

10.6   AVAILABLE COMPUTER PROGRAMS

This exercise illustrates the need for computer programs, especially when utilizing several elements in the analysis of a structure. Any manual attempt in the solution of the resulting system equations is certainly headed toward error and frustration. Fortunately, many programs have been devised for finite element analysis of structures. A few of these programs are shown in Table 10.1.

The selection of a program must be done on the basis of the desired application. However, the selected program should make the use of the finite element analysis technique less frustrating. For example, one of the most tedious processes in finite element modeling is the generation of meshes (outlines of the

Program	Source	Application
ANSYS	Structural Dynamic Research Corp., Cincinnati, OH	General-purpose finite element analysis program
ASTRA	Boeing, Seattle, WA	General-purpose finite element program
MAGIX	MARC Analysis Corp., Providence, RI	Nonlinear finite element modeling analysis
NASTRAN	NASA	Structural finite element modeling analysis
SAP	University of Calif., Berkley, CA.	Finite element modeling program for analysis of linearly elastic structures
SUPERTAB	Structural Dynamic Research Corp., Cincinnati, OH	General-purpose finite element modeling program

T A B L E 10.1

Finite element programs.

model elements). Therefore, it is important for the selected program to be capable of automatic mesh generation. The mesh generation program should preferably be linked with graphical display capabilities to ensure that the generated mesh approximates the geometry of the structure being modeled. The importance of automatic mesh generation can be seen from Figure 10.10. According to [7] Figure 10.10a was generated in 30 hours using the manual method and Figure 10.10b was created in 14 hours using an automatic mesh generator.

There are certain requirements for a good automatic generator, as suggested in [8]. Some of these necessary capabilities are summarized here:

1. **Ability to handle any general *n*-sided boundary.** If the generator cannot process nonlinear planar boundaries, manual creation of the mesh becomes a necessity.

2. **Various element types.** The generator must be capable of handling any element typology (triangular, quadrilateral, and so on) and any element order (linear, parabolic, or cubic displacement functions).

3. **Element distribution.** The generator should automatically decrease the element size in places of high displacement gradients and increase the element size in places where high gradients do not exist. This capability will lead to a decrease in computational cost (see the cited reference for further details).

Another factor in selecting a program is the type of computer on which the program is to be run. If a personal computer (PC) is to be used, it is much better to select a program that is written so that the operating commands are not machine dependent. It is often frustrating to discover that to make a transition from a PC version of the program to a mainframe version requires additional training. A program without this drawback is the ANSYS.

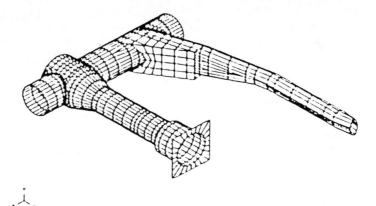

(a) Created manually (time — 30 hours)

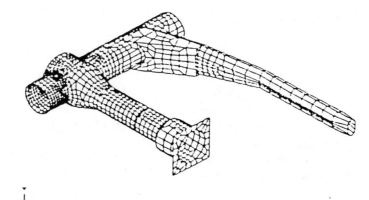

(b) Created with the Triquamesh free generator (time — 14 hours)

FIGURE 10.10

Mesh generation for a suspension model [7].

CONCLUDING REMARKS

Although the treatment of finite element analysis in this chapter has been confined primarily to structures, you should understand that finite element is applicable in more than the analysis of structures or machine elements. The finite element method proliferates in many engineering disciplines and is useful both for modeling heat transfer equipment and fluid flow in pipes and for circuit analysis. The impression that we want to create is that finite element method has tremendous potential for many engineering analyses and designs.

EXERCISES

1. Determine the displacements of nodes 2 and 3. (Ans.: $u_2 = u_3 = 0.00067$ in.)

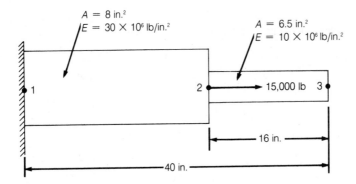

2. The axially loaded member is fixed at both ends. Compute the displacements of nodes 2 and 3.

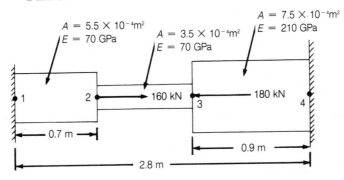

3. For the statically indeterminate structure shown, determine the displacement of the free node. (Ans.: $u_{2x} = .0043$ m, $u_{2y} = -.0097$ m).

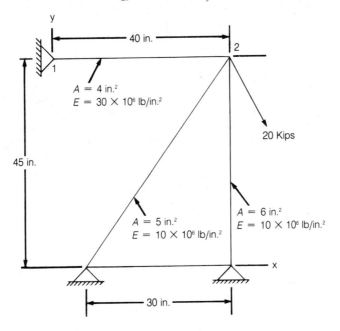

4. The structure shown is supported by a roller at joint 1. Find the displacement of the roller as a result of the applied loads.

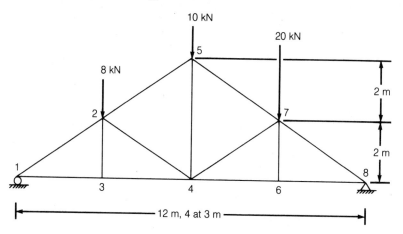

REFERENCES

1. Norrie, D. H., and G. Devries. *Introduction to Finite Element Analysis.* New York: Academic Press, 1978

2. Grandin, H. *Fundamentals of the Finite Element Method.* New York: The Macmillan Publishing Co., Inc., 1986.

3. Wait, R., and A. R. Mitchell. *Finite Element Analysis and Applications.* New York: John Wiley & Sons, Inc., 1985.

4. Cheung, Y. K., and M. F. Yeo. *A Practical Introduction to Finite Element Analysis.* London: Pitman Publishing Ltd., 1979.

5. Logan, D. L. *A First Course in the Finite Element Method.* Boston: Prindle, Weber & Schmidt, 1986.

6. Huston, R. L., and C. E. Passerello. *Finite Element Methods.* New York: Marcel Dekker, Inc., 1984.

7. Rudd, B. W. "Impacting the Design Process Using Solid Modeling and Automated Finite Element Mesh Generation." Finite Element Methods, Modeling, and New Applications, Proceedings of the 1986 Pressure Vessels and Piping Conference, ASME, CED 1, PVP 101, 1986, pp. 5–9.

8. Sluiter, M. G. C., and D. L. Hansen. "A General Purpose Automatic Mesh Generator For Shell and Solid Finite Elements." *Computers In Engineering* 3 (1982): 29–34.

CHAPTER 11

Application of Computer-Aided Design

11.1 INTRODUCTION

In the preceding chapters, we have examined the software and hardware components of computer-aided design (CAD). Because the hardware components discussed in Chapter 2 are used most often in automated drafting, most people think of computer-aided design only in terms of this application (i.e., drawing). But a complete CAD system, especially for the mechanical engineer, should allow for various operations, including engineering analysis (which includes finite element analysis and mass properties calculations), automated drafting, shape modeling, and computer-aided manufacturing. These operations are possible only if the CAD system is capable of a three-dimensional representation of the mechanical elements.

Such a representation enables the engineer to see the potential problems of both manufacturing and assembling the designed parts. The assembling aspect of design has not traditionally received attention; hence, many automobiles designed in the past have lacked the so-called good fit and finish, meaning that the overall tolerance of the assembled system has not always conformed to the desired overall tolerance of the design. Often, designers of the various components have maintained the tolerance in their specific part of the system without giving any consideration to the entire system. As a result, many parts have been "hammered" into the system, and it is no wonder that in a relatively short time, they begin to fall apart. This occurrence could be avoided if engineers were to think in terms of the total system design instead of *component design*; one means of facilitating such thinking is to use CAD systems, which are capable of three-dimensional representation. Therefore, in this chapter, we introduce the concept of geometric modeling and also present a case study of how computer-aided design may be applied in the industry.

11.2 GEOMETRIC MODELING

The main problem in geometric modeling is describing a three-dimensional, continuous object in a finite and discrete digital computer. The representation and display of three-dimensional objects in the computer have been accomplished by using either of two schemes: wireframe or solid model.

In the wireframe scheme, objects are represented only by their edges in a collection of lines, arcs, and curve segments. While this is useful in visualizing objects and in the generation of Numerical Control (NC) tapes, there are many drawbacks, the most serious of which are the ambiguity involved in representing objects (for an illustration see reference [1]) and the fact that physical properties of components, such as volume or moment of inertia, cannot be determined. The second drawback limits the application of the wireframe scheme, especially since no dynamic analysis or computer simulation of mechanisms is possible.

Solid modeling, a term used to describe the solid model scheme, is a newer branch of computer-aided design that deals with the theory, techniques, and systems for geometric representation of objects in the form of solids. Solid models have no ambiguity in representation and permit the automatic calculation of certain geometric properties. Often solid systems are independent of other CAD methods. The *solid modeler* is responsible for creating, manipulating, storing, and transmitting spatially complete data on the geometric form of a three-dimensional object. Because the representation of surfaces discussed in Chapter 6 was wireframe modeling, further discussion of geometric modeling is restricted to solid modeling schemes.

11.3 METHODS FOR REPRESENTATION OF A SOLID

Although various schemes for solid modeling have been proposed [2], only two of these schemes are widely used: the constructive solid geometry and the boundary representation schemes. These two schemes are briefly discussed.

CONSTRUCTIVE SOLID GEOMETRY

In constructive solid geometry (CSG), a solid is represented as a collection of primitive shapes such as blocks, cylinders, spheres, and cones. These shapes are stored in a binary tree consisting of a set of Boolean operations (union, differ- ence, and intersection). A tree node represents an intermediate solid, which is a combination of primitive solids and intermediate solids lower in the tree. The root node is the complete object. A typical representation of an object using the CSG representation is shown in Figure 11.1.

The formation of objects using CSG is not as simple as described earlier be- cause of the difficulties in developing algorithms to perform the Boolean opera- tions. Any such algorithms developed must address at least two cases: the case when the primitive shapes touch each other but do not intersect, and the case when the primitive shapes intersect. An efficient algorithm for dealing with these cases for objects bounded by planar or cylindrical surfaces has been developed [3].

The CSG scheme offers several advantages. It requires less data storage than the other schemes in the formation of simple parts that are commonly and easily machined. Even for complex parts, the number of nodes in the CSG tree is ap- proximately equal to the number of distinct surfaces on the part. It is more ap- pealing to the designer who is accustomed to thinking of objects in terms of vol- ume of materials rather than in terms of faces and edges. Perhaps the most important advantage of this scheme is that it allows the designer to emulate the manufacturing process of an object by following the operations described in the CSG tree.

BOUNDARY REPRESENTATION

A solid in a boundary representation (B-rep) scheme is represented by its bound- ing faces, each face being rendered in terms of its boundaries (as a union of edges and vertices) and the data required to define the surface in which the faces lie. The creation and manipulation of a B-rep model are done by use of Boolean op- erations, although these are, strictly, not part of the B-rep model in the same

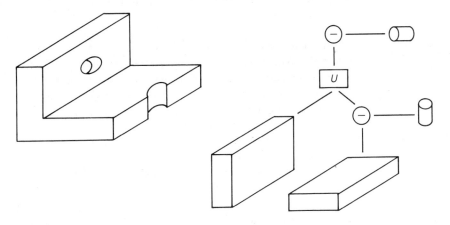

FIGURE 11.1

CSG representation of an object.

sense as that of the CSG scheme. A typical solid constructed by a B-rep scheme is shown in Figure 11.2. The B-rep is similar to the wireframe scheme, with the ambiguity removed. In addition, B-rep is applicable to mass-property calculations and two-dimensional finite element meshes.

Although the B-rep is a stepwise method of constructing a solid model, it requires much computer storage and involves significant computation. Of course, one advantage of B-rep is that it allows the greatest variety of construction methods, such as extruding and sweeping to create surfaces. With B-rep, data generation for NC tapes is based on surfaces to be formed rather than volumes to be removed. Despite these advantages, the B-rep system may represent a non–physically realizable object.

11.4 SOLID MODELING SYSTEMS

Most of the modeling systems available today utilize one or both of the two methods of representation described in the previous section. Some systems, such as BUILD, DESIGN, and ROMULUS, depend on boundary representation for internal representation of the objects. Others, such as PADL (Part And Design Assembly Language) and GMSOLID, rely on the CSG method for a primary internal representation of objects and on the boundary method for creation of displays. Such a combination draws on the strength of each method of representation.

Table 11.1 gives a partial list of available solid modeling systems. Most of the modeling systems are for the design and manufacture of simple mechanical parts; a handful of them are capable of being applied to complex parts.

It is not the intention of the author to discuss any system in detail but rather to make you aware of the available tools in solid modeling. No one system can be considered as "the best"; the user's need must dictate which system is most applicable.

Among the questions that the potential user should ask are: (1) What are the graphics capabilities of the system—does it include, among other requirements, automatic dimensioning? (2) What are the analysis capabilities? Can it be used for finite element analysis (automatic mesh generation) or interference analysis? Will it permit kinematic simulations? (3) What manufacturing features does the system have? Is it capable of automatic process planning, automatic NC program generation, and assembly planning?

Obviously, there is no one system (known to the author at the time of writing) that would answer all these questions in the affirmative. Therefore, one must use his or her own judgment in compromising the demands put on the modeling system.

This section has been included to introduce you to the growing field of geometric modeling and the tools available for it. The discussions presented here are based on [1] through [5]; the interested reader may consult these works.

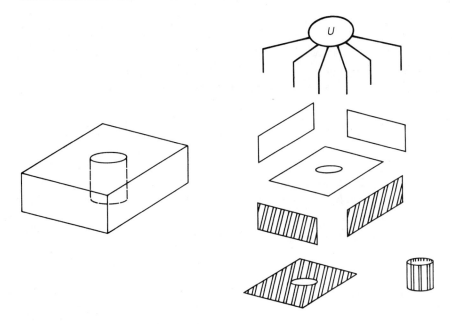

FIGURE 11.2

B-rep of an object.

Modeler	Vendor/Distributor	Representation
PATRAN-G	PDA engineering	Cell decomposition
MEDUSA	Prime	B-rep
ROMULUS	Evans & Sutherland	B-rep
SOLIDESIGN	Computervision	B-rep
CATIA	IBM	B-rep
DDM-SOLIDS	Calma	B-rep
PADL 1,2	U. Rochester	CSG
ICEM SOLID MODEL.	CDC	CSG
SOLIDS MODELING-II	Applicon	CSG
UNISOLIDS	McAuto	CSG

TABLE 11.1

Partial list of available solid modelers.

11.5 SUPERQUADRICS IN GEOMETRIC MODELING

We have mentioned that a CSG model consists of a collection of primitive shapes that are combined by Boolean operations. We now introduce, as an illustration of shape modeling, the concept of quadrics, which are useful in shape modeling using the CSG model.

The concept of quadrics has already been researched by many [8], [9], but the idea of superquadrics has recently been introduced by Barr [10]. The ensuing discussion is based primarily on the works of Barr and Zarrugh [11]. A quadric surface is of the form

$$f(x,y,z) = c_1 x^2 + c_2 y^2 + c_3 z^2 + c_4 xy + c_5 yz$$
$$+ c_6 zx + c_7 x + c_8 y + c_9 z + c_{10} = 0 \qquad \textbf{(11.1)}$$

Using homogeous coordinates $(x, y, z, 1)$ and following Levin [8], equation (11.1) can be represented in matrix form

$$f(x, y, z, 1) = [x \ y \ z \ 1] \begin{bmatrix} c_1 & 0.5c_4 & 0.5c_6 & 0.5c_7 \\ 0.5c_4 & c_2 & 0.5c_5 & 0.5c_8 \\ 0.5c_6 & 0.5c_5 & c_3 & 0.5c_9 \\ 0.5c_7 & 0.5c_8 & 0.5c_9 & c_{10} \end{bmatrix} \begin{bmatrix} x \\ y \\ z \\ 1 \end{bmatrix} \qquad \textbf{(11.2)}$$

The 4×4 matrix is called the discriminant of the quadric surface.

To use equation (11.1) or (11.2) for modeling requires the determination of all the constants, which is not easily achieved. In addition, the determination of intersection curves between two quadrics presents a challenge. For these reasons, quadric surfaces have been of limited application in CSG models. However, Barr's superquadrics are more useful in shape modeling.

MATHEMATICAL DEVELOPMENT OF SUPERQUADRICS

Recall from Chapter 6 that a surface patch is formed by intersecting curves. We use this concept in developing the mathematical basis for superquadrics. Let two-dimensional curves be defined as

$$\mathbf{h(v)} = \begin{bmatrix} h_1 (v) \\ h_2 (v) \end{bmatrix} \quad v_0 \leq v \leq v_1 \qquad \textbf{(11.3)}$$

and

$$\mathbf{g(u)} = \begin{bmatrix} g_1 (u) \\ g_2 (u) \end{bmatrix} \quad u_0 \leq u \leq u_1 \qquad \textbf{(11.4)}$$

where u is a north-south parameter (latitude) and v is an east-west parameter (longitude); see Figure 11.3. Then the spherical product $\mathbf{y} = \mathbf{g} \otimes \mathbf{h}$ defines a surface, S, given by

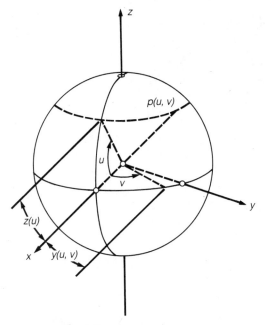

FIGURE 11.3

Coordinate system.

$$S(u, v) = \begin{bmatrix} g_1\,(v)h_1\,(u) \\ g_1\,(v)h_2\,(u) \\ g_2\,(v) \end{bmatrix} \quad \begin{array}{l} u_0 \leq u \leq u_1 \\ v_0 \leq v \leq v_1 \end{array} \qquad \text{(11.5)}$$

S can be scaled by a vector **a**, yielding

$$S = \begin{bmatrix} a_1 g_1\,(v)h_1\,(u) \\ a_2 g_1\,(v)h_2\,(u) \\ a_3 g_2\,(v) \end{bmatrix} \qquad \text{(11.6)}$$

The spherical product derived its name from the surface of a unit sphere, which is produced when a half-circle

$$g(u) = \begin{bmatrix} \cos u \\ \sin u \end{bmatrix} \quad -\frac{\pi}{2} \leq u \leq \frac{\pi}{2} \qquad \text{(11.7)}$$

is crossed with a full circle (see Figure 11.4)

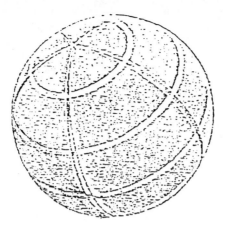

FIGURE 11.4

Formation of a sphere by crossing half-circles and full circles.

$$\mathbf{h}(u) = \begin{bmatrix} \cos u \\ \sin u \end{bmatrix} \quad 0 \le u \le 2\pi \tag{11.8}$$

giving

$$\mathbf{S} = \begin{bmatrix} \cos v \cos u \\ \cos u \sin v \\ \sin v \end{bmatrix} \begin{array}{l} -\dfrac{\pi}{2} \le u \le \dfrac{\pi}{2} \\[2ex] 0 \le v \le 2\pi \end{array} \tag{11.9}$$

Using this concept, Barr produced superquadric solids from the basic quadric surfaces.

SUPERELLIPSOIDS

We now consider the modeling of superellipsoids as an illustration of the usefulness of the superquadrics. The equation of a superellipsoid is given in the form

$$\left(\frac{x}{a}\right)^2 + \left(\frac{y}{b}\right)^2 + \left(\frac{z}{c}\right)^2 = 1 \tag{11.10}$$

Using the concept of superquadrics and following Barr, the implicit form of equation (11.10) is

$$\left[\left(\frac{x}{a}\right)^{2/\alpha_2} + \left(\frac{y}{b}\right)^{2/\alpha_1}\right]^{\alpha_1/\alpha_2} + \left(\frac{z}{c}\right)^{2/\alpha_1} = 1 \tag{11.11}$$

and in parametric form, a point **P** on the surface is given as

$$P(u, v) = [x(u, v) \ y(u, v) \ z(u, v)] \tag{11.12}$$

where

$$
\begin{aligned}
x(u, v) &= a \cos^{\alpha_1}\!u \cos^{\alpha_2}\!v \\
y(u, v) &= b \cos^{\alpha_1}\!u \sin^{\alpha_2}\!v \qquad -\frac{\pi}{2} \le u \le \frac{\pi}{2} \\
z(u, v) &= c \sin^{\alpha_1}\!u \qquad\qquad\quad 0 \le v \le 2\pi
\end{aligned}
\tag{11.13}
$$

The parameters α_1 and α_2 control the surface curvature, and the constants a, b, and c define the maximum extent of the superellipsoid along the coordinate axes. Varying the parameters α_1 and α_2 will produce different shapes (see Figure 11.5).

Equation (11.11), given by Barr, may not produce certain shapes; because of this, Zarrugh [11] introduced a third parameter to ensure that certain shapes can be modeled. The form given by Zarrugh is

$$\left[\left(\frac{x}{a}\right)^{2/\alpha_3} + \left(\frac{y}{b}\right)^{2/\alpha_2} \right]^{\alpha_3/\alpha_1} + \left(\frac{z}{c}\right)^{2/\alpha_1} = 1 \tag{11.14}$$

or, in explicit parametric form,

$$
\begin{aligned}
x(u, v) &= a \cos^{\alpha_1}(u)\cos^{\alpha_3}(v) \\
y(u, v) &= b \cos^{\alpha_1\alpha_2/\alpha_3}(u)\sin^{\alpha_2}(v) \qquad -\frac{\pi}{2} \le u \le \frac{\pi}{2} \\
z(u, v) &= c \sin^{\alpha_1}(u) \qquad\qquad\qquad 0 \le v \le 2\pi, \ \alpha_1, \alpha_2, \alpha_3 > 0
\end{aligned}
\tag{11.15}
$$

Equation (11.15) reduces to equation (11.13) if $\alpha_2 = \alpha_3$. The shapes that can be produced using equation (11.15) are left as an exercise for the student.

ADVANTAGES OF SUPERQUADRICS

Superquadrics provide a simple way of introducing the student to the concept of geometric modeling. They also provide an easy method of producing primitives shapes useful in CSG modelers. It is amazing how various shapes can be produced from a single equation by simply altering the shape parameters.

The superquadrics are truly solid models, since the inside and the outside can be differentiated from each other and it is easy to determine in which region an arbitrary point falls. For example, in the case of a unit sphere of the form

$$f(x, y, z) = x^2 + y^2 + z^2$$

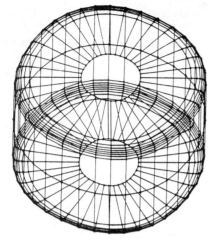

$\alpha_1 = 0.1$
$\alpha_2 = 0.9$

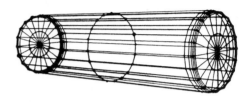

$\alpha_1 = 0.05$
$\alpha_2 = 0.99$

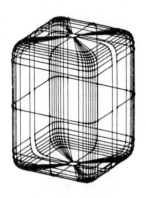

$\alpha_1 = \alpha_2 = 0.2$

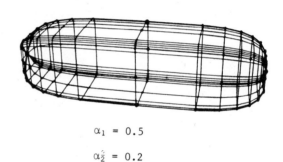

$\alpha_1 = 0.5$
$\alpha_2 = 0.2$

FIGURE 11.5

Effect of varying the control parameters α_1 and α_2 in using Barr's superquadrics.

a simple test can applied to any point, such as (x_o, y_o, z_o), as follows:

If $\begin{cases} f(x_o, y_o, z_o) = 1, \text{ the point is on the surface} \\ f(x_o, y_o, z_o) > 1, \text{ the point lies outside the sphere} \\ f(x_o, y_o, z_o) < 1, \text{ the point lies inside the sphere} \end{cases}$

In addition, it is relatively easy to compute mass properties (such as volumes and moment of inertia) using superquadrics [11].

This section has been included to give the student a feel for geometric modeling, with a brief introduction to the subject of solid modeling. A reader interested in more advanced study may consult the book by Mortenson [12]. It has a good treatment of the subject but requires more mathematical skills than may be possessed by the intended user of this book.

11.6 CALCULATION OF GEOMETRIC PROPERTIES

We present methods required to calculate the area, centroid, and the moment of inertia (second area of moment). In addition, we examine the methods for determining the surface of revolution and the volume of revolution. The need for calculating these properties lies in their engineering applications—both in the design and the manufacturing phases.

AREA

Consider an arbitrarily shaped cross-sectional area (Figure 11.6). The area of the vertical element is the area of a trapezoid; therefore,

$$\Delta A = \frac{(x_{i+1} - x_i)(y_{i+1} + y_i)}{2}$$

If we subdivide the given cross-sectional area into $n - 1$ finite elements, then the area is

$$A = \sum_{i=1}^{n-1} \frac{(x_{i+1} - x_i)(y_{i+1} + y_i)}{2} \tag{11.16}$$

Since equation (11.16) is an approximation to the given area, its accuracy depends on the size of the element. The more finely the area is subdivided, the more accurate is the approximation.

CENTROID

The centroid of a given cross-sectional area is

$$\overline{X} = \frac{\int x \, dA}{A}$$

$$\overline{Y} = \frac{\int y \, dA}{A} \tag{11.17}$$

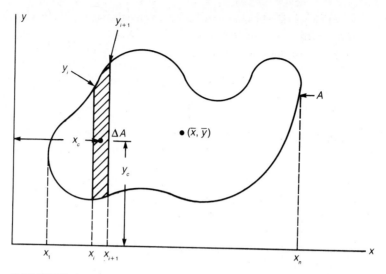

FIGURE 11.6

The integral $\int y\, dA$ is the first moment of area. From Figure 11.6, the centroid of the element is

$$x_{c,i} = \frac{x_{i+1} + x_i}{2} \qquad (11.18a)$$

$$y_{c,i} = \frac{(y_{i+1})_u + (y_{i+1})_l}{2} \qquad (11.18b)$$

If the boundaries of the area are irregular, a better approximation for y_c is

$$y_{c,i} = \frac{(y_{i+1} + y_i)_u + (y_{i+1} + y_i)_l}{4} \qquad (11.18c)$$

The subscripts u and l refer to the upper and lower boundary of the given cross-sectional area. For the entire sectional area, the centroid may be approximated using

$$\overline{X} = \frac{\displaystyle\sum_{i=1}^{n-1} x_{c,i} A_i}{A}$$

$$\overline{Y} = \frac{\displaystyle\sum_{i=1}^{n-1} y_{c,i} A_i}{A} \qquad (11.19)$$

MOMENT OF INERTIA

The moment of inertia, being the second moment of area, is defined as

$$I_x = \int y^2 \, dA$$

$$I_y = \int x^2 \, dA$$

(11.20)

where y is the moment arm measured from the x axis and x is the moment arm measured from the y axis. For use with the computer, equation (11.20) can be put in the form

$$I_x = \sum_{i=1}^{n-1} y_i^2 \, \Delta A_i$$

$$I_y = \sum_{i=1}^{q-1} x_i^2 \, \Delta A_i$$

(11.21a)

where n and q are the number of points in the x and y axes, respectively. In equation (11.20) horizontal and vertical elementary strips are used.

However, the same vertical element can be used to compute the moment of inertia about both axes. In this case we have

$$dI_x = \frac{y^3 \, dx}{3}$$

and

$$dI_y = x^2 y \, dx$$

Then

$$I_x = \frac{1}{3} \sum_{i=1}^{n-1} y_i^2 \, \Delta A_i$$

$$I_y = \sum_{i=1}^{n-1} x_i^2 \, \Delta A_i$$

(11.21b)

In an application, the moment of inertia is normally determined about the centroid of the given area. Using the parallel axis theorem,

$$I_x = \sum_{i=1}^{n-1} [y_i^2 \, \Delta A_i + \Delta A_i d_{y,i}^2]$$

$$I_y = \sum_{i=1}^{q-1} [x_i^2 \, \Delta A_i + \Delta A_i d_{x,i}^2]$$

(11.22)

where

$$d_{x,i} = \overline{Y} - y_{c,i}$$
$$d_{y,i} = \overline{X} - x_{c,i}$$

Frequently, it is necessary to subdivide the given cross-sectional area into m sections. In this case equation (11.22) may be cast as

$$I_x = \sum_{r=1}^{m} \sum_{i=1}^{n-1} [y_{ir}^2 \Delta A_{ir} + \Delta A_{ir} d_{y,ir}^2]$$

$$I_y = \sum_{r=1}^{m} \sum_{i=1}^{q-1} [x_{ir}^2 \Delta A_{ir} + \Delta A_{ir} d_{x,ir}^2] \qquad \textbf{(11.23)}$$

SURFACE AREA OF REVOLUTION

The area of the surface generated by a plane curve about a given axis in the plane of the curve (Figure 11.7) is

$$A = 2\pi \int y \, dL \qquad \textbf{(11.24)}$$

Using Pappus's theorem, which states that

> If an arc of a plane curve is revolved about a line that lies in its plane but does not intersect the arc, then the surface area generated by the arc is equal to the product of the length of the arc and the distance traveled by its center of gravity.

we have

$$A = 2\pi \bar{y} L \qquad \textbf{(11.25a)}$$

where y is the centroid, which is defined by

$$\bar{y} = \frac{\int y \, dL}{L} \qquad \textbf{(11.25b)}$$

To use equation (11.25b) requires the determination of the length of the curves and the evaluation of the integral $\int y \, dL$. From Figure 11.7, a linear approximation of the arc length ds by dL gives:

$$dL = [(x_{i+1} - x_i)^2 + (y_{i+1} - y_i)^2]^{1/2}$$

Hence

$$L = \sum_{i=1}^{n-1} [(x_{i+1} - x_i)^2 + (y_{i+1} - y_i)^2]^{1/2} \qquad \textbf{(11.26)}$$

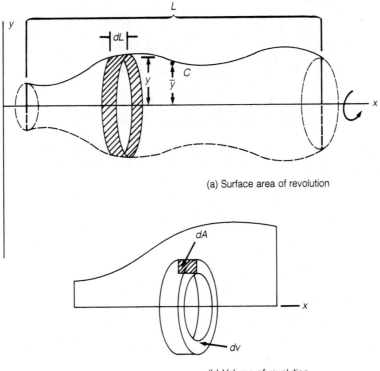

(a) Surface area of revolution

(b) Volume of revolution

FIGURE 11.7

Determination of area and centroid.

and

$$\int y dL = \frac{1}{2} \sum_{i=1}^{n-1} (y_{i+1} + y_i) [(x_{i+1} - x_i)^2 + (y_{i+1} - y_i)^2]^{1/2} \qquad \textbf{(11.27)}$$

If dL is written in the form

$$dL = \left[1 + \left(\frac{dy}{dx}\right)^2\right]^{1/2} dx$$

it is easy to see that the integral $y\,dL$ is in the form $g(x)\,dx$, which is more suitable for computation by numerical approach. For example, Simpson's rule may be used to compute the integral $g(x)\,dx$ as

$$\int g(x)\,dx = \frac{\Delta x}{3} \left[g_1 + 4 \sum_{\substack{i=2 \\ (\text{even})}}^{n-1} g_i + 2 \sum_{\substack{i=3 \\ (\text{odd})}}^{n-2} g_i + g_n\right] \qquad \textbf{(11.28)}$$

where

$$g_i = g(x_i)$$
$$\Delta x = (x_n - x_1)/m$$
$$m = \text{any positive integer} \quad (m \text{ determines accuracy})$$

VOLUME OF REVOLUTION

The volume of revolution is that generated by revolving an area about an axis in its plane (Figure 11.7). It can be calculated using

$$V = 2\pi \int y \, dA \tag{11.29}$$

Again, using Pappus's theorem (for volumes, see Figure 11.7), we have

$$V = 2\pi \bar{y} A \tag{11.30}$$

But

$$\bar{y} = \frac{\int y \, dA}{A}$$

We can evaluate the integral $\int y \, dA$ by means of double integration. For example, suppose we wish to evaluate

$$\int f(x, y) \, dy \, dx$$

If we keep y constant and apply Simpson's rule (11.28), we have

$$\int_c^d f(x, y) \, dy \, dx = J_y$$

where

$$J_y = \frac{y}{3} \left(f_1 + 4 \sum_{i=2}^{n-1} f_i + 2 \sum_{i=3}^{n-2} f_i + f_n \right) \tag{11.31}$$

and

$$f_i = f(x_i, y)$$

Applying Simpson's rule to each term in equation (11.31), our final result is

$$\int_a^b \int_c^d f(x, y) \, dy \, dx = \frac{\Delta x \Delta y}{9} (G_1 + 4G_2 + 2G_3 + 8G_4) \tag{11.32}$$

where

$$G_1 = f_{11} + f_{1m} + f_{n1} + f_{nm}$$

$$G_2 = \sum_{\substack{i=2 \\ (\text{even})}}^{n-1} (f_{i1} + f_{im}) + \sum_{\substack{j=2 \\ (\text{even})}}^{m-1} (f_{1j} + f_{nj})$$

$$G_3 = \sum_{\substack{i=3 \\ (\text{odd})}}^{n-2} (f_{i1} + f_{im}) + \sum_{\substack{j=3 \\ (\text{odd})}}^{m-2} (f_{1j} + f_{nj})$$

$$G_4 = 2 \sum_{\substack{i=2 \\ (\text{even})}}^{n-1} \sum_{j=2}^{m-1} f_{ij} + \sum_{\substack{i=2 \\ (\text{even})}}^{n-1} \sum_{\substack{j=3 \\ (\text{odd})}}^{m-2} f_{ij} + \sum_{\substack{i=3 \\ (\text{odd})}}^{n-2} \sum_{\substack{j=2 \\ (\text{even})}}^{m-1} f_{ij} + \sum_{\substack{i=3 \\ (\text{odd})}}^{n-2} \sum_{\substack{j=3 \\ (\text{odd})}}^{m-2} \frac{f_{ij}}{2}$$

$$\Delta y = (y_m - y_1)/(m - 1) \quad (\Delta x \text{ is as previously defined})$$
$$f_{ij} = f(x_i, y_j)$$
$m, n =$ positive integers

Equation (11.32) is based on the assumption that the region under consideration can be defined as rectangular. However, if the boundaries vary with respect to x, as is often the case (Figure 11.8), then the step size must be modified using

$$h = \frac{v(x_i) - u(x_i)}{2m} \qquad (11.33)$$

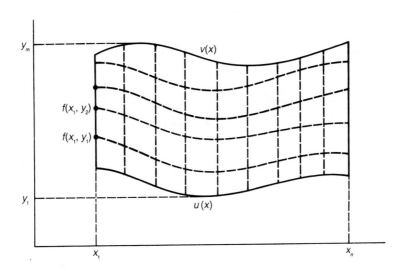

FIGURE 11.8

Determination of surface area of revolution and volume of revolution.

Let

$$S_i = \int_{y_1}^{y_m} f(x_i, y)\, dy$$

Then

$$S_i = \frac{h}{3}\left[f_{1i} + 4 \sum_{\substack{j=2 \\ (even)}}^{m-1} f_{ij} + 2 \sum_{\substack{j=3 \\ (odd)}}^{m-2} f_{ij} \right] \quad i = 1, 2, \ldots, n \qquad \textbf{(11.34)}$$

where

$f_{ij} = f(x_i, y_j)$
$i = 1, 2, \ldots, n$
$j = 1, 2, \ldots, m$

The integral

$$\int_{x_1}^{x_n} \int_{y_1}^{y_n} f(x, y)\, dy\, dx$$

can be approximated by

$$\int_{x_1}^{x_n} \int_{y_1}^{y_m} f(x, y)\, dy\, dx = \frac{\Delta x}{3}\left[S_1 + 4 \sum_{\substack{i=2 \\ (even)}}^{n-1} S_i + 2 \sum_{\substack{i=3 \\ (odd)}}^{n-2} S_i + S_n \right] \qquad \textbf{(11.35)}$$

A sample program for calculating the above properties is shown in Figure 11.9 and a sample program for double integration is given in the appendix.

```
10    '*******************************************************
20    '* THIS PROGRAM IS FOR MASS PROPERTY CALCULATIONS *
30    '*******************************************************
40       PI = 22/7
50       PRINT"*******************************************************
60       PRINT"THIS PROGRAM IS DESIGNED TO:"
70       PRINT
80       PRINT" 1.   CALCULATE THE AREA
90       PRINT
100      PRINT"    THE SURFACE AREA OF REVOLUTION OF A LINE (ARC)"
110      PRINT
120      PRINT" 2. THE AREA, CENTROID, THE MOMENT OF INERTIA, THE VOLUME
130      PRINT      "OF REVOLUTION FOR A GIVEN AREA."
140      PRINT"*******************************************************
150      PRINT
160      INPUT"DO YOU WISH TO CONTINUE (Y/N)";Q$
170      IF Q$ ="N" THEN 820
180   INPUT"WOULD YOU LIKE A DISPLAY OF THE GEOMETRY ";DH$
190      INPUT"DO YOU WANT THE PROPERTIES FOR A LINE/ARC  (Y/N)";L$
```

FIGURE 11.9

A sample program for mass-property calculations.

```
200        IF L$ = "N" THEN 220
210        GOSUB 1130  : GOTO 820
220        INPUT"DO YOW WANT THE PROPERTIES OF A GIVEN AREA (Y/N)";R$
230        IF R$ = "N" THEN PRINT "PROGRAM'S CAPABILITY EXCEEDED": GOTO 82
240        INPUT"CAN THE AREA BE SUBDIVIDED INTO RECTANGLES ONLY (Y/N)";P$
250        IF P$ = "Y" THEN 290
260        GOSUB 1610  : GOTO 820
270  ' COMPUTING PROPERTIES OF AN AREA THAT CAN BE SUBDIVIDED INTO
280  ' RECTANGLES
290        INPUT" THE NO. OF REGIONS AREA CAN BE SUBDIVIDED";M
300        DIM XA(2,M),XB(2,M),YA(2,M),YB(2,M),P1(50),P2(50)
310        IF DH$ ="N" THEN 330
320        SCREEN 2 : CLS : WINDOW (-10,-10) - (10,10)
330        FOR I = 1 TO M
340        FOR J = 1 TO 2
350        PRINT "FOR REGION";I
360        PRINT"WHAT ARE THE X,Y COORDINATES OF THE START OF BOUNDARY";J
370        INPUT"X,Y";XA(J,I),YA(J,I)
380        IF I = 1 THEN PSET (XA(J,I),YA(J,I))
390   II = II + 1 : P1(II) = XA(J,I) : P2(II) = YA(J,I)
400        IF INT(II/4)*4 = (II/4)*4 THEN SWAP P1(II-1),P1(II)
410        PRINT"ENTER THE X,Y COORDINATE OF END POINT FOR BOUNDARY";J;"RE
420        INPUT"X,Y";XB(J,I),YB(J,I)
430        IF DH$ ="N" THEN 460
440        II =II +1 : P1(II) = XB(J,I) : P2(II) = YB(J,I)
450        IF INT(II/4)*4 = (II/4)*4 THEN SWAP P1(II-1),P1(II)
460        NEXT J
470        NEXT I
480        IF DH$ = "N" THEN 540
490        CLS
500        FOR JJ = 1 TO II
510        LINE - (P1(JJ),P2(JJ)) :  JI = JJ + 1    : J3 = JJ-3
520        IF INT(JJ/4) = JJ/4 THEN LINE - (P1(J3),P2(J3)) : PSET (P1(JI),P
530        NEXT JJ
540        N = 40
550        FOR I = 1 TO M
560        H1(I) = (XB(1,I) -XA(1,I))/N : H2(I) = (YA(2,I) - YA(1,I))/N
570        NEXT I
580        DIM X(N,M),A(N,M),HX(N,M),XBAR(N,M),Y(N,M),AY(N,M),VBAR(N,M),VH(
590        FOR R = 1 TO M
600        FOR I = 0 TO N
610        X(I,R) = XA(1,R) + I* H1(R) :  Y(I,R) = YA(1,R) + I*H2(R)
620        NEXT I : NEXT R
630        FOR R = 1 TO M
640        SUM = 0
650        DELY =(YB(2,R) - YB(1,R)) + (YA(2,R) - YA(1,R))
660        DELX =(XB(1,R) - XA(1,R))
670        HY(R) = DELY
680        YBAR(R) = (YB(1,R) + YA(1,R))/2 + DELY/4
690        FOR I = 0 TO N-1
700        HX(I,R) = X(I+1,R) - X(I,R)
710        A(I,R) = (X(I+1,R) -X(I,R))*DELY
720        VH(I,R) = Y(I+1,R) - Y(I,R)
730        AY(I,R) = DELX*VH(I,R)
740        SUM = SUM + A(I,R)
750        NEXT I
760        SUM2 = SUM2 + SUM
770        NEXT R
780        AREA = .5*SUM2
790        PRINT"AREA=";AREA
800        GOSUB 830
810        GOSUB 980
820        END
830        FOR R = 1 TO M
840        SUMX = 0: SUMY = 0
```

F I G U R E   11.9

(Continued).

```
850      FOR I = 0 TO N-1
860      XBAR(I,R) = X(I+1,R) + X(I,R)
870      VBAR(I,R) = Y(I+1,R) + Y(I,R)
880      SUMX  =   XBAR(I,R)*A(I,R) + SUMX
890      SUMY  =   YBAR(R)*A(I,R) + SUMY
900      NEXT I
910      SUMCX = SUMCX + SUMX
920      SUMCY = SUMCY + SUMY
930      NEXT R
940      XC =SUMCX*.25/AREA :YC = .5*SUMCY/AREA
950      PRINT"XC = ";XC ;"YC=";YC
960      RETURN
970      'FIND THE MOMENT OF INERTIA
980      FOR R = 1 TO M
990      SIX = 0 : SIY = 0 : ADX = 0 : ADY = 0
1000      FOR I = 0 TO N-1
1010      SIX  = VH(I,R)^2*AY(I,R) + SIX
1020      ADX  = AY(I,R)*(YC - (VBAR(I,R)/2))^2  + ADX
1030      SIY  = HX(I,R)^2*A(I,R) + SIY
1040      ADY =A(I,R)*(XC - (XBAR(I,R)/2))^2 + ADY
1050      NEXT I
1060      IX = IX + SIX     : AD1 = AD1 + ADX
1070      IY = IY + SIY     : AD2 = AD2 + ADY
1080      NEXT R
1090      IX = (IX + AD1)
1100      IY = (IY + AD2)/2
1110      PRINT "IX=";IX;"IY=";IY
1120      RETURN
1130      '--------------------------------------------------
1140      '   SUBPROGRAM COMPUTES THE CENTROID AND AREA OF
1150      '   REVOLUTION OF A LINE (ARC).
1160      '--------------------------------------------------
1170      DIM X(100),Y(100)
1180      PRINT"WHAT ARE THE LIMITS OF INTEGRATION ON X OR Y"
1190      INPUT"THE LOWER LIMIT IS ";XO
1200      INPUT"THE UPPER LIMIT IS ";XM
1210      INPUT"IS THE REVOLUTION ABOUT THE X -AXIS (Y/N)";A$
1220      ' DEFINE THE GIVEN FUNCTION
1230      DEF FNA(X) =    X^3/3 + 1/(4*X)
1240      M = 40 : DSTEP = (XM - XO)/(2*M) : N = 2*M
1250      IF A$ = "Y" THEN 1300
1260      FOR I = 0 TO N
1270          Y(I) = XO + I*DSTEP
1280          X(I) = FNA(Y(I))
1290      NEXT I  : GOTO 1340
1300      FOR I = 0 TO N
1310          X(I) = XO + I*DSTEP
1320          Y(I) = FNA(X(I))
1330      NEXT I
1340      FOR I = 0 TO N-1
1350      YYI = Y(I+1) + Y(I)   : XXI = (X(I+1) - X(I))^2 + (Y(I+1) - Y(I)
1360      XXX = XXI^.5
1370      ' COMPUTE THE LENGTH OF THE GENERATOR
1380      LENGTH = LENGTH + XXX
1390      YDL = Y(I)*XXX + YDL
1400      XDL = X(I+1)*XXX + XDL
1410      IF A$ = "N" THEN 1470
1420      ' COMPUTE THE SURFACE OF REVOLUTION "SREVX"
1430      SREVX = ABS(Y(I))*XXX + SREVX
1440      ' COMPUTE THE FIRST MOMENT OF AREA
1450      MOMX = X(I)*ABS(Y(I))*XXX + MOMX : GOTO 1500
1460      ' COMPUTE THE SURFACE OF REVOLUTION "SREVY"
1470      SREVY = ABS(X(I))*XXX + SREVY
1480      ' COMPUTE THE FIRST MOMENT OF AREA
1490      MOMY = Y(I)*ABS(X(I))*XXX + MOMY
```

FIGURE 11.9

(Continued).

```
1500        NEXT I
1510        YARC = YDL/LENGTH    : XARC = XDL/LENGTH
1520        IF A$ = "N" THEN 1540
1530        XREV = MOMX/SREVX    : SREVX = PI*SREVX*2 : GOTO 1550
1540        YREV = MOMY/SREVY    : SREVY = PI*SREVY*2
1550        IF A$ = "N" THEN SREVOL = SREVY ELSE SREVOL = SREVX
1560        PRINT"LENGTH OF THE GENERATOR = ";LENGTH
1570        PRINT"THE CENTROID OF ARC IS : ("XARC;YARC;")"
1580        PRINT"THE CENTROID OF SURFACE OF REVOLUTION IS (";XREV;YREV;")"
1590        PRINT"THE SURFACE OF REVOLUTION ABOUT X AXIS =";SREVOL
1600        RETURN
1610        ' --------------------------------------------------
1620        ' SUBPROGRAM COMPUTES THE CENTROID, VOLUME OF
1630        ' REVOLUTION, AND MOMENT OF INERTIA OF IRREGULARLY
1640        'SHAPED AREA.
1650        ' --------------------------------------------------
1660        DIM X(100),Y(100),S(100),Z(100)
1670        ' COMPUTING THE AREA OF REVOLUTION
1680        PRINT"WHAT ARE THE LIMITS OF INTEGRATION ON X OR Y"
1690        INPUT"THE LOWER LIMIT IS ";XO
1700        INPUT"THE UPPER LIMIT IS ";XM
1710        M = 25 : DSTEP = (XM - XO)/(2*M) : N = 2*M
1720     INPUT"IS THE AREA BOUNDED BY EITHER X OR Y AXIS (Y/N)";D$
1730     IF D$ = "Y" THEN 1760
1740     DEF FNC(X) = X^2
1750     DEF FND(X) = X
1760        DEF FNA(X) = X^2
1770     IF D$ = "Y" THEN 1800
1780     F1 = FND(XO) - FNC(XO) : FM = FND(XM) - FNC(XM)
1790     GOTO 1810
1800        F1 = FNA(XO) : FM = FNA(XM)
1810        SUMT = F1 + FM
1820        FOR I = 0 TO N
1830        X(I) = XO + I*DSTEP
1840     IF D$ = "Y" THEN 1870
1850     Y(I) =FND(X(I))  : Z(I) = FNC(X(I))
1860        S(I) = Y(I) - Z(I) : GOTO 1880
1870        S(I) = FNA(X(I)): Y(I) = S(I)
1880        NEXT I
1890        GOSUB 2350  : AREA = SUM
1900        AREA = SUM : PI = 22/7
1910        SUMT = XO*F1 + XM*FM
1920        FOR I = 1 TO N
1930        IF D$ = "Y" THEN S(I) =X(I)*Y(I) ELSE S(I) = X(I)*(Y(I)-Z(I))
1940        NEXT I
1950        GOSUB 2350 : XDA = SUM
1960        CENTX = XDA/AREA
1970        SUMT = F1^2 + FM^2
1980        FOR I = 1 TO N
1990        IF D$ = "Y" THEN S(I) = (Y(I))^2 ELSE S(I) = Y(I)^2 - Z(I)^2
2000        NEXT I
2010        GOSUB 2350
2020        YDA = SUM/2  : CENTY = YDA/AREA
2030     IF D$ = "N" THEN 2130
2040     ' CALCULATE THE VOL. OF GENERATION
2050        VOLUME = 2*PI*CENTY*AREA : VOLUME = ABS(VOLUME)
2060     SUMT = XO*F1 + XM*FM
2070     ' COMPUTE THE CENTROID OF THE VOL. OF GENERATION
2080        FOR I = 1 TO N
2090        S(I) =X(I)*(Y(I))^2
2100        NEXT I
2110        GOSUB 2350  : XV = SUM*PI/VOLUME
2120     ' COMPUTE MOMENT OF INERTIA
2130        SUMT = F1^2 + FM^2
2140     IF D$ = "N" THEN 2190
```

FIGURE 11.9

(Continued).

```
2150      FOR I = 1 TO N
2160        S(I) = (Y(I))^3
2170      NEXT I
2180      GOSUB 2350  :  IX = SUM/3  : GOTO 2230
2190      FOR I = 1 TO N :  S(I) = Y(I)^3 : NEXT I
2200      GOSUB 2350  : IX1 = SUM/3
2210      FOR I = 1 TO N : S(I) = Z(I)^3 : NEXT I
2220      GOSUB 2350 : IX2 = SUM/3  : IX = IX1 - IX2
2230      SUMT = XO^2*F1 + XM^2*FM
2240      FOR I = 1 TO N
2250        IF D$ ="Y" THEN S(I)=X(I)^2*Y(I) ELSE S(I) = X(I)^2*(Y(I)-Z(I))
2260      NEXT I
2270      GOSUB 2350 :  IY = SUM
2280       PRINT" THE CENTROID = "; "(";CENTX;",";CENTY;")"
2290       IF D$ = "N" THEN 2320
2300       PRINT" THE VOLUME OF REVOLUTION = ";VOLUME
2310      PRINT" THE CENTROID OF THE VOLUME GENERATED IS" ;XV
2320       PRINT"MOMENT OF INERTIA ABOUT THE X-AXIS IS";IX
2330       PRINT"MOMENT OF INERTIA ABOUT THE Y-AXIS IS";IY
2340      RETURN
2350    ' INTEGRATION BY SIMPSON'S RULE WITH MODIFICATION
2360    ' SUMT = SUM OF FIRST AND LAST TERM OF SIMPSON'S EQUATION
2370    ' SUME AND SUMO ARE THE SUMS FOR EVEN AND ODD TERMS
2380    ' DEFINE THE FUNCTION
2390      SUME = 0 : SUMO = 0
2400      FOR I = 0 TO N
2410      IF I = 0 OR I = N THEN 2430
2420          IF I/2 = INT(I/2) THEN SUME = SUME + S(I) ELSE SUMO = SUMO
2430      NEXT I
2440      SUM = DSTEP*(SUMT + 2*SUME + 4*SUMO)/3
2450      PRINT" THE INTEGRATION RESULT = ";SUM
2460      RETURN
```

F I G U R E 11.9

(Continued).

11.7 APPLYING COMPUTER-AIDED DESIGN

We have examined the various components of computer-aided design as defined in Chapter 1. Most books on the subject leave the impression that CAD is automated drafting or computer graphics. Actually, computer graphics, as previously mentioned, is only one portion. Therefore, this section is included in keeping with our concept of CAD. Before continuing, it is important to realize that complete automation of the design process is currently impossible. Representation of the entire design process or design methodology must wait for the current research efforts in artificial intelligence to yield meaningful results. This notwithstanding, we now present what we consider to be an appropriate CAD approach in design.

Problem Statement

An aircraft company wishes to apply the concept of computer-aided design in the design of some of the components of a landing gear. The desired configuration of the gear is shown in Figure 11.10. This is the design to reduce the load borne

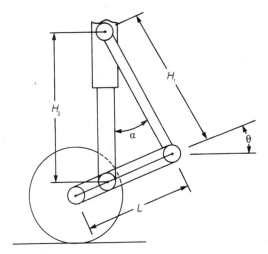

FIGURE 11.10

Landing gear.

by the hydraulic cylinder. It is assumed that the reaction on the wheel is known from another analysis and therefore should be an input parameter in the design process.

The real need is to design the various links and pins. The sizes of the links are to be constrained by the values of the angles θ and α that will produce minimum load on the cylinder. Furthermore, it is desired that when the design has been automated, detailed drawings of the parts to be manufactured by the company must be generated. The company, however, subcontracts with another company that manufactures hydraulic cylinders and therefore would like to be able to specify the desired stroke of the cylinder as well as the minimum load that the piston rod must sustain.

SOLUTION   There are many possible approaches to this problem. We chose what may be considered the simplest approach, in order not to get bogged down with a lot of details and lose sight of the CAD application we wish to present. For example, we are ignoring the use of finite element codes in detailing the stresses around the holes in the links and are simply using the stress concentration factor. In keeping with our concept of computer-aided design, this problem can be viewed as a four-stage process: analysis, optimization, software design, and automated drafting (see Figure 11.11).

ANALYSIS

We begin by analyzing the forces in the various links.

$$\sum M_A = 0 = -0.5RL \cos \theta + 0.5L(F_{BC} \sin \alpha \sin \theta + F_{BC} \cos \alpha \cos \theta)$$

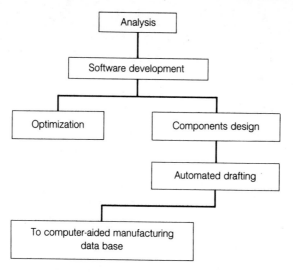

FIGURE 11.11

Schematic for solving sample CAD problem.

giving

$$F_{BC} = \frac{R \cos \theta}{\sin \alpha \sin \theta + \cos \alpha \cos \theta}$$

$$\sum F_y = 0; \quad F_A^y = R \left[\frac{\cos \theta \cos \alpha}{\cos (\alpha - \theta)} + 1 \right]$$

$$\sum F_x = 0; \quad F_A^x = R \left[\frac{\cos \theta \sin \alpha}{\cos (\alpha - \theta)} \right]$$

Therefore,

$$F_A = R \left\{ \left[\frac{\cos \theta \sin \alpha}{\cos (\alpha - \theta)} \right]^2 + \left[\frac{\cos \alpha \cos \theta}{\cos (\alpha - \theta)} + 1 \right]^2 \right\}^{1/2}$$

Consider triangle ABC. Using sine rule, we have $h_1 = 0.5L \, (\cos \theta / \sin \alpha)$ and $h_2 = h_1 \, [\sin (90 + \theta - \alpha)/\cos \theta]$.

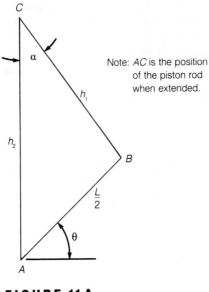

Note: AC is the position of the piston rod when extended.

FIGURE 11.A

Components Design

Member BC:

ASSUMPTIONS

1. Load fluctuates from F_{BC} to zero
2. Infinite life
3. 99.99% reliability
4. Full-notch sensitivity
5. End condition (for buckling analysis) of one
6. Surface finish—ground

MATERIAL

AISI 9255 (quenched and treated at 400C).

PROPERTIES

Yield stress = 1980 MPa, tensile stress = 2140 MPa, modulus of elasticity = 207 MPa.

Design against Buckling: Consider Figure 11.12. In (a) for buckling in the plane of the paper, we have radius of gyration $r_a = (tw^3/12wt)^{1/2} = 0.2886w$ and the moment of inertia about a is $0.0833tw^3$.

Similarly, for case (b), radius of gyration $r_b = 0.2886t$ and the moment of inertia about b is $0.0833wt^3$. For a conservative design, the critical stresses corresponding to the two modes (cases [a] and [b]) of buckling must be equal. This means that the effective slender ratios for both cases must be equal. For case (a), the effective length is $2h_1$ and for case (b) the effective length is $0.71h_1$; hence,

$$\frac{0.7h_1}{t/\sqrt{12}} = \frac{2h_1}{w/\sqrt{12}}$$

giving $t = 0.35$ w.

From [6] Euler's equation for buckling applies if $Q/r^2 > 2$ and Johnson's formula applies if $Q/r^2 < 2$, where

$Q = S_y h_1{}^2/C\pi^2 E$

C = end condition

r = radius of gyration

Simplification of the preceding equations leads to

$$P_{cr} = 0.35w^2\left(1 - \frac{24.8978Q}{w^2}\right)S_y \quad \text{if} \quad \frac{Q}{r^2} < 2$$

$$P_{cr} = \frac{0.003529w^4S_y}{Q} \quad \text{if} \quad \frac{Q}{r^2} > 2$$

Use of these two equations is satisfactory only for a static condition; therefore, we repeat the process, replacing the yield stress with the endurance limit, to design against fatigue failure. Once the width and thickness have been determined, we can size the pin at B for bearing load using

$$d_b = \frac{F_{BC}}{S_b t}$$

where d_b is pin diameter and S_b is the permissible bearing stress.

At this point it should be noted that an iterative process is necessary, and any one of the methods covered in Chapter 4 may be used in determining the width of member BC.

Member OAB: See Figure 11.13a.

ASSUMPTIONS

Same as applied in member BC.

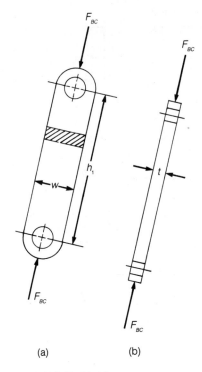

(a)   (b)

FIGURE 11.12

Member *BC* (Free Body Diagram).

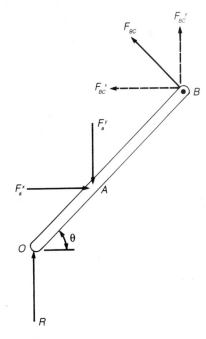

FIGURE 11.13a

Member *OAB*.

MATERIAL

The same as that of member *BC*.

DESIGN EQUATIONS

Bending is to be avoided; therefore, we design based on flexural stress, σ, given by

$$\sigma = \frac{Mc}{I}$$

$$I = \frac{t(w^3 - d^3)}{12}$$

The maximum moment can be determined using the moment and shear diagram given in Figure 11.13b.
     Also

$$\frac{Sy}{N} = \frac{kM_{max}}{I/c} = \frac{6kM_{max}w}{t(w^3 - d^3)}$$

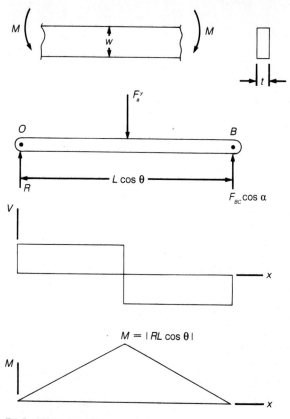

FIGURE 11.13b

Shear and moment diagram for member *OAB*.

Note that k is the stress concentration factor, and according to [7] its value is 2 regardless of the value of the ratio d/w.

Again, we must check against fatigue failure, and once we have obtained satisfactory values of the width, we can determine the appropriate thickness of member *OAB*. It is assumed that the same size pin used at *B* is to be used at *A* and *O*.

Optimization

The optimization aspect of the design can be stated in the form shown:

OBJECTIVE

Minimize the force F_A by finding the "best" values of α and θ.

CONSTRAINTS

None.

SPECIFIED

Length of *OAB*.

With the problem in the preceding format, it becomes a simple matter of selecting the appropriate optimization algorithm.

The result of the optimization leads to fixing the length of links *BC* and the distance *AC*. By simple geometric calculation, we can determine the permissible stroke for the cylinder.

Software Design

Having completed the analysis, we see that software design becomes quite straightforward, once we apply the concepts learned in Chapter 3. The software for this problem was developed in stages. First, the optimization program was developed and tested. Second, the program for the design of the components parts was developed, then incorporated into the optimization routine, and then tested. The complete listing of the program used for this design is shown in Figure 11.14. Note that the program is interactive and is, therefore, of a general nature for design of the landing gear for different sizes of airplanes.

```
10     REM ***********************************************
20     REM * PROGRAM FOR THE FINAL APPLICATION          *
30     REM * PROBLEM IN CHAPTER 11.                      *
40     REM ***********************************************
50     PRINT"***********************************************"
60     PRINT"*   ENTER MATERIAL PROPERTIES               *"
70     PRINT"*   ENTER STRESSES IN MPa OR PSI.           *"
80     PRINT"*   ENTER DIMENSIONS IN mm OR IN.           *"
90     PRINT"***********************************************"
100    PRINT
110    INPUT"WHAT IS THE YIELD STRESS OF MATERIAL-MPa OR PSI-";SY
120    PRINT
130    INPUT"ENTER THE MODULUS OF ELASTICITY  IN - MPa- ";E
140    PRINT
150    INPUT "TENSILE STRESS (ULTIMATE) IN - MPa- ";SU
160    PRINT
170    REM CL IS CLEARANCE
180    CL = .0625 : PI = 22/7
190    INPUT" WHAT IS THE PERMISSIBLE SHEARING STRESS";SS
200    INPUT"ENTER THE PERMISSIBLE BEARING  (MPa) ";SB
210    PRINT
220    INPUT"WHAT IS THE LENGTH OF MEMBER OAB (mm)";LL
230    PRINT
240    INPUT"WHAT IS THE LOAD ON THE TIRES ";R
250    PRINT
260    INPUT"WHAT IS THE FACTOR OF SAFETY";N
270    PRINT
280    INPUT"ARE YOU USING THE S.I. UNITS (Y/N)";A$
290    PRINT
300    IF A$ = "N" GOTO 350
310    GOSUB 2300
320    REM ----------------------------------------
330    REM -- OPTIMIZE FOR BEST ANGLES ------
340    REM ----------------------------------------
```

FIGURE 11.14

Program for the landing gear problem.

```
350      GOSUB 460
360        H1 = .5*LL*COS(X(2,L))/SIN(X(1,L))  : Z=PI/2
370        H2 = H1*SIN(Z+X(2,L)-X(1,L))/COS(X(2,L))
380      STROKE = H2 - SQR(H1^2 -(LL^2/4))
390      FBC = R*COS(X(2,L))/COS(X(2,L)-X(1,L))
400      FAX =    SIN(X(1,L))*COS(X(2,L))/COS(X(2,L) -X(1,L))
410      FAY =   (COS(X(1,L))*COS(X(2,L))/COS(X(2,L) -X(1,L)))+1
420      FA = R*SQR(FAX^2 + FAY^2)
430      GOSUB 1220
440       GOSUB 1640
450      END
460  REM  -----------------------------------
470  REM  ---   HOOK AND JEEVES METHOD OF ---
480  REM  --- MULTIVARIABLE SEARCH METHOD --
490  REM  -----------------------------------
500  DIM X(6,30),PX(6,30),U(6,30),V(6,30),H(6)
510  DEF FNX(A,B) =SQR((COS(A-B)+COS(A)*COS(B))^2+(COS(B)*SIN(A))^2)*R/C
520    TOL = .0001 : N = 2: L =1
530    FOR I = 1 TO N
540    READ X(I,L),H(I): NEXT I
550    DATA 0.2,0.02,0.2,0.02
560    P = L
570    FOR I = 1 TO N
580    U(I,P) = X(I,L) : NEXT I
590    GOSUB 970
600    FOR I = 1 TO N
610      X(I,L) = U(I,P) : NEXT I
620    FOR I = 1 TO N
630      X(I,L+1) = V(I,L) : NEXT I
640 REM  T
650    FOR I = 1 TO N
660       IF H(I) < = TOL GOTO 920
670    NEXT I
680 REM T    B
690     FOR I = 1 TO N
700        IF X(I,L)< > X(I,L+1) GOTO 750
710      NEXT I
720      FOR I = 1 TO N
730        H(I) = .5*H(I) : NEXT I
740      GOTO 560
750      J = 1: L = L + 1: KC = KC + 1 : P = J
760     FOR I =1 TO N
770        PX(I,J) = 2*X(I,L) - X(I,L-1) : NEXT I
780      FOR I = 1 TO N
790         U(I,P) = PX(I,J) : NEXT I
800      GOSUB 970
810       FOR I = 1 TO N
820          XP(I,J) = U(I,P) : NEXT I
830    REM T
840  DEF FNX(A,B) =SQR((COS(A-B)+COS(A)*COS(B))^2+(COS(B)*SIN(A))^2)*R/C
850    PATN = FNX(V(1,J),V(2,J))
860    BASE = FNX(X(1,L),X(2,L))
870    IF PATN < BASE GOTO 890
880    GOTO 560
890    FOR I = 1 TO N
900      X(I,L+1) = V(I,J) : NEXT I
910    L = L + 1 : KC = KC + 1 : J = J + 1 : GOTO 760
920    FOPT = FNX(X(1,L),X(2,L))
930     THETA = X(2,L)*180/PI : ALPHA = X(1,L)*180/PI
940       PRINT "ALPHA = ";ALPHA;"DEG.";" THETA = ";THETA;" DEG."
950      PRINT " FOPT =";FOPT
960    RETURN
970    REM
980  DEF FNA(A,B) =SQR((COS(A-B)+COS(A)*COS(B))^2+(COS(B)*SIN(A))^2)*R/C
990      FOR I = 1 TO N
1000        V(I,P) = U(I,P) : NEXT I
```

FIGURE 11.14

(Continued).

```
1010       FOR I = 1 TO N
1020         U(I,P) = V(I,P) + H(I)
1030         FO = FNA(V(1,P),V(2,P))
1040         FF = FNA(U(1,P),U(2,P))
1050         IF FO > FF THEN V(I,P) = U(I,P) : GOTO 1110
1060         U(I,P) = V(I,P) - H(I)
1070          FB = FNA (U(1,L),U(2,L))
1080          FON = FNA(V(1,L),V(2,L))
1090        IF FO  > FB THEN V(I,P) =U(I,P) : GOTO 1110
1100          V(I,P) = V(I,P)
1110       NEXT I
1120          KC = KC + 1
1130      RETURN
1140     REM -------------------------------
1150     REM --  COMPONENTS DESIGN -----------
1160     REM -------------------------------
1170     REM
1180     REM -- DESIGN OF MEMBER BC AND PIN ---
1190     REM -------------------------------
1200     REM -  DESIGN AGAINST STATICS FAILURE-
1210     REM -------------------------------
1220      ST = SY: PCR = FBC*N: GOSUB 1520
1230      WSTA = WBC: TSTA = TBC: PINSTA = PINC
1240     REM -------------------------------
1250     REM -- DESIGN AGAINST FATIGUE FAILURE-
1260     REM  -------------------------------
1270       K = 3: GOSUB 2000
1280        ST = SE: PCR = .5*FBC*N: GOSUB 1520
1290      WFATG = WBC: TFATG = TBC: PFATG = PINC
1300     REM -------------------------------
1310     REM  -- SELECTION OF DESIGN PARAMETERS--
1320     REM -------------------------------
1330     IF WFATG>WSTA THEN WBC = WFATG: TBC = TFATG: PINC = PFATG:GOSUB 1
1340     WBC = WSTA: TBC = TSTA: PINC = PINSTA :GOSUB 1360
1350     RETURN
1360     PRINT"THE DESIGN SPECS. FOR MEMBER BC ARE:"
1370     PRINT
1380    IF A$ = "Y" GOTO 1400
1390     GOTO 1450
1400     CV =1000!: WBC = WBC*CV: TBC = TBC*CV: H1=H1*CV: PG = PINC: PINC
1410     PRINT "WIDTH =";WBC;" mm";"THICKNESS = ";TBC;" mm"
1420     PRINT"LENGTH =";H1;" mm";"PIN DIAMETER =";PINC;" mm"
1430     PRINT
1440     GOTO 1490
1450     PRINT"WIDTH =";WBC;" IN.";" THICKNESS =";TBC;" IN."
1460     PRINT
1470     PRINT" LENGTH = ";H1;" IN. ";"PIN DIAMETER AT  B =";PINC;" IN."
1480     PRINT
1490     RETURN
1500     RETURN
1510     REM -- SUBROUTINE FOR DESIGN OF MEMBER BC --
1520     Q = ST*H1^2/(PI^2*E)
1530     WBC = ((PCR*Q)/(.003573*SY))^.5 :  W = WBC
1540      TBC = .35*W  : T = TBC
1550      RB = (TBC)^2/12
1560     IF Q/RB > 2 GOTO 1590
1570     W = SQR(((PCR/SY) + 8.57143*Q)/.35)
1580     WBC = W: T = .35*W : TBC = T
1590     DB = FBC/(SB*TBC)
1600     DS = SQR(2*FBC/(PI*SS))
1610      IF DB > DS THEN PINC = DB ELSE PINC = DS
1620     RETURN
1630     REM
1640     REM -----------------------------------
1650     REM --  DESIGN OF MEMBER OAB ------------
1660     REM -----------------------------------
```

FIGURE 11.14

(Continued).

```
1670   REM - DESIGN FOR STATICS CONDITIONS -----
1680   REM ------------------------------------
1690     DS = PG : K = 2: ST = SY: SP = SB
1700     TS = FA/(SB*DS)
1710     MMAX = .5 *LL*COS(X(2,L))*(R - FBC*COS(X(1,L))): MMAX = ABS(MMAX)
1720       X1 =    PINC : GOSUB 2090
1730     WS = X2: WOAB = X2 : GOSUB 2000
1740   REM ------------------------------------
1750   REM --- DESIGN AGAINST FATIGUE FAILURE --
1760   REM ------------------------------------
1770     ST = SE : FA = .5*FA : SB = SE : MMAX = .5*MMAX
1780     X1 =    DS : K = 2: GOSUB 2090
1790     WF = X2:  TF = FA/(SE*DS)
1800   REM -- SELECTION OF SATISFACTORY SIZES --
1810   REM ------------------------------------
1820     IF WS  < WF   THEN TOAB = TF :W = WF
1830     W = WS : TOAB = TS
1840     PRINT"DESIGN SPECS. FOR MEMBER OAB ARE: "
1850     IF A$ = "Y" GOTO 1870
1860       GOTO 1950
1870     W = W*CV : LL = LL*CV : TOAB = TOAB*CV: DS = DS*CV
1880       STROKE = STROKE*CV
1890     PRINT" WIDTH = ";W;" mm";"THICKNESS = ";TOAB;" mm"
1900     PRINT
1910     PRINT" DIAMETER OF PIN AT O = ";DS;" mm";"LENGTH =";LL;" mm"
1920       PRINT
1930     PRINT "NOTE: THE PERMISSIBLE STROKE FOR CYL. = ";STROKE;" mm"
1940       GOTO 1990
1950     PRINT""WIDTH =";W;" IN.";"THICKNESS = ";TOAB;" IN."
1960     PRINT
1970     PRINT"DIAMETER OF PIN AT O = ";DS;" IN.";"LENGTH =";LL;" IN."
1980       PRINT "NOTE: THE PERMISSIBLE STROKE FOR CYL. = ";STROKE;" IN."
1990     .RETURN
2000     REM -- ENDURANCE LIMIT CALCULATIONS -----
2010     D1 = SQR(.05*T*W/.0107)
2020     IF D1 < = 8.000001E-03 THEN KB = 1
2030     KB = 1.189*(D1^(-.097))
2040     KF  = 1/K : KC = .753
2050     SEP = .45*SU
2060     SE = KB*KF*KC*SEP
2070   PRINT "SE =";SE
2080     RETURN
2090     SYT = ST*FA/N
2100       DEF FNX(W) = SYT*(W^3 - (DS+CL)^3) - 12 *MMAX*W*(DS + CL)*SP
2110       DEF FNP(W) = 3*SYT*W^2 - 12*MMAX*(DS+CL)*SP
2120   REM ------------------------------------
2130   REM --ITERATION BY NEWTON RAPHSON METHOD ---------
2140   REM ------------------------------------
2150 ER = .00001  : LN = 1
2160   YX = FNX(X1)
2170 YP = FNP(X1)
2180 X2 = X1 -(YX/YP)
2190 F  = FNX(X2)
2200  IF F < =ER GOTO 2270
2210 X1 = X2
2220 LN = LN + 1
2230 GOTO 2160
2240 REM ------------------------------------
2250 REM  OUTPUT THE RESULT OF ITERATION
2260 REM ------------------------------------
2270   X2 = ABS(X2)
2280 PRINT " THE WIDTH IS OBTAINED AFTER ";LN;" ITERATIONS
2290 RETURN
2300   REM CONVERSION FOR S.I. UNITS
2310     SS =  SS*1000000! : SB = SB*1000000! : SU = SU*1000000!
2320     SY = SY *1000000! : LL = LL*.001  : CL = CL*.025 : E = E*1000000
2330     RETURN
```

F I G U R E 11.14

(Continued).

Automated Drafting

At this point, the components of the landing gear are drawn using sketches made of the components. A digitizer is used to digitize the various components into the CAD system. Once this has been done, the drawings can be used for future components by simply changing the dimensions in the components. This ability to change only the dimensions instead of generating new drawings each time a different-size airplane is designed is the main advantage of computer-aided drafting. The component drawings, along with the design specification, are shown in Figure 11.15.

It is worth mentioning that although we did not do any kinematic simulation, computer graphics could be applied to simulate the motion of the various components of the landing gear to help dictate any error or a problem-prone member.

CONCLUDING REMARKS

The author feels that the approach demonstrated throughout this book and in this chapter should form the main basis for a true CAD process. There are cases in which computer-aided design has been effectively used in the automotive and

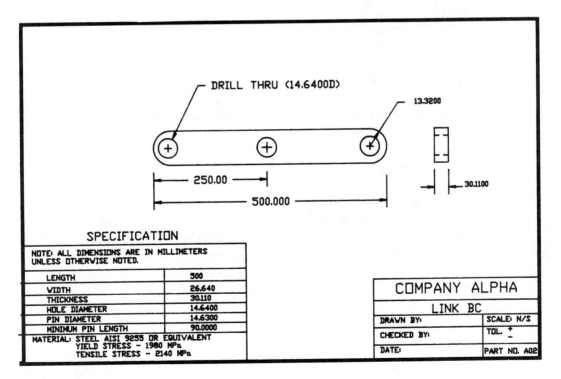

FIGURE 11.15a

Component drawings.

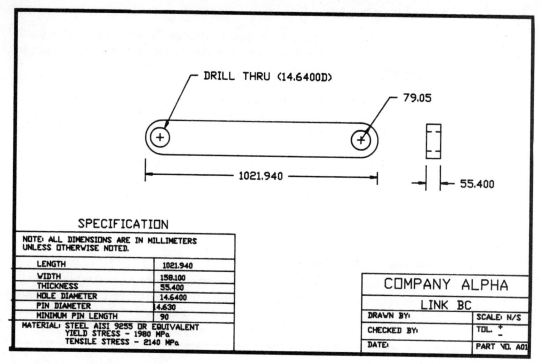

FIGURE 11.15b

Component drawings (continued).

aircraft industries, but because of the proprietary nature of some of these applications, the author is unable to cite them.

EXERCISES

1. Using Zarrugh's equation (11.15), generate a solid with the parameters $\alpha_1 = 0.05$ and $\alpha_2 = \alpha_3 = .99$. Use $a = b = c = 1$.

2. Compute the volume of the solid generated in Exercise 1. (*Hint*: Zarrugh has shown that the volume of an ellipsoid may be evaluated using

$$V = 32 \int_0^1 \int_0^{\pi/4} \left(\frac{R}{2}\right)^2 d\theta \, dz$$

   where

$$R^2 = [(1 - z^{2/\alpha_1})^{\alpha_1/\alpha_2}/(\cos^{2/\alpha_2}\theta + \sin^{2/\alpha_2}\theta)]^{\alpha_2}$$

3. The outline of a duct system can be approximated using the curve that fits the following data:

x: 1.00 1.20 1.40 1.60 1.80 2.00 2.20 2.40 2.60 2.80 3.00

y: 0.58 0.78 1.09 1.52 2.08 2.79 3.66 4.71 5.95 7.41 9.08

Find the centroid of this curve. If the curve is rotated around the x-axis, what is the surface area of revolution? What is the centroid of the surface of revolution? [Ans.: (2.31, 4.66), (2.55, 0)].

REFERENCES

1. Requicha, A. A., and H. B. Voelcker. "Solid Modeling: A Historical Summary and Contemporary Assessment." *Computer Graphics and Applications* 2, no. 2 (March 1982): 9–24.

2. Requicha, A. A. "Representations for Rigid Solids: Theory, Methods, and Systems." *ACM Computing Surveys* 12, no. 4 December 1980): 437–64.

3. Braid, I. C. "The Synthesis of Solids Bounded by Many Faces." *Communications of the ACM* 8, no. 4 (1975): 209–16.

4. Hillyard, Robin. "The Build Group of Solid Modelers." *Computer Graphics and Applications* 2, no. 2 (March 1982): 69–84

5. Casale, M. S., and E. L. Stanton. "An Overview of Analytic Solid Modeling." *Computer Graphics and Applications* 5, no. 2, (February 1985): 45–56.

6. Hindhede, U., J. Zimmerman, R. B. Hopkin, R. Erisman, W. Hull, and J. D. Lang. *Machine Design Fundamentals.* New York: John Wiley & Sons, Inc., 1983.

7. Roark, R. J., and W. C. Young. *Formulas for Stress and Strain.* 5th ed. New York: McGraw-Hill Book Co., 1975.

8. Levin, J. Z. "A Parametric Algorithm for Drawing Pictures of Quadric Surfaces." *Communications of the ACM* C9, no. 10 (1976): 555–63.

9. Sabin, M. A. "A Method for Displaying the Intersection Curve of Two Quadric Surfaces." *The Computer Journal* 19, no. 4. 336–38.

10. Barr, A. H. "Superquadrics and Angle-Preserving Transformations." *IEEE, Computer Graphics and Applications* 1 (January 1981): 11–23.

11. Zarrugh, M. Y. "Display and Inertia Parameters of Superellipsoids As Generalized Constructive Geometry Primitives." *Computers in Engineering (ASME)* 1 (1985): 317–28.

12. Mortenson, M. E. *Geometric Modeling.* New York: John Wiley & Sons, Inc., 1985.

Some Useful Programs

```
**********************************************************************
*          PROGRAM SOLVE                                              *
*          THIS PROGRAM SOLVES SYSTEM OF LINEAR EQUATIONS OF THE     *
*          FORM :   [A][X] = [B].                                     *
*          THE NUMBER OF UNKNOWNS IS LIMITED TO 15.  TO INCREASE     *
*          THE NUMBER OF UNKNOWS CHANGE THE DIMENSION OF THE         *
*          ARRAY [A] AS A(M,M), WHERE M = 2*N AND N IS THE NO. OF*
*          UNKNOWNS.                                                   *
**********************************************************************
*.....................................................................*
           REAL A(30,30),B(15),C(15)
           COMMON A,B,C,N
           OPEN(6,FILE='PRN')
*.....................................................................*
*                       INPUT DATA                                    *
*.....................................................................*
           WRITE(*,*)'HOW MANY VARIABLES?'
           READ(*,*)N
           DO   5 I = 1,N
           DO   5 J = 1,N
               WRITE(*,*)'A(',I,J,')='
               READ(*,*)A(I,J)
      5    CONTINUE
           CALL XINVES
*.....................................................................*
*          MULTIPLICATION OF THE INVERSE MATRIX WITH THE SOLUTION    *
*          MATRIX I.E. [C] = [A][B]                                   *
*.....................................................................*
*                                                                     *
           DO 40 I = 1,N
           SUM = 0.0
           DO 30 J = 1,N
           C(I) = A(I,J)*B(J) + SUM
     30    SUM  = C(I)
*.....................................................................*
*                     OUT PUT SOLUTION                                *
*.....................................................................*
           WRITE(6,35)I,C(I)
     35    FORMAT('X(',I2,')=',E14.7)
     40    CONTINUE
           END
**********************************************************************
*          THIS SUBROUTINE XINVES FINDS THE INVERSE OF THE [A]       *
*          MATRIX.                                                    *
**********************************************************************
           SUBROUTINE XINVES
           REAL A(30,30),B(15),C(15)
           COMMON A,B,C,N
*          THE AUGEMENTED MATRIX OF THE SIZE A(N,NX)                  *
*                                                                     *
           NX = 2*N
           NY = N + 1
*                                                                     *
*.....................................................................*
*          FORM THE AUGEMENTED MATRIX BY ADDING AN IDENTITY          *
```

```
*         MATRIX                                                            *
*.............................................................................*
*                                                                            *
          DO 50 I = 1,N
          DO 50 J = NY,NX
          IN = I + N
          IF(IN.EQ.J) THEN
              A(I,J) = 1
          ELSE
              A(I,J) = 0
          END IF
  50      CONTINUE
*                                                                            *
*.............................................................................*
*         BEGIN ROW OPERATIONS                                               *
*.............................................................................*
          K = 1
  55      J = K
          S = A(K,K)
          DO 60 J = 1,NX
  60      A(K,J) = A(K,J)/S
          I = 1
  65      IF (I.EQ.K) THEN
              I = I + 1
          ELSE
              J = K
              S = A(I,K)
              DO 70 J = K,NX
  70          A(I,J) = A(I,J) - S*A(K,J)
              I =I + 1
          END IF
          IF (I.LE.N) THEN
              GO TO 65
          ELSE
              K = K + 1
          END IF
          IF(K.LE.N) THEN
              GO TO 55
          ELSE
              DO 80 I = 1,N
              DO 80 J = 1,N
              A(I,J) = A(I,J+N)
              WRITE(6,75) A(I,J)
  75          FORMAT(5X,E14.7)
  80          CONTINUE
          END IF
          RETURN
          END
```

```
******************************************************************
*   DOUBLE INTEGRATION USING SIMPSON'S COMPOSITE METHOD          *
*   VARIABLES:                                                   *
*              XU,XL :=  THE   OUTER LIMITS OF INTEGRATION       *
*              FU,FL : = FUNCTIONS DEFINING THE INNER LIMITS OF  *
*              OF INTEGRATION.  THIS ASSUMES THAT THE INNER LIMIT*
*              IS A FUNCTION OF X.   IF THIS IS NOT THE CASE THEN*
*              APPROPRIATE MODIFICATION MUST BE MADE I.E. EVERY  *
*              OCCURRENCE OF FU AND FL SHOULD BE TREATED AS CONST.*
*              HSTEP := STEP SIZE IN THE X DIRECTION             *
*              VSTEP := STEP SIZE IN THE Y DIRECTION             *
*              N,M   := INTEGERS THAT DETERMINE THE STEP SIZES   *
*              SUMT :=  SUM OF 1ST AND LAST TERM OF OUTER INTEGRAL*
*              SUME,SUMO := SUM OF EVEN AND ODD TERMS OF OUTER    *
*                          INTEGRAL OF SIMPSON RULE              *
*              TERM1,TERM2,TERM3 := THE SUM OF THE FIRST AND LAST*
*                          EVEN, AND ODD TERMS OF THE INNER INTEGRAL*
******************************************************************
*                                                               *
*...............................................................*
*            DEFINE THE FUNCTION TO BE INTEGRATED THE BOUNDARIES *
*...............................................................*
*
          INTEGER N,M
          REAL S,FU,FL,F,C,D,SUMT,SUME,SUMO,TERM1,TERM2,TERM3,
     .    VSTEP,HSTEP,XL,XU,SUM,VALUE
*            INPUT N AND M                                       *
          F(X,Y) = X**2 - X*Y
          FL(X)  = X
          FU(X)  = 3*X - X**2
          OPEN(6,FILE='PRN')
          M = 20
          N = 20
*      DOUBLE THE VALUES OF M AND N FOR GREATER ACCURACY         *
          M = 2*M
          N = 2* N
          NN = N + 1
          MM = M - 1
*    INPUT THE LIMITS OF INTEGRATION                             *
          XL = 0.
          XU = 2.
          HSTEP = (XU - XL)/N
*    INITIALIZE THE SUMMATION TERMS FOR OUTER INTEGRATION        *
          SUMT = 0.
          SUME = 0.
          SUMO = 0.
*...............................................................*
*   BEGIN INTEGRATION OF INNER INTEGRAND FOR A FIXED VALUE OF    *
*   OF OUTER VARIABLE                                            *
*...............................................................*
          DO 50 I = 1,NN
               II = I-1
               X = XL + (II)*HSTEP
               C = FL(X)
               D = FU(X)
```

```
                     VSTEP = (D-C)/M
                     TERM1 = F(X,C) + F(X,D)
*         INITIALIZE SUMMATION TERMS FOR INNER INTEGRATION              *
                 TERM2 = 0.
                 TERM3 = 0.
                 DO 40 J = 1,MM
                     Y = C + J*VSTEP
                     S = F(X,Y)
                     IF(J.EQ.(2*(J/2))) THEN
*          SUM EVEN TERMS                                               *
                         TERM2 = TERM2 + S
                     ELSE
*          SUM ODD TERMS                                                *
                         TERM3 = TERM3 + S
                     END IF
 40          CONTINUE
*                                                                       *
*         FIND THE VALUE OF INTEGRATION FOR A FIXED OUTER VARIABLE*
             SUM = (TERM1 + 2*TERM2 + 4*TERM3)*VSTEP/3
             IF((II.EQ.0).OR.(I.EQ.NN)) THEN
*              SUM THE FIRST OR THE LAST TERMS                          *
             SUMT = SUMT + SUM
             ELSE IF (II.EQ.(2*(II/2))) THEN
                 SUME = SUME + SUM
             ELSE
                 SUMO = SUMO + SUM
             END IF
 50          CONTINUE
*         COMPUTE THE TOTAL VALUE OF THE DOUBLE INTEGRAND               *
             VALUE = (SUMT + 2*SUME + 4*SUMO)*HSTEP/3
*.......................................................................*
*                    OUT PUT THE RESULT                                 *
*.......................................................................*
             WRITE(6,60)VALUE
 60          FORMAT(4X,'THE VALUE FOR THE DOUBLE INTEGRATION IS:',
     .       E14.7)
             END
```